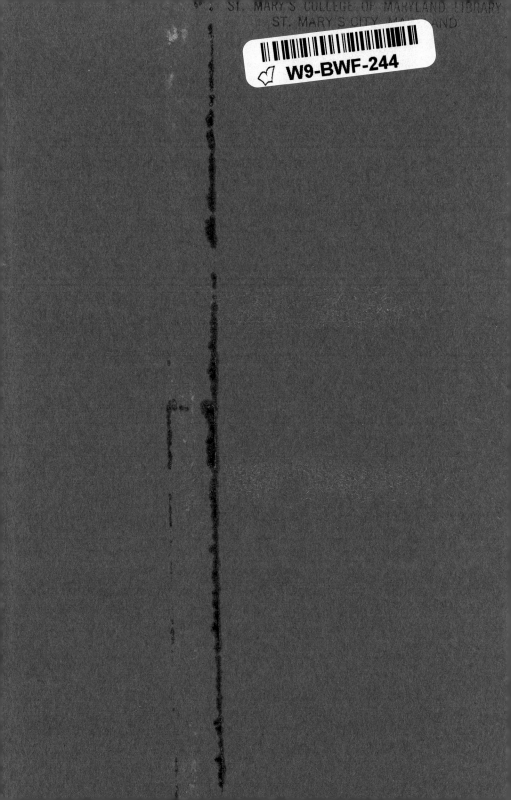

Bismarck

WERNER RICHTER

Translated from the German by Brian Battershaw

FOREWORD BY F. H. HINSLEY, M.A.
*Fellow of St. John's College, Cambridge
and Lecturer in History at Cambridge University*

G. P. Putnam's Sons
New York

First American Edition, 1965

© 1962 S. Fischer Verlag GmbH, Frankfurt am Main
This translation © 1964, Macdonald & Co. (Publishers) Ltd.

Library of Congress Catalog
Card Number: 64-23090

Second Impression

MANUFACTURED IN THE UNITED STATES OF AMERICA

FOREWORD

by F. H. Hinsley, M.A.

Herr Richter's book on Bismarck was widely acclaimed when it first appeared, and with justice. It will be surprising if it does not receive an equally warm welcome from the wider public to which it is now made available in an English translation. That the translation is accurate—this goes without saying. That it is lively the reader will soon see for himself. Still more to the point, however, is the fact that the original work, whose liveliness is thus preserved, has other prominent merits.

Its readability has not been purchased at the expense of scholarship. The author takes account of the mountain of information that has come to exist on his subject and it would be hard to find anything of real significance that has escaped his attention. Then, secondly, he has not confined himself to Bismarck the man, though he has come to understand him well. Bismarck's life spanned a large part of the nineteenth century; his activities were close to the heart of much that happened in that century's most stormy years; and anybody attempting his biography must study the man in his time. But Herr Richter's book is notable for its excellent grasp of the character of the period, no less than of Bismarck himself; and in this respect no less than as a biography his work is abreast of the most recent scholarship.

And then, finally, since scholarship and sound judgement do not always go together, it is worth emphasising the sanity and sobriety of the author's judgements. Any man writing about Bismarck and his time has to move among a bewildering variety of arguments and verdicts. If Herr Richter moves easily among them it is primarily because his touch is as sure as his grasp of his subject is complete. There have been many biographies of Bismarck. Some have been for him, others against. Herr Richter is neither for nor against. He is not the first writer to attempt to paint him "warts and all". But there are few other books on Bismarck which, attempting this impartiality, so nearly succeed in conveying an integrated, a balanced and a convincing portrait.

LIST OF PLATES

following page 132

The author and publishers wish to thank the following for supplying photographs: Privatsekretariat, Fürst von Bismarck for 6; Historisches Bildarchiv for 7; and Ullstein for the remainder.

CONTENTS

CONTENTS

BABELSBERG OVERTURE

The Havel is a broad and gentle river with a flow that is leisurely without being sluggish. It comes from the lonely lakes of Mecklenburg and, moving south-westward, debouches ultimately into the Elbe. During its course it often broadens into yet more lakes, and a number of these enclose the island on which stands the city of Potsdam. Shortly before this point the Havel is joined by the Spree which comes from Berlin in the east; the ancient fortress of Spandau lies at the junction of the streams. Nearly all the important events in the history of the Kingdom of Prussia took place in the triangle formed by these three cities of Potsdam, Spandau and Berlin.

Shortly before the Havel reaches Potsdam it flows past the park of the little castle of Babelsberg, a structure of yellowish brick which has been furnished with small towers and sundry other projecting features, a happy example of that compromise so often effected by nineteenth-century Gothic between the congenital parsimony of the bourgeois and the insistencies of his characteristic taste. The park itself, created with great difficulty in that barren soil, rises and falls with the gentle undulations of the terrain.

On September 20th, 1862, two officers in the dark-blue uniform of Prussian generals were moving along its winding paths. They were engaged in lively and at times distinctly heated conversation, and though outwardly they presented a picture that was ordinary enough, their conversation was to have consequences that changed the course of history.

The man, in whose blond side-whiskers there was already a considerable amount of whitish grey, was King William I of Prussia. He held himself stiffly erect—as though to meet with dignity the advance of age. The figure of the other had the slimness of youth and there was a certain looseness in his movements. This younger man was the King's son, the Crown Prince Frederick William.

It was only two days since he had arrived from Thuringia, whence the King had summoned him by telegram. The fact is that the relations between father and son often left something to be desired and it was sometimes prudent to extend the geographical distance between the two. Early on the day after his arrival, however, the King had surprised his son with the news of his intended abdication, which meant that the Prince, now thirty-one years of age, would within a matter of hours be King of Prussia.

It was barely two years since his childless brother's death, when William I had ascended a throne which he had never coveted and for which he had never been intended: for he had never desired more than to be the first soldier of the realm. Now, as King, he found himself in a position from which he would have been glad to escape. He could never—and this especially irked him—establish a good working relationship with parliament, an institution that had only existed for a decade and one which was a product of the revolution of 1848. That revolution had compelled him to flee to England in disguise and his pride had never forgiven the humiliation. And so it came about that he enjoyed little popularity in Prussia while in the rest of Germany he was quite heartily disliked, for it was under his command that in 1849 Prussia had brutally suppressed a revolt of troops in Baden, an incident that had caused him to be known as the "Kartätschenprinz" or Cartridge Prince.

As King he had found the Army in what seemed to him a neglected state and had immediately instituted reforms. The Landtag had at first granted him the means to carry them out, though it had done so grudgingly and merely provisionally. When, however, the King had sought to turn such expenditure into a permanent item in the military estimates, parliament had refused to concur, though it had suggested a compromise. It had agreed to meet the King's wishes if he would agree to reduce the period of service from three years to two. This last, however, was opposed by William with all the stubbornness of a professional soldier of sixty-four—whereupon it looked as though parliament were going to reject the whole Army estimates. According to the constitution it was fully entitled to do this, whereas the King was clearly in the wrong, and it was this that prevented his ministers, essentially men who obeyed the rules of the game, from putting his views before the Landtag.

That is what made William declare to his son that he felt himself forsaken by all the world and that, rather than dispense with the three-year period of service, he would renounce the throne. He said he had already drawn up the instrument of abdication which was now complete except for the signature.

The young prince was thus faced with a difficult decision. He was an eager, ambitious optimist, and these qualities, which were native to his youth, were encouraged by his wife, a daughter of Queen Victoria. The young couple were convinced that Prussia needed to be remodelled from the bottom up if it was to become the land they desired—which meant, if it was to follow the pattern of England, the ideal state of that day.

The two enthusiasts were sure that they could achieve their aim as soon as Frederick William inherited the throne in the natural course of things. But was it possible that this moment (wholly unexpectedly) had already arrived? The Prince knew that in the matter of the period of service a compromise would be easy to reach. Indeed to this young and handsome man, with his popularity and his faith in progress, a wholly different degree of co-operation with parliament would be possible than was the case with his sour-tempered father who was so universally disliked.

Yet from the very start Frederick William had refused even to look at the instrument of abdication. He had gone from Babelsberg directly back to Berlin and throughout the night had tried to make the ministers change their attitude. But he was unsuccessful, and so on this 20th of September he was again wandering through the castle park at the side of his father without clear plan or counsel, but firmly resolved not to accept the crown.

What was it that prevented him from relieving the King of his undesired burden? Was it a childlike tenderness that sought to safeguard the old man against what would necessarily be a humiliating experience? Or was it the thought—which in point of fact he actually expressed—that an abdication constituted an arbitrary interference with the existing system of hereditary parliamentary monarchy and so a confession of the latter's inadequacy? Such interference would not only impair the monarchic principle, according to which the inheritance of the crown was governed by the grace of God and could not be affected by any human agency; it would equally destroy the respect for parliament. It was on this last institution that the Prince's heart and indeed his whole future depended, precisely because in Prussia it had till now only struck tenuous roots. As previously, the dialogue between father and son was a wearisome and torturing affair and failed entirely to achieve any result.

The talk dragged along. Meanwhile in the distance beyond the Havel and behind a screen of peaceful villages, behind poorly yielding acres and grazing cattle, there lay the city of Potsdam, the very heart and symbol of that Prussian kingdom. When the wind was blowing in the right direction, you could hear within that little castle the music of drums and fifes coming from Potsdam's barrack squares. In the Garrison Church King Frederick II lay buried. Because he had outlasted a severe internal German civil war waged against the imperial power of the Hapsburgs, he was called "The Great". Now the shrunken dwarflike body of this old man rested behind the altar almost at surface level, because of the nearness of the ground water, and in so confined a space that the flags which had fluttered above his regiments were positively crowded above his coffin.

At hourly intervals the carillon in the church tower jingled a simple peaceful tune into the streets below, streets through the midst of which passed a number of tree-lined canals, while the modest classicism of the house roofs and portals spoke of bourgeois comfort and of modest but merited affluence. Everything was a little on the economical side and had the air of a coat tailored with a sharp eye to expense, for soldiers cost money. Yet the idyll that had once marked these Havel islands lived on—even as in the life of the Prussian state there had been long periods when she had been open to the world and had turned towards the quiet arts of peace and to the pleasures vouchsafed by the Muse.

William I had ended by wearily shrugging his shoulders. Since his son persisted in his refusal, he said, there was nothing he could do save continue to carry the burden alone, and seek for other solutions, hopeless as the prospect seemed of finding them. There was one remark that he repeated several times. It was that he would not dream of making a minister of Herr von Bismarck, the Prussian ambassador in Paris, though for years, whenever there was a Cabinet crisis, Bismarck's name had been mentioned as a candidate. He felt, the King said, a secret repugnance towards this man,* a remark with which the Crown Prince eagerly agreed, saying that he too felt unsympathetic towards Bismarck, particularly because he was considered a partisan of France and looked on as a friend of the Emperor, Napoleon III.

The young man who returned that same evening to Thuringia, well nigh in despair, had, during those two days in Babelsberg, held the fate of many human beings and much good and ill fortune in his hands—and had let it all drop from his grasp. Had he not done so, the face of Prussian and indeed of European history during the nineteenth century would have been different. As Crown Prince, Frederick William had shown himself an upright humanitarian liberal. As King he would assuredly have been the same. More than that can scarcely be said. To seek to calculate in detail the results of a change of monarchs and how it would have interacted with other liberalising trends is an enterprise beyond the capacity of man. It will not be attempted here, all the more so since a quite different actor is about to come upon the stage.

---

* As Prince Regent William had already observed, in reference to a possible candidature of Bismarck, that it would be marvellous . . . to have at this juncture of affairs a man who would turn everything upside down.

On September 22nd, two days after the desultory conversation described above, King William was again walking along the winding paths of Babelsberg. Now, however, he was not in the company of his son but in that of the very Herr von Bismarck whom he had mentioned two days earlier. It was only on the previous day that Bismarck, alerted by a telegram from his friend von Roon, the Minister of War, had arrived in Berlin. After a railway journey of twenty-five hours Bismarck had hardly caught up with his sleep, yet he was now being received by the King, who was under the impression that Bismarck's presence in Berlin was due to nothing more than chance and that he had gone there to collect his family and take them to Paris.

Two days had wrought some changes. Autumn weather had set in and there were small waves on the Havel and the swans kept in hiding. And in place of the youthful Prince the King's companion was a tall man whose hair was already receding from his forehead and whose face, the lines of which were broken by heavy eyebrows and a moustache, already showed some traces of age. Disraeli, who had seen him some weeks previously, describes him as a pale slender man, with a wasp waist, but meanwhile Bismarck had been in the south of France and had also bathed in the Bay of Biscay. His paleness had vanished and his Berlin friends found him "gaunt and sunburnt" as though he had been journeying by camel through the desert.

The King received him in Babelsberg Castle and once again the instrument of abdication lay upon the table—still unsigned. Bismarck was not surprised by this. In Berlin it had been an open secret that the King was tired of his office and it was as part of an eleventh-hour attempt to prevent him from abdicating that Roon, who feared such abdication like the devil, had sent an appeal to his friend in Paris.

Bismarck therefore was already prepared for the royal opening gambit in which the King declared that he could no longer find any ministers ready to carry on their office without a surrender to the majority in the Landtag. To this argument Bismarck had long known what his reply would be. He was ready, he declared, to accept ministerial office, and when the King asked to know the conditions of such acceptance, he answered, "None whatever. My sentiments are those of a vassal of the Elector of Brandenburg who sees his liege lord in danger. My abilities, such as they are, are at your Majesty's disposal."

Did this mean, the King then asked, that he would support the military estimates together with the three-year period of service? And when Bismarck answered in the affirmative, he put a further question. Would he be prepared to do so against the majority in

the Landtag? Once more Bismarck replied with a simple "Yes".
We can hardly suppose that the King was particularly pleased
with these very candid replies which barred his escape through
the door of abdication. Nevertheless he declared, in that dry and
rather inhibited way in which he was in the habit of communicating his decisions, that it was now his duty to join Bismarck in
continuing the fight. The question of the constitutionality of such
warfare, carried on as it would be directly against the budgetary
rights of Parliament, was never raised. Possibly the King was
unaware and Bismarck deliberately oblivious of its existence.

Agreement in principle having thus been achieved, the details
concerning the changes in the government were to be discussed
during a walk in the park. And here the King, too, was far from
unprepared. He produced a sixteen-page memorandum written
in his own hand, which was a programme of government to which
the minister, a man notorious for the pursuit of his own glory, was
to pledge his unqualified loyalty. Obviously the King's conscience
was bothering him because of the promise that he had made, not
only to the Crown Prince but to Queen Augusta herself, that he
would never summon Bismarck to take office. Once Bismarck's
signature had been secured to a programme of moderation,
however, he might hope to weather the storm that threatened
him within his own household.

Yet Bismarck had only to pass a rapid glance at the memorandum in order to realise that he could never sign it. He saw that it
held a pair of handcuffs open and ready for him which, like a
magician, he must conjure out of existence. The walk in the park
gave him the opportunity to do just that.

The King did not lack a certain distrust of this newly won ally,
an ally who had a reputation as an odd and even a rather sinister
sort of person. Had not Bismarck, only a few months after his
appointment as ambassador in Paris, already achieved such
intimacy with the upstart Napoleon, that the latter had suggested
an *"entente intime et durable"* with Prussia? The King had immediately caused his Foreign Minister to inform the ambassador that
he could never agree to an alliance with France, and even now
the "secret repugnance" towards Bismarck, the existence of
which the King had admitted to his son, had not disappeared.

Actually the conduct of the new minister was impeccable,
despite the fact that there had been much talk of his overbearing
manner. It is true that there was pride in the tall man's bearing,
even when he was near the King. Yet he was able somehow to
express in his attitude a certain knightly devotion. His large, light-
blue and rather bulging eyes were always turned attentively
towards his sovereign's face. And yet he never failed to observe

that measure of distance from him which etiquette prescribed. What a contrast with the scene in which the King had walked along the same paths with the Crown Prince, with that young general who felt little constraint in his father's presence, made no attempt to conceal his emotions and who, when something displeased him, was quite capable of sharp words and a sudden impatient half-turn on a spur-jingling heel. Bismarck was utterly different. Every nerve, every thought, every word was under control. He seemed to be all respect, consideration and even reverence. And yet he was full of a manly tension; he gave the impression of one who knew exactly what he was at and showed not an ounce of servility.

At this first encounter William suffered defeat at Bismarck's hands, as he was invariably to suffer it throughout his life. For Bismarck had long known that the King was in the habit of seeing analogies between his own immediate position and the fate of Charles I of England, though the Prussians of 1862, schooled as they were in obedience, bore as little resemblance to the ragged Puritans of 1649 as did that simple soldier William I, who was so anxious to be left alone, to the pompous and provocative Charles and his Stuart pride.

Needless to say, Bismarck understood all this as well as the next man. Yet William's obsession was not without its uses, for by directing the talk towards the King's darling theme Bismarck was able to distract his attention from the fatal memorandum. He now declared that the conflict which faced them was no longer concerned with liberal or conservative predominance. The issue was between royal and parliamentary rule (a skilful return to the King Charles theme—via the problem which had cost poor Charles his head). To wage war against the supremacy of parliament, he continued, was something for which he was unreservedly prepared. He therefore did not look upon his decision as that of a constitutional minister in the conventional sense of that term, but simply as that of a servant of the King.

That at least was, no doubt, the general gist of his remark though Bismarck was notoriously untrustworthy as an autobiographer and we cannot be certain of his actual words. It is probable enough that he said, as he claims to have done, that even if he disagreed with the course the King was pursuing, he would go under with him "rather than leave Your Majesty in the lurch in your battle with parliament". For this dramatisation of the rather banal Prussian crisis and all the mood of catastrophe that it conjured into being were things admirably suited to the sombre temperament of the King, hag-ridden for so long by the nightmare of a scaffold on the Opernplatz.

William was essentially a sober-minded man, yet—perhaps for
that very reason—one could usually, if one was reasonably lucky,
impress him with a romantic gesture, and this, of course, was
precisely what Bismarck had managed to do. How different, the
old man must surely have reflected, was Bismarck's language
from that of the Crown Prince, who, despite his general's uniform,
was still a civilian at heart and loathed to pick a quarrel with any
man. How different a man was this ambassador from Paris,
whose clear and lapidary pronouncements, despite his civilian
trappings, were more like those of some legendary general—the
only subject so far who had declared his readiness, whatever the
risk, to take his stand beside the King. It hardly seemed decent
to put constraint upon so perfect a vassal; yet what other purpose
than this had the royal memorandum been intended to serve?

Having no doubt arrived at the climactic point of these reflections, the King slowly proceeded to tear the document to pieces.
Bismarck was delighted: he had contrived to talk the threatened
handcuffs out of existence. However, when the King was about
to throw the fragments of the memorandum from a bridge into a
small artificial gorge with which the park was conveniently
equipped, Bismarck, once more the cool-headed man of business,
reminded him that the papers containing the well-known handwriting should not be allowed to fall into unauthorised hands,
whereupon the King obediently allowed the ruins of his manuscript to disappear into the pocket of his coat.

Next day he signed Bismarck's appointment as minister and as
President of the Ministerial Council. Three days later Bismarck
wrote from Babelsberg to his wife in Berlin: "You will have seen
an account of our miserable condition (*unser Elend*) in the papers."

He had attained the goal for which he had striven for years; and
at long last the power of the Prussian Crown was concentrated in
his hands. Yet he spoke of this simply as "*unser Elend*". Otto von
Bismarck was that kind of a man.

Those who knew him were hardly surprised, least of all Bismarck himself. "My unhappy disposition is such that every
situation in which I could possibly find myself seems a desirable
one—only to become boring and wearisome once I have actually
attained it." Bismarck had written these words to his brother at
the age of twenty-seven—and the words were true.

Part I

THE LONG MORNING

I

THE YOUNG MAN

Let us for the moment allow the curtain to fall on the Berlin of
1862. Let us reach back four decades into the past. We shall
then catch sight of the little seven-year-old schoolboy Otto von
Bismarck, the son of Ferdinand von Bismarck, the owner of a
Rittergut, or knightly estate, called Kniephof, in Pomerania, and
we shall encounter him in the unfriendly Spartan rooms of an
educational institution known as the Plamannsche Lehranstalt,
in Berlin. Here the child was subjected to an educational disci-
pline that derived from the coarse-grained ideology of Turnvater
Jahn.* But that was not all. He was tortured in that strange,
dreary city by wild dreams and was moved to tears if, at the edge
of the town, he happened to catch sight of a yoke of ploughing
oxen.

They will understand the child's emotion who know something
of the hidden yet intimate charms of the North German plain,
those who know how one's gaze loses itself in that unlimited
expanse of heath and fields and in that vastness of sky in which
there is always room for enormous formations of white cloud.
Those who know the bright coppices of oak and elm and the
dark pine forests, who know the willow-shaded brooks and the
will-o'-the-wisp that haunts the damp depressions in the ground,
will understand. A picture of young Bismarck from this period
shows us a chubby-faced country lad with a round head, thick
unruly hair, a snub nose and large eyes that have a look of slyness
in them.

At the age of twelve he left the Plamannsche Lehranstalt and
attended first the Friedrich-Wilhelm Gymnasium and then the
Gymnasium zum Grauen Kloster, two Berlin schools of a rather
sober bourgeois character which contrived to communicate a
certain amount of knowledge but conveyed nothing of the intellectual culture of the day and were strangers to German classicism

* Friedrich Ludwig Jahn. German educator, famous for his efforts to foster a
spirit of national self-confidence in Prussia after the latter's defeat by Napoleon,
through the practice of gymnastics. "Turnvater" means Father of Gymnastics.
"With all the gymnastics and reminiscences of Turnvater Jahn people led a
thoroughly unnatural kind of life that I personally loathed." Robert von Keudell,
Fürst und Fürstin Bismarck (1901), p. 161.

21

(even, if anything, inimical to it). When he left school in 1832, Bismarck was, to use his own words, a normal product of the state grammar schools, the "Gymnasia", of that time, which means that he was "a pantheist, but not a Republican, though convinced that the Republic was the most rational form of state".

"National German" influences which could be traced to Plamann, however, could make no headway against his innate prusso-monarchical sentiments. Those inclined towards that kind of thing may perhaps see something symbolic in the date of Bismarck's birth. It was the first of April, 1815, two and a half months before the Battle of Waterloo, which brought the era of Napoleon and the revolution to a close and made room for a new one.

The estate of Schönhausen, on which Bismarck was born, lay in that part of the Altmark which at that time belonged to the Prussian province of Saxony. It lay near to the right bank of the Elbe and was therefore in East Elbia. When Otto was barely a year old the family transferred itself to their Pomeranian estate of Kniephof, and it was here that the child spent the first years of his life. The first chronicled mention of the Bismarck family occurs in 1270. They appear to have come from a farming settlement in the West Elbian Altmark called Bismarck and had migrated to the town of Stendal, which in the Middle Ages was a respected member of the Hansa. They gradually came to be included among the great mercantile patricians and ultimately around the year 1300 had become members of the landowning knighthood. From that time onwards the Bismarcks were counted as members of the nobility of the Altmark.*

Bismarck's father, who was twenty-four when his son was born, had joined the cavalry regiment, the "Leib-Carabiniers", at the age of twelve and had left the Army at the age of twenty-three in order to devote his energies to the estate which he had inherited. We know little of this man. His portraits show a jovial and open face. Like the rest of the Bismarck family, he was no doubt physically robust though without any excessive urge to action, the kind of man who would be satisfied with the pleasures of a life of quiet comfort, and who was marked by an equanimity that could not easily be disturbed. As a person he had little influence on the formation of his son's character; however, as a type he is highly significant.

For he bore the unmistakable marks of the Prussian Junker,

* In Stendal, today a small town with a certain amount of Gothic trimmings, there saw the light of day a century before the birth of Bismarck a cobbler's son named Winckelmann, who was to open the world of antiquity to the West. It was in honour of this man that a century later one of Napoleon's officers named Henri Beyle took the pseudonym Stendhal.

that most curious breed of men which evolved over the last thousand years east of the Elbe-Saale line. Before the arrival of these newcomers, this territory was inhabited by that branch of the Western Slavs who at the time of the folk wanderings had penetrated furthest west, the Wends. As will be seen in a moment, these facts may even today have a certain significance.

Around the year 900 cultivatable land began to grow scarce within the Holy Roman Empire, and since landed property was everything, one wave of German migration after another began to move across the Elbe. The usual process which leads to the formation of colonies began. The alien soil was annexed, the newcomers settled upon it, the native population, though vigorously resisting, was enslaved and forcibly converted to Christianity.

The clashes on the Wendic frontier territories were horrible affairs, but nowhere did the Germanic newcomers dream of anything in the nature of a root-and-branch extermination of the native population. The superior methods of German agriculture made even that light soil fruitful and so there was room for all. Moreover, every Wend who became a Christian came by that very act under the protection of the Church and so there came into being in East Elbia a state of affairs in which all that was Wendic disappeared from the surface but by no means ceased to exist. On the contrary, to the Celtic-Germanic-Roman elements, of which the stream of invaders had been composed, there was now added a fourth, the Slavic element. German peasants, German knights and burgesses, gradually formed unions both legitimate and illegitimate with the Wends, who, with that tough but elusive vitality that marks the Slav, continued to survive. All those noble East Elbian families whose names end in "itz" and "ow" are, so we believe today, of Slavonic origin, while Wendic place names that still survive are innumerable.

Something Wendic seemed actually to slip into the soul of the conquerors and imparted to their bearing and behaviour an element which in their homes west of the Elbe would have been regarded as strange. In six or seven centuries the type of the East Elbian German had become fixed and along with him a wholly unique variant, the Prussian Junker. His manner had retained some of that natural sense of superiority acquired by all those who had made their homes as colonists on conquered soil. Yet in addition to the orderliness and trustworthiness that he had brought with him from Lower Germany, qualities which often degenerated to mere cheese-paring and bad manners, he developed a certain largeness of thought and action which the seemingly limitless nature of the East Elbian plain appears to inculcate.

For the Junker the dominant motive was that land hunger which had driven his forebears across the Elbe—the overwhelming value attaching to landed property. True, it was Junkers who largely officered the Prussian Army and supplied the Prussian administration with its officials. But this was for the most part done by younger sons. Their elders refused to be parted from the soil. Again and again we discover in Bismarck these hidden peasant instincts. An excellent example is provided by the father who, though he was a professional soldier, obstinately refused to budge from his estates even when the Prussian state had been destroyed by Napoleon and the royal family had fled to the extreme eastern edge of the country. Nor did he act differently when the wave of the War of Liberation flooded past him on its return westward.

Whenever they stood with their own land beneath their feet, the Junkers were their own masters, even in their relationship to the King. So long as the Prussian monarchy lasted there was always a fronde of Prussian Junkers, sometimes open, sometimes rather more concealed. It was only a few years before Bismarck was born that a Junker revolt in the Lithuanian village of Tauroggen had forced the King to join with Russia in her war against Napoleon.* The King knew what he possessed in his Junkers, while of course the Junkers knew how valuable the King was to them. There were good-for-nothings among them and there were slave-drivers. There were obstinate, wooden-headed men and there were men of the purest crystal, in whom there was concentrated the very essence of culture and good breeding. The latter, in so far as they had a great part of the lower judiciary posts in their hands, were better protectors of the peasants of their districts than the royal judges, who were strangers to the countryside and administered justice in the towns, could ever be.

Bismarck's mother, however, was quite a different sort of person. Her name was Wilhelmine. She was the daughter of Geheimer Kabinettsrat† Ludwig Mencken, and thus of bourgeois origin. Her family, which came from Oldenburg, had for two hundred years resided in central Germany and particularly in Leipzig and had produced a long line of professors of jurisprudence and practical jurists.

The office of Kabinettsrat, which Mencken held, was highly respected and enabled him to participate directly in the conduct of public affairs. For a time he was a diplomat at the royal court

* In Tauroggen negotiations were also conducted on the Russian side by Prussian Junkers in the service of the Russians, Diebitsch, Dohna, Clausewitz.

† The title of an official who acted as link between the Monarch and the departments. Now no longer in use.

in Sweden. His physical appearance showed him to be the off-spring of a race of highly-bred intellectuals. He was narrow-chested and suffered from poor health, but his mind was always active and receptive to new ideas. He was liked well enough at the Prussian court, so much so that his daughter, even after his early death, was favoured as a playmate of the Crown Prince (later to become Frederick William IV). In so far as it was possible for a Prussian official, Mencken was influenced by the ideas of the French Revolution. But the matter was not taken too seriously in court, where Mencken was jestingly called "a Jacobin".

Mencken's intellect, which so strongly favoured the Enlighten-ment, his lively and ever-wakeful Saxon common-sense, had been inherited by his daughter, who showed these qualities in an even more marked degree than Mencken himself. Her children, too, were to have the mould impressed upon them, for she wanted to turn them into what the Germans so untranslatably call *Gebildete Menschen*, a term which carries a slightly solemn moral connotation that is largely or even wholly lacking in the phrase "educated people", the nearest English equivalent.

With the naïveté that always marks self-imputed omniscience, she was convinced that "higher intellectual culture . . . would of its own accord one day lead us to God". Her considerable intellectual activity was sometimes marked by a kind of hysterical sharpness, while her lack of inward balance was often perceptible in an over-sensitive introspection and in the fear of ever-varying forms of illness, though whether or no there was here anything like foreknowledge of her end (she died of cancer) is difficult to say.

There were times when she believed herself to be possessed of second sight, which caused her husband to express regret that she had not foreseen the fall in wool prices on the Stettin Exchange. Unlike her husband, who seemed satisfied with a pretty ordinary and bourgeois way of life, she had a flair for elegance, and family means allowed her to indulge it, particularly during their winter stay in Berlin when there were court balls.

Much in Bismarck's character can be traced back, though usually in a negative sense, to his mother's influence. His resistance to schooling and later his unwillingness to apply himself systema-tically to his studies represent his answer to her pedagogic ambi-tions. Instead of engaging a tutor, as was customary among noble families, she sent the sensitive child away from his accustomed surroundings and exiled him to a town school "in order to break his aristocratic pride".

Bismarck seems never quite to have got over this. Nor, during the whole of his life, did he ever lose a dislike not only of his mother but of the whole social stratum from which she came, namely the higher bureaucracy—which argues a violent attempt to force all thought of his mother into oblivion.*

Yet, whether he wished it or not, he received endowments from the Mencken family which did more to shape the course of his life than the half-peasant inheritance from his father— his razor-sharp intellect, the lightning speed with which he could grasp a situation and the unerring instinct with which he reacted to it. His wealth of ideas, his capacity for extricating himself from any difficulty, even for downright cunning, especially where the interpretation of a law or an agreement was concerned, may be described as inherited characteristics; inherited also was that cold bureaucratic indifference with which he ignored everything that was unlucky enough to stand in his way.

At the age of seventeen Bismarck became a student at the University of Göttingen. The fact that he did not choose a Prussian university but that of the kingdom of Hanover, which at that time stood in personal union with the British Crown, shows his desire to make a sharp break with the past, and to recompense himself for all that he had suffered as a schoolboy. The form in which that desire first expressed itself seems to have been a kind of childish pleasure in simply hitting out. In his first semester alone he was involved in no less than twenty-five student duels, and for this reason was often in confinement. He wore the red cap of the Hanovera Corps on his head. His life followed the pleasant pattern that seemed unvarying for the sons of the landed nobility. There was the *Fechtboden* where the aforementioned duels were fought. There was also some drinking—and some harmless adventures in love.

The solemn boredom of the lectures could not fetter his lively spirit. He soon felt himself to be superior to the professors, which in point of fact he was, and realised that he could afford to be much more lazy than the average student. His dashing appearance caused something of a sensation in the musty little town. These were the last days of the coloured dress coat, of the exquisite linen which foamed out from the opening of the waistcoat and of those collars whose starched points almost stabbed the corners of one's mouth.

* It was very rarely that Bismarck admitted that he had inherited his actual intelligence without which he would never have amounted to anything, from his mother's side of the family (Philipp, *Vertrauliche Gespräche mit Bismarck* (1927), p. 140). Occasionally he would also say that the Mencken family was descended from Field-Marshal Derflinger who had originally been a tailor's apprentice and so had also not been a Junker. One branch of the Mencken family settled in America, and to this belonged the circus rider Ada Mencken, who was the friend and possibly the mistress of the elder Dumas, and also H. L. Mencken, the publicist, of whom it was said that every literate American had written to him at least once.

He was also capable of moving through the streets in a light-coloured garment rather like a dressing-gown, wearing, according to an eye-witness's account, "a strangely constructed cap, and carrying a twisted staff of iron in his hand, while a huge whitish-yellow hound followed in his train". He was now a tall young man with a proud bearing but "as thin as a knitting needle". His head was not over large, his thickly-growing hair and sprouting beard were reddish blond, while his skin had the pastel delicacy that is usual with red-headed people.

In the three following semesters which he spent in Berlin, his manner of life was the same as at Göttingen. Indeed he wrote to his lifelong friend Keyserling, whom he first met in that city, that he was devoting himself once more to "his old mistress, the bottle" and then in the evening behaving "as boorishly as possible in the dress circle at the Opera".

What is remarkable is that not only did he reveal the high spirits normal in a young man with a privileged background, but that those bright days of his youth were continually darkened by deep fits of melancholy. In strength of intellect and brilliance of wit he stood forth as the unquestioned superior of the young men of his own age, yet he could at times attain a cold cynicism, a positively cruel readiness to reject all those illusions which are the gentle privilege of youth. He was healthy, so healthy that he could afford to be inconsiderate towards himself, and careless of the treatment he meted out to his body. Yet at times it appeared that this wild waste of his energy was due to an actual weariness of life. Certainly there was in all this an element of pose, something of Lord Byron's fashionable shudders at the transitoriness of life. But at the same time there was a genuine inability to find any purpose in his own existence.

Naturally her son's way of life caused agonies to the ambitious Wilhelmine von Bismarck. Yet he passed all his exams with a quite ridiculous ease—in 1835 the final legal exam which gave him the rank of an *Auskultator* and in the following year that which raised him to the rank of *Referendar*. As such he was transferred to the government at Aix. The Rhineland had only been Prussian for twenty years. French laws were still in force there and it had referred to its union with Prussia as "our poor marriage".

To the East Elbian it was a strange country and not a particularly pleasing one. But Aix was at that time a spa visited by all the world. Compared with it Berlin was a provincial backwater. No wonder that the glittering flood of cosmopolitan life soon carried the young man away. He had his mother's weakness for an elegant style of life and his father's habit of making himself as comfortable as he could. His name and office provided him with credit. And so Referendar von Bismarck could be seen strolling in the Kurpark, dining in the more epicurean restaurants, or disporting himself in the theatre on both sides of the curtain.

Quite as often he would be encountered at the gaming tables where the gold pieces into which the corn, wood and cattle of his paternal estates had been transformed, rapidly disappeared on the green tablecloth. His hope of thus finding a way of settling his debts, debts which went right back to Göttingen, soon proved vain, indeed the debts merely grew larger.

He made the acquaintance of some of the very wealthy English, among whom it was at that time the fashion to travel in Germany. It was among the latter, whom Goethe considered to be "people who were not anything by halves and had nothing unbalanced about them . . . but were always rounded and complete" ("*ohne Halbheiten und Schiefheiten . . . immer durchaus komplette Menschen*"),* that young Bismarck's hitherto somewhat erratic love life took on a more stable form.

A Miss Laura Russell, a granddaughter of the Duke of Cleveland, so bewitched him that he regarded himself as being engaged to her. Some months later a certain Isabella Lorraine, a clergyman's daughter and a famous beauty from Lancashire, caused (the metaphor is as strange in German as it is in English but Bismarck's metaphors are often a little wild) "his poor inflamed blood to burn up like steam". He followed her and her family, whom he already referred to as "my relatives", like a troubador through Central Europe, visiting Frankfurt, Wiesbaden, Strasburg and Basle, and finally achieved a genuine engagement, only to have the prize diverted from his grasp some two months later by "a wretched colonel aged fifty with four horses and fifteen thousand reichsthaler in revenues".

Meanwhile he had, on his own authority, extended the fortnight's leave which had been granted him in Aix to four months, and had sought to satisfy his rapidly growing need for cash at the gaming tables. The attempt proved abortive and, as he later wrote, he lost some seventeen thousand talers, which had been "set aside for other purposes".† It was not till October that he reported from Berne to the Aix government, which, however, dispensed with his further services. And so in November he returned contrite and penniless to Kniephof resolved to become a farmer.

Yet his parents persuaded him to make a fresh attempt at a career in the government service, and for three months he once

* To Eckermann, August 11th, 1828.
† Letter dated 3rd September, 1837, to Karl Friedrich von Savigny "Regierungsreferendar" in Aix, Bismarck, Collected Works XIV, p. 10.

more worked as a Referendar in Potsdam. Then, to fulfil his military obligations, he donned, though very unwillingly, the green uniform of the *Gardejäger*. He was, however, granted frequent leave, for the mortal illness of his mother had now been diagnosed. Moreover, the Bismarck properties, which had also been the object of her reforming zeal, were in a critical condition. His parents therefore demanded his presence at home.

Wilhelmine died on New Year's Day 1839. Now his father raised no objection to Bismarck's resignation from the state service, and was ready for him to "take over the management of the estates and attempt a resolution of all the difficulties into which they had run". Bismarck settled down at Kniephof at the age of twenty-four. To himself he justified this step on the grounds that the Prussian official "was like the single player in an orchestra, whether he played the triangle or first violin . . . but I want to make music which I recognise as good or none at all".* His superiors in Potsdam, however, expressed their views in a more pedestrian fashion, saying, "If Herr von Bismarck can succeed in overcoming his personal laziness, then he will be capable of filling the highest offices in the state."

---

* Bismarck, *Briefe an Braut und Gattin*, p. 27.

2

THE SQUIRE

The world to which Bismarck returned had been familiar to him since childhood and it was a unique world which (to him) existed in a vacuum. For much as the Elbe had formed the frontier between Germans and Slavs, so too East Elbia was a kind of special enclosure in the Europe created by the Vienna Congress.

Here, in the old whitewashed houses of an aristocracy that had been impoverished by the war, and in the midst of parks that were now running to seed, the end of the Napoleonic era was mistaken for the beginning of undisturbed peace. It was believed that there would simply be a return to that mode of life to which these people had always been accustomed, a life governed by the categorical necessity of work, a life in which there was always a clear distinction between those who gave the orders and those who received them, in which there had been a reasonable kind of loyalty towards the dynasty, while on one's own land there was patriarchal domination. When papers brought the news that barricades were being built in Paris, it all seemed to be happening upon another planet.

Living as it did in a world that was not of the times, the East Elbian nobility also found refuge in the timeless, namely in the Bible. For since the clergy sent out by the government had become too deeply permeated by the spirit of the Enlightenment, the Junkers withdrew and busied themselves unaided with biblical interpretation. There was divine service in the home, meditations and biblical instruction, while religious themes were often passionately discussed.

For eight years Bismarck lived as an East Elbian squire. At Easter 1839 he and his brother Bernhard took over the paternal estates of Kniephof, Külz and Jarchelin, while their father retained Schönhausen.

It was only now that Bismarck got to know his sister Malwine, called Malle for short, who had been born in 1827 long after he had himself been packed off to Plamann. Meanwhile he had hardly ever seen the child and now quite suddenly there she was, some thirteen years old, half as big as he was himself, with a fair skin and reddish blonde hair much like his own, and twinkling, sapphire eyes. Had it not been for an obstinate hardness about the mouth, she might well have ranked as a little beauty.

Until now Malwine had passed the greater part of her life in educational institutions in Berlin. It was not till April 1843, after her confirmation, that she finally returned to the country, under the supervision of her elderly governess, Antonie von Blanckenburg, who, in Bismarck's view, exerted what he called a "wintry influence" on her surroundings. When the Blanckenburg disappeared the whole house became more comfortable; also Malwine began, as he says, to thaw.

For the rest of her life Malwine was destined to stand closer to Bismarck than any other person, save possibly, at a later stage, Herbert, his son. In the deep solitude of the country, left wholly to themselves, with only their ailing father for company, brother and sister found themselves united in an intimacy which could only proceed from a certain feeling of pre-existent oneness. Such a predestined affinity between brother and sister is often found in old families with a strong tradition behind them. Classical examples of it are Frederick the Great and Wilhelmine von Bayreuth, and also Goethe and his sister Cornelia. It is as though exceptional people, fearing the loneliness imposed on them by their very uniqueness, sought to attach themselves all the more closely to those with whom, from the very beginning of their lives, they have had a tie, with those who have been their oldest intimates.

Bismarck and his sister hardly needed words to understand each other. They possessed intelligent and practical minds and both had inherited the realistic business sense of their parents. They were unromantic, they were natural mockers. They had a leaning towards eccentricity. They ran the house together like a married couple. Their mutual affection was obvious to all. Otto played the part of the gallant protector and delighted in that role. "He treated her like a bride," people in Schonhausen would remark. She watched with housewifely zeal over his creature comforts.

Soon, however, this young country lass was spied and wooed by the friend of Bismarck's youth, Oscar von Arnim, a bearded man who, with his freckles and his reddish blond hair, suggested nothing so much as the old robber baron of the marches. Malwine was seventeen at the time, and since she was accustomed to Berlin and felt bored in the country, she married him as early as October 1844, leaving her brother alone with the "green linen chair". Upon this chair—as he now wrote to her—she had been in the habit of "kissing and whispering with Oscar", and, seated on it, he was now setting down his reflections upon the "unnatural and

selfish conduct of a young lady who has a brother and an un-
married one to boot, and yet inconsiderately gets married herself".*

His letters to Malle make strange reading. He addresses her as
"Mein Schatz", *"Mein Herz"*, rough equivalents of the English
"my darling", and also as "my angel", "my adored one", and he
concludes his letter with such words as "Farewell for now, my
love", *"Ganz Dein engener"* (wholly your own). When answers to
his letters were delayed, his anguish is that of a lover. In 1856,
when Bismarck had himself long been married, one of his letters
to her says, "Daily after writing I ask quite coldly, 'Will she ever
again write to me in this life'?" †

Throughout half a century the certainty on the part of both
brother and sister that they could always count on each never
grew less. At seventy-nine, Bismarck could still write to that sister,
"The first person I think of when I want to lay bare my soul is
yourself." When he could issue his orders to the whole of Europe,
petitioners could be certain of success if it was through her that
they addressed their petitions. She was the only woman by whom
he let himself be influenced, and that influence extended even
to official matters. Her daughter, Sibylle, became his daughter
in-law.

After the death of his father in 1845, Bismarck moved to
Schönhausen, which, together with Kniephof, became his property
when the inheritance was divided. It had been the property
of the Bismarcks since 1502 and was therefore very dear to their
hearts. It was a box-like baroque building rather like a fortress
and furnished, though very sparely, in eighteenth-century style.
Actually only three rooms out of the thirty could be considered
as being properly furnished at all. The colour of the damask wall
coverings could often only be recognised by the few rags that
remained.

Here he lived in the same rooms in which, as he was fond of
pointing out, his forefathers had been born and had died, "lonely
as a bear in its winter habitation". Here he was able to do what
he had always wished, namely, "to make music which I considered
to be good". Nobody could interfere with him.

Yet, as time went by, Bismarck found that he was wholly
unfitted for the utter stillness of the hedged-in world of his
ancestors. Perhaps he had lived outside East Elbia for too long.
Here too, as elsewhere during his life, periods of intense exertion
were followed by those of idle drift and of torturing unrest.

At first Bismarck sought escape in the semi-official tasks which
were still at that time performed by the owners of a squire's

* Bismarck, *Briefe an Schwester und Schwager*, p. 61.
† Moritz Busch, *Tagebuchblätter*, II, p. 119.

estate. Within the confines of his lands Bismarck held police power in his hands and administered justice. Thus, as a vassal of the reigning sovereign, he was still a minor territorial overlord. These rights had been enjoyed by his family for centuries and so there had grown up among them a curiously familiar relationship with many generations of the inhabitants. Some evidence of this is provided by a remark of one of Bismarck's own rank, who states that he treated the peasants over whom he held this authority "as though they were members of his own social circle" and so got along very well with them. No doubt both sides were the happier for this.

It was much the same when he was given a post making him responsible for the dams which guarded the acres of the Schönhausen district against the treacherous floods of the Elbe. He treated this office of "river god", as he called it, very seriously and was compelled on account of it to engage in much bureaucratic wrangling. Yet all this made little difference, for there flowed through his veins not merely the torpid blood of the Bismarcks but also that of the restless Menckens, who were never content to leave well alone. The net result was fury and frustration—which caused him in later years to remark, not quite justly perhaps, that these country years were a time of "*bescheidener oder blöder Unselbständigkeit*", of modest, not to say imbecile, dependence on others.

There were also attempts to escape into the outside world. As early as 1842 he disappeared from July to October on a journey of which we know very little. It took him to England, Scotland, France, Switzerland and possibly to Italy. In 1844 he got away to Norderney, which at that time was a Royal Hanoverian island in the North Sea. Here he moved in the same circles as the blind Crown Prince George, whose fate it was to be deprived by Bismarck twenty years later of his land and all his inheritance. On his return he grew a beard which caused his peasants to mutter to each other that he had said something against the King at an inn, in which the King had been present though unrecognised. When Bismarck had spoken, the King was said to have got up and displayed the great star upon his breast in order that Bismarck might know who he was. Bismarck, however, had thrown him down the stairs. As a punishment he was forbidden to shave. Supposedly the public executioner visited him on New Year's Eve to trim his beard.

There were other stories that circulated about him, all of them bearing witness to his readiness for light-hearted violence. It was said that he announced his visits to friends by firing a pistol into the ceiling, that he sometimes went about accompanied by four

young foxes which stank quite abominably. It was also said
that unless he could have a bottle of champagne and a lobster
for breakfast his stomach was queasy all day.

Women of the most varied background now played an ever-
increasing part in his life—and were quickly but invariably left
lying by the wayside. He moved, he was later to declare, "in
every sort of bad company", and had looked upon every kind
of sin as permissible. In the not-too-distant Bad Polzin he was
attracted by lady visitors from abroad and by female members
of the "Kurtheater". Mounted on Caleb, a large brown horse, he
seemed to be restlessly on the move, both by day and by night.
Occasionally he told Malwine something about this twilight
territory of his mind, as for instance that the "mild damp weather"
caused him "in a melancholy and dejected fashion to feel himself
in love".

By and large he seemed at this time to have plumbed some very
dangerous depths. His friend Keyserling did not mince matters.
He states in his diary that Bismarck "in his love for women
followed his natural instincts without any scruples". Bismarck
himself used to shudder a little when he spoke of these days, and
as he cast his gaze over Schönhausen spoke "full of sadness and
remorse about his blind appetite for pleasure, in the pursuit of
which he had aimlessly squandered all the rich gifts of his youth,
his mind, his fortune and his health, without having anything
to show for it".*

Small wonder that for his more sober neighbours he was "a
prodigy of wild arrogance", an Alicibiades of the Marches, a
splendid greyhound who delighted men with his mad extravag-
ances, but whose presence caused them to keep an eye on their
daughters. Externally he was in those days a most attractive
person with close-cropped blond hair, a carefully trimmed beard,
and eyes that bulged a little but were very bright, and in ordinary
conversation a remarkably gentle voice.

Yet it was unquestionably in these East Elbian years that
Bismarck underwent the most important and the most profoundly
disturbing experience of his private life. In 1843, at the still
impressionable age of twenty-eight, he got to know Marie von
Thadden, the daughter of his neighbour, Adolph von Thadden,
who owned the estate of Trieglaff, and was one of the heads of the
Pomeranian Pietists. Marie was at that time twenty and a famous
beauty. She was engaged to Bismarck's old schoolfellow, Moritz
von Blanckenburg. She was tall, powerful in a rustic sort of way
(which verged on Pomeranian coarseness) and yet with noble
features and magnificent eyes. The spirit of the parental home had

* *Briefe an Braut und Gattin*, p. 80.

shaped her upbringing and she was therefore a pious Christian
though by no means a recluse.

She visited theatres and concerts in Stettin and Berlin, planned
journeys to distant parts, and delighted in the very fashionable
romantic movement, in Brentano, Tieck, Bettina, and above all in
the bizarre but pregnant obscurities of Jean Paul. His famous work,
"Titan", she said she had dashed down like a glass of champagne.
She read Goethe, but "Faust" and "Wahlverwandschaften"
seemed still to disturb her well-ordered world. Her conversation
tended to be slightly erratic but was always distinguished by the
freshness and naturalness of the country-woman. Perhaps it
was this that caused her to criticise Bismarck's "cold elegance"
and a certain "smoothness of the man of the world".

Marie von Thadden became the great passion of his life and
it was a passion which, because it could not attain its object,
never died. For, as the betrothed of his friend, Marie was surrounded by an invisible fence which he could never cross. Most
certainly Marie returned his love, and it is almost equally certain
that they never openly confessed it to each other. Both no doubt
realised that it was their duty to avoid each other, but so great a
measure of self-control was beyond their power.

Nothing could shake Marie's faith and that was no doubt
her good fortune. For the very first time that she talked about
religion with Bismarck she encountered an indifference, a conscious incapacity for belief which Bismarck was not afraid to
emphasise and which she later admitted almost reduced her
to tears. Since it was impossible for a girl of Marie's openness of
heart to see the soul of this man of all men threatened by unbelief, she exerted herself to the utmost to awaken in him a genuine
longing for Faith and sought to make him turn the words "help
thou mine unbelief" into a kind of basic prayer. To which Bismarck replied on one occasion, his face red with excitement, that
faith must "open up within him" without his willing it or doing
anything to bring it into being.

It would be much too crude to say that their religious talks were
mere pretexts for seeking the loved one's company, nor can there
be any doubt that their deep mutual feeling in these matters was
genuine. For Bismarck too—and this is quite beyond dispute—
was profoundly affected, since Marie was leading him back
towards paths deserted by him since childhood.

Remote as it was from the world, the simple East Elbian
manor house was the scene of a drama of mingled longing and
renunciation, a drama in which the actors continued to leave
unuttered the feelings of their hearts. Only the minutest of
symptoms, words half spoken here and there, betrayed the true

nature of their condition. As when once, in the garden, Marie pinned a blue flower on to the coat of her betrothed, blue being the colour of faithfulness, but on that of Bismarck a rose, "the flaming colour of love".

Marie was not so naïve that she failed to notice the danger which confronted her. In his presence, she said, she always had the feeling of standing on ice that might break at any moment, but she wrote to her friend, Elizabeth von Mittelstädt, "I think I can trust him, for to him I am holy."*

In October 1844 Marie and Moritz von Blanckenburg were married. During the celebrations there was an evil omen; rockets set fire to some farm buildings, and the guests, Bismarck among them, had to help put out the flames. He was a frequent guest at Kardemin, the Blanckenburgs' estate, and there enjoyed such entertainment as their slender means could provide. In those days people were fond of giving what they called "aesthetic teas"; thus in Kardemin they used to meet at regular intervals to read Shakespeare, with parts suitably distributed. In a letter to Malle, Bismarck tends to make fun of the pineapple punch which was tasted on that occasion and of the prayer which initiated the proceedings.

As before, his talks with Marie dealt almost exclusively with religion, and Moritz too was concerned for the welfare of his boyhood friend. The crux of the matter was always the same. The Blanckenburgs believed that faith in a personal God could be forced into being by willpower and prayer, whereas Bismarck could see nothing in man save an incidental by-product of creation who came into being and passed away like dust disturbed by the rolling of wheels. Thus the success of the two friends' efforts seems to have been negligible. Marie was moved to tell her friend Mittelstädt: "I am always depressed when experience teaches me anew that one human being cannot help another. It is a melancholy thing to behold one who suffers as much as Otto Bismarck under the coldness of unbelief."

However, the rustic gossip of Pomerania tended more and more to seize upon the strange triangular friendship of Kardemin, and as it did so, the weight on Bismarck's conscience grew heavier. His excursion to Nordeney had been an attempt at flight. It was much the same with a somewhat over-chaperoned journey into the Harz mountains which he undertook in 1846 together with the Blanckenburgs, a certain Pastor Wangemann, and two friends of Marie, Johanna von Puttkamer and Elizabeth von Mittelstädt.

---

* In letters from Marie von Thadden to Johanna van Puttkamer—who later became Bismarck's wife—there is reference made to "the special one" and "the Platonic one".

But the journey undertaken in two carriages proved a pleasantly light-hearted affair. The pastor distinguished himself as a singer of Mendelssohn's songs, champagne was drunk at the different hotels and there were romantic walks by moonlight. People would hardly have guessed that these were Pietists.

In the autumn that followed, however, an epidemic swept East Elbia, against which apparently nothing could be done. It seems to have taken the form of an inflammation of the brain. In August Marie's youngest brother succumbed to it and her mother in October. On the night of November 11th, Marie herself passed away.

In the whole of Bismarck's life we know of no death that shattered him so dreadfully as this. He was, Blanckenburg tells us, "full of nothing but tears, which he showed publicly before people". Bismarck is reported to have said "this is the first heart that I lose of which I know that it truly beat warmly for me". He never forgot Marie. Those with a liking for historical conjecture may seek to try and estimate how different the fate of Europe might have been if Marie von Thadden had not been betrothed and if she had not died at twenty-six.

It was not merely the loss of Marie that thus turned Bismarck's world upside down. It was the manner in which in all the firmness of their Christian faith both she herself and those who were close to her encountered death. He told Malwine that Marie had faced her death with "unclouded cheerfulness" and that during her illness both her husband and her father had been "full of confidence". He envied the certitude with which they regarded this death "as being hardly anything more than a journey ahead of the rest, a journey which must ultimately be followed by joyful reunion". It is certainly not to be wondered at that the spectacle of such firmness of faith, a firmness to which his own eyes were witnesses, aroused in him the wish to be the equal of such people as these, a wish which, in the days that followed, full as these were of all too much disquiet, attained its ultimate fulfilment.

For Marie had not died without leaving him an inheritance. When she regained consciousness for a matter of hours, she had sent a message to him which "she earnestly insisted on being delivered, that he must now be converted and that the time was all too short". He also knew that she had long desired that he should marry Johanna von Puttkamer, so that the whole of his life should thenceforward be under the tutelage of her friends, on the firmness of whose faith she knew she could rely. Given the way she looked at life, could Marie have done more, and what other answer could Bismarck have made to that last message than to do all in his power to enable her wish to be fulfilled?

Johanna von Puttkamer had none of Marie's radiant beauty, but she was delicately made, her hair was raven black, her eyes Bismarck described as "grey blue black with large pupils".* A letter of Marie refers to her as "a fresh, gushing fountain of health, a true physic for our poor ailing hearts". She was a cooler person than Marie and more inclined to keep her thoughts to herself, but once one contrived to get her out of her ivory tower, she could be both cheerful and witty. She was said to be very musical.

To win Johanna von Puttkamer, however, was far from easy. The same spirit of unswerving piety governed Johanna's parental home, Reinfeld, in Further Pomerania, as dominated those of the Thaddens and the Blanckenburgs, though in Johanna's case there was a lack of that little pleasant element of worldliness which was present among the two others.

The Puttkamers, however, lived, as Marie put it, in "further, further Pomerania". Moreover, Bismarck's reputation was such that the gates of Reinfeld were only opened to him with some hesitation. Johanna had learned from the Blanckenburgs something of Bismarck's struggles with his conscience and was thus a little frightened of him and inclined to keep him at arm's length. But a correspondence had been going on for months between the two and it was only the shock that Marie's death had given both of them that put an end to it. In an interview which the widowed von Blanckenburg arranged for them on his estate, Zimmerhausen, Johanna finally consented to become Bismarck's wife, though that consent was qualified by it being made dependent on the approval of her parents.

To obtain this last Bismarck wrote to her father, Heinrich von Puttkamer. He had, he said, now won the battle for faith in a personal God and so considered himself entitled to ask for Johanna's hand. From the age of seventeen he had ceased to pray, since prayer seemed to be contrary to reason. Yet when Marie lay dying, "the first fervent prayer had burst forth from my heart without any brooding on my part on whether or no it was contrary to reason". His prayer, he continued, had remained unheard by God. Yet it had not been rejected. "For I have never again lost the ability to petition to Him, and though I have no sense of peace, yet I feel within me confidence and a zest for life to a degree which I have never previously experienced."

There is no need to suppose that these words were anything but a perfectly sincere expression of feeling, but there is equally no need to attach to them, as some who have spoken of a "conversion" have perhaps tended to do, a greater importance than

* Others speak of Johanna's brown eyes, though the pupil is said to have been so large that the whole eye would sometimes seem to be black.

they deserve. For there is nothing here of the road to Damascus or of any total breaking and remaking of a human being. The fact is that Bismarck had been deeply moved by the solicitude of a beloved woman for the welfare of his soul, that this had brought him nearer than he had ever been before to the domain of religion as such, and that the overwhelming shock of her death had produced upon him a profoundly cathartic effect, traces of which remained to the end of his days.

Certainly Johanna's father accepted Bismarck's words at face value, and the parents' consent having been given, Bismarck and Johanna became formally engaged. In the letters that were exchanged between them during the months that followed we can discern the growth in Bismarck of a sense of quiet happiness that was wholly new to him, a happiness in which there was nothing of that volcanic passion that, like a subterranean fire, had glowed within him for Marie. Life had tossed Bismarck around and now the man who, till that moment, had never been at rest, began to experience something of the sense of security that was to come to him through always having at his side one who was completely and utterly faithful.

On June 28th, 1847, the marriage was celebrated. Shortly before this a horse's rib had been found at the Kniephof while some digging was going on, and Bismarck had identified it as that of Caleb, the great brown horse which for seven years had untiringly carried him to the scenes of his gallant adventures. It was clear that all this was now at an end.

Bismarck was never again an entirely irreligious man, but in the course of time his religion became a purely personal affair. If a timely frost saved the dykes of the Elbe from floodwater, then it was for him, Dyke Captain Otto von Bismarck, that God had sent it. When he no longer acted as an isolated human being but as administrator of the state, however, that relationship no longer seemed to be relevant. He did indeed in various ways express the thought that the statesman did nothing alone; he could only listen till he heard God's footsteps in events and then leap forward and catch the hem of His garment; but in the course of time he propounded the theory that the state was governed by its own laws which need not conform to those of Christianity, and that the statesman who, to set his own Christian conscience at rest, made his politics conform to the principles of the Gospel rather than those of political life, was acting from a personal and arbitrary predilection and was permitting "the embryo of faithlessness towards the state" to come into being.*

* Letter to Gerlach, May 2, 1857. From Bismarck, *Gedanken und Erinnerungen* (1922), I, p. 180.

Never in any case was his whole being, like that of the Pietist members of the East Elbian aristocracy, permeated in every fibre by the presence of God. Never was his Christian faith, like theirs, the central sun which determined the direction of all earthly aims, as the physical sun brings about the flowering of plants. Bismarck's religious feeling was rather like that of the men of antiquity, who received both suffering and good fortune from the hand of an insensitive Zeus, a God who can now and then be diverted from His purposes by prayer and sacrifice, and who communicates his intention by means of ambiguous oracles. Bismarck too had his oracles. For many years he read when retiring to bed in *Lösungen und Lehrtexten der Brüdergemeinde* (Watchwords and Instructional texts of the Community of Brothers), a collection of biblical texts and hymnbook quotations for every day of the year, and time and again he believed that in these chance juxtapositions he could discern the counsels of God in the business of every day.*

After the terrible shock of Marie's death, his ordinary life resumed its course. In a letter which he wrote to his brother on January 31, 1847, months before he wrote to Puttkamer asking for his daughter's hand, he could already say of Johanna, "To put the matter bluntly, she is 'facile à vivre' to an extent which I have never before seen in any female." One recognizes afresh the old condescending tone of an ironical man of the world. Small wonder that in the circle of his gambling and hard-drinking friends he was laughed at when he said something about reading from the Bible. In Johanna's parental home, they declared, they would have said the same kind of thing, "but it is ridiculous to try and lead your oldest acquaintances up the garden".†

---

* He also read regularly from a book entitled *Daily Refreshment for Christians*, containing some words of Holy Scripture for every day of the year with added expositions by Dr. Martin Luther, A. O. Meyer, *Bismarcks Glauke* (1933), p. 2.

† *Briefe an Braut und Gattin*, p. 9.

3

THE COUNTER-REVOLUTIONARY

With the coming of early summer in 1847, Bismarck began to disengage himself more and more from the sphere of religious discussion. Instead, the earthly goddess of politics increasingly took possession of him. It was the barest chance that led him towards her.

A certain Herr von Brauchitsch, a member of the United Provincial Estates which had been sitting in Berlin since February, was struck down by illness. Bismarck was selected to take his place as the representative of the knighthood of the Altmark, and although at that time he was midway between his betrothal and his marriage, and although Johanna at that very time was seriously ill, Bismarck agreed to accept the position.

The assembling of the Provincial Estates was an experiment—and one not without risk—which was being attempted for the first time in the history of Prussia. The peaceful and contented tenor of East Elbian life was by no means typical of the kingdom as a whole. In East Elbia people had no fault to find with the conduct of affairs—and so—this is as true of Bismarck as of any of them—believed things to have been managed in the best possible way. They failed to observe that the rest of Europe had in greater or less degree grown weary of the system which thirty years previously the participants at the Vienna Congress had constructed with such admirable artifice.

At the heart of that system was the German Bund, a loose conglomeration of German states containing, amongst others, the Prussia now mightily enlarged by her Rhenish and Westphalian provinces. But the generation of the Napoleonic wars was dying out, and its descendants, who had never known war, and despised the outmoded safeguards of peace, succumbed to the all-too-human urge for change. The novelist, Theodore Fontane, at that time a young chemist's apprentice in Berlin, declared that people were "fed up with the old set up", not that they had endured any marked degree of suffering under it, "but everything seems out of date". There was a mass of dissatisfaction and disquiet, but it was only gradually that concrete and recognisable wishes began to emerge. All of these could be brought together under the elastic concept of "freedom".

Always and under every system of government there will be people who feel themselves to be underprivileged and oppressed, and that is why whenever freedom is asked for, he who demands it will never wholly lack followers. Here in the Germany of the forties that most ancient concept of personal freedom, for which Prometheus had already had to suffer, had united with the very novel concept of the nation, a legacy of the French Revolution. The revolution, being in need of a formula for its mass conscriptions, had replaced the terms people and state, which were associated with royalty, and for that very reason unserviceable, by the word "nation", which up till now had only been used in intellectual discussions, but soon became the mightiest slogan of the century, one which, though no one could satisfactorily define its meaning, enjoyed religious veneration and could claim the heaviest sacrifice. Was nationhood a metaphysical fact which destiny demanded, was it the empirical result of common speech and a common way of life, or was it simply the product of an act of will by which the majority imposed its desire upon a minority? No one could say, yet precisely because nationalism was rationally inexplicable, it could plunge a world which was helpless against it into the murderous age of the nation-states.

The development of German nationalism paralleled Bismarck's own development. Throughout his life he had in one way and another to argue and come to terms with it. Sometimes he made use of it if there was a chance of a useful alliance, but he never forgot its questionable nature, was never its true friend, and remained always fundamentally its enemy. He was against it as he was against everything that had its origin in the French Revolution. But above all he recognised in it an enemy that threatened the very existence of Prussia.

He was much too intelligent to think of Prussia as though it were objectively the most valuable of states, and thus himself to stray into nationalist ways of thought. For all that, Prussia was the state into which he had been born and so the state to which, organically and irretrievably, he belonged. A German national state, however, could do nothing but bring about a diminution of Prussian power. Yet this was precisely the goal of that motley company who had a general appetite for change.

It was in particular the middle class which, encouraged by growing economic power, felt the Prussian form of state to be antiquated and obstructive, as did the intellectuals of Berlin whom that social group had produced. In these circles people referred to themselves as progressives, and to be progressive was the hallmark of the upper strata of bourgeois society and the stamp of their intellectual maturity. Genuine want of a kind that threatened life itself, want that left its victims no escape save by an overthrow of the existing order, such want existed in a few narrowly circumscribed localities—among the weavers of Silesia, for instance. It existed nowhere else.

After 1830 the defences erected by the Congress of Vienna had been broken into more than once. The Bourbons had been driven out of Paris. Belgium had broken away from the kingdom of the Netherlands. Russian Poland had again and again risen against the Czars. There had been revolts in Upper Italy and in the states of the Church. In Germany there had been disturbances in a number of towns—in Brunswick, Dresden and Kassel. Baden and the Palatinate were the territories most affected by the unrest. In Prussia the Rhenish provinces, which in 1815 had been made subject to that state without their consent, had always felt themselves more closely tied to the West than they were to the East. In the universities the students' corps were voicing their discontent, as were quite a few of the professors, to say nothing of higher bureaucrats like the Menckens. There were also the industrial workers, a class that had only recently come into being, and these naturally enough were discontented with their lot, though their numbers were inconsiderable. Yet what weight did all these elements possess compared with the millions of Prussian inhabitants who continued the even tenor of their lives?

Frederick William IV was probably the most un-Prussian of all Prussian monarchs. Popular history has got back at him for this, by speaking of him with a sort of sneer as "witty" (*geistvoll*), so that in the end people began to think of him as a weak babbler. Actually he was a man who clung firmly to his ideals, which unfortunately became less and less identical with those of his own age. His judgment was both quick and sound, but he lacked the faculty to convert his insights into action, when action was required. He had a deep and genuine feeling for Humboldt and Ranke, Savigny and Schinkel, and acted as a patron towards them to a degree that went far beyond the minimum that his office entailed. There was, in fact, concentrated in his cultured person what might well be called the Other Potsdam, all that legacy of classical German humanism, a legacy now permeated and enriched by a romantic feeling about life. In this respect he was a child of his mother Queen Louisa, who in so far as one can disentangle her figure from the accretion of patriotic legend, appears to float through Prussian history like some gentle elf.

His father, Frederick William III, had left behind him a

promise, a promise that had been rather vaguely formulated but had certainly remained unfulfilled. The promise was that Prussia should attain "popular representation", and the son was receiving ever more stormy reminders of this fact. He had now summoned to Berlin the four estates of his eight provinces, consisting of the high aristocracy, the knighthood, the burgesses and the peasantry. These formed a "united landtag". This was, of course, no parliament after the French or English models, but precisely because it was based on the old German principle of community of rank and function (*genossenschaftlich-ständisches Prinzip*), it was for the King a much more faithful mirror of his people than something brought mechanically into being by some electoral device. The conception of a commonwealth of estates carried in those days at least as much weight as the rationalist idea of universal suffrage. Even Freiherr von Stein, the ultimate originator of Prussian reforms, had never considered any form of popular representation that was not based on the estates. Certainly Frederick William was convinced that, by calling together his parliament of estates, he had kept his father's promise.

It was to this parliament, in which, with studied eloquence, a conservative minority and a liberal majority sought to provoke each other, that Bismarck belonged. He was ill at ease, and when it was his turn to speak his words seemed clumsy and witnesses spoke of a stammer. Actually, he just spoke as the spirit moved him, as though he were carrying on some kind of a conversation with himself, and made no attempt to curb his peculiarly arrogant sense of humour. At the very start he attacked the great dogmas of liberalism. He utterly rejected the view that the Prussian people had gone to war in 1813 on the strength of a promise of popular representation which the King had made them as a recompense for their service in the war, and that this recompense they now had a right to demand. To argue thus, Bismarck declared, was "to render a poor service to our national honour". His words were received with immense indignation, although he was certainly in the right, for the peasants and petty bourgeoisie probably cared a great deal less about some future parliament than about getting rid of the burden of the French occupation.

At the end of June the united landtag was dissolved and Bismarck celebrated his marriage and went off on his honeymoon with Johanna—incidentally in quite a modest way, for he had with him only one small piece of luggage, "one suit I wear, the other is in the trunk". They were in Venice in September and there they met the King. In Berlin he had avoided Bismarck because of his questionable reputation. Here, however, he invited him to his table and showed him "encouraging approval".

His was a spirit sympathetic to every kind of human character, and the feeling he had for this individualist of the Altmark was wholly genuine.

The young couple returned in time for the harvest. Autumn came and with it the hunting season. Then came the feast days that marked the year's end. Soon it was New Year and it looked as though 1848 would be pretty much like the years that had preceded it. Even when in Paris, on February 24th, the Orleans dynasty was driven out, this caused little stir east of the Elbe—until it became evident that this Paris revolution had a very disturbing quality. It was highly infectious.

For it was only a matter of days before revolting masses were parading the streets all over western Germany, including Baden, Hesse, Württemberg and Bavaria, and everywhere they were making what were roughly the same demands: introduction of a liberal democratic constitution, new ministries, abolition of the censorship and arming of the people. And everywhere the panic-stricken courts were in retreat before them. On March 12th revolution broke out in Vienna. On the 13th, Metternich resigned. On the 18th the sparks leapt over to Berlin.

Frederick William, surrounded as he was by his thoroughly reliable guard, was under no necessity to make concessions, but the fall of Metternich, who had carried the whole epoch on his shoulders, had disturbed him very deeply, so much so that he issued an order which met all the usual demands: a constitution for Prussia, reorganisation of the German Bund into a federal state, even a German fleet. Peace was once more restored and the joyous Berlin crowds surrounded the palace like a flood.

Then the infantry which was guarding the palace gates fired two shots. The shots were fired without order and into the air; but in an instant the mood of the crowd had changed into a raging fury. As church bells sounded the alarm, barricades seemed positively to shoot out of the ground, which on the morning of the 19th the guards had more or less successfully contrived to storm. But a confusion of orders, which to this day remains inexplicable, caused the troops, which, since Jena, had remained undefeated, to withdraw first to their barracks and then to Potsdam.

At a later date the suspicion arose—it was particularly rife in officer circles—that at the sight of the slaughter the King had had a stroke and had at the time been bereft of his reason. Whatever the cause, he remained behind under the protection of the Citizens' Guard. Fortunately this consisted of Prussians who took their duties seriously and his life was never in danger.

In East Elbia the news of these events spelt the end of the world. Bismarck heard of them on March 19th on the estate of a neighbour, Count Wartensleben, to which some Berlin relations had fled. Bismarck's first reaction was a desire to lose no time in meeting force with force, to hurry to Berlin accompanied by armed peasants and rescue the King from the men of the barricades. But in Potsdam, whither he went on March 20th and where he found the Berlin guards bivouacking in the streets, their officers talked some sense into him. They had no need, they assured him, of a peasant army. They did need supplies from the farms. The troops would at any time be capable of freeing the King, as soon as the latter ordered them to do so. In a mood of frustration, Bismarck rushed to the railway station, travelled to Berlin and contrived to reach the castle, where he would have seen the King, had not the Citizens' Guard inconsiderately refused him admittance.

Next day he was again in Potsdam—with nothing less in mind than a coup d'état which, since the King no longer enjoyed his liberty, was to place power in the hands of his successor. However, William, the brother of the King, who was the immediate heir to the throne, continued to keep in hiding. Bismarck had therefore to lay a plan before the latter's wife, Princess Augusta, according to which she was to seize the Regency in the name of her son, Frederick William, who at that time was still a minor. The Princess was shrewd enough to see that here was a man who had simply gone berserk with rage and, not unnaturally, refused to lend herself to such a scheme. She declined the offer, and the interview, carried on in a quiet servant's room in Potsdam Castle, became the beginning of the deadly hatred between the two which, though the politest forms continued to be observed, was only ended by death.

Bismarck saw himself faced by the ruin of all that had been achieved by the Congress of Vienna, which, so he thought, had finally buried the ideas of the French Revolution. This was an error which Bismarck shared with many of his contemporaries, an error which completely dominated his formative years, and one of which for that very reason he could never wholly rid himself. That the ideas of 1789 had by no means suffocated under the gravestone of the Congress of Vienna and had ultimately claimed the sole right to govern men's minds—these were facts which Bismarck never came to realise.

Actually destiny was kind to him on this occasion. By subjecting him to this triple rebuff she ensured that he never appeared in the pages of history as the hero of a mildly farcical military coup.

On April 2nd the United Landtag reassembled in order to make arrangements for the election of the new Prussian parliament which the King had promised. Yet once again Bismarck rose to speak and once again he allowed himself to be carried away by his feelings, feelings of anger, of sorrow and contempt. It had been moved that the King should be thanked for his concessions. "No," cried Bismarck. He accepted the present situation but only because he could not help himself. The past had been buried "after the crown itself had thrown the earth upon its coffin". But he could not leave that assembly with a lie on his lips. He could not declare that he was either thankful or glad about it. The speech remained unfinished. An urge to weep constricted his throat and he was compelled to leave the tribune.

With his reputation of an extreme reactionary, he could hardly hope to enter the new parliament for which a general election was now being held. And so he retired to Schönhausen. Witnesses describe him about this time as rather inclining to fat and note that his hair was thinning. His appetite for elegance had disappeared. For the most part he would sit smoking in silence in the corner of a sofa, dressed in one of his father's old coats.

Bismarck's exclusion from practical politics had one important effect. He was now for the first time able to take a wholly dispassionate view of recent developments. These various localised German revolutions had brought out into the open a mass of vague ill-will and discontent. Nowhere, however, had they inspired great masses to risk their lives.

The reigning powers had utterly failed to form a correct assessment of these matters. Because the flames of revolt shot up so brightly for a short time, they had failed to see that there was relatively little fuel on which they could feed. Wherever the troops remained reliable, no revolution could last. In Prussia it had not extended much farther than the pavements of Berlin.

When Bismarck made an estimate of the forces on both sides, those supporting the revolution could hardly have seemed very formidable. Of what did they consist save a few narrow bourgeois strata, a handful of the nobility whom he regarded as renegades, the workers in the newly-created industries, and a certain number of artisans? The great masses of humble folk had marched willingly enough against Napoleon. Now, however, they had remained at home. They were unwilling to sacrifice their lives for the privilege of electing a parliament or belonging to a unitary state. Thus Bismarck, who had first been obsessed by a furious resolve that the revolution must in no circumstances succeed, began to grow calmer as he realised that such success was in point of fact quite out of the question. His instinct, which was much sounder than that of the German courts, showed him that he had only a weak enemy to contend with and was thus under no necessity to negotiate. In that quiet summer of Schönhausen there was born to him on August 21st his first child, a daughter, who—how could it be otherwise?—received the Christian name at baptism of Marie, in memory of Marie von Thadden.

Bismarck's marriage developed in the manner which, given the circumstances in which it took place, should not have been difficult to foresee. Most certainly he knew that his offer of marriage had resulted from a transient process of auto-suggestion which, but for the tremendous effect on him of Marie's death, could never have occurred at all. As with the course of time the power of his feeling diminished, he could not but realise that Johanna could never be so perfect a companion as Marie would have been for him, and that she could never have that intimate understanding of every aspect of his life.

Politics in particular—and this was soon to be the only thing that really mattered to him—remained a sealed book to her. When in his letters he inadvertently started to talk politics, he would apologise and almost feel sorry for her, addressing her as "*mein armes Herz*" (my poor darling). This lack of interest and understanding must surely often have irritated him, as did the lighthearted way in which she expressed her likes and dislikes, her superficial judgments about people, her proneness to gossip and to trivialities in general. But if he had such feelings, he always sought to prevent her from being aware of them. For he never forgot that he was the one who was responsible for the existence of this marriage. He genuinely loved Johanna but only indirectly, as a kind of heirloom, as though she were a jewel which some dear departed friend had left him. The charm which Johanna herself exercised upon him, the charm of that gentle, fragile figure with the raven-black hair, and the depths that seemed to lurk in the pupils of her eyes, was obviously due to the attraction which from time immemorial fair and dark people had for each other. Again and again in the letters written before their marriage Bismarck uses the word "black" in reference to Johanna.

Of any actual passion on Bismarck's part there is little to tell; there was more on Johanna's side. Indeed, had she not to some extent at least controlled herself, he might well have wearied of her. For the most part, however, she was pleasant enough, a well-brought-up and considerate lady, though there were times when her words could display a streak of quite savage cruelty. To a virile type like Bismarck this kind of thing must have seemed embarrassingly unfeminine. Yet of this she was obviously unaware.

In the sphere of her immediate interests, in the house and in the family, Johanna reigned supreme. In all that pertained to this she was sensible and could show good judgment. Moreover, in her attitude towards her husband she never lost her self-control, and forced herself never to be jealous, either of people or of things. Also she kept that faith in which she had been brought up, while successfully maintaining towards her world that position of subjective superiority with which it endowed her.

Meanwhile in Berlin the first constitutionally elected landtag had assembled. In the ministry which it called into being there were for the first time representatives of the now rich middle class, men from the western provinces to whom Bismarck scornfully referred as "commercial travellers in Rhenish wine". He held that such a system would soon outlive any usefulness it possessed and in this he was not alone. In 1848, before that fatal March had ended, groups of men had emerged like unassailable islands from the revolutionary flood, groups of men who held that the old authorities had been taken by surprise and had indeed sustained a blow which had thrown them off balance. But the damage, it was believed, was not irreparable and they were still capable of enforcing their will. The most powerful of these groups had gathered around two brothers, Ludwig and Leopold von Gerlach. Leopold was adjutant-general to the King and Ludwig *Gerichtspräsident* in Magdeburg, which meant that he was the highest judicial authority in the Prussian province of Saxony. The Gerlachs were related to the Thaddens, and this brought Bismarck within the sphere of their influence. Ludwig von Gerlach was a Christian and a conservative, and ruthlessly consistent in his views.

In outward appearance he rather resembled a monk. He had thin lips and sharp eyes which Frederick William used to describe as "piercing", and his influence on Bismarck, who was twenty years his junior, was both deep and lasting. In 1851 Bismarck wrote in his album, "I have never regretted taking your advice and often regretted doing the opposite."

Ludwig's brother Leopold was intelligent with an aptitude for diplomacy. His frequent meetings with the King, whom he saw daily at the *Kaffeevortrag* ("coffee report") gave him excellent opportunities of securing the latter's support.

Two more adjutant-generals were members of the Gerlach circle, von Rauch and von Manteuffel. Von Rauch was an eminently practical man but with a strange habit of lapsing into grammatical solecisms. The King said of him that "he has more common sense than all of us" but that he would never learn German. Von Manteuffel was for many decades to play a prominent part in Prussian history. He was a self-willed man but with a great breadth of culture. He was in fact the cultured soldier par excellence.

This group, which referred to itself as the Camarilla, was the chief and almost the official organizer of reaction. Its aim—or at any rate that of its more intransigent members—was counter-revolution, with which end in view it gave itself over—amongst other things—to the persistent stiffening of the King's back. For Frederick William, though anything but a coward, as Bismarck was quite ready to admit, had nevertheless shown himself deplorably accommodating to the revolutionaries. He had, on those fatal March days, talked with them, donned their detestable colours and gone in procession behind their dead. It was a performance the Camarilla found profoundly disedifying. Yet attention to the Royal Person far from exhausted its energies. These were also directed towards organizing reaction as a popular movement, or at least—and this very largely for the King's benefit—towards giving it the appearance of one.

The King meanwhile had moved to Sanssouci, and here on the terraces of Frederick the Great he was able during the summer months to renew the conversations which he had had with Bismarck in Venice. Bismarck on these occasions would reproach the King with the "softness" of his policy, and when he did so he did not mince his words. The King accepted such criticism with patience and good grace and his liking for this turbulent subject was evident enough—this at a time the two Gerlachs regarded Bismarck as no more than just a landed Junker, though one who, simply because he had the courage to go to extremes, seemed rather to tower above his peers.

The first open trial of strength with the revolution came when the government produced plans for the abolition without compensation of the privileges of landed proprietors. Four hundred East Elbian Junkers immediately joined together in the "Association for the Protection of the Interests of Landed Property", an organisation popularly known as the "Junker Parliament", in the foremost ranks of which stood Bismarck himself. The diligence of this body soon degenerated into mere perverted ingenuity, and it was unfortunate its aims were so crassly material that Ludwig von Gerlach was markedly estranged. In Bismarck, however, something seemed to rise from the depths when landed property was the issue. There came to the surface on these occasions some atavistic element in the character of an ennobled colonising peasantry who occupied lands conquered by their forefathers and held on to them with an almost childish stubbornness. This was a basic and elemental East Elbian trait, and one which was not to be found in West German aristocrats like Metternich or Von Stein.

As summer drew near its end, new opportunities for the counter-revolution began to be discerned. In Prussia, as everywhere else, hybris had begun to affect the leaders of the revolution, and an ill-considered "little man's radicalism" was gaining the upper hand in the Berlin National Assembly. As Bismarck was later to write, an attempt was being made, by the offer to peasants and workers of glorious things to come, to win sympathy for the revolution "of which not so much as ten thousand people really approve". Thus a situation was arising which was positively ideal for the counter-revolutionaries. The revolution was playing directly into their hands.

All over Europe it was using up its strength. In Paris, at the end of June, General Cavaignac had in a series of street battles already opened the road to the bourgeois empire of Napoleon III. During the course of the summer Austria had suppressed all revolts in upper Italy. Revolutionary Vienna surrendered on October 31st. Meanwhile in Berlin in September the Liberal Ministry had been unseated by the radical left.

There followed a long Cabinet crisis, in which, as in March, Bismarck once more developed a feverish appetite for action, though on this occasion he did not act as a lone and slightly ludicrous figure, but as the agent of a great political movement.

During these weeks he was perpetually moving to and fro between Schönhausen, Berlin and Potsdam, for which, he tells us, the knights of his district quite cheerfully paid an allowance comparable to that of a landtag member. The appointment of a Ministry under General von Pfuel represented an interim solution of the problem which in the end satisfied no one. Meanwhile the Prussian National Assembly was coming more and more under the influence of the Berlin mob, and both ministers and members of the parties of the right were in danger of being lynched when they ventured into the streets.

On October 31st a certain Waldeck, a member of the Assembly, proposed a motion that Prussia should immediately go to the aid of "Imperilled Popular Freedom in Vienna" which meant, in effect, that she should go to war with the Austrian government. Thus was created the perfect setting for a coup d'état—and the opportunity was duly seized. The King dismissed Pfuel, removed the National Assembly to Brandenburg, where it was shortly afterwards dissolved, and sent the guards back to Berlin under General Wrangel, who instructed the rather helpless Civil Guard which had marched up against him to "evaporate" (*Verduften*), an order which they obligingly obeyed by returning to their homes. Count Brandenburg, a relative of the Hohenzollerns through a morganatic connection, was made Prime Minister, and on December 5th, the revolution now being over, the King complied, from the plenitude of his own power, with its more reasonable requests. It was from the plenitude of that power that he granted a constitution whose essential features were a copy of what was then the most modern constitution in existence, namely that of Belgium, and so differed very little from the plan which the National Assembly had left behind it.

During the week when the coup d'état took place, Bismarck seemed to be everywhere at once. To the King he called himself *"Hof-und-Kammerintrigant"* (Court and chamber intriguer). By September 9th Ludwig von Gerlach had gained the impression that Bismarck was "almost offering himself for a ministerial post", and indeed while the coup d'état was being prepared he was actually considered as a possible ministerial candidate. But the King, attached to him though he was, rejected the idea. He should only be used, he declared, "when the power of the bayonet becomes unlimited". This kind of thing was to be repeated many times, with Bismarck's name coming up whenever a list of ministers was being prepared, and then disappearing again—presumably because men were afraid of those powers of destiny whose presence they sensed in the depths of his being. For the present he remained what Gerlach's words described him as being, "a very, efficient and intelligent adjutant of our Camarilla headquarters", a useful partisan but no more than that.

Yet the revolution and the counter-revolution proved to be his first political educators. They had begun to turn this wild creature, who had hitherto been wholly guided by mere feeling, into a statesman capable of objective thought, one who no longer believed in the necessary identity of the desired and the attainable. He was making decisive progress in his grasp of the nature of the real world, and it is at this stage, surely, that we can already discern the first signs of what was later to be called his realpolitik, though actually that word does not mean very much, since every policy that is not doomed in advance to failure must be built up on the given reality.

The second Prussian Landtag opened in February 1849 and once more Bismarck was a member. It had not been easy to secure him a seat. The electors said that they were of course conservative but they were not "Bismarckisch". It was mere chance that turned the scale in his favour. Franziska von Putt-kamer was a close relative and a childhood friend of Johanna. She had married a certain Hermann Barschall, the governor of Brandenburg Prison, and Barschall used the very considerable influence that he enjoyed among the burgesses on behalf of the kinsman with whom marriage had united him—this despite the fact that Barschall was a Jew and Bismarck had in Parliament opposed Jewish emancipation.*

His outward appearance was undergoing a change. He was broadening out, but the original image of the powerful, healthy Junker still remained. Also he still had the same round head which racial theorists classify as Slavic. Haym, the literary historian, speaks in February 1849 of his red side-whiskers, and continues, "in the softer, fleshy lower parts of the face, there was a mocking smile". He describes the nose as "ugly" and "somewhat flat, while the eyes are clear and suggest cleverness, even guile".

In the spring of that year the fate of Prussia was once again following a quieter road. But in that spring Bismarck began for the first time seriously to consider the problem that was to dominate his life, the problem of turning the mid-European land mass which was inhabited by Germans into a state.

To create a constitution for such a state was a task at which the National Assembly, then sitting in the Paulskirche in Frankfurt, had been labouring for an entire year. That body had been gathered together from all the countries of the German Bund under the pressure of the revolution of 1848, and, like the revolution itself, it was Janus-headed. One of its two faces was turned towards the Holy Roman Empire which the Germans, as soon as it had disappeared in 1806, so painfully missed. For all those instincts which for centuries had come to find satisfaction in loyalty to the Emperor and his Crown were now left reaching out into the void. Of course, the new concept of nationhood, like a new kind of spice, had entered even into this ancient longing. Nationhood—such at least was the desire of the Frankfurt Assembly—was to form the basic principle of the new political construction. The catchword "as far as the German tongue is spoken" was actually elevated to the dignity of a programme, and as a result the annexation of Alsatia was demanded just as easily as that of Holland, Switzerland and of the Baltic provinces of Russia. As against this, all those old Hapsburg territories which were not inhabited by Germans were to be excluded. Of course— and here one sees that other face of the assembly—the internal structure of this new "Reich" would be very different from that of the old. For it was to be the preserver to all eternity of all the things which the revolution was supposed to have won. The sovereignty of the princes was to be virtually abolished. All real power was to be vested in parliament, though it was to be shared

* The complete emancipation of the Prussian Jews did not take place until 1869 as a result of legislation by the North German Bund.

with an Emperor of parliament's choice. The Reich ministries, however, were to be responsible to parliament alone and not to the monarch.

All this the National Assembly thought it could bring about by the simple processes of legislation, for it held itself to be the sole instrument in Germany in which sovereignty was vested. Actually, it vastly over-estimated the extent of this sovereignty which at best had been provisionally granted it by the dynasties under temporary pressure. These misapprehensions were rich in farcical results. Solemn debates were carried on in the Paulskirche as to whether Austria and Prussia should not on the resolution of a simple majority be split up into their constituent parts. That both these states enjoyed a considerable measure of real power escaped observation. Or again, the desirability of a "war of principle" against Russia was seriously examined. Such a war would of course have had to be carried on by the armies of the two states in question.

Rarely in history have some hundreds of men, many of them genuinely gifted, striven so eagerly to shape something anew, of whose real nature they had so little knowledge. The National Assembly was a spirit without a body. In the realm of feeling it was a giant; in that of fact, a child that had lost its way. It summoned ministries into being and selected incumbents. It created diplomatic posts and the office of *Reichsverweser* (or imperial administrator), and even produced the first beginnings of a fleet. In short, it created the apparatus of a government that had neither the protective power which a genuine state could have provided nor any real foundation of popular support. It hung in the air and was too impotent even to close the gaming houses in the immediate vicinity of Frankfurt.

The helplessness of the whole undertaking became apparent in March 1849. A Reich constitution had been drawn up, a rigidly centralised affair which virtually deprived the individual states of all authority. The Hapsburg dynasty being excluded, Frederick William IV of Prussia was elected Emperor. But the King refused to accept the offer. He could only receive the imperial crown at the hands of the German princes, who alone had the right to dispose of it. The National Assembly, he held, had offered him something which it was not theirs to bestow. No doubt it would have been possible for him to throw Prussian power into the scales and so endow the phantom creations of the Paulskirche with real life. But what enemies it would by that very action create for itself! Certainly Austria, which had just broken the revolt in Hungary as it had broken that of the Italians, would have offered armed resistance, and Austria might well have been joined by Central Germany, by Saxony, Hanover, Bavaria and Württemberg, whose governments had only accepted the Frankfurt constitution through fear of the Prussian Army. It was even possible that France and Russia would join with Austria and the coalition of the Seven Years War would thus have been re-created.

As on that occasion, Prussia would have been able to count on the sympathies of England but for the fact that the National Assembly's naval plans had made the island kingdom uneasy. It was therefore no romantic folly that led the King to his decision but a very sound calculation of forces. Donoso Cortès, at that time Spanish Ambassador in Berlin, and not yet the philosopher of history of later years, referred in a report to his government in March 1849 to "the interest which the King of Prussia had and which he understood very well in resisting a temptation which must inevitably lead to his ruin, a temptation to steer a rock-strewn course at the end of which lay first an inevitable war and after that dethronement".

Bismarck's attitude was identical with that of the King. It is not difficult to imagine how he trembled inwardly before the decision had been made and how great was his joy when it was made known. The Assembly in the Paulskirche had for him always belonged to the realm of cloud-cuckoo-land. He had a word for it: "Frankfurterei". At other times he would bluntly refer to it as "the German swindle". The Frankfurt constitution made him its open enemy, for under it the fate of Prussia would be determined by a parliament with a non-Prussian majority. To turn the King of Prussia into a vassal was, he declared, "constitutionalised anarchy". Everyone wanted German unity but "I don't want it with such a constitution as this". For both the King and Bismarck, Germany meant the ancient empire that was coterminous with Hapsburg rule. And so he spoke of "our South-Eastern frontier districts, Styria and Illyria". For all that, however, such concepts as "Empire" and "Emperor" carried little weight with him when compared with the central significance of Prussia and of the Prussian dynasty.

Bismarck knew that the offer of Frankfurt's imperial crown could only ensure an enhancement of Prussian prestige if it was refused. He sought, he declared, in the Landtag, to protect Prussian honour by ensuring that Prussia avoided all "dishonouring connections with democracy". Democracy meant for him that the French Revolution, his arch enemy, had broken out afresh together with its nationalism, a nationalism whose character he recognised in the misuse made by the National Assembly of the ideas of race and language. He knew enough history to be aware of the fact that it is the weaker governments, those most desperately in need of popularity, that "force wars upon us in order to strengthen their own position", that it is much rarer for princes to bring wars about and so to risk their thrones, than for eager masses to do so, who imagine that they are running no risk at all, an illusion that persists until the publication of the first casualty list.

This was the attitude maintained by Bismarck throughout the years that followed, while, guided by his friend and minister, Radowitz,* Frederick William IV endeavoured to obtain by way of the dynasties that prize which, out of regard for those dynasties, he had refused to accept from the hands of a parliament. Burgesses had held up a crown to his gaze—the crown of an imaginary empire. They had no power to dispose of it and yet their action had not been without its seductive after-effects.

This affair has its intriguing aspects. Radowitz in particular is a curious figure. Descended from Catholic Hungarian stock, very ambitious, he seemed a strange person to act as representative of Protestant and Puritanical Prussia, and is indeed only explicable as the Paladin of the most un-Prussian Frederick William IV. At first, while the Frankfurt Assembly was in process of disappearing without a trace, luck seemed to be on his side. As an anticipatory form of the new German unity, he brought into being in May 1849 a league of three kings, namely the kings of Prussia, Saxony and Hanover, a league which the smaller states wedged in between them were compelled for better or worse to join. By the end of August the new formation, named a "Union", embraced Central and Northern Germany and also Baden in the south. It was to be a federal state under Prussian leadership and was to enter into an indissoluble League with Austria. In March 1850 the Union summoned a parliament to Erfurt, where it was to draw up a constitution.

Bismarck again was a member of this body although for him the Union was always something essentially childish, a game that could be played as long as Austria was occupied in Italy and Hungary. As soon as the old imperial power reappeared upon the German stage and was acclaimed, as it would be, as the liberator by the German states, who bore the Union's yoke very unwillingly, this game would rapidly come to an end. Radowitz was for Bismarck a "funereal figure", a man of "immense vanity", while the Union itself was simply "humbug", a "still-born child".

Six months later an unimportant conflict was to prove him right.

* Joseph Maria von Radowitz, originally an artillery officer in the Westphalian-French army, was taken prisoner at the battle of Leipzig and thereafter entered the service of Kurhessen and later of Prussia. In 1842 he became Prussian ambassador in Karlsruhe and Darmstadt.

The Elector of Hesse had fallen out with his subjects and in September had been compelled to flee. Yet although Hesse belonged to the Union, he did not summon the latter's help, but turned to Austria, the presiding power of the German Bund which was, after all, still in existence.

Nothing more fortunate could have happened to Austria, which had just suppressed the Hungarian rebellion even though she had done so with Russian help. Having thus gained a new access of strength, she was eagerly awaiting the opportunity to show the whole world that she had no intention whatever of accepting her exclusion from Germany, which the Union was tacitly endeavouring to bring about. Prince Schwarzenberg, whose iron hand had converted the post-revolutionary Hapsburg Empire into a greater Austrian unitary state, summoned the Diet of the Bund to meet on September 2nd. He was a man who detested the revolution, but he also detested incompetent conservatives and had taken on a number of liberal ministers such as Stadion, Bruck and Bach.

The clash between the two German state systems, the Union and the Bund, grew rapidly more acute. Both sides mobilised. Prussia saw herself confronted by a war against her old ally of 1813, while France, governed by a new Napoleon, lay at her rear. In this situation she was compelled to rely on an army whose value was widely doubted. On November 8th the first engagement took place with Bavarian and Austrian troops. These last had occupied Hesse at the orders of the Bund and so severed the western provinces of Prussia from those in the east. A strongly worded communication from his uncle, the Czar, made Frederick William realise that there was only one possibility open to him, to drop Radowitz. Bismarck celebrated Radowitz's fall with champagne.

Otto von Manteuffel, a cousin of the royal aide and a coolheaded, sensible man, was now appointed Prime Minister in a new "cabinet of the saving deed", and was charged with the task of negotiating with Schwarzenberg and coming to terms with him. At the meeting in Olmütz both sides agreed to demobilise, though Prussia had to demobilise first, while the Austrian and Bavarian troops were granted the right of transit through Hesse. The political problems which still awaited solution after this military détente were dealt with at conferences in Dresden and Olmütz during the course of which the Union was silently dissolved and the German Bund took on a new lease of life.

In the narrowly nationalist school of Prussian historiography these arrangements are referred to as the "humiliation of Olmütz". But Bismarck defended them in the Landtag, declaring that, given the facts of the situation, no better arrangement could have been arrived at.

It was in many ways a remarkable speech and an excellent example of Bismarck's rather unusual theory of political ethics. Hesse's party political quarrels, he maintained, "are not sufficiently important to risk the horrors of a war". Though it is all too easy for a statesman to move with "the popular wind and blow the war trumpet, leaving it to the musketeer, who lies bleeding in the snow, to decide whether a particular political system is to win honour and victory or no. . . . Woe to the statesman who does not search for a ground for war which will still remain valid after the war is over. . . . Why nowadays do great states wage war? The only sound foundation of a great state is political egoism (*der staatsrechtliche Egoismus*) and not romanticism, and it is unworthy of a great state to pick a quarrel for a cause that does not serve its own interests."

It was some years now since Bismarck had begun to sit in parliament and he was already beginning to look upon himself as a professional politician. He had leased his estates, and in 1849 rented a house in Berlin at the corner of the Wilhelm- and Behrenstrasse, half of which was occupied by himself and his family while the other was taken over by his brother-in-law Arnim, Malle's husband, who was also a Member of Parliament. But the two families did not continue to live alongside each other for long. The reason could well have been that Arnim was rich. He had seven estates and could well afford in a single day to spend twelve thousand thalers for a purchase of three pedigree horses, whereas Bismarck was continually under the necessity of saving, an unhappy condition which at the beginning of 1851 had driven him, as a means of increasing his income, to seek a ministerial post in the Duchy of Anhalt, where "the Duke was crazy and the minister was a duke".*

What is more to the point, however, is that Malle and Johanna were women of such diametrically opposite characters. Johanna was a simple and unassuming provincial, whereas Malle, now a person of outstanding charm, was the darling of Court society. "Society is spoiling her too much," wrote Bismarck to Johanna, "and it will be to her honour if she is not the worse for this experience". No doubt Johanna was aware of the fact that the intimacy which existed between brother and sister had opened a sphere to both of them which it was impossible for her to enter.

---

* It is stated that he asked von Schätzell, Minister in Anhalt, for a post even if it only carried a thousand thalers since his income was no longer sufficient to cover essential expenses.—Horst Kohl, *Erläuterungen zu Bismarcks Briefen an Braut und Gattin*, pp. 36-7.

This must have saddened her, but people of her nature tend to be uncommunicative, and she never spoke of the matter.

So in the summer of 1849 Johanna joined her parents in Reinfeld, while Bismarck remained behind alone in Berlin and lived in a furnished room, where he complained of bedbugs and of his landlord's four screaming children. Naturally he refused to fall in with Johanna's wish that she should live permanently in Reinfeld and so he found a less expensive home than the one he had shared with the Arnims, a ground-floor flat in the Behrenstrasse. Here in December his first child, Herbert, was born. At the beginning of April 1850, however, while Bismarck was sitting in the Union Parliament at Erfurt, Johanna was back in the country again.

She had neither the desire nor the ability to push herself forward, although she can hardly have been too happy when Bismarck described to her how on official occasions, at social gatherings, concerts, in St. Matthew's Church to hear the fashionable preacher Büchsel, and also on a visit to the graves of those who had fallen in March 1848, he was accompanied by his elegant sister. On the last-named occasion Bismarck was moved to observe that Christ had also died for these mutineers. "But my heart swells with poison when I see what they have done to my country."

Meanwhile the more Bismarck stood out in the public view, the more obviously Johanna lagged behind, not merely physically in Further Pomerania, but in what in this context is the more obvious sense of the term.

4

THE AMBASSADOR

At Olmütz all the German revolutions of 1848 had been liquidated.
The counter-revolution was victorious on all fronts. The united
power of the German states was once again represented by the
German Bund. In the spring of 1851 Prussia had once again
to send an ambassador to Frankfurt, and Frederick William's
choice fell on Bismarck.

It was entirely unprecedented for Prussia that a parliamen-
tarian, and a very eccentric one at that, should be entrusted with
a diplomatic post. Bismarck was right when, during the audience
granted him by the King before his departure, he said that it was
not he who had shown courage by accepting the appointment
but the King in offering it to him. Undoubtedly he derived
pleasure from those mingled feelings of outrage and amazement
which his appointment aroused, and it must have intrigued him
when the Prince of Prussia, displaying that ill-humour that so
often marks an heir to a throne, expressed his displeasure that
"this Landwehr lieutenant" should be made ambassador to the
Bund. Bismarck felt that he enjoyed the confidence, nay possibly
even the admiration, of the King, and indeed the King, himself
anything but an ordinary man, had no doubt recognised the
uniqueness of his ambassador and was enjoying the originality
of his style, the quality of his wit, and his thoroughly unbureau-
cratic appearance, with all the zest of a playgoer watching a
play.

To Johanna, Bismarck insisted that he had never "uttered a
syllable or even wished" for what had actually happened but that
he was "God's soldier" and "where He puts me there must I
go". Johanna being what she was, it is probable that the suggestion
of being under the direct orders of the Almighty made the move
more palatable—and no doubt it was for this reason that Bismarck
argued as he did, for he knew that the frivolities of Frankfurt
would make little appeal to her. For the time being, however,
she did not accompany him and he took up residence alone in
a Frankfurt hotel.

The impression made on him by the Frankfurt of that day was
not disagreeable. It was a sovereign city republic with seventy thou-

sand inhabitants, and a member of the German Bund. Its air
was balmy and it was situated in rolling fruitful country. The
graceful line of the Taunus Mountains rounded off the scene
while the steel-grey waters of the Main, that river which has
throughout history acted as a means both of union and division,
flowed past it through a broad valley. Frankfurt had had gas
lighting since 1828 and a regular steamship connection with
Mainz since 1845. It was also accounted one of the most expensive places in Europe.

At the very beginning of his stay Bismarck visited the Paulskirche, which he found exactly as the National Assembly had left
it, empty and deathly still after so many months of noisy and
desultory activity, a cold, pedantic circular building, the audi-
torium of a professor of chemistry which could serve on occasion
as a divine habitation. For the moment, however, as Bismarck
wrote to Johanna, its facilities as a place of divine worship continued to be withheld. No doubt there was an insufficiency of
worshippers.

One small but significant incident marked these first weeks.
Very soon after his arrival he received an invitation from the
head of the Frankfurt House of Rothschild, Meyer Amschel, who
had been ennobled in 1817 and quite obviously took as little
exception as had the prison governor Barschall in Brandenburg
to the fact that Bismarck a few years previously had spoken
against the emancipation of the Jews. The two men, each in
his own way a highly original creature, took an obvious liking
to each other.

In his personal life Bismarck was now enjoying an enhanced
freedom. In recent years he had been forced to practise not
inconsiderable self-denial. Now he had a salary of twenty
thousand thalers. He was rid of the relatively subordinate part
he had played at the Camarilla, the part of a mere intermediary.
He held a great position and the waves of the world were carrying
him along. The social life of Frankfurt, empty as it might be,
the luxury in which aristocratic diplomats and bourgeois practi-
tioners of high finance jointly indulged, were not only part of his
official duties, but were, he found, extremely enjoyable. The
most humdrum business of daily life was enacted against a background of delight, of silk upholstered furniture and damask wall
coverings. There were choice wines, lobsters, caviar, things which
in East Elbia, where they were a little close-fisted in such matters,
were reckoned as only suitable for the most festive occasions.

There was always a riot of receptions, balls dinners, with
gleaming uniforms whose wearers often wore the star of some
noble order, and with the sparkle of ladies' jewels as their wearers

moved through the throng in their hugely bulging dresses. The taste for life in the great world, the taste which had already been discernible at Aix, and was the heritage of the Mencken blood, was once more in evidence. He felt "as strong as a lion", also he had his beard removed, after which he looked "like a young girl with a bit of a moustache". All this did not prevent him from trying to save on his official allowance. Too much of the peasant Junker Bismarck had come out in him for him to do otherwise.

The Bundestag, in which Bismarck had to represent Prussia, was the visible embodiment of the German Bund, of that constitution which the Vienna Congress had given to thirty-eight German states with the object of maintaining a balance between the three effective powers, namely Austria, Prussia and the whole body of the other states. Thus, by putting a curb on excessive ambition in the sphere of inter-state policy, it was hoped to render each state innocuous towards its neighbour. Gentz* rightly described the organisation as being "incapable of aggression, invincible in defence".

Generations of docile students have since then had the idea hammered into them that the German Bund was a miscarriage, a contemptible ridiculous thing utterly unfitted to survive. This is not surprising when one reflects that the historiography of the succeeding epoch had a vested interest in such denigration, since the prestige of its own regime was thus enhanced. Bismarck, whose destiny it was to destroy the German Bund, avoided having any part in this injustice. Indeed, from the tribune of the Landtag in 1851, he challenged the House to show him "any period of history since the days of the Hohenstauffen in which, save for the Spanish sovereignty of Charles V, Germany commanded greater respect abroad, showed better judgment and commanded greater authority in its diplomacy, than during the time when the Bundestag directed Germany's affairs".

The Bund was an attempt to enable Germans to live with one another in peace and security, and the expedients employed to secure this end were sensible ones, though of course their success depended on the good will of all concerned. The constitution permitted such reforms to be made as the changing times demanded, though naturally enough it did not provide for partition of the kind that took place in 1866 and brought about the death of the Bund itself. When all is said and done, it lasted for half a century, which is longer than the life of any of its successors.

* Political publicist (1764–1832), translator of Burke's *Reflections on the French Revolution*. Acted as political adviser to both the Austrian and the British governments and drew pensions from both. Confidential adviser to Metternich, it was he who drafted the Carlsbad Decrees. Began life as a liberal but later became a strong reactionary.

The Bundestag was at one and the same time a permanent diplomatic conference and a kind of permanent senate, which dealt with the common affairs of the German states in accordance with the instructions of their governments. The Presidency was in the hands of the representative of Austria, who also held the purse strings, and where the voting was equal had a casting vote, as befitted his unique position as heir to the rulers of the Holy Roman Empire.

Bismarck, who did not feel himself called upon to change the world, was at first quite content with the situation as he found it. Indeed, he definitely believed his duty to lie in the conservation of the existing order. This meant that he must go along with Austria, which, like Prussia, had mastered the revolution. His radical enmity towards Radowitz and his determination to eliminate him root and branch made him feel that in this particular, at any rate, he and Schwarzenberg were very much of one mind.

The matter did not quite end there, however. Bismarck believed that this community of aims would turn Austria and Prussia into "Germany's two equal protecting powers", and this phrase was actually used by him in his Olmütz speech on December 3, 1850, though the remark was, to say the least, a little presumptuous, since the constitution recognised only a single presidential power. It failed to grant Prussia a single right that was not enjoyed by any other member of the Bund.

Any change in this state of affairs would, above all else, depend on the good will of Austria, and it was on this that Bismarck was obviously counting. Actually, however, at that particular moment the government of Vienna felt that it had emerged out of a sea of crises with a new access of strength, and, having duly humbled Prussia at Olmütz, had no intention of conceding to her anything resembling what Bismarck termed "a dualistic equality of rights". It was one of the many pieces of ill-chance that marked Austria's history that she drew out for too long the enjoyment derived from her triumph at Olmütz and so forgot Metternich's advice never to weary of making advances to Prussia. She thus ended by doing the very opposite and disastrously wounded Prussian *amour-propre*—a blunder that changed the whole course of her history. For Bismarck was quite incapable of enduring any inferiority of rights for long, though in this case Austrian "primacy" was hardly more than a mere formal tradition that carried no real weight.

Austria resisted, and though her resistance was elastic and carried on under the politest of forms, it remained inflexible. Bismarck was roused to dumb fury, for not only had he been betrayed by one whom he believed to be both his debtor and his friend: he had also been made to look ridiculous. To make matters worse, the Austrian representative in Frankfurt, Count Thun, was a man with whom from the very start Bismarck could not get anywhere at all. Thun was very much a grand seigneur who came from a wealthy Bohemian family. The Pomeranian Junker, whom he took to be a party politician playing at diplomacy, made little impression on him. Also he was a follower of the lazy man's wisdom, according to which the best way of dealing with unpleasant problems is to mislay them, forget them or leave them to solve themselves.

This caused Bismarck—and here as a heavy-blooded North German he ran thoroughly true to type—to suspect that his proposals were not really being dealt with seriously at all, and, as always in such cases, he took this as a personal affront. Naturally he understood that there were good reasons for Austria's attitude. Prussia, a state whose territories were scattered across Central Europe, with other states stuck in between them, was greatly inferior to the imperial power of Austria whose land mass stretched without a break from Lake Constance to the Turkish border. If the facts were really allowed to speak, Austria was really the only great power in the German Bund. Prussia indeed had the right to designate herself as such, but this was not so much a fact as a concession which the Vienna Congress had granted through an anxiety to avoid disputes. Why then should Austria share with Prussia the privileges which she owed to her unique position?

Yet Bismarck's whole aim was the destruction of these privileges. The way to achieve that end was to alter the Bund's constitution. If the military-geographical power relations made this impossible, then these very military-geographical power relations would themselves have to be changed. Bismarck had begun by seeking to transform the very nature of Austria's primacy so as to make it extensible to Prussia. But he had a further and more distant end in view. It was to put an end to Prussia's territorial fragmentation, and to set beside Austria a Prussia that was as much a closed political body as Austria herself. This meant that states still surviving in between the various territories which in the course of time had come under the Prussian Crown, began to be viewed with an increasingly unfriendly eye, and this in its turn produced a corresponding and understandable distrust on the part of the states concerned, a mistrust which, as Bismarck himself remarked, "not even an angel could talk out of their heads, so long as there was a map for them to glance at".

Yet even if his aim was to secure for Prussia a position of greater authority within the Bund, he had not at this stage begun to question the usefulness of the Bund itself or to cast doubts on its right to exist. For the moment he was concerned with Austria, and his aim was to diminish the respect in which she was held and thus to shake her self-confidence, undermine her whole position and ultimately isolate her. Often the issues raised were petty to the point of being ludicrous, such as the custom whereby the Austrian plenipotentiary was the only one allowed to smoke. Bismarck called this privilege in question by deliberately lighting a cigar. This banal triumph involved him in what to our present way of thinking was a singularly mild exchange with a deputy, von Vincke. Fortunately the resulting duel was something of a farce. Before the order to fire was given, Bismarck removed his hat in order to pray. Vincke thought that he was saluting him and also removed his hat. Each of the contestants then fired a shot which hit nothing, whereupon there was a general shaking of hands.

Having once resolved to attack Austria, Bismarck was unswerving in carrying out his purpose and quite ruthless in the choice of means. He indulged in hair-splitting at which he often showed considerable wit, in pinpricks, in gross self-righteous dogmatism, and would pick a quarrel for almost no reason at all. He thus reduced the representatives of Austria to the verge of despair and all the time he was showing an equal degree of skill in representing himself as the victim of aggression.

These disputes about trivialities between the two German powers ultimately became so scandalous that Czar Nicholas I, who regarded himself as the executor of the Holy Alliance, sent the Russian ambassador in Stuttgart, Gortschakow, to Frankfurt as a peacemaker. This was the first meeting between Bismarck and this shrewd, diligent, and enormously ambitious man, who was some twenty years his senior and who was so often to cross his path. His first impression was certainly incorrect. Gortschakow, he said, was "a solemn and misguided fool, a fox in wooden shoes". That the Russian effort produced no practical results is in the circumstances hardly surprising.

In April 1852 Schwarzenberg died at the comparatively early age of fifty-two. It was one of those many premature deaths that marked the history of the Hapsburgs. In the summer of the same year, Arnim, the Prussian ambassador in Vienna, fell ill and Bismarck was sent provisionally to take over his duties. There is little doubt, however, that the real reason for the appointment was Frederick William's desire to give his protégé further education in "the great school of diplomacy".

Bismarck was received in Vienna "with more honour than I should have expected". He found himself in a new and highly centralised state in which Count Buol was in charge of the Foreign Office. The young Emperor, Francis Joseph, who regarded himself as the heir and pupil of Schwarzenberg, had reserved for himself the supreme direction of all affairs of state, but Bismarck believed that the real political "Faiseur" was his mother, the Archduchess Sofia.

The immediate issue was that Austria wished to join the customs union which Prussia had formed with a number of the central German states. Prussia, however, was afraid that in this customs union she would again be outvoted by Austria and was doing her utmost to exclude her from membership. In the end she succeeded in her endeavours, which might perhaps be regarded as a modest compensation for Olmütz.

For Bismarck the chief advantage of his stay in Vienna was that he was able to meet and so size up the very people with whom in the immediate future he was to have dealings. Meanwhile in Frankfurt the ranks of his opponents were being steadily strengthened and this was logical enough, for Bismarck was obviously trying to weaken Austria's position in the Bund. This undermined the Bund's constitution and so the Bund itself; and since it was the Bund that for the other German states constituted the only sure guarantee of their own existence, they were forced on to Austria's side, and thus drew upon themselves the downright enmity of Bismarck.

Having lasted for forty years, the system of world peace constructed by the Vienna Congress fell to pieces in 1853. Russia's centuries-old pressure on Turkey to secure possession of the Dardanelles had become so acute that France and England had come to Turkey's aid and had sent troops through the Black Sea to land in the Crimea. Vienna, moved by a not unreasoning fear that Russia's urge towards expansion, which had already been directed towards Turkey, might tomorrow threaten Austria on the Lower Danube, was at first quite prepared to join the Allies. Even in Prussia important personalities, among them Prince William, the heir to the throne, were ready to join Austria, though the King described an alliance with "heathen Turkey and Napoleonic France" as "an incest".

In the end both German powers remained neutral, though Austria went so far as to mobilise in Eastern Galicia and so pin down two hundred thousand Russians who might have won a decision for Russia in the Crimea. Prussian neutrality was much more strict, and two hundred thousand Russian troops were thus released for the theatre of war. Without realising it, Frederick William IV was accumulating the great capital of Russian friendship which later on brought such excellent interest in the form of Russian neutrality during the wars of 1866 and 1870.

Naturally enough during the Crimean War, Bismarck was

wholly on the side of the King. He cared little for the fact that the campaign of the Western Powers was represented as a kind of crusade. If it influenced him at all, it did so in a negative sense. He was, however, genuinely afraid that Austria might suddenly join the West and so turn Germany into a battleground. In May 1854 he remarked with a certain not untypical complication of metaphor that "next year Cossacks and Paris gamins will use our bones to knock apples from the trees". Since he always looked upon himself rather as Prussia's ambassador than as a member of the central body of the German Bund, he had no inhibitions about intriguing against Austria, with Glinka, the Russian ambassador in Frankfurt, for Austria, though a member of the Bund, was for all practical purposes to him as much a foreign country as Portugal.

In 1855 he visited the World's Fair in Paris, and, surrounded by the glittering splendour of the new empire which had so suddenly emerged out of a kind of conspiratorial darkness, he gazed for the first time into the grey, enigmatic eyes of Napoleon III. A strong bond of sympathy seemed immediately to establish itself between himself and the mysterious man of whom no one knew whether he was really the nephew or the son of the first Emperor, the offspring, that is to say, of a union between step-father and stepdaughter.

He was in Paris again in the spring of 1857. The dispute between Prussia and Switzerland over Neuchatel,* in which Napoleon acted as arbitrator, gave Bismarck occasion to get himself appointed as representative of the German Bund, although the Bund's concern with this particular matter was extremely remote—and this, too, had agreeable consequences. He felt, he wrote to Malle, "extremely edified by the people and things around me and especially by the Emperor". He spoke of the Empress Eugenie as a "woman who excited lively admiration", but most of all he was drawn toward Napoleon himself.

At the imperial table or walking along the quiet garden paths of his palaces, Napoleon showed this diplomatic beginner, who still held a very unimportant and insecure post and was now visiting him on a wholly superfluous mission, an astonishing degree of openness. Thus he told him that he was planning to attack Austria and was counting in this connection on an alliance

---

* As a result of certain hereditary rights the Swiss canton of Neuchatel had once been subject to the sovereignty of the King of Prussia from which it contrived to free itself in 1848. In 1856 a conservative group sought to restore the monarchy by a coup d'état but were made prisoners. Prussia prepared an offensive through Baden in order to bring aid to the conspirators and Switzerland was about to oppose it in Baden itself. In the end the King renounced all claims on Neuchatel in return for the liberation of his supporters.

with Prussia, to which Bismarck replied that the Emperor had made this communication to the only Prussian diplomat who would not use it to the utterer's disadvantage. From this Napoleon could infer that Bismarck did not share the dislike which the various courts felt for Napoleon as an illegitimate ruler, and that so far as Bismarck was concerned the idea of legitimacy was confined to the Prussian dynasty. Each of the two recognised in the other a man who was capable of being conservative or revolutionary, who cared little for labels and was quite ready to enter into an alliance with anybody if such a thing seemed to be to his advantage. No doubt it was this that made Napoleon so communicative.

The fact is that for some time a change had been developing in Bismarck's outlook. He no longer felt that he owed a duty to the common political philosophy which was supposed to actuate the Holy Alliance. His duty lay where the interest of Prussia demanded that it should lie, and nowhere else. He had, to put the matter almost over-concisely, elevated a lack of principle into a principle, or, to be more exact, he had narrowed down all principles to one, namely Prussia, with which he entirely identified himself.

His change of outlook was utterly uncompromising. It meant that he must withdraw from the circle of those who, from likeness of mind, he had hitherto regarded as his friends, in particular the Gerlachs, whose whole existence had been governed by the principles of Christian morality and who made their decisions dependent on a changeless authority that was not of this world. For Leopold von Gerlach, for instance, Napoleon was "a half-fantastic, half-gruesome politician for whom right and honour were concepts devoid of substance". Whereas for Bismarck such considerations were irrelevant; for him France was never more than a piece in the game of political chess, though it was one that could never be overlooked whoever might be the personage temporarily at its head.

In Vienna the more intelligent minds had long ceased to have any illusions concerning Bismarck's undeviating hostility. Prokesch, the Austrian representative in the Bund, a person who had travelled all over the world and had an excellent knowledge of men, wrote when leaving Frankfurt in 1854, that "no consideration, no treaty" would deflect Bismarck's efforts. This could only be achieved "by force and a diminution of (Prussian) power".

Prokesch's successor, Count Rechberg,* a career diplomat

---

* Johann Bernhard Count von Rechberg, descended from a Swabian family, was born in Regensburg in 1806, became a career diplomat, was civilian aide to Radetzky in Italy, and in 1855 Austrian ambassador to the Bundestag.

with a gentle manner, endeavoured despite all that had occurred to reach an understanding. Bismarck told him quite openly, "I am a Prussian ambassador and have to represent the interests of Prussia and not of the Bund." Nevertheless Rechberg remained prepared to make reasonable concessions and was ready to agree that Austria, as the presiding power of the legislative assembly of the Bund, should only lay before it such bills as had previously been agreed on with Prussia. This would have meant a common Austro-German veto, and in effect a dictatorship by the two great powers which actually would have been to the disadvantage of the Bund itself and to the whole of the rest of Germany. But it was already too late for any such cool-headed and realistic solution. It was not long before Rechberg, an upright though somewhat simple man, had for Bismarck become "the little bottle of poison".

In the autumn of 1857, however, the King of Prussia, who for some time had been suffering from high blood pressure, had several strokes which impaired his powers of speech, so that, although his mind was still sporadically active, he could no longer find the words which he needed and had become unfit to rule. His brother William acted first as his representative and was then made Regent.

One of the changes resulting from this was Bismarck's recall from Frankfurt and his transfer to St. Petersburg. Technically this was promotion. Actually Bismarck accepted it with very ill grace, and it may well be that men who considered his policy too aggressive may have had a hand in the matter. What chiefly irked him, however, was leaving Rechberg in possession of the field.

St. Petersburg was not ungracious. In Czar Alexander II, and also in Gortschakow, who had now become Chancellor, Bismarck found an agreeably sympathetic understanding for his enmity towards Austria, and when in the summer of 1859 the Italian war broke out between France and Austria, he could experience much satisfaction in the pleasure which in the Russian capital was aroused by Austria's defeats.

Strangely enough, the Crimean War had left Russia with a hatred of England and Austria, but none of France. Indeed, hardly was the peace signed when Gortschakow was already seeking an alliance. Here, too, then, Bismarck was at one with his hosts. Indeed, there were such open French sympathies in St. Petersburg that court society was already adopting the characteristic Imperial of Napoleon III.

His greatest anxiety at this time was that the Prince Regent, a veteran of the wars of liberation, might think that, as on that occasion, he would have to take the field against France side by side with the Hapsburgs. He feared, as he himself put it, that in Berlin people would "get drunk with an imitation of 1813", and would go to war "because of the bleating of the herd". The Prince Regent had already ordered mobilisation, and it was only because the latter wanted to assume command in any German theatre of war, a command which he might perhaps never have relinquished, that Francis Joseph preferred to make a quick peace with Napoleon rather than enter into such an alliance. For this, of course, he had to pay with a great part of the fair province of Lombardy, an amputation which made the Hapsburgs' Italian possessions perilously small.

Even now Bismarck was not satisfied, however, and came out with a project that was to alienate the Prince Regent even more than he was alienated already. He proposed that the Franco-Austrian war should really be allowed to "dig itself in" (*sich einfressen*), then the whole Prussian army was to march southwards "carrying boundary posts in its knapsacks which it would set up at Lake Constance". Alternatively, it would "move forward where the Protestant religion came to an end and found a kingdom of Germany where the other princes would simply be mediatised". Only Bavaria, which was "too fat for such a system", should "remain outside" enlarged by Catholic Swabia.* That the Prince Regent, a professional soldier, for whom after sixty-two years of life correct behaviour had become second nature, would have had little sympathy for such a wild fantasy—it was nothing less than an attempt to blow the whole of Germany sky-high— is something that his uninvited counsellor should surely have known.

In August of that year Bismarck, while hunting in Sweden, struck his leg against the edge of a rock and injured the shin bone. He did not concern himself much with the matter until the pain became unendurable. Then, in St. Petersburg, he fell into the hands of a quack who called himself Dr. Walz, although he had never got his degree. But since the so-called Dr. Walz was also the son of a Heidelberg confectioner, he managed to get himself recommended by his sovereign lady, the Grand Duchess of Baden. He put a blister in the hollow of Bismarck's knee, and tore open a wound as large as a man's hand, destroying a vein. Bismarck returned to Prussia by sea in great pain. During the journey a Russian surgeon told him that amputation of the leg would be unavoidable.

In Nauheim, after a partial recovery, he had a serious relapse,

* Memorandum for the Prince Regent, William, addressed to Adjutant General von Alvensleben, May 1859, Rothfels, *Bismarck und der Staat* (1925), p. 113.

for he suffered from a thrombosis, together with so severe an inflammation of the lungs, that his life was despaired of. Tortured
by great pain, he himself awaited the end "with complete resignation". Before so resigning himself, however, he made a final
disposition which prevented any interference by the law with the
arrangements made by him for the tutelage of his children, a vote
of no confidence against Prussian justice with which it was his
intention to depart from the world.

It was not till May 1861 that, after an absence of ten months,
he was back at his Russian post. He had always looked upon it
as a provisional appointment and that is why he never set about
"making a house" in St. Petersburg. Probably, however, as in
Frankfurt, his Junker's passion for economy may, of course, have
had something to do with this, but certainly he was acutely conscious of straitened means. "With a salary of thirty thousand
talers," he wrote, "one was compelled in St. Petersburg drastically to cut down one's expenditure." For this reason he hardly
ever accepted a luncheon invitation, rarely went out after five
o'clock and had very little to do with the real society of the place.
He considered the older generation of the aristocracy to be the
best educated in the world, "the cream of European good
manners", though he was less enamoured of their descendants,
whom he found already infected by the disease of Western
nationalism, which here took the form of Panslavism and therefore tended to be unfriendly to Germany.

The Czar, a nephew of the Prince Regent of Prussia, continued
to show him good will, as did also Gortschakow, whom he now
referred to as "the best mind in official Russia" and towards
whom he seems to have developed some warmth of feeling.
Johanna describes what may well have been a typical scene. She
tells how, after a funeral, the two sat together on the black velvet
catafalque trimmed with silver skulls, "planning and plotting as
though there were no such thing as death". The Czarina Mother,
Charlotte, who was something of an invalid and yet reminded
one, with her intelligence and charm, of her mother Queen
Louisa, liked to have the Prussian Ambassador sitting chatting
by her bed. Here, too, then was a friend.

But there were other things than friendship that now began to
stir him. With that respect for Russia that was peculiar to the
older generation of Prussians, there had begun to mingle a deep
sense of the monstrous uniqueness of this giant, who just about
this time was reaching the Pacific Ocean. Sakhalin was occupied
in 1859 and Vladivostok founded in 1860. Russia cast a spell on
him by the very vastness of her space. It was this, and not the
cold that had broken Napoleon. It was this with all its military

and political implications, that captured Bismarck's mind. The great white bear held him hypnotised, *"ich sehe dem Eisbären ins Gesicht"* he wrote, and thenceforward whenever he sought to calculate forces, Russia's huge power-potential dominated the equation.

Holstein,* at that time a young attaché at the Prussian embassy, tells us that at this stage little notice was taken of Bismarck because of his retiring way of life. In 1862, however, interest suddenly exploded like a pyrotechnic display. This may or may not have been occasioned by a report from the Russian ambassador in Berlin naming Bismarck as a future prime minister, a prediction that would by no means have been incredible.

Of course by any rational assessment Bismarck should have been regarded as side-tracked beyond redemption. Yet he had contrived with an almost impish skill to remain the subject of political gossip and so ensured that his reputation as a man with a future achieved a robust and gratifying persistence. The death of his well-wisher Frederick William and the succession of the Prince Regent, who had little liking for Bismarck, changed nothing of this. He continued to make appearances in Berlin with well-nigh horological regularity—attending, amongst other things, the coronation of William I, with which he had no shadow of official concern. He was labelled a careerist and was looked on as something of a joke, but he achieved his end, for he was not forgotten.

There were times when he cried sour grapes and affected a complete indifference to the prospects of his career, a mood which finds not infrequent expression in his letters to Malle. He would at times during such phases make remarks to his superiors which were quite terrifyingly ill-considered—such as that to Bernstorff, "If you want a war, appoint me your under-secretary of state. I will within four weeks undertake to deliver to you a civil war of the very highest quality." According to Holstein, Bismarck

* Friederich von Holstein (1837–1909). One of the most mysterious figures in recent German history. He contrived to establish himself in a position of strength in the German Foreign Office, where almost every piece of important business passed through his hands and he really had more power than any Minister. Just how he contrived to acquire this is something of a mystery. That he was a man of great ability we cannot doubt, otherwise he would never have got where he did, but seen in retrospect he seems to have had a positive genius for being wrong. He constantly asserted that neither France nor England would ever become the ally of Russia and based all his policy on that. He started off being Bismarck's spy at the Paris Embassy. Later the two became estranged from one another and many think he was the real author of the latter's fall. Philip Eulenberg, the favourite of William II, is responsible for the statement that Bismarck spoke of him as the man with the hyena eyes. He was a crack shot and fought a duel with the editor of the comic paper Kladderadatsch. There is a very readable account of him in Emil Ludwig's *William Hohenzollern*.

gave the impression of being a dissatisfied man who was also something of a hypochondriac and insufficiently resigned to the quiet
life of a Prussian representative at St. Petersburg. He was anything but a jovial person, even when he was telling a funny story.
... In every one of his remarks he seemed to suggest that life and
action were for him interchangeable terms. He had an itch for
ministerial office, and though he seemed to know that even that
would fail to satisfy him, the itch remained. (*"Wird mir der
ministerielle Gaul vorgeführt, so kann mich die Sorge über den Zustand
seiner Beine nich abhalten aufzusitzen."*)

His recall came in March 1862—and it did not come too soon
—but Bismarck's effect on the King had always been vaguely disturbing and it required something of an effort to decide how he
was to be used. Of this the King, a prudent but essentially a
simple man, was not immediately capable. It was only recently
that he had contemptuously referred to him as a Landwehr
lieutenant. How could he give such a man even a share in the
power over the Prussian state. The King took refuge in inaction.
It was not till the end of May that he appointed Bismarck Ambassador to Paris.

When Bismarck presented his credentials, both Emperor and
Empress treated him as an old acquaintance. He found Eugenie
"prettier than ever". As for his political contact with Napoleon,
it was not long before that was resumed. During a leisurely walk
at Fontainebleau, on the 26th June, the Emperor reviewed and
expanded his offer of an out-and-out Franco-Prussian alliance.
Bismarck was somewhat taken by surprise and hesitated with his
reply, whereupon the Emperor remarked that Austria had been
panic-stricken by Bismarck's activity in Paris and had made
quite incredible proposals. It was a promising beginning.

Then suddenly Paris had become unendurably dusty and hot
(the early summer had been damp and cool) and Paris society fled
post-haste to the watering places, as did the government itself.
Bismarck was alone in the city with almost nobody to talk to
except Thiers, then a man of sixty-five, and already to some
extent an embodiment of tradition. Neither knew that eight
years later they were to talk together in a very different fashion
and that history would be made by their dialogue.

During these weeks of solitude one question was always in the
forefront of Bismarck's mind. Who was to hold the power in
Prussia? He began to realise that the answer could not long be
delayed. One way or the other, there would have to be a decision.
Writing to Roon, he declared himself willing to serve but accompanied this with fulsome promises of discretion. He was, he
declared, *"bereitwillig"* but not *"mutwillig"*. This time there

would be no pranks. But he was obviously straining at the leash, and eager for action. He felt, he declared—pregnantly but with a certain zoological imprecision—"like that animal that goes dancing on the ice when it feels too well".

In the end he applied for six weeks leave, hoping thus to put out of his mind the uncertainty of his own future. He was in a highly nervous state and had no fixed plan, but went first to London,* then back to France and along the Atlantic coast up to the Spanish border. On the 4th August he was in Biarritz and here was joined at the Hotel de l'Europe, where he lived, by Prince Orlow, the Russian ambassador in Brussels who arrived on the 7th and whom he knew from his St. Petersburg days.

Prince Orlow was a veteran of the Crimea who had had his right arm shattered and wore a black silk eye shield to conceal the loss of an eye. Princess Orlow—her name was Katharine, and she was by birth a Trubetzkoi—was twenty-two years old and utterly bewitching. She had been brought up in France and spoke French, English and German and hardly any Russian. She was a stranger to Bismarck but there rapidly developed between them a companionship which, though our information is scanty, seems to have gone rather beyond the permitted informalities of a holiday resort.

Bismarck and the Orlows took their meals together in the Orlows' rooms. Apart from this, a small company gathered daily together consisting of Bismarck, the Orlows, the Princess's French lady-in-waiting, and a Russian diplomat named von Hamburger, Gortschakow's *homme de confiance*, whom Bismarck described to his wife as "hunch-backed, intelligent and a good fellow". The Princess called Bismarck "uncle". The Prince, a great gentleman of the old school, always more or less of an invalid, gave his wife, his junior by some thirteen years, the maximum of freedom and left her no opportunity of asking for it. For Bismarck the idyll was all too short, but while it lasted politics seemed to be forgotten, nervous tensions relaxed. Indeed, when von Galen, the Prussian ambassador in Madrid and an old friend of his, called to see him, Bismarck did not find this visit altogether welcome.

To Malle who, as always, was again his confidante, he declared quite openly that he had fallen slightly in love with the "*niedliche principessa*". "You know that this type of thing sometimes happens to me"; and to Johanna he wrote, with rather less candour, that the Princess was "original, jolly, intelligent and friendly, pretty

* It was after this visit that Beaconsfield remarked: "Be careful of that man, he means what he says." According to the memoirs of Lord Loftus, British Ambassador in Berlin at the time, Bismarck said that he was planning to re-organise the Prussian army and would then declare war on Austria and unite Germany under Prussian leadership.

and young. . . . When you meet her you will forgive my being somewhat épris." Johanna at that time was writing to Keudell, "If I had any disposition towards envy or jealousy, I could no doubt let these passions tyrannise over the very depths of my being . . . but there is no aptitude for that kind of thing in my soul. I am only always very glad indeed that my dear husband has found this charming woman." In all this Johanna showed a very magnanimous side of her character. There can be little doubt that she did experience jealousy and suffer from it, although the knowledge of her own worth compelled her to be silent.

But Bismarck was full of the careless fun of a new adventure. The time seemed to have returned when the truant Referendar had followed the lovely Englishwoman through half of Central Europe. Now, twenty-five years later, the story was to some extent to repeat itself; when on September 1st the Orlows left Biarritz, he accompanied them to Pau, to Lourdes, to Cauterets, and, as on that previous occasion, he overstayed his leave.

On September 12th a letter from Roon reached him in Toulouse. It stated that though the King was still undecided, the time was drawing near when Bismarck would have to take up the burden of duty. "So I pretend that I have your consent and advise that you should provisionally be appointed Prime Minister without Portfolio." Bismarck replied that all he asked was an immediate decision whether he was to be made prime minister or was to remain as ambassador in Paris. "Let me know for certain whether it is to be the one thing or the other and I shall paint angel's wings on your photograph."

At last he contrived to tear himself away, Avignon being the scene of the parting. The Orlows left for Geneva while he himself took the train for Paris. The farewell party which at the age of forty-seven he had given to his own youth was over. All that remained was a little twig of olive which the Princess had plucked at Avignon and which he always carried about in his cigar case. And yet this recent interlude on the shores of the Atlantic was still overshadowed by that other overwhelming experience vouchsafed him on the peaceful estates of East Elbia some twenty years ago. Writing to Johanna, he could still say of his young Princess that the best of her was "a bit of Marie Thadden".

Those weeks with the Orlows seemed to mark the close of a chapter in Bismarck's life. It was as though he had resolved to let feminine charm have no further influence over him. Not that he had become insensitive to it. On the contrary, he admired and delighted in it even in extreme old age. He never wearied in gallantry and was the darling of the ladies in every drawing-room. But the boldness with which he threw himself into adventures of passion had disappeared, although life under William I, who, unlike his contemporary on the throne of England, had much understanding for human weakness, held many opportunities for those inclined to go astray.

In Paris, Bismarck once again saw German newspapers, which since they were short of material during the summer, gave all the more space to the grave difficulties which the King of Prussia was experiencing with his Parliament. Shortly after his arrival in the city Bismarck received a telegram from the Foreign Minister Bernstorff, urging him to come to Berlin immediately. Two days later, on September 18th, came the now historic telegram from Roon: "Periculum in mora".

He arrived in Berlin early on the 20th. In the evening the Crown Prince asked him to come and see him and tried to get him to say something of his intentions, but Bismarck remained a model of courteous uncommunicativeness. On the 21st, a Sunday, Roon went to Babelsberg to see the King to obtain an audience for Bismarck. The King seemed ill-humoured and sceptical. He was well informed and knew that Bismarck had already been to see his son. Nevertheless, on September 22nd Bismarck came to Babelsberg and met the King, and before it was evening he was Prussian Minister of State and President of the Ministry. A fortnight later he was Prime Minister and Minister for Foreign Affairs.

Part II

HIGH NOON

5

THE LEAP TO POWER

The Kingdom of Prussia, whose fortunes had now been placed in Bismarck's hands, was a state of middling size, lying largely in the North German plain, stretching to the east across the Vistula and to the west across the Rhine, and containing nearly twenty million inhabitants. On the map it shows a curiously jagged outline. To the heartland, the Electorate of Brandenburg, there had been added in the course of centuries towards west, north, and south-east, large complexes of territory which were like bastions that had been pushed forward. Towards the north lay Pomerania which, after the old Slavic dukes had died out, had been peacefully inherited. In the north-east there was East Prussia, originally the territory of the German knights, which in the Reformation had been transformed by the High Master, Albrecht von Hohenzollern, into a secular Protestant dukedom, a dukedom of which Albrecht had appointed himself to be the first incumbent. Later, in the course of ordinary inheritance, it had come into the hands of the Brandenburg Hohenzollerns.

It was only since the end of the eighteenth century that the annexed territories of Poland, which became the provinces of West Prussia and Posen, connected it with the Brandenburg heartland. In the south-east lay Silesia, wrested in three wars from the Hapsburgs, rich, fruitful and still full of the Austrian baroque tradition. Finally, there were the highly-developed territories of the west, that were incorporated with—nay positively thrust upon—Prussia (which would have been far better pleased with the simple annexation of Saxony); the chief agents of this embarrassing largesse being (of all people) Talleyrand and Metternich, for whose countries this enlargement of Prussian power was to have such regrettable results.

It was only since 1807 that these territories had enjoyed the blanket cognomen of Prussia. Till then they had been referred to with a certain engaging vagueness as "All his Royal Majesty's lands and provinces". And since large portions of what was now called Prussia jutted out into the world like peninsulas, they were in continual danger of being subjected to pressure from both sides and of thus ultimately being squeezed off the body of the Prussian state. Indeed, the whole block of the western possessions was cut off completely from the central and eastern provinces.

Actually Prussia was not the only sufferer from this kind of disability which was not without its peculiar temptations to an aggressor. But these things were the outcome of organic historical growth, and in the main the Bund, which maintained a fairly stable equilibrium between states, safeguarded quite effectively against such dangers. Indeed, its "ordering of peace" has rightly been called by Gerhard Ritter "the most stable the West has known since the days of the high Middle Ages".

Admittedly, the Bund was a league not between states and between peoples. It was a clumsy arrangement and essentially difficult to survey, and the fact that some of its members only belonged to it with a part of their territory (Austria and Prussia, for instance, whose Slavonic lands lay outside the Bund), while others, such as Holstein and Luxemburg, were the properties of foreign sovereigns, namely the kings of Denmark and Holland, must have reduced any political architect to despair. But in the words of Oliver Wendell Holmes, "A moment's insight is sometimes worth a life's experience."

Under the Bund the Germans were not living under a state system that had no future. Still less were they living under intolerable conditions. What was meant by "intolerable conditions" they were only to learn in the thirties of the following century. Their ancient, small and medium-sized states were not driven together by force but were united by a community of basic principles. They lived, as the Germans have always lived when left to their own devices and when nobody misdirects their feelings, industriously and economically, and they continually displayed inventive power. Their old commercial relations which stretched across the continent developed anew, and gradually the country roads were turned into railways. Many and varied were the industries that burst into life. In all probability the Germans had never been better clothed or better fed during the whole of their past.

The Bund had at its disposal all the riches of Europe from the French to the Turkish frontier. It had been designed as a league not for aggression but for mutual defence, and for fifty years it had performed that function. It had ensured that German states were not involved in the crises which had disturbed the rest of Europe—in the French Revolution of 1830, for instance, in the disturbances that rocked Belgium, Holland and Luxemburg, or the quarrels concerning the Spanish throne. Finally it was the machinery of the Bund which allowed that strange Franco-German war psychosis that boiled up around 1840 to be harmlessly dispelled—and indeed, apart from some differences of opinion concerning the Turco-Egyptian question, there had never been any real grounds for its existence.

The worst that can be said is that during this period the popular nationalism of undisciplined mass instinct blazed up like summer lightning, ominous as the knife of the guillotine. It was the same popular nationalism which, in the following century, was to bring this proud continent to the edge of the grave. Even the internal tensions of the Bund—and, as in every human form of symbiosis, there were plenty of these—never came near imperilling its actual life. Whatever derogatory things may have been said about it, the Bund was, to quote Erich Marks, "the old empire in a less pretentious and more realistic form".

Over Brandenburg, after it had been united with the sometime possessions of the German Order in Prussia, there seemed to hang a special and peculiar destiny. For many years the life of the Electorate had been distinguished by the same quality of phlegmatic equanimity that marked the other North German members of the Empire. Even the Hohenzollerns, who originally came from Swabia, had to adapt themselves to this unenterprising mood.

Along with the territory of Prussia, however, Brandenburg appeared to have inherited something of the acquisitive talents of its original possessors, of that strange German Order whose members so ingenuously endeavoured to make the best of both worlds, and whose white mantles, marked with the Cross of Christ, so imperfectly concealed their highly serviceable armour. They made their mark in many fields as administrators on the grand scale, as soldiers, and in diplomacy. All over eastern Europe they helped to shape its history and, as we have seen, their spirit survived them. Barely twenty years after Prussia had come into its possession, Brandenburg embarked on a course which, to say the least, was remarkable in a state of that size. The Great Elector, Frederick William (1620–1688), who may well have inherited from his mother some of the skills of rulership possessed by the House of Orange, plunged his country into the whirlpool of world politics, and let his small but excellent army engage itself all over Europe, now in the service of the Emperor, now in that of France, then in that of Holland, of Sweden or of Poland.

The result was a modest enlargement of his territory. What was of even more importance, however, was that the old relationship of vassalage to Poland was ended and that the Elector acquired full sovereign rights.

His son Frederick III of Brandenburg (1657–1713), drew the logical conclusion from this and assumed the title of Frederick I of Prussia in 1701, though Prussia lay at a distance of many days' journey and had never belonged to the German Empire. His grandson, Frederick William I of Prussia (1688–1740), went still further and built up an army scarcely matched by any of the great powers. People regarded this Prussian army as little more than the crazy hobby of an absolute monarch—until this same army made it possible for his son Frederick II (1712–1786) to display over a period of years a quite exemplary strategic skill, and so created the myth of Prussian glory.

Even Frederick the Great, however, never departed from the traditional Prussian policy of leaning on the stronger powers and rendering them service; much as the Great Elector was the sword of France or Sweden, as circumstances appeared to dictate, so his great-grandson lent his army to Britain during the Seven Years War. With the Napoleonic wars Russia set about casting Prussia for a similar part. The winter of 1812 which had destroyed Napoleon's army had made the Czars into the decisive power of Europe. So long as Prussia believed that she had to play a rôle in world affairs, she was compelled to make up for the inadequacy of her means by a bold and resourceful diplomacy, and since she often lacked diplomats of the necessary calibre, she was compelled to resort to intrigues, to the concealment of her true aims and to frequent changes of front. It was this that won for Prussian policy a reputation for quite exceptional disingenuousness.

The people who were theoretically at least the intended beneficiaries of such questionable ingenuity were men and women whose outlook had been widely affected by the harshness of their environment. Prussia was poor and there was a limit to the numbers its soil could support, and even then that soil exacted a heavy price in hard physical toil.

Since 1807 the last vestiges of serfdom had disappeared, and the former serfs became free labourers of the estates. But this did not soften the hardness of their life. A state therefore which put what a man earned under the protection of an honest and sparingly remunerated bureaucracy was thoroughly welcome, and since one had to make do as best one could with the niggardly gifts of nature, order was gradually elevated to the dignity of a moral principle. When these peasants married, the novelist Fontane has told us, they did not speak of love or passion. What they said was "*Ich muss doch meine Ordnung haben*", which means "I must have my order", though it means somewhat more than that. A wholly Germanic and almost lovable quality of self-righteousness wholly incommunicable in English is packed into the "*Doch*".

Yet order, even when coupled with integrity, can have its disadvantages, and its close connection with the martial virtues can sometimes cause its devotees to be misunderstood. So it may well have been with the unhappy Prussians, for people were at this time already asking whether they were not an unusually warlike race, since they so obediently followed the harsh music of fife and drum whenever their rulers desired.

Such an assessment may of course well have been less than just, and the fact that the army was popular—as by the middle of the nineteenth century it most certainly was—may well have been due to more amiable affections than the Prussian's allegedly incurable propensity to fall upon his neighbours with fire and sword. The fact is that soldiering had other and more innocent features to recommend it. It was in those days still a relatively simple business, and the demands it put upon the recruit's intelligence were small, while the relief it afforded over a number of years from the worry of having to make a living was an even more positive advantage.

But there was more to it. A smart uniform, martial music and parades—all this made a pleasant change in the humdrum course of ordinary life, and, finally, when the citizen soldier was discharged from the reserve, he felt himself to be a person of some importance even though he had once more become an ordinary suppressed rural worker.

And yet it must be admitted that the military cult may also have satisfied less innocuous appetites. Certainly since the days of the first King of Prussia we can recognise something which a recent writer, Otto Heinrich von der Gabelentz, calls "the Prussian impatience"—a restless ambition, a complete inability to be content with one's own smallness—a thing which other states manage quite successfully to do. Bismarck, who knew a great deal more about these hidden motivations than he was usually ready to admit, once wrote the following: "The Prussian is a bigmouth (*der Preusse ist grossschnäuzig*). If you allow him to act like that towards the outer world, you can, so far as internal matters are concerned, do what you please with him."*

Quite obviously there was something about Prussia that repelled people. From the days of Klopstock all Germany's great literary figures detested her. Lessing called her "the most slavelike country in Europe". Herder, who came from East Prussia, thought that the best thing that could happen to Prussia was that she should be split up, while Novalis, round about 1800, was saying that "no state is administered more like a factory than is Prussia".

In spiritual quality there was little to choose between the peasants and the landed gentry, or, for that matter, between

*Ziekursch, *Geschichte des neuen deutschen Kaiserreichs*, pp. 26–7.

townsfolk and countryfolk, especially now that the many little
country towns were bursting out from the brick town walls that
surrounded them. Railways were connecting them with one
another, railways that were respectfully marvelled at as miracles
of technology.

About 1850 the main lines in the Prussian railway system had
been completed and the great period of bourgeois business activity
began. Textile industries grew up on the Rhine; iron works in
the Ruhr, though these enterprises were still largely financed by
French and Belgian capital. Thus the bourgeoisie, which in 1848
had suffered political defeat, was not only gaining a new sense
of its own importance but real power which it had never had
before. For though in theory the three-class voting system* was
an instrument of conservative power, it really made for middle-
class and upper middle-class majorities, since it tended to favour
those who paid the higher tax rates. Prosperity had, of course,
considerably impaired the revolutionary ardour which these elements had once displayed and even the petty bourgeois, who
was also moving into higher economic levels, was losing his
propensity for conspiratorial radicalism. That was now only to
be found in the working-class.

There were, however, certain tensions. The industrial development in the West had been much more intense than in the old
provinces, and places which even in Roman times had already
attained metropolitan status and were now under the influence
of a progressively minded upper middle-class were very reluctant
to let themselves be governed by East Elbian Junkers. Von Stein,
that typical West German, who despite his origin became the
reformer of Prussia, referred in a moment of anger to the inhabitants of "these sandy steppes, crafty, wooden, half-educated
people (*pfiffige, hölzerne, halbgebildete Menschen*), fit for nothing save
to be corporals and clerks".

Berlin, the Prussian capital, when Bismarck took up his residence there, was little more than a collection of unimportant
provincial houses and small shops with little pretence at elegance.
One or two very tall buildings towered above the roofs. There
was the cupola of the royal castle and the Brandenburg Gate,
both connected by four rows of linden trees. Such avenues were
often constructed by small East Elbian towns along their former
fortifications.

* Under the Prussian voting system the electors were divided into three groups
according to the amount of direct taxation paid and the votes in each group were so
weighted that the total cast by each group was equal in elective power to the total
of each of the other groups, irrespective of the number of voters each group contained. The system favoured the moneyed and landed classes as against the social
democrats. It was abolished in 1918.

Somewhat forlornly, in the centre of the town stood two medieval churches, already somewhat warped by the weather. Schinkel* had been busy in the not-too-distant past putting up government offices, first in the neo-Gothic, then in the Graeco-Roman style, with circles and squares as the principal motif. After him, his work had been continued by his pupils. Lenné had replanted the Tiergarten and made it worth looking at. Between this and the Brandenburg Gate express railway coaches were dragged by horses from one station to another, together with their passengers. Meanwhile hard work was being done in the new industries which, together with barracks and cemeteries, encircled the city. Berlin was badly over-populated. Unlovely working-class quarters had come into being, showing all the signs of hasty and careless construction. From roof to cellar they were crammed with humanity. Much hunger and misery lay hidden here.

But changes were already discernible and they were not always for the better. The noble restraint that had marked the work of Schinkel was to a prosperous bourgeoisie becoming only an embarrassing reminder of a time in which it had been necessary to economise. The new architecture gave evidence of ever-increasing means and ever-deteriorating taste. Despite its wealth, Berlin had nothing to compare with the princely magic of the old residences in southern and central Germany. Berlin was thus not a city with which men easily fell in love. Even its food and drink excited the displeasure of strangers, while many felt that the great plains to the east, with their infinite and frightening distances, were really the beginnings of the Russo-Asiatic steppes.

It was this city that was the scene of all Bismarck's further activities. He lived in the Wilhelmstrasse, a long, straight street of modest palaces, all of the same type and all with gardens at the back. In manner and appearance he was now the accomplished man of the world. His tall figure was clothed in a dark frock coat, the fashion at that time, and keen observers could certainly already note a tendency to corpulence. His black silk tie wound twice around his neck was a masterpiece. His face, with its finely-domed forehead, its light-blue and slightly protruding eyes, seemed to be always perfectly under control. A witness tells us something of Bismarck's first appearance in the Chamber of Deputies. "The bow which he made in the direction of the Praesidium deserved to be studied. It was so perfectly

* German architect and town planner (1781–1841). His work was based on various historical styles. The monument to Queen Louise of Prussia is one of the earliest examples in Europe of the Gothic revival.

calculated that it did not in any way fall short in courtesy, but did not perform the duties of courtesy to any excess."

His problems were only too evident. A glance at the map showed him the twisted, jagged frontiers of Prussia all too clearly, and he had but to compare them with the enclosed quality of the old powers, of France, Austria and Spain. Only when Prussia had such an enclosed territory herself would she be a great power, not in name only but in fact. Never again would it be necessary for Prussia to allow herself to be used by a stronger power in return for payment of a subvention. Never again was Prussia to enter the arena with borrowed crutches. If she entered into any alliance, then the whip hand was to be her own.

Two years previously, in St. Petersburg, a Prussian diplomat named Schlözer, who was working under Bismarck at the time, had written privately of him, "*Ein höllischer Kerl ist er, aber wo will er hinaus?*" (He's a hellish fellow all right, but just what is he getting at?) That was worth saying in 1860 and it was still worth saying. Bismarck was at first, even when he was Prime Minister, in the position of a prisoner who passes his hand along the walls of his cell to find out where it would be easiest to break through them and so to make a dash for liberty. He was seeking the road that would lead Prussia to great power status, though he was doing so for the time being with the utmost caution.

The number of his trustworthy friends was small and steadily getting smaller, that of his declared enemies enormous. Bismarck was no unknown quantity. Indeed life had put upon him a very recognisable mark. Many who saw him pointed to the thinning hair on his head, to the circles underneath his eyes, and said that the fate of something so old and solid as Prussia, whose consols were counted as the most reliable of gilt-edged papers throughout the world, should not be entrusted to a roué and a gambler. Few had confidence in him. The petty bourgeois still remembered him as a kind of poltergeist, a disturber of the peace in sessions of the German Bund in Frankfurt. The reputation that he had acquired, which he had in part deliberately manufactured for himself, was similar to the rumours spread by his peasants when they muttered that only the public executioner was allowed to trim his beard. They thought of him as a man whose eyebrows had been scorched by the fires of hell. Some prophesied a Napoleonic future for him, full of blood and tears. Others were more succinct and declared he would live to be hanged.

Nor did such predictions issue only from those who had never seen him. They came from men with whom he was personally acquainted, from conservatives who, during the counter-revolution of 1848, had sensed in Bismarck a man whose place was really on the other side of the barricades, a revolutionary who was capable, if he thought fit, of following the example of Frederick II and turning all Germany upside down. Gerlach at this time was writing in his diary, "May God the Lord protect him from himself, from the temptations of his ambitions and his selfishness, and make him realise in time that the little catechism applies even to politicians." Moreover, the new Foreign Minister had the whole of Prussia's diplomatic machine ranged solidly against him.

Even the King did not fully trust him. In calling him to office he felt he had merely fulfilled a rather sinister duty. "What can I do," he had plaintively remarked to the Queen, "if people ask me to go against my duty and my conscience and destroy the Army, the palladium of Prussia?"

The fact is that the stars in their courses were working for Bismarck. William was essentially an unenterprising man who liked other people to push him along, and this worked strongly in Bismarck's favour. Under his predecessor, Frederick William IV, a man with a mind and a will of his own, his task would have been much more difficult.

Even so, the entire royal family stood in opposition to him. Queen Augusta, at that time still as lovely as her portrait, with her dark hair and large passionate eyes, never forgot the interview she had had with him in the servants' room in Potsdam, where he had suggested a coup d'état to her that would nullify her husband's claim to the throne and so her own. After that, Bismarck came to take Augusta's enmity for granted. In 1852 he had said that so long as Augusta lived he would never get into the saddle. In 1862, after his appointment, he said, "Yes, I'm in the saddle now, but how long she leaves me there is anybody's guess." The Crown Prince, who was honestly convinced that the British system was the most desirable for Prussia, an opinion in which he was unceasingly confirmed by his wife, to whom he was deeply devoted, rejected the new Prime Minister from the start.

All this caused Bismarck to put a curb on himself, to proceed with the utmost caution, and to endeavour, if indeed such a thing was possible for him, to offend nobody. This was not easy. In the Chamber of Deputies there had been since May 1862 a considerable left-wing majority. This was dominated by the "German Progressive Party", which had only come into existence a year ago, its supporters coming mostly from the petty bourgeoisie. The moderate Liberal majority which had preceded it had at least sanctioned the expenditure for army reorganisation. The new majority, however, completely cancelled this as early as

September 23rd—immediately, that is to say, after Bismarck's appointment. This step was equivalent to nothing less than a hurried last-minute declaration of war against the new Prime Minister.

Bismarck, however, contrived so to handle matters that there was no actual breach. On September 29th he simply withdrew the estimates. The Upper House thereupon rejected the decimated estimates, which had reached them from the Chamber of Deputies, and instead accepted the government's proposals, which was practically of no effect whatever and, incidentally, contrary to the constitution, since the Upper House was only authorised either to pass or to reject the estimates presented to them by the lower one. It could not undertake any alterations in them.

Two days later Bismarck prorogued both Houses without having got any estimates passed at all. In this way, he managed to extricate himself and his government from the conflict and turned it into one between the two Houses of Parliament. Thus he was now compelled to govern without estimates, which was entirely in accordance with his wishes.

On the day previous to that, however, he had, while addressing the finance committee of the House, been somewhat unfortunate. In a thoughtless moment, he had relapsed into his old and careless way of speaking, and in that peculiar voice of his, which was shrill rather than powerful, had declared, "It is not by speeches and majority resolutions that the great questions of our time are decided. That was the great mistake of 1848 and 1849. It is by iron and blood."* These few words, that were in reality little more than a kind of slip of the tongue, were to adhere to his name like pitch. His audience, which was as tense as he was himself, believed that his real opinion had slipped out, that he believed the weapons of war had first to shed human blood before great decisions were possible.

The general indignation was intense. "When I hear so shallow a Junker as this Bismarck boast of blood and iron," wrote Treitschke, "by means of which he intends to put a yoke on Germany's back, then the blackguardly nature (*Gemeinheit*) of such an utterance seems to be only outstripped by its absurdity."† Attempts were made to give the words a relatively acceptable interpretation. All he had meant, it was argued, was that the King needed a strong army and that speeches in the Chamber did not provide him with the necessary support. All this was in

---

* For some unknown reason popular usage has reversed the order of this quotation and has turned it into "blood and iron".

† Zechlin, *Bismarck und die Grundlegung der deutschen Grossmacht* (1930), p. 33.

vain. It was all too clear that the formula meant exactly what it said, and that Bismarck himself had long come to believe that it was true.

The hostile reaction against Bismarck spread with lightning speed all over Germany. The King heard of it while he was celebrating the Queen's birthday in the company of her relatives from Baden. In order to have a word with the King before the latter's return to Berlin, Bismarck, the Prime Minister, waited for William's train on an upturned wheelbarrow amid workmen and commercial travellers at the station of the small town of Jüterbog.

The King was sitting by himself, like any banker, in an ordinary first-class compartment—things were as homely as that in the Prussia of that day—and was not easy to find. He had had the light turned down so that his thoughts—and they were none too cheerful—should be undisturbed, and Bismarck found, as he had expected to find, that his words about blood and iron had revived his ever-present fears of an imminent Prussian revolution.

William declared that he could already see Bismarck's head falling on a scaffold erected before the royal palace, and it would not be long before his own fell too. *"Et après?"* asked Bismarck. "Yes, *après,"* said the King, "afterwards we'll be dead." "We will indeed," said Bismarck, "but we must all die at some time, and could we die more honourably?" Both of them, he continued, were now compelled to fight. Surrender was impossible, and again, as he had done a few weeks previously in Babelsberg, he showed how well he knew how to handle the King.

He did not try to introduce logic into the argument, but treated William's fears as though these were well grounded. Thus he won his confidence and was able successfully to appeal to the feelings of the old army officer. Even if he had to perish, Bismarck argued, that would be death in the line of duty and every soldier had to reckon with that. And so as the train hurried through the dreary pine-studded plain, Bismarck contrived to lead the King away from politics and into that sphere of purely military thinking with which he was entirely familiar and so once more gave that troubled spirit a sense of security. Before they ever reached Berlin, William was already displaying a kind of genial pugnacity.

That Bismarck should have sought to dispel the fog of fear and mistrust that surrounded him was no more than ordinary common sense. For however much he might appeal to the example of Frederick the Great, he had in reality no desire whatever to do battle with such mighty coalitions as had been gathered together against that monarch. On the contrary, he hoped one day when Prussia was truly a great power to construct and control such alliances himself.

Among all such alliances, that with France easily rated first. Franco-Prussian friendship was at that time far from chimerical. It was not the Germany of Prussia but that of Austria which France, since the encirclement policy of Charles V, regarded as the hereditary enemy, and even in 1866 Napoleon would not permit any military attaché to accompany the Bohemian campaign lest any Frenchman should be a witness to the Prussian defeat which the French Emperor regarded as a certainty.*

Bismarck had only been in office for a few weeks when at the end of October he once more travelled to Paris, ostensibly to take his official departure as Prussian ambassador, although he had really never properly begun to exercise that office. The world was to be made to feel that the new regime in Prussia had no warmer friend than the powerful Emperor.

There was, however, rather more behind the visit, for the King of Prussia had not yet even given serious consideration to Napoleon's rather astonishing offer of an alliance. Would the Emperor now turn to Austria? It was soon evident that such fears were groundless and Bismarck, after the farewell audience, could confidently telegraph to Berlin that the imperial utterances had been more friendly to Prussia than ever.

If Napoleon continued to weight the scales in favour of Prussia and against Austria, he was naturally doing so in the hope of the compensation which even an expansionist-minded Prussia would be more willing to grant him than conservative Austria. Like Bismarck, Napoleon wanted to enlarge the territory of France, and for both it was a matter of supreme importance to see their wishes fulfilled. In Napoleon's case, it was the left bank of the Rhine on which his gaze was fixed. Here he hoped to see a restoration of the frontier of 1814 or 1792. If the defeats of Napoleon I could thus be wiped out, his dynasty, he calculated, would have been made well-nigh irremovable.

With an exquisite virtuosity, though his methods may at times have been a little devious, Bismarck suggested rather than openly averred that there was a community of interest between them, that one good turn deserved another, that services rendered by one member of the pair would surely be of benefit to both. For years, relying on the Emperor's sympathy and so on his patience, he was able to pursue his policy in Germany without any kind of interference from France and (this is the truly astonishing thing about this whole period of history, the thing which has never been explained) without making any kind of a down-payment on these implicit bargains. Bismarck used sometimes to account for these successes by saying that people had over-rated Napoleon's

* Holstein, *Private Papers* (1956), pp. 1, 29.

intelligence, but that is to take rather a superficial view of the matter.

One factor that may have been operative is a certain bond of sympathy that subsisted between the two from the start, and this may well have made Napoleon more pliable. What the origin of that sympathy was is difficult to say, but it was perhaps due to a certain similarity in their respective lives. The ascent of both had been adventurous, and they had each reached their goal after battling with circumstance. Each had his wounds to show, and each, incidentally, brought to the business of ruling a quite unusual breadth of experience. They even were like each other in yet another matter. Each spoke French with something of a foreign accent. For Napoleon had been brought up in Germany and in the German-speaking part of Switzerland.

The general conception which formed the starting point of negotiations was very simple. If Prussia could increase her territory sufficiently at the expense of neighbouring states—Bismarck usually treated the line of the Main as Prussia's natural frontier—then Prussia would no longer be dependent on Austria and Russia, and could enter openly into an alliance with France. If France should then chance to occupy Belgium and were thus to destroy what he called "a nest of demagogues", Berlin would certainly do nothing to stop her. To what extent the subject of Luxemburg, and other territories on the Rhine, was brought up in these talks, it is difficult to say. Both men were much too prudent to leave any written evidence of their real decisions. As Bismarck was fond of saying, the important thing was "what didn't get into official documents".*

There were, of course, matters concerning which Bismarck and Napoleon failed to reach an understanding and occasions where mind failed to meet mind. Thus, during his farewell visit in 1862 the Emperor expressed his regret that revolution would surely soon make an end of the new regime in Prussia, to which Bismarck replied, "In our country, the people do not put up barricades. In Prussia it is only Kings who make the revolutions." Napoleon could make absolutely nothing of this, and his comment, "*Il n'est pas un homme sérieux*", marks the extent of his incomprehension. As against this, there were times when Bismarck would find Napoleon equally baffling—when he used French troops and the French taxpayers' money to support foreign revolutions, for instance. Such action appeared to Bismarck as a veritable luxuriance of sentimentality.

As to France's old rival, Russia, Bismarck believed that there were bonds uniting that country with his own, even though there

* Moritz Busch, *Tagebuchblätter*, II, p. 171.

were no formal instruments to prove this. The dynasties were closely related to each other, and the Empire of the Czars had twice saved Prussia's life—in the days of Frederick the Great and in 1812. Prussia's service in remaining neutral during the Crimean War had been gratefully recognised. Prusso-Russian friendship thus seemed to Bismarck to be so solid a thing that it was quite superfluous to negotiate for a binding alliance. In St. Petersburg he had of course not been unaware of the rapid growth of certain anti-Prussian sentiments. The fact is, however, that he under-estimated this, as was shortly to appear.

Even Austria, which obstructed him so continually in his plans for a reorganisation of the German states, he sought, during all the difficulties that confronted him in the early stages of his career, to keep in a tolerably good mood. Early in December he had an interview with the Austrian ambassador, Karolyi, in which he spoke with extreme frankness, thus perhaps showing a greater degree of respect for the ancient imperial power than he could have rendered any other way. He said that Prussia "must be able to move freely and without hindrance in North Germany, which was its natural sphere, and must have enough air to keep alive".

The state of Hanover and the Electorate of Hesse were the two greatest obstacles to this. That is why "they must not be acces-sible to any influence save that of Prussia". If Austria would leave Prussia the North German sphere of influence, Prussia would be prepared to promise Austria help against all European powers and against all revolutionary movements within Austria's own boundaries.

Bismarck was nothing if not persuasive. "It will be a long time," he said, "before you find another Prussian politician who is ready to pursue '*Kabinettspolitik*' (i.e., to pursue the interests of his state as seen at the highest governmental levels independently of all ideological considerations), with so much determination and with so little regard for public opinion. Nobody despises public opinion as I do."

Though he was unaware of this, Bismarck by these remarks confirmed what the Austrian ambassador in Paris, Prince Richard Metternich, the son of the Chancellor, had said about him. Reporting to his government, Metternich had declared that the new Prussian Prime Minister desired "by every means to set up a firm military and political control of northern Germany. He would do this without any scruple whatever, but also, if it should prove at all possible, without entering into disputes with anybody and without hypocrisy. He would act boldly and honestly and—again if this were possible—within an understanding and close partnership with Austria."

These views received yet further confirmation at the beginning of 1863, when Bismarck received a visit from his old colleague in the Bundestag, Count Thun, who was now ambassador in St. Petersburg. As he had done in the case of Karolyi, so once more on this occasion he sketched his programme for Germany, which was in reality a programme for breaking up the Bund, with a complete lack of inhibition. But the pill was skilfully sugared by a vehement disavowal of any liking for German nationalism, in which he was certainly sincere—though quite capable of overcoming this dislike should the occasion require—and by a profession of readiness to make war on Hanover or Bavaria or any other German state with the same determination which he would display —should this prove necessary—in waging war against France.

He assured his visitor and gave his word of honour on the point that nothing could be further from his mind than a conflict with Austria, enhancing the impression of bluff honesty by the candour with which he declared that treaties between Prussia and Austria served no good purpose since great states like these were guided by pure selfishness and would break the treaties if their self-interest were not served by keeping them. The obvious implication was that Prussian and Austrian interests marched so closely together that all possibilities of a conflict were ruled out.

England, at that time at the height of her greatness, had for Bismarck a deplorable way of doing things, though fortunately the things she did were unlikely to do Prussia much harm. But the intrusion of English ideas and the English way of life into the Crown Prince's household aroused in him something very like fury. In England, he complained, aristocrat and statesman had been deposed, and "the press bounders run the show" (*die Pressbengel führen das Regiment*). He was of course aware—and this did not sweeten his temper—that England's opinion of Prussia was not very high. That Queen Victoria believed Bismarck to be ruining his King together with the latter's children and grandchildren, grandchildren which incidentally were her own, seems to have left the author of the alleged mischief undisturbed; but that England saw in Prussia little more than a state of medium size, locked in by other states at the heart of the Continent, a state which, like so many others, was glad enough to get a subsidy and do precious little in return—that was a much more galling consideration.

But this was not without its advantages, for the indestructible Palmerston—he was nearing eighty at the time—was all the less inclined to pay much attention to the bickerings of such nugatory political entities. Palmerston would keep his eye on larger matters, on India where the Mutiny was still of painfully recent memory,

on the American Civil War where British intervention seemed by
no means improbable, on the projected Suez Canal and on the
other overseas adventures, in Mexico and Cochin-China, in
which Napoleon was even more directly interested. For Napoleon's
enterprises were initiated by a sense of rivalry with England.

Italy, the most recent of the great powers, a kind of South
European variant of liberal nationalism, had just been recognised
by Prussia. From the nature of things, she was an enemy of Austria, and her arrival on the scene was for that very reason highly
relevant to Prussia's Prime Minister. To Bismarck, the man,
however, as indeed to the whole of old Prussia, figures like that
of Victor Emmanuel and Garibaldi were thoroughly distasteful.
King William hardly ever spoke of Victor Emmanuel otherwise
than as "the robber captain", and Bismarck himself might very
easily have been one of those Prussian noblemen who sent a
shield of honour to the King of Naples after Garibaldi had driven
him out. He was sceptical about Garibaldi's declared intention
of invading Venetia; he had formed too low an estimate of that
leader's military value. But the revolutionary attitudinising of
Garibaldi's men, their red shirts and all the rest of it, got thoroughly
underneath his skin. There was, in fact, in this case a head-on
clash between political interests and personal dislike.

Actually immediate danger did not threaten Bismarck from
without. It threatened him from within. His only political
capital at the moment was the confidence of the King, and that
asset was still distressingly unstable. There was thus nothing left
for him to do but to seek an accommodation with parliament that
would not be utterly intolerable. We have seen how cautious he
could be in his dealings with that institution—in his withdrawal
of the estimates, for instance. We have seen how eager he was to
relegate to oblivion that unfortunate phrase about iron and blood.
But that was not all. He was to demonstrate his skill as an architect
of alliances not only abroad but within the confines of his own
country. Despite the clear implication that the counter-revolution
of 1848 had failed to destroy them, he sought—and that quite
openly—to cultivate its enemies upon the neutral ground of
social intercourse. He engaged in an odd succession of courtesy
calls on the leaders of the opposition—Vincke, Sybel, Simson,
Twesten—during the course of which he expressed the hope that
by winter the King, who was of course to blame for everything,
would have been brought round to accept the two-year period
of service. For that matter, he may have meant what he said, for
the three-year period of service was for Bismarck anything but
an article of faith.

This was the first clear proof that Bismarck was no longer an uncompromising opponent of the West European type of parliamentary system. Indeed, provided it granted him what he wanted, he would have greatly preferred to deal with a parliament than with an obstinate monarch. He was in fact no longer concerned with questions of principle but solely with those of expediency. As early as 1860 he was already advising the conservatives "not to be too squeamish in accepting a representative popular assembly". All this is of a piece with certain remarks, remarks which were made as though they were little more than plays of fancy, in which he declared that in order to attain its object Prussia might have to "enter into an alliance with the German people". Legend has treated this as proof that even at this early stage Bismarck had already come to believe in Germany, a Germany which the Prussian Army was to forge into unity.

Unfortunately, the truth is just the opposite, and what Bismarck had in mind was to use the wishful thinking of liberal nationalism against those states which stood in the way of Prussian expansion. Thus he was quite ready to make an alliance with the liberal nationalists of Hesse Kassel against their own dynasty. The North German princes were to be subjected to a double pressure, from the Prussian Army on their frontiers and from hostile popular movements in the interior. They were thus to be induced to enter into treaties with Prussia which would virtually place them in the position of satellites. The whole matter was succinctly put in a letter to the liberal von Auerswald: "In the long run we have certainly one thing on which we can always rely. It is the national strength of the German people, so long as it sees its champion and the hope of its future in the Prussian Army."

But whatever may have been the truth about these plans, whether they can be taken seriously or treated as more or less airy fantasies, Bismarck must have been well aware that into the old, careless, stratified Prussian state, which depended on the two factors of feudalism and bureaucracy, a third had now intruded, that of liberal nationalism. It was impossible to do other than come to terms with it. It had outgrown the ideas of the forties and was no longer dependent on an impotent petty bourgeoisie but on the middle class that was growing steadily stronger economically and was often connected with the higher ranks of officialdom.

This situation once more demonstrated the law governing all ideologies, for these do not owe their success to the devotion of their first adherents, but rather to the subsequent approval by the masses who are resigned to the belief that they must not seem to hold out against the trend of the times. Thus in Germany liberal nationalism had now reached the stage of popular success and progressive vulgarisation. Gatherings of every kind were popular at this time, gatherings of singers and gymnasts, of railwaymen and agriculturists and of every sort of professor. On such occasions it was an inevitable item in the programme that expression should be given to the desire for a unified German state.

On such occasions the black, red and gold flag, which had been outlawed in 1848, would be massively displayed. Nor would there be any end to the singing of "*Was ist des Deutschen Vaterland?*" (What is the German's Fatherland?) Most famous of all was the Frankfurt marksmen's festival in July 1862, of ten thousand armed men, among them Tyrolese and Swiss. No practical politician could refuse to note the sources of power that here stood revealed. Nor did Bismarck fail to use them.

Of course, Bismarck knew too much history to overestimate the possibility that now seemed to be opening up. He knew that a cause whose articulate defence, whether expounded on the platform or by means of printer's ink, was still largely in the hands of intellectuals and littérateurs always looked stronger than that of its opponents. Those opponents may actually be in a majority, but because they are unfamiliar with the use of words, and so voiceless, nobody notices the fact.

Yet Bismarck would not have been the man he was had he not at the same time been starting the search for other allies with whom he might hold the liberal bourgeoisie in check. Even in those days he sought always to have the apparatus of re-insurance ready to hand. It was this that was behind his relations with Lassalle, the importance of which has tended to be exaggerated simply because of the bizarre picture which they present to the world. Actually there was already a remote connection between the two. Barschall, the Brandenburg prison governor, who had been more instrumental than anybody else in getting Bismarck elected to the Landtag, was a relative of Bismarck's wife and also a relative of Lassalle, a fiery, ambitious, brilliant, though slightly equivocal character of Silesian Jewish extraction.

A lawyer by profession, and in bearing and way of life an aristocrat, he had acquired considerable reputation through the divorce proceedings lasting ten whole years which he had conducted on behalf of a certain Countess Hatzfeldt. Before this he had undergone some months of imprisonment for participating in the disturbances of 1848. He subsequently founded a socialist sect among the industrial proletariat which was at that time unquestionably living in the most wretched conditions. He called this organisation the *Allgemeiner deutscher Arbeiterverein* (General German Workers' Union), and he ruled it in a quite dictatorial fashion.

In his conversations with Bismarck he was concerned with a possible alliance directed against the liberal middle-class. This common enemy, they both agreed, could be robbed of its power if universal suffrage could be introduced in place of the existing three-class voting system. For then peasants and workers would be evenly matched at the ballot box with the bourgeoisie. Left and extreme right would then have a huge majority and the bourgeoisie would be squeezed out.

That Lassalle, a true disciple of Hegel, wished to give the state a dominant position of power—"the state is God" he was in the habit of saying—met in principle with Bismarck's approval. What was less reassuring was that this state of which Lassalle was dreaming was to be the unified German nation state which was to bring about the liberation of the worker, though all that Lassalle was prepared to promise in return was that "the worker would be prepared to regard the Crown as the natural vehicle of a socialist dictatorship".

Bismarck saw quite plainly that the young man was trying to bluff him, that he was trying to exact vast concessions, for which he was in no position to give any consideration whatever. Even so, he submitted to Lassalle's visits with mingled feelings of tension and good will. Later he was to say that he had always had the line from Faust in mind, "What hast, poor devil, thou to offer me?" Yet Lassalle, Bismarck averred, had been one of the most amusing and lovable men that he had ever met. "There had," he declared, "never been any real question of negotiation because I never could get a word in edgeways." When, shortly after this, Lassalle was involved in a duel—it was rather characteristically fought about a lady—and was killed, the episode for Bismarck came to an end.

It was not till the early part of 1863 that Bismarck gradually relaxed his efforts for peace and allowed the conflict in the Landtag once more to assume really serious proportions. During the debate on the Address which it was customary to make to the King at the end of the year, he coolly explained the manner in which he was ready to carry on the government, even if he failed to secure the support of the people's representatives. He fell back on the theory which his tame Press had developed for him. According to this theory, when the constitutional powers, that is to say Crown and Parliament, were unable to reach agreement on a Bill, then it was obvious that a gap in the constitution had opened up which it was the government's duty to fill.

Actually the constitution obliged King and Parliament to co-operate in legislation, but to turn the "and" which formed the mandatory link between the two into an "either/or" was to adopt an untenable position. Bismarck was at least honest enough to admit that what had now arisen was a power conflict, and that the party that held the power must now go ahead and act as it thought fit.

Parliament was quite unable to defend itself. The liberals of 1863 were what they were, bourgeois pedants—and bourgeois pedants they remained even in their justifiable indignation. These administrators, judges, lawyers, town councillors, landed proprietors and professors, were far too fond of life to risk their all to safeguard their undoubted rights. They did indeed resolve, by 274 votes to 45, that the minister should be made accountable in his person and his goods for his unconstitutional expenditure. But this was an empty gesture, and in disciplined Prussia an appeal to the public to withhold the payment of taxes would merely have made its authors ridiculous. On the contrary, business was so good that the yield of taxation grew steadily greater—as did the income from Crown property and its forests and mines. Thus Bismarck had no cause to worry about the financing of his policies. Officials continued to receive their regular salaries and were as conscientious as ever in their work. Parliament in a word demonstrated its complete inability to change the hard facts of the situation.

In themselves the Army reforms in which this conflict had originated meant nothing whatever to Bismarck. Indeed it was his personal opinion that a two-year period of service was quite sufficient. But generals who insatiably asked for larger armies were nothing new to him. It happened in every country of the world, and William was above all else a general. If William had demanded a ten-year period of service, Bismarck would cheerfully have defended the request.

Of course there was more to the whole thing than mere finance. Amongst other things, the reforms were to minimise the importance of the Landwehr, by incorporating it, as far as practicable, in the troops of the line, and for Bismarck this was a matter of rather greater importance. For Prussian liberalism had a soft spot in its heart for the Landwehr which it regarded as a sort of democratic militia on the Swiss model. For the liberal the Landwehr had been "sanctified by glorious memory" in so far as he ascribed to it victory in the war of liberation which had in reality been gained by the newly organised Standing Army. King William, however, had no such illusions. He could never forget that in the Baden campaign the Landwehr had frequently to be pushed into action by the bayonets of the troops of the line.

The matter, however, that most immediately concerned Bismarck was the constitutional question. He was desperately anxious that the royal power should be extended and preserved, for he was completely dependent on it. That the wishes of his opponents might be those of the Prussian people, as those opponents claimed, was an idea that never once entered his mind. For that matter these men were themselves only too well aware how singularly they failed to touch the depths of the people's hearts. A Deputy, von Hoverbeck, was to bear testimony to that in 1865. On the great mass of the people, he wrote, "Our debates have no influence at all. . . . The immediate future may well show how slight a thing is our people's much belauded political maturity."

Outside of parliament, Bismarck continued to battle against the Opposition with the same vigour that he had displayed inside that institution. Members who were state officials found themselves selected for special abuse. Their promotions were blocked and they were subjected to other penalties. Here at last he could give vent to his old dislike of the higher Prussian bureaucracy. Here he could hit back at the ideas and values of his grandfather, Mencken, which he had himself so largely inherited.

It was during these weeks that he had to meet his first external crisis. A revolt had broken out in Russian Poland, in the repression of which Czar Alexander II, the "Czar-Liberator" who had quite recently freed the serfs, endeavoured to display genuine self-restraint. This did not deter Bismarck from sending General von Alvensleben to St. Petersburg to conclude a military convention, according to the terms of which Prussian and Russian troops in the border areas were to assist each other against the rebels.

The convention remained a dead letter. Nevertheless, it had occasioned the wildest indignation against Bismarck all over Western Europe, including Germany and Austria. People spoke of Bismarck putting the "hangman Alvensleben" at the Czar's disposal. But what was almost worse was that in Russia itself only the Czar, a man of moods easily moved by sentiment, seemed to appreciate what Bismarck had done. Gortschakow's reaction was very different. He made no effort to conceal his displeasure at these uninvited services, the object of which, in the form of reciprocal yet unspecified Russian favours, was perfectly well known to him. Bismarck obviously wanted to establish a credit balance of gratitude on Russia's books, of much the same kind as Russia had herself established in the ledgers of Austria when she assisted that country to break the Hungarian rebels in 1849. Unfortunately Russia had no need of such help against the Polish rebels, and even the offer of it was something in the nature of an insult.

So Bismarck was completely isolated and had incurred the displeasure of Russia quite as much as he had that of England and Germany. Even the sympathies of Napoleon, who saw himself in the part of a self-appointed patron saint of nationality in Poland, seemed to have grown cooler. Bismarck now tried to terminate the Alvensleben convention but was met by the malignant refusal of Gortschakow. Russia, the latter declared, never drew back. Indeed, quite the contrary happened, for now the Czar, greatly over-estimating the value of Prussian readiness to help, proposed a full-scale alliance between Prussia and Russia against the Western Powers. This, needless to say, Bismarck was bound to refuse. It was impossible for him to get involved in all manner of complications for the sake of Russian prestige. Unfortunately, however, his refusal cost him the only support that was left to him in Russia, namely that of the Czar himself. Bismarck, in fact, had made a palpable blunder and a very bad one at that. Russian neutrality, which was later to safeguard the Prussian rear, was certainly not attributable to the intervention of Alvensleben. In so far as there was not more behind it than calculated self-interest, it was due to Prussia's neutrality during the Crimean War, when that neutrality was of genuine value.

Bismarck appears to have learnt two lessons from his experience. First of all, he never repeated the mistake of initiating a diplomatic action in the brusque and hasty manner he had displayed when dispatching Alvensleben. Further, he was now sure that the relationship of the Hohenzollerns and the Romanovs was not a rock upon which the Prussian eagle could build its nest. It took some time to arrive at this conclusion, for it was in Russia that, under Napoleon, the French Revolutionary flood had exhausted itself, and so, like many others, he had tended to regard Russia as the great stabilising factor in Europe, and had overlooked the fact that for centuries it had been a force of such dynamic expansive power that, compared with it, the powers of France or Prussia seemed ludicrously small.

There was indeed in those days still a general tendency to ignore the fact that what had once been the Grand Duchy of Moscow had—within a period of time that for such an achievement seems relatively short—pushed eastwards as far as Alaska and westwards to the defences of Thorn. Bismarck had convinced himself during his stay in Russia that there was an innate conservatism in the Russian character, an almost obstinate veneration for the status quo. It was only gradually that he was able to discard that belief.

His attitude towards Poland was in equally palpable need of

reappraisal. The Prussian reformers of 1813, West Germans for the most part, had regarded Prussia's Polish provinces as an alien ballast of which on the whole they would have been glad to rid themselves. Von Stein's last hours had been made easier by the Polish revolt of 1831. Bismarck's views, on the other hand, had been wholly those of the East Elbian, of the coloniser, who sees his livelihood threatened by an uprising of the native population. They were the views of the land-hungry Junker who would in no circumstances yield land, be it his own or that of the state. With the ruthlessness that was so typical of his kind, he had written to his sister in 1861, "Hit the Poles till they despair of their very lives. I have every sympathy for their position, but if we are to survive, our only course is to exterminate them."

Nevertheless, throughout his life he was haunted by the question whether the partitions of Poland had not done Prussia more harm than good. To that question he never found an answer, and so his Polish policy was always one of vacillation. Again and again there is evidence of the suspicion that, thanks to the Polish territories, the death-watch beetle had entered the rafters of the well-built Prussian house. He was too much of a realist not to recognise that, despite all the partitions, Poland had un-mistakably retained its historic identity. Marx and Engels in distant London might well give each other illusory advice "to take whatever one can from the Poles in the West, to send them into the fire and eat up their land". Bismarck, who was on the spot and responsible, continued to search for compromises.

As early as 1863, when the Czar was planning to withdraw from Poland, Bismarck was considering a "Personal union" between Russia and a Poland that went as far as the Narev. In 1870 he said much the same. He had had occasion to remark that the Great Elector of Brandenburg had had the opportunity of extend-ing his power in Western Poland, whereupon a hot-headed nationalist broke in with the remark that Prussia would then no longer have remained a German state. Bismarck replied that this would not have mattered at all. "Something would then have existed in the North that was very like Austria in the South. What Hungary was for Austria Poland would have been for ourselves." The idea of the Hohenzollerns ruling over a "nation-alities-state" on the Hapsburg pattern was thus far from being unacceptable—which showed how little he was a prisoner of the "national-German" ideology.

Later still, in 1879, he was quite ready to consider an in-dependent Poland as a bastion against Russia; and again in 1883, though he did not like the idea, he thought it "a lesser evil than a Russian invasion". Quite early in his life—indeed it was during

those quiet years in Schönhausen—he had begun to learn Polish,
and he never wearied of repeating that all the rulers of Brandenburg Prussia up to Frederick the Great had been familiar with
that language. Again and again he importuned the Crown
Prince to let his children learn to speak it. Frederick William
with that curious incomprehension for the national sentiments
of non-Germans which so often bedevilled the German liberals
and which they had shown so clearly in the Paulskirche in 1848,
rejected the idea. Let the Poles learn German, then the problem
would be solved.

On the very day on which he received the Russian offer of an
alliance, an offer which formed the climax of his external embarrassment, he was able in his internal struggle to strike one of
his most effective blows. He had sent the Landtag packing at the
end of May. He now (it was June 1st) issued the so-called Press
ordinance in which he assumed power to suppress any periodical,
even the most innocuous, on the slightest provocation. The
anti-parliamentary dictatorship was becoming more naked every
day.

Parliament was, of course, repeatedly convened, but it only
produced repetitions of the original performance. The Lower
House rejected the estimates while the Upper one accepted them.
Whereupon the King proceeded to act as though he had been
granted the full authority he required. Parliament stood by
passive and impotent, but the King was not to enjoy his victory
undisturbed. The Crown Prince for once abandoned the restraint
he had imposed upon himself and at a reception in Danzig
publicly deplored the breach which the Press ordinance had
brought about between government and people. He himself,
he declared, wished to have no part in it. It was an affront to
Bismarck, though the King was far more deeply hurt than
Bismarck himself, who advised his master to "deal gently with the
boy Absalom". If the Crown Prince chose to cast himself for
the part of a popular martyr he was welcome to do so.

For so violent a man Bismarck, despite all his difficulties,
remained astonishingly calm and even astonishingly patient.
Only those in the closest touch with him knew of the physical
handicaps by which he had been afflicted since the beginning of
the year, of his insomnia and the violent headaches which compelled him for days on end to do his work lying on a sofa. His
wife hardly saw him at all. Yet when during that summer of 1863
a few friends gathered in the Prime Minister's drawing room and
the door leading to the old garden stood open, while Keudell sat
at the piano and filled the stillness of the Berlin night with his

music—for Berlin still had the quiet air of a provincial town—then it would sometimes happen that Bismarck would appear towards eleven o'clock, would take a glass of beer or a bowl of thick milk and would chat away quite guilelessly about the most embarrassing events of the day.

Few at this time would have said that Bismarck's affairs were prospering. An atmosphere surrounded him not so much of fear as of failure and futility. He had built his hopes on Russian gratitude and everybody knew that the speculation had not come off. Parliament was bitter, while abroad there was glee at his ill-fortune. The government was on the rocks and he was sustained only by the uncertain favour of the King. Everywhere there were whispers that his resignation could not long be delayed.

Now Prussia's unpromising situation had presented the Austrian government, which was at that time enjoying a new sense of its own strength, with the opportunity for a bold and timely stroke, a stroke which might restore to Austria that which the constituent instrument of the Bund had given her reason to expect, namely the leadership of all Germany. The Emperor summoned a gathering of the German princes to Frankfurt, with the object of initiating a revision of the Bund in a manner suited to the needs of the age, a project which, incidentally, was well within the bounds of practicability.

But Bismarck knew that reform of the Bund, the chief obstacle to his plans for Prussia, would merely enhance its capacity for survival. For himself, therefore, the success of the conference might well spell irretrievable disaster. He saw that he was thrown back upon his own resources, and in so desperate a situation could only resort to the counsels of despair. He did not hesitate to follow them. At whatever price, he had to prevent the King of Prussia from joining the other princes at Frankfurt. The conference might then pass resolutions, but in the absence of Prussia, the second most important member of the Bund, they would carry very little weight. But what hopes could the petty East Elbian squire entertain of wrenching his sovereign from out of that dynastic world in which, like his brother princes, the latter had his roots?

And yet he made the attempt. Once he had made up his mind, he never let the King out of his sight. He accompanied him on a state visit to Dresden. He was with him at Karlsbad and thereafter at Gastein. It was at the latter place that William, on August 2nd, met the Emperor himself, who personally handed him the invitation to attend the assembly of princes on the 16th, and it was perhaps unfortunate that Bismarck was absent during the first encounter between the two royal personages. He had become absorbed in the contemplation of a bird's nest, so he himself recounts, and was delayed accordingly.

As a result William showed a depressing inclination to go to Frankfurt after all, and so Bismarck had to bring up his heaviest artillery in his efforts to dissuade him. He argued almost frantically that the notice was too short, that William had been left no time to consider the matter, that his much-needed holiday had been inconsiderately interrupted, that in fact the invitation was nothing less than an insult, and he continued this line of argument for so long that William ultimately felt that he had actually been insulted. The whole performance, in which indignation completely usurped the place of rational argument, was typical of a method which Bismarck employed again and again with the King.

Even so, the game was far from being won. The princes foregathered at Frankfurt, and their first resolution was to send a new invitation to the King of Prussia, an invitation which was brought to him by the venerable and profoundly respected King John of Saxony. Meanwhile, with Bismarck continuing apprehensively to gyrate around him, the King had migrated to Baden-Baden, and it was here that the Nestor of the German princes encountered him and appealed to all those feelings of fraternal solidarity by which for centuries the German dynasties had been united.

Bismarck, if he was to gain his end, had now to achieve a well-nigh incredible tour de force. Almost the entire family of the King had been gathered together and all were against the minister. Moreover, there could now no longer be any question of an insult, since a King had acted as a messenger for thirty princes.

What exactly transpired between Bismarck and the King on this occasion we do not know. It may well be that in the mild air of this ancient watering place there was enacted one of the wildest scenes in German history. When at length, towards eleven o'clock at night, Bismarck had at last succeeded in obtaining the royal signature to a letter of refusal. William lay sobbing upon a sofa, a broken old man, while Bismarck was so exhausted that his legs were shaking. An agonised note from the King of Prussia written that same evening to King John gives us some indication of the kind of experience those concerned had undergone. William wrote that he could not see the King of Saxony, that "twitching nerves" compelled him to take to his bed immediately. "God bless you for the friendship you have shown me. Your faithful friend, William."

The conference of princes duly took place, however, and the city of Frankfurt thoroughly rose to the occasion. To the beholder's

eye it was a splendid affair and an unqualified success. All
Germany seemed to welcome it. The popularity of Francis
Joseph was unbounded, but since Prussia was absent from the
gathering, its deliberations—exactly as Bismarck had foreseen—
did no more than construct castles in the air.

During King John's visit to Baden-Baden it had been agreed
that the constitutional proposals of the princes' conference were
to be submitted to the Prussian government for its consideration.
This was done, and Bismarck in his reply refrained from all
detailed comment and instead expounded a scheme of his own
which provided, rather surprisingly, for the introduction of
universal suffrage throughout Germany. We know today that
he had been considering this idea for some little time. When he
came forward with his proposals, however, all that people saw in
them was an attempt to revive his popularity—which had sunk to
almost nothing after the conference of princes—by some startling
and radical suggestion. If this was his intention, he utterly failed
to realise it.

The strain was already beginning to tell. In September, on the
anniversary of his appointment, he said to Keudell, "It seems to
me as though I have in this one year grown fifteen years older.
You know, people are really much more stupid than I thought
they were." Keudell states that the day he made this remark he
looked pale and tired.

In October there were new elections to the Prussian Landtag
and these spelled an unqualified defeat for Bismarck, who could
only count on thirty-seven votes to back his government. The
prospect was grim. All the future appeared to offer was a series of
petty squabbles with parliament, unending arguments with the
ageing King which used up his nervous energy and got him nowhere—and more trouble with the Crown Prince, who might
succeed to the throne at any time and made no secret of his enmity.
That he was feared and yet nowhere enjoyed any true human
authority was well known by Bismarck himself. He was losing all
confidence and might actually have agreed objectively with the
Crown Princess, when, in a letter to her mother, she referred to
him as a "world calamity". Was it really worth struggling on?

Then quite suddenly, in November 1863, King Frederick of
Denmark died. The situation was aptly summarised by Prince
Charles Anthony, the head of the Catholic branch of the
Hohenzollerns. "This," he remarked, "is a quite incredible piece
of luck for Prussia." And actually it was the first of those enormous
pieces of luck that were to continue throughout the years without
interruption. It was the first upward step in that triumphal ascent
which destiny had prepared for Bismarck.

6

THE TRIUMPHAL WAY

The Duchies of Schleswig and Holstein, situated between the North Sea, the Baltic and the Lower Elbe, are made up of rich marsh lands which alternate with barren heath, of farmland with little towns. These territories, which contain the natural harbour of Kiel, had for many centuries been connected by personal union with Denmark. Holstein had originally belonged to the Holy Roman Empire and was consequently now a member of the German Bund. "Platt-deutsch" was spoken throughout Holstein, and in Schleswig it was spoken by a slight majority of the population. The others spoke Danish.

Throughout the centuries no one so far had found this an objectionable state of affairs. There is little point in recounting here the chequered history of these two countries. Suffice it to say that both duchies had of old enjoyed certain privileges which naturally enough they continually sought to extend and which, equally naturally, the central Danish power endeavoured to limit. This was a permanent state of affairs and in 1848 had developed into a violent nationalist explosion and into an armed uprising. On the orders of the assembled delegates in the Paulskirche, the rebels were supported by troops of the German Bund. In 1848 Prussia, as Frederick William IV had put it, had had to perform a "bond-slave service for democracy", while in 1849 the Düppel fortifications, Denmark's strongest line of defence, had been stormed by troops of Saxony and Bavaria.

Matters did not quieten down till 1852, when the great powers, weary of having their maritime trade disturbed by unending petty warfare, brought pressure to bear, and enforced a compromise known as the London Protocol. This confirmed Danish sovereignty over the duchies but compelled Denmark to respect their administrative privileges and their German character.

The compromise London Protocol satisfied nobody—German opinion least of all; beneath the surface the hatred of Denmark lived on. Thus for a decade neither Denmark nor the duchies knew any effective peace. At length the Danish government resorted to drastic means to end this state of affairs. It worked out "a Unitary Constitution" which incorporated Schleswig.

This was unquestionably a violation of the London Protocol. But Denmark was relying on the great powers having more pressing business elsewhere. She feared no difficulties from Prussia, her next-door neighbour, since Bismarck had been continually kept informed through the Danish embassy of the nature of the proposed new constitution and had raised no objection. A few days before King Frederick's death, on November 9th to be exact, parliament accepted the constitution, but on the 13th, to Copenhagen's embarrassed astonishment, Bismarck was already protesting against it on the ground that it violated the Treaty of London, a fact which had been known to him for months.

No one knew what to make of this sudden change of front. That Bismarck had no sympathy for the irredentism of the duchies was known to all. Moreover, Denmark's understanding with Prussia had been excellent. Unlike Schleswig, Holstein was, as we have seen, a member of the Bund, but by express direction of the King of Denmark almost invariably cast its vote on the same side as Prussia. Bismarck had condemned the uprising of 1848 as a revolt against the lawful sovereign. It is, therefore, unlikely that he would have raised objections to the new constitution had it not so conveniently coincided with the death of the King.

For there were special circumstances surrounding the succession. On the death of King Frederick VII, Christian of the House of Glücksburg inherited the throne, but he did so by Salic law which was valid in Denmark and Schleswig but not in Holstein. Here the lawful heirs were the Holstein-Augustenburgs. This difficulty had, however, been foreseen by the London Protocol, which had laid it down that the head of the House of Augustenburg was to renounce his right against an indemnity paid in money. His son, Frederick, however, a Prussian guards officer, a friend of the Crown Prince and an intelligent, sceptical, rather colourless man, with vague liberalising tendencies and on the whole, one would have thought, anything but a very warlike sort of person, nevertheless believed that he owed it to his family to refuse to acknowledge the financial transaction.

Indeed, on November 16th, on the very day on which the heir of the Glücksburgs had himself proclaimed as Christian IX of Denmark, Duke of Schleswig and Holstein, Frederick had himself proclaimed as Frederick VIII of Holstein, and had simultaneously claimed the Duchy of Schleswig on the strength of a royal decree of the fifteenth century, according to which both countries were to be "for all times united" (*up ewig ungedeelt*). The whole affair was hopelessly involved. According to Palmerston there were only three men who really understood it, the Prince Consort who was dead, a German professor who had been driven mad by it, and he himself, but he unfortunately had forgotten all about it.

There can be no shadow of doubt that as early as the 13th of the month, when he made his surprising protest to Copenhagen, Bismarck had been informed that King Frederick's end, which actually took place two days later, was already approaching. He knew that this would bring the question of succession to a head and it was surely in this moment and not later that the great idea flashed into his mind. He would allow neither Schleswig nor Holstein to be handed over to either of the two pretenders but would get them incorporated into the state of Prussia. In a word, he resolved in this moment to set forth on the road of expansion, the road that would lead to the transformation of Prussia from a country that enjoyed great power status by courtesy only into one which was a great power in fact.

Schleswig and Holstein would, of course, not yet provide a connecting bridge between old Prussia and her provinces in the West. To reach them one still had to pass through either Mecklenburg or Hanover. Yet their acquisition would extend Prussia's sea coast and would bring her nearer to the oceans of the world. Above all, it was a step in the right direction and a step which covered a very useful amount of territory.

But the prize would not be an easy one to secure, and there were those who for the most diverse reasons would be only too eager to withhold it from his grasp. There was Denmark which would certainly not yield up the provinces without a struggle. There was Augustenburg who wanted them for himself. There was the Bund, there was the Prussian parliament and there was all over Germany a wildly excitable public opinion, prepared with infantile simplicity to apply to a terrifyingly complex problem solutions which were no solutions at all. There was the King, who would certainly reject the whole adventure on moral grounds. There was London and there was Paris, each eager to see the entrance to the Baltic safely in the hands of a small independent power. Above all else, there was Austria whom for years Bismarck had treated as an enemy and whose recent congress of princes he had deliberately turned into a farce. Now suddenly he must at all costs bring Austria over to his side. If he failed in this, the whole project collapsed.

It is impossible to study the history of these few weeks without feeling that if all the circumstances are taken into account, they represent the most brilliant of all Bismarck's diplomatic achievements. Never at any subsequent time of his life was Bismarck so alone, so utterly bereft of friends and influence, so encompassed by the mistrust and hatred of men more powerful than himself, and for that matter so lacking in experience as a leading statesman. How delicate was that sensibility which, in situations which changed from hour to hour, enabled him to know exactly when to retreat before an opponent who would yield no further and when a slackening opposition made it safe to press forward.

Traps were set with every step he took. He avoided them all. He contrived to make everyone with whom he had dealings believe that he was the sole recipient of his confidences, the only one who had been initiated into his secrets. He showed himself a master player with all, and he needed all he played with, each in a different capacity—the King, his ministerial colleagues, the diplomats of the German Bund, the ambassadors of the European powers. He influenced decisions in London, in Paris, in Vienna, in Copenhagen. In the latter case, he strengthened the Danish government's belief that England would come to their country's aid, and he did this so that they should in no circumstances give way to him, lest by doing so they should bring to nothing his plans for conquest.

As we have seen, his most difficult task still remained the winning over of Austria, the arch enemy of Prussian expansion, whom he had already secretly condemned to death, and who must nevertheless, before the ultimate stroke was administered, be persuaded not only not to interfere with the first step of Prussia's expansion but actually to assist her with it. For if Austria were now to join with England and Russia, Bismarck's bold plan would be utterly defeated. He could not carry it out with three great powers opposing him, but if Austria made common cause with him, then it would be a case of two great powers against two, and the risk would then become a legitimate one.

On one point Prussia and Austria had already reached agreement. It was Prussia and Austria, and not the German Bund, which had signed the Treaty of London. These two countries therefore were the sole guarantors of the privilege of Schleswig which Denmark had violated. But Austria and Prussia were also both opposed to the Augustenburg claim, now favoured by the Germans, though for two entirely different reasons. Austria believed that Duke Frederick would become a Prussian vassal, while Prussia feared that he would always side with Austria.

At this point Bismarck was assisted by yet a further coincidence. Count Rechberg, whom Bismarck had called "the little bottle of poison" while he had been his colleague in Frankfurt, had recently been appointed Austrian Foreign Minister. Now actually Bismarck had misread his man. Rechberg was a high-principled lawyer, though not a strong personality, and profoundly admired Bismarck as a model conservative, the only true heir of his own

unforgettable master, Metternich. He was one of the first of those
admirers of Bismarck whose number was subsequently to be
legion and who, themselves insecure, were deeply impressed by
the signs of the ruthless assertion of power which they thought to
discern in Bismarck and which they so painfully missed in themselves. What such men were hoping to achieve by associating
themselves with Bismarck was, to quote Rechberg's own words,
"to crack German democracy over the head".

Here then was the bond that drew the two powers together and
that caused them on November 28th to declare in the Bundestag
that they stood by the London Protocol and—this was the obvious
inference—would support Denmark in her claim to be sovereign
over the duchies. The indignation that swept over Germany left
them unmoved; indeed, it was actually in the name of this same
detested Protocol that they moved that the Bund should call upon
the Danish government to suspend the new constitution which
violated the London Protocol, and should occupy Schleswig in the
event of a refusal. Needless to say, it was impossible to get a majority
in the Bundestag to favour such a demand and actually a substantial
majority rejected the motion. Austria and Prussia then declared
that they would act on their own account, which was tantamount
to refusing recognition to a perfectly legitimate resolution of the
German Bund, clearly an unfriendly act towards the Bund, if not
an actual violation of its constitution.

In January the plan was put into effect. Prussia and Austria
summoned Denmark to abolish the new constitution within
forty-eight hours, which itself was a technical impossibility,
since in so short a time it was impossible for a resolution of the
Danish Parliament to be made effective. Thereupon, the Austro-
Prussian Army marched in under the eighty-year-old Prussian
Marshal Wrangel, who was unmistakably showing signs of old
age, and who, for a campaign against a cruelly inferior enemy,
could find no more suitable watchword than "Forward with
God".

Once the avalanche had begun to move, Bismarck raised the
mask which he had worn so cautiously since the beginning of the
crisis. He had always given the assurance that it was his object
to keep Denmark inviolate, in accordance with the spirit of the
Treaty of London, and he now declared in a ministerial council
that he proposed to gain the duchies for Prussia. Nobody agreed
and nobody opposed, but nobody was surprised. The fact is that
in the preceding weeks the whisper had gone round the ballrooms
of Berlin about plans which the Prime Minister had in mind. His
few friends had heard the news with anxiety, and the general
opinion was that "that sort of thing just can't be done in the

present age". That it could be done very well indeed was soon to become apparent.

Meanwhile the Danes defended themselves as best they could. They reckoned on help from England which Palmerston had hinted at. The Saxon and Hanoverian troops who were acting in Holstein under orders from the Bund were pushed aside by Prussia and Austria without a shot being fired. At the start the Austrian troops had more success than the Prussian,* till the Prussians, goaded on by this, stormed the Düppel fortifications, much as the Saxons and Bavarians had stormed them six years before. General von Schweinitz, who was later to become ambassador and of whom there will be further mention in these pages, had some caustic comments to make on this. "It was no great triumph," he wrote, "after two months' siege to drive the poor Danes out of a few earthworks when they had only smooth-bore cannon, while we had artillery from Krupps and needle guns." King William, however, was delighted that the glory which Prussian arms had won in the past was still as untarnished as ever.

The German nationalists now found themselves in an agonising dilemma. For decades they had been clamouring vainly, though at the top of their voice, for the liberation of the duchies from Danish control, and now this very thing had been achieved by a man who kept on assuring them that the nationalist ideology meant nothing whatever to him, and that he would have been quite as ready to make war on the King of Bavaria or Hanover as he was on the King of Denmark. Here then was the dilemma. If you showed yourself hostile to Bismarck you were against the war, which the nationalists had been asking for for years. If you favoured the war, then you supported Bismarck, who had openly shown his colours as the most dangerous enemy of the national idea. What were the nationalist leaders to tell their ever-more excited followers to do?

When, therefore, the Queen of England, who, through the marriages of her children, was connected to the Courts both of Denmark and of Prussia, contrived to bring about an armistice and a conference of the powers, the German nationalists breathed a sigh of relief. The conference took place in London on April 25th and lasted till June 25th, and rejoicing was universal throughout Germany when, under pressure from the other conference members, the Prussian government, on May 28th, declared itself ready to accept the succession of Augustenburg.

---

* The Austrians had brought quantities of élite troops to Schleswig (Holstein, I, p. 27) and had expended them overlavishly, incurring greater casualties than was necessary.

Needless to say, Bismarck never for a moment took this declaration seriously, but by making it he enabled the British Cabinet to accede to the passionate wish of Queen Victoria and to withdraw from its promise of assistance to Denmark. By the end of June it had finally abandoned any idea of intervention. And it was not long before Denmark was suing for peace.

The next task which confronted Bismarck was no easy one. He had now to reverse his acceptance of the Augustenburg claim. Things were made no easier by the unrelenting efforts of the Crown Prince, who was convinced of the juridical soundness of his friend's case and who had indeed already won over the King. It should be added that Augustenburg had already renounced so many of his sovereign rights in regard to the duchies that he was by now little more than a Prussian vassal, and this circumstance would make it even more difficult to deprive him of the last vestiges of his authority. Prussia had hardly made her declaration of May 28th before Bismarck had an interview with Augustenburg which lasted till midnight and the substance of which is only imperfectly known. But it was an interview in which he certainly attained his object, which was to make the Prince's position so impossible that the question of further concessions could hardly be said to arise.

The methods employed were simple in the extreme. Bismarck informed Augustenburg that the duchies would have to take over the costs of the Prussian and Austrian troops in the fighting against Denmark, whereupon the terrified Frederick replied that the duchies had never invited the allies to come. It was an unfortunate observation, all the more unfortunate perhaps because it was true, and it laid the foundations for the reputation of ingratitude which now began to pursue the unfortunate man wherever he went and which even estranged the King, who somehow found that this was a slur upon his fine new army.

All this was grist to Bismarck's mill. The May declaration had, as he told the Saxon minister, Beust, compelled him "to harness the Duke to his plough", but he added—and here the metaphor grows slightly imprecise—"the plough was now in motion", and, thanks to the Duke's unhappy indiscretion, he "was able to unharness him again".

Peace was signed on October 30th. The King of Denmark's rights in the duchy were duly transferred to Prussia and Austria. It was a little unfortunate that the nature and extent of those rights were still as obscure as on the outbreak of the war, which that very obscurity had occasioned. Even the provisions of the London Protocol, to safeguard which the allies had leapt to arms, now became veiled by a convenient mist of oblivion. In the meantime, the duchies were placed under the military administration of the two powers concerned, while the other great powers, on whom Denmark had relied, appeared vaguely embarrassed and affected not to notice. The Augustenburg claims were submitted to the scrutiny of the Crown's legal advisers a happy touch in so far as this involved delay, and the greater the delay the smaller the public interest would become.*

When it became obvious that the duchies had experienced nothing that could conceivably be called liberation, that they had actually lost any power which they had ever possessed to decide their own affairs, and had become the object of a naked military dictatorship, there was a marked change of feeling, and Bismarck was furiously attacked. But Bismarck had been successful, and as usually happens in such cases, large sections of the public began after a time to go along with him and even to clamour for outright annexation. Among these were representatives of the young Westphalian industry who sniffed profits in the prospects of a Navy, the probable development of Kiel harbour and the construction of a North Sea-Baltic canal.

In the duchies themselves the citizens contemplated Prussia's high taxes and military service with feelings of something very like horror. The peasants, however, were indifferent, and the nobility actually hoped that annexation would get them out of having to pay the costs of the war. By and large, therefore, it seems to be true that had Bismarck now proclaimed annexation as a *fait accompli*, there would, save for his nominal ally Austria, have been little resistance.

At a ball some time previously, Bismarck had—gleefully and with well-nigh exhibitionist candour—remarked that Austria would be working "*pour le roi de Prusse*", a current euphemism for doing a piece of work without reward. But things were not to be quite so easy. In July, when he came to Vienna, he was "gaped at like a new hippopotamus at the zoo", but the general astonishment, if such indeed there was, failed to rob the Austrian negotiators whom he met at Schönbrunn of all sensibility to their own interest, and it soon became clear that working for "*le roi de Prusse*" was an occupation in which Rechberg refused to engage,
Bismarck excelled himself in suave insinuations. The duchies, he urged, were a long way from Austria and she could have but little interest in them though she had a very great deal of interest

---

* The findings of the eighteen Prussian Crown jurists were finally delivered at the beginning of 1865. A minority of seven found for Augustenberg since his father had not renounced his rights but merely refrained from their exercise while his sons had not renounced anything.

in good relations with Prussia, and Prussia would of course always be delighted to come to her aid should there be any little difficulty in Italy.

But it was all to no avail. Rechberg would have none of these hypothetical compensations. There had from the start in Austria been much powerful opposition to the war, particularly in the Reichsrat, in which there were men perceptive enough to see in this little Schleswig campaign the beginning of the end for Austria. Rechberg would have been swept away had he surrendered the booty against no more than a Prussian "Thank you". Nevertheless, since Bismarck had himself brought up the subject of Lombardy, Rechberg made an effort to draft some kind of a treaty giving Prussia a free hand in the duchies against a promise of military aid in the reconquering of Lombardy where the unfriendly Piedmontese were still far from having extinguished all Hapsburg sympathies.

But such a firm guarantee would certainly have set Bismarck at cross-purposes with Napoleon, and he drew back from it. Nor was anything to be hoped for from minor territorial concessions such as the surrender of the Silesian county of Glatz, for the King would not surrender an inch of the glorious conquests of Frederick the Great and utterly set his face against such a step.

When the two negotiators came to part they had to admit that they had got nowhere, that there was nothing for it but to leave matters as they were and hope that the future would supply some solution. In any case, however, Rechberg's days were numbered, for at the end of October he retired.

Meanwhile Bismarck had been back in France. In Biarritz he had again met Princess Orlow. Each found that the other had grown older and more serious. Then he started to negotiate with Napoleon in St. Cloud. Again, there is no record of the substance of their conversations. One thing, however, was obvious to the whole of Europe. If the Austrian ally, with whom Bismarck had travelled the first half of the road towards annexation, were now to desert him, he would have to look around for another to accompany him along the second half.

On the great stage that lies between the North Sea on the one side and the Baltic on the other, there was enacted once more that tragi-comedy which Bismarck had produced fifteen years previously before the more select audience of the Bundestag. There was the same policy of unrelenting pressure against Austria, the policy of pinpricks and hair-splitting over trifles—all this alternating with massive protests and ever-varying complaints concerning the brutality of his opponents whenever the latter hit upon the whimsical idea of defending themselves. Interminably

Bismarck demanded the expulsion of Augustenburg from Kiel, all of which that unhappy man and his phantom Court endured in discreet silence. Interminably he made Austria the subject of his attacks. Never to leave her alone even for a day, to make her very existence a misery, to drive her step by step towards renunciation—it was the old Frankfurt technique, but now on a vastly greater and consequently a much more dangerous scale.

Whether he really believed he would get anywhere with it we do not know. At times he may well have persuaded himself that he would do so, yet unconsciously he must have known that his efforts were useless. How could he expect Austria to do something which he, had he been in charge of Austrian affairs, would certainly never have permitted? What great power of Austria's standing would voluntarily consent to reduce its own influence by half and to surrender that half to a parvenu and unfriendly rival? If any great power went to such lengths of long suffering, it would immediately cease to be a great power at all.

Bismarck's sense of history was much too real for him not to have been aware quite early of the inevitability of a solution by force of arms, though naturally he was compelled to keep the knowledge to himself if he was not to risk the moral alibi he would certainly require when the moment of the big break arrived. Orthodox Bismarckists of course see in the fact that Austria could not desert the road which destiny had prescribed for her a proof of quite exceptional wickedness, and so try to find an objective justification for Bismarck's essentially personal and subjective resolve on Austria's ruin. But history and hagiography are two distinct sciences w' ich must not be confused with each other.

One thing must have been plain. If it came to the use of force between the two great powers much more would be at stake than the duchies. Bismarck must have experienced all the feelings of a gambler in those last few moments before the roulette wheel begins to hum. He saw the stakes growing larger and the temptation increased to add to his own. If luck was with him, he would win much more than two relatively unattractive pieces of territory in the far north. All Germany would be in the hollow of his hand. But if he were to lose, then the encounter would be of a very different order from that with the unfortunate Danes. What then? For him personally it would mean death in the final retreat, a death which would virtually be suicide. But his own fate would be a negligible matter compared with that of Prussia. For Prussia defeat would mean not only a fourfold Olmütz, it would mean a reversal of the whole of Prussian history since Frederick the Great.

During all this period Bismarck was lonely, indeed he was lonely throughout his life. Whatever happened, the real drama took place in provinces of his mind into which he would allow no other man to look. These inward disturbances, which he repressed and of which he would speak to no man, produced outward effects in acute physical suffering, which took such forms as neuralgia of the face and legs. "I was never free from anxiety about his health," writes Keudell, in reference to the winter of 1864–5.

Prussia and Austria made another attempt to reach a peaceful settlement in 1865. This was largely due to the efforts of Count Moritz Esterhazy,* the Minister without Portfolio, who in the meantime had gained great ascendancy over the Austrian Emperor and whose counsel was in most matters decisive. Esterhazy was a great admirer of Bismarck, and saw in him a promising ally in the suppression of European liberalism. There were conferences in Salzburg and Gastein, and Esterhazy was so warm an advocate of appeasement that the Austrians agreed to put an end to the condominium in the duchies. Schleswig was placed under Prussian administration, which meant—and here no one was deceived—that it was annexed to Prussia. The same was true of the harbour of Kiel and of Lauenburg, the southern tip of Holstein. "There is something I could never have believed," said Bismarck afterwards. "Fancy being able to find an Austrian diplomat who was ready to sign a thing like that."

The results of the conference, negligible though they were, aroused a storm of indignation throughout the world, for the two powers were now ignoring the slogan *"up ewig ungedeelt"* and were quite unmindful of the professedly righteous indignation that had in the previous year driven them to war. They were indeed ignoring these things as lightheartedly as they ignored the claims of Augustenburg. The King was pleased enough about getting Lauenburg and elevated Bismarck to the rank of Count, though he was giving more pleasure to himself by this than to Bismarck. Indeed, Bismarck and Johanna's family pride made them regard the new title as a wholly unnecessary inconvenience.

Bismarck had little confidence in the Gastein settlement and only a few weeks were to pass before he was once more conferring, and again in Biarritz, with Austria's opposite number, Napoleon. On arrival, he had suffered yet another disappointment. Princess Orlow had failed to arrive. She said she feared the cholera, but

---

* Moritz Count Esterhazy was born in 1809 and was in the diplomatic service from his youth on, and according to the contemporary view was a man of penetrating intelligence. He was capable of overwhelming charm which "held men captive and drove women to madness" but was also capable of ill-humoured misanthropy and intolerance. He was a strange person and ended his life a madman.

it is quite likely that she was now shrinking from the rather sinister monster that for so many of his contemporaries Bismarck had become.

The weather was dull. He walked with Napoleon in the gardens of the Hotel Villa Eugenie, where the Emperor and Empress were passing the summer, and sought to gather the fruits of the understanding that for many years had subsisted between the French Emperor and himself, an understanding that there should be moral support with Prussia if she were at war with another German state.

Again, we do not know what Bismarck offered in return, for there were neither witnesses nor written records of their conversations—purely verbal engagements are, after all, so much easier to repudiate—but we do know from French embassy reports that were made somewhat previous to this that Belgium was at that time a subject of discussion, as were certain territories on the left bank of the Rhine belonging to the South German states, and on occasion "all territories in which French is spoken", which meant Belgium, Luxemburg and Western Switzerland. Faced as he was with an early decision by force of arms, we can well believe that Bismarck was generous enough with any property other than that of Prussia.

Even so, Napoleon remained increasingly evasive and Bismarck began to realise that the Emperor was a changed man. He had for months been suffering from gallstones, and when the pain grew very severe his attention was diverted. Then, as though awakening from a dream, he would probably ask Bismarck if he had gone mad. He approved Prussia's annexation of the duchies, as he had always done, because Prussia thus became at least a second-class naval power and might thus help France to counter British superiority at sea. Of course he laid down the condition—he felt that he owed this to his old ill-starred love, the principle of nationality—that a plebiscite should give a verdict in favour of Prussia and that the Danish-speaking frontier territories should be given back to Denmark, a condition to which Bismarck remained conveniently deaf. Beyond that, the Emperor would not go. Bismarck was still satisfied that the Emperor's personal liking for him had not grown less, but he was convinced that Prussia could no longer regard him as a stable factor in her policy calculations. On his return, Seebach, the Saxon ambassador, saw Bismarck in Paris. He said that his face had become that of an old man.

It was about the turn of the year that Bismarck reached his final and irreversible decision; only a war would make possible his programme of expansion. Actually it was in November that, according to the records of Under-State Secretary von Thile, he directed the military government of Schleswig to make continual complaints in Vienna concerning the Austrian administration of Holstein, and to keep all grievances open which "might in certain circumstances be capable of more intensive exploitation". The unhappy Augustenburg in particular, he insisted, despite the latter's undiminished popularity, was an "arbitrarily imposed territorial overlord", and his continued presence in Holstein was "incompatible with the King of Prussia's indefeasible sovereign rights".

In January there were demonstrations in Altona, that is say within the Austrian sector, in favour of Augustenburg. Bismarck protested vehemently, and when he received the unanswerable rejoinder that such a matter lay solely within the competence of the Austrian Emperor, he took up the attitude of a deeply injured man and declared that he would no longer answer any communication from Vienna and that the intimacy between the two courts which had subsisted till now was at an end.

Meanwhile, he began to arrange the pieces on the German chess-board in readiness for the great game. He sought to persuade the states lying south of the Main to remain neutral, assuring them that he had no desire to usurp their territories since they did not lie in Prussia's way. But here he was unsuccessful. The South Germans knew that they had nothing save the German Bund to safeguard their existence as states, and it was that Bund that Bismarck was obviously seeking to destroy.

How could they remain neutral? For years they had been concerned with a defence plan, the so-called "Trias", a military alliance of all German states except Prussia and Austria. In a word, they were concerned with a "third Germany" which was to be ready to come to the aid of whichever of the two great powers was attacked by the other, and might thus be in a position to prevent fratricidal war between the two. King Max II of Bavaria was the originator of the idea. Everyone found it excellent.

Unfortunately nobody attempted to realise it. For in South Germany, during that long period of peace for which the German Bund was responsible, the dislike of all things military had become as deep-rooted as the envy that had always existed between its dynasties. North of the Main things were very different. The North German states, which were already enclosed by Prussian territory, were naturally compelled to come to Prussia's support. Those, however, who had the misfortune to lie along the Prussian line of attack wished for that very reason to remain neutral at all costs, an object which—again naturally enough—Bismarck could not allow them to achieve.

The position of Hanover was particularly distressing. She had not yet forgotten that, half a century before, she had been annexed by Prussia, a present from Napoleon I. Unlike the South German states, she had not formed any alliance with Austria, since Bismarck might have regarded it as a breach of neutrality and it was for this reason that King George refused to allow his army to be strengthened by an Austrian brigade which was just leaving Holstein.

In the middle of May Bismarck declared himself to be ready to respect Hanoverian neutrality, but a week later he demanded that King George should further undertake to ignore any resolution by the Bund for general mobilisation. Bismarck had had previous dealings with this blind and strongly legitimist monarch, and knew very well that he would never consider such a breach of the Bund's constitution, and of course Bismarck was right— which was just too bad for Hanover.

As to the great powers, Bismarck was counting on the neutrality of Russia, for that country would surely not let slip the opportunity of repaying Austria for her neutrality during the Crimean War. England, too, he assumed, would remain neutral, for the Danish war had so increased the dislike in which both the German powers were held that if these were now to set about their mutual extermination, such an event could only be regarded as the punishment inflicted by a just God. The attitude of France, as he had himself recently all too clearly seen, remained an enigma, but for any aid which France might give to Prussia, she would inevitably send in a staggering bill.

So all that remained was Italy—the revolutionary power, wholly dependent on the graces of the equally revolutionary usurper, Napoleon—Italy, still looked on by all the Courts as a plebeian upstart, but a country whose interests, in so far as she now coveted Austrian-held Venetia, marched with Prussia's own.

Violently suppressing his own personal antipathies, Bismarck had for months been endeavouring to establish some kind of confidential relationship with Italy. Unfortunately this was rather difficult, since in Florence, at that time the capital of the new state, the anti-Italian sentiments of Berlin were all too well known. The King's resistance to the plan was well nigh violent, and it was not till the end of 1865 that he could bring himself to present the "robber captain" Victor Emmanuel with the order of the Black Eagle. Unfortunately, even this produced no results, for Italy, who was all too conscious of her military inferiority to

Austria, was at that time still trying to settle her differences
concerning Venetia by peaceful means, though, thanks to the
fact that the Hapsburgs would never recognise the propitious hour
when it came, those attempts had failed. It was only then, at
the end of February, that Italy informed Berlin of her readiness
to enter into an alliance.

This was a great step forward, and at the Crown Council on
February 28th Bismarck proceeded suitably to exploit it. The
report which he made on that occasion was a quite masterly
distortion of the facts of the immediate past, facts which were
perfectly well known to all that heard him. All that had happened
in recent months—his persistent interference with the Austrian
administration of Holstein; indeed, the very patience of Vienna—
were actually made to appear insults to Prussia which would
make war unavoidable, a war which, if it were now to come,
they must in no circumstances refuse to wage.

The demands he now made were the natural and well-nigh
inevitable corollaries of his position. Negotiations, he insisted,
should be opened forthwith with Italy with a view to an alliance
and with France with a view to ensuring her neutrality. Such was
by now the suggestive power of his personality that almost none
dared gainsay him. Indeed, that shrewd and observant woman,
the Crown Princess, was not far wrong when she wrote to her
mother about this time that no absolute monarch could be migh-
tier than Bismarck. Only the Crown Prince and von Bodelschwingh, the Finance Minister, the latter under the influence of
Ludwig von Gerlach, offered a modicum of opposition, the Crown
Prince saying that the war would render a most acceptable service
to Napoleon and that he could see no good whatever from it.
But nobody was in the habit of taking much notice of the Crown
Prince, and nobody did so now.

As to the King, he allowed himself to be persuaded along with
the rest, though only after considerable hesitation. He also insisted on the inclusion of a minute to the effect that the war
should not lead to the dethronement of any German prince.
Where he showed real mulishness, however, was in his reluctance
to sign a personal letter to Napoleon (Bismarck dragged the
concession out of him on the following day), a letter written in
cordial, not to say fraternal, terms in which he suggested to the
Frenchman, nay positively begged him, to enter upon a "special
and intimate entente" with him—save for its form the identical
project that Napoleon had proposed to Bismarck in '62, only to
have the King indignantly reject it.

But circumstances had changed—for both the parties concerned. William was faced with the possibility of a major war

and Bismarck, not so long ago a mere Junker going through
diplomatic motions, was now a figure who was internationally
famous and internationally feared. As things stood at the time,
it was wise when dealing with such a man to maintain a certain
freedom of action, and so Napoleon's answer was friendly, but
said exactly nothing—and that, in the circumstances, is not
surprising.

Actually Bismarck's policy of alliances became ever more repugnant to the King and his scruples grew. When an Italian delegation appeared in Berlin, he used the pretext of indisposition to
avoid receiving them. Immediately after this, he instructed the
Crown Prince to write to Queen Victoria, his mother-in-law,
that he was prepared to accept the offer of mediation which had
been made to him verbally by her ambassador, Loftus.* A copy
of the letter was sent to Bismarck who, as the Crown Princess
reported to her mother, was beside himself with rage.

Politics, Bismarck clearly felt, was no occupation for princes,
or at any rate no suitable field for independent princely initiative,
and the Prussian ambassador in London was instructed to treat
the princely letter as non-existent, and also to state as forcefully
as possible at the Foreign Office that the Elbe duchies were indispensable for Prussia. The British government, which had never
recognised the full seriousness of the situation, allowed itself to
be both annoyed and browbeaten by these tactics, the Queen
saying in the end that Bismarck's methods of procedure made it
quite impossible for her to tender her good offices—which was
precisely what Bismarck wanted her to say.

It was no novelty for a German prince to enter into an alliance
with a foreign potentate against one of his own order, but it was
something which had not occurred since the formation of the
German Bund, which indeed explicitly forbade such an arrangement. The alliance with Italy, and to a lesser degree William's
letter to Napoleon, were thus flagrant breaches of the Bund's
constitution and as such weighed heavily on the sensitive conscience of the King. The matter was so painful to him that
throughout his life he sought to suppress all memory of the
circumstances in which the Italian alliance had been initiated.
Even so, the treaty of alliance was signed on April 8, 1866.

The signature was followed by a somewhat surprising event.
One day after it had taken place the Prussian ambassador got
up in the Bundestag, and by Bismarck's direction moved that a
new parliament based on universal suffrage should be convened

* Lord Augustus Loftus. Career diplomat. Envoy at Vienna (1858), Berlin (1860),
Ambassador Berlin (1866), then Envoy to North German Confederation, Ambassador
St. Petersburg (1871-9). Ultimately Governor of New South Wales.

which was to set about reforming the Bund itself. The ambassador did not specify along what lines such reform was to follow, but this merely served to emphasise the fact that it was on universal suffrage that the new parliament was to be based. This proposal was of course not wholly new. Bismarck had already made it after the Frankfurt princes' diet, but it was none the less startling for all that, and the question remains just why it was made.

Actually Bismarck had already provided the answer to that question on the previous evening when he informed the Italian military mission that this motion would plunge Germany into confusion and might conceivably lead to war. Obviously he was assuming that hotly contested issues like that of the suffrage— Bismarck was actually harking back to the revolutionary legislation of 1848—would serve to add new bitterness to the relationship between the princes and their peoples. The King himself had remarked, "What you are proposing to me is a revolution," and perhaps he was not so far wrong. For Bismarck needed such a revolution as this in order to disturb the negotiations between the different states of the Bund and between these and Austria. Later he declared that he had made this motion with a view to providing public opinion with a more valid ground for war than could be found in the question of the duchies. It may well be that this was one of his motives.

The first results of the manœuvre was a Stock Exchange collapse, while the Bundestag, as a face-saving measure, referred the matter to a select committee. It is doubtful whether much else was achieved by it, though the fear of war mounted during May, the whole of Europe being affected by it. When for a time the prospects grew brighter, Bismarck's physical health was quite visibly affected. He lay, said Karolyi, on a sofa "like a wounded boar" with violent pains in his legs, and other witnesses bear similar testimony.

It was becoming obvious that what this audacious man had in mind was out-and-out separatism, the splitting of a political entity to whose existence in the centre of Europe the world had for centuries grown accustomed, and the more obvious his intentions became, the more violent on all sides grew the opposition. Queen Victoria surpassed herself in the darkness of her foreboding. William was being deceived. The belief was being implanted in his mind, wrongly, that he was the victim of aggression. At such a time she could not keep silent, etc., etc. The Czar warned vaguely against revolutionary policies and city fathers protested all over Prussia while Treitschke, himself anything but a moralist, wrote after a long and heated discussion with Bismarck, "He simply has no conception of the moral forces existing in the world."

On May 7th Bismarck, returning to his house which he had left earlier during the day, greeted Johanna with the words, "Don't be alarmed, my dear, I've been shot at," and indeed in Unter den Linden a pale young student had fired several times at him with a revolver. Bismarck had hurled himself upon his assailant, seized his throat and wrists, and overpowered him. His assailant was a certain Ferdinand Cohen Blind, a stepson of Karl Blind, who came from Baden, was one of the revolutionaries of 1848, and now lived in London. It was the young man's intention to save Europe from the threatening catastrophe of war. Shortly after his arrest, he seems to have contrived to cut his veins, though the full story behind this affair has never really come to light.

As chance would have it, on the very day which he was spared the loss of his life Bismarck incurred a loss almost equally grievous, the loss of a friend. Already after the end of the Danish war Ludwig von Gerlach had set his face against what he called "the Prussian greed for territory" which was driving "the rest of Germany into the arms of Bonapartism". After that, the estrangement between himself and Bismarck had rapidly increased. In a private letter which he composed about this time we find the words "that the Lord is King of all peoples is for me of more importance than the very existence of Prussia". It would be difficult to conceive of any sentiment more alien to Bismarck's ideas. Now, in the *Kreuzzeitung* Gerlach drew a line of division that was public and unmistakable. "Let us beware," he wrote, "of the hideous and mistaken doctrine that God's holy ordinances do not apply to the sphere of politics, of diplomacy and war. Do not let us speak as though these spheres were governed by no higher law than that of patriotic egoism." He condemned Bismarck's preparation for a war against Austria and the German Bund, which had given Germany fifty years of peace, prosperity and freedom from outside interference—a remark unmistakably directed against Bismarck's negotiations with France and Italy, which had long become public knowledge.

Bismarck had a message conveyed to Gerlach that the latter's words had wounded him more deeply than Blind, the would-be assassin, and when Gerlach, then in his seventy-fourth year, visited the much younger man in the hope that their purely personal friendship might still be saved, he was compelled to leave without a handshake. This was the end, not only of one of the few friendships enjoyed by Bismarck with one who measured up to him as a man, it was the end of Prussian Conservatism as an essentially spiritual movement. Gerlach, accompanied by a small minority, left the party whose rank and file became a government party without a will of its own, mere putty in Bismarck's hands.

Suddenly, on May 24th, a communication was received from Napoleon. Till then he had regarded a German civil war as inevitable and so had started negotiating with Austria in order to see whether she was more ready than Bismarck to make concessions. But he had obviously thought better of it, and now, rather than sign with either of the potential belligerents, preferred to work for a general pacification and so invited Prussia, Austria, Italy and the German Bund to a conference.

Bismarck immediately accepted; though such a conference might well interfere with his warlike preparation, he realised that he should not seek to evade it. Austria, however, which might have been saved by such a conference before things had come to powder and shot, sent a reply, which, though technically justified, was in the circumstances somewhat infelicitous. For she stipulated that no increase in the size or power of any state should form the subject of discussion. In this Napoleon saw a criticism of his proposals for "compensation" and so regarded his invitation as having been refused. Thus the conference collapsed before it had begun. Bismarck was jubilant: "Long live the King. This is war."

But Napoleon had not finished with Austria yet. Like Bismarck, a master of diplomatic reinsurance, he had, under the threat of a Franco-Prussian alliance, extracted a secret treaty from her which in the event of an Austrian victory left him master of Venice. In consideration of this, Austria was given a free hand against Prussia which meant that Prussia stood to lose Silesia and the province of Saxony, to say nothing of the neutralisation of Italy. For himself Napoleon claimed the revision of France's eastern frontier and the formation on the Rhine of a new state which was to be received into the German Bund.

The blackmail was successful. On June 12th the treaty was signed. Two days later war broke out.

For in the meantime blow had followed blow. On June 1st Austria had brought the whole Schleswig-Holstein question before the Bundestag and summoned Holstein's Estates to meet. Bismarck's reply was to declare that the treaty of Gastein had been violated and to despatch troops into Holstein before whom, to Bismarck's not inconsiderable annoyance, the Austrians retreated. Baulked of the collision he had desired, Bismarck addressed a letter to Manteuffel, the general officer commanding, which was conspicuous neither for its courtesy nor its restraint.

On the 10th Bismarck circulated the blueprint of a new constitution to all members of the Bund. It was anything but an eloquent document, though its main points were startling enough. These comprised the exclusion of Austria from Germany, the division of the command of the Bund's forces between Prussia and Bavaria and—once more—universal franchise. The proposals were again not treated seriously, and under the stress of more turbulent events were soon forgotten.

On the 11th Austria tabled a motion for the mobilisation against Prussia of all the Bund's non-Prussian troops. The motion was voted upon on the 14th. Austria was given nine votes, against the six of the states of Northern and Central Germany who had naturally enough been overawed. Thus it was resolved that the German Bund should make war on Prussia. The Prussian representative hereupon declared the Bund dissolved, though his authority to do anything of the kind was, to say the least, obscure. The action had as little significance as his assurance that the King of Prussia was still prepared to negotiate on the basis of the draft constitution circulated three days before.

All this was to no purpose so far as Bismarck was concerned. The world was of one mind in regarding the war as an outbreak of Prussian lust for conquest. Nor were there many doubts that Austria was doing no more than defend her just rights.

The prospect was disturbing. It was only a year since the American Civil War had ended, leaving behind it vast losses and enormous devastation. What, after a German civil war, would remain of Germany, which offered a much more restricted theatre of operations and possessed a much higher degree of vulnerability? Of all this men were keenly aware, nor could the passionate hatred that was growing up all around the figure of Bismarck be assuaged by paper constitutions or by any proliferation of phrases from the liberal textbooks. Bismarck had no illusions about this. He knew the world well enough to know that there was only one infallible means of converting such universal detestation into universal applause. It was victory.

7

THE DECISIVE BATTLE

The prospects of victory were doubtful indeed. Would the Prussian army, which had not met a serious opponent for half a century and whose performance in Schleswig was distinctly unconvincing, be a match for the Austrian veterans? What vast forces stood on the Austrian side! The armies of some of her German allies, Saxony, Bavaria and Württemberg, for instance, had won the profound respect of Napoleon I, while, save for Italy, the allies of Prussia were forced by considerations of geographical proximity to furnish their infinitesimal contingents very much against their will.

It is true that the Prussian infantry possessed the needle gun, which was capable of four times the firing rate of the Austrian muzzle-loaders. One-fifth of the artillery was equipped with rifled guns, with barrels not of bronze but of steel. They had been delivered by Krupp, who was in no way perturbed by the fact that there was as yet no parliamentary sanction for the expenditure, as part of a two-million thaler credit. In May, von Bodelschwingh, who hated the idea of war, had suddenly declared that he had no money to pay for any further mobilisation, and for the moment it appeared as though the whole mobilisation plan were in danger of collapsing. But Bleichröder, Bismarck's banker, advised the selling of the operating rights of the Cologne-Minden railway. Bodelschwingh's predecessor, von der Heydt, was asked whether, should he be made Finance Minister, he would undertake such an operation; he answered in the affirmative, on condition that the Landtag would subsequently be approached for an indemnity. So Bodelschwingh was dismissed and Heydt replaced him, and matters took their course.

On June 15th a twenty-four-hour ultimatum was handed in by Bismarck's orders in the Central States, which lay between the two parts of Prussia. It demanded their disarmament and their agreement to the exclusion of Austria from the German Bund. In all cases it was rejected.

When midnight sounded from the towers of Berlin, the hour when the ultimatum expired, and when Prussian troops began marching into Saxony, Hanover and Hesse, Bismarck was walking in the old garden of the ministry with the British ambassador. He said, "The fight will be bitter. If we are beaten, I shall not return here. I shall fall in the final attack. One can only die once, and if one is conquered it's better to die."

In Hesse the Prussians encountered no resistance and the same thing happened in Saxony, since the Saxon army had already withdrawn towards the upper reaches of the Elbe into Bohemia. In Hanover there was a clash and the issue was not too favourable for Prussia. A combined Prussian-Thuringian force was beaten at Langensalza. However, two days later the entire Hanoverian army was surrounded here and forced to surrender. So Northern Germany was conquered.

The South German armies which should have joined up with the Hanoverian were now isolated. They continued to operate against the Prussians for some time but did so clumsily, for they were hampered by a not wholly unjustified mistrust of each other and made hopelessly uncertain of themselves as a result of petty domestic jealousies. They took part in a number of engagements, the results being for the most part unfavourable for them. But there was never a decision.

There was, however, one factor which was very decisive indeed. It was that the South Germans remained separated from the Austrian main force, which was concentrating as the "Northern army" in Bohemia, strengthened by the Saxons alone. This force, which Moltke, the Prussian commander, now sought out, was commanded by a general of infantry named Benedek, a Protestant Hungarian and a good soldier, but one who had as yet failed to prove himself as a strategist. Actually the man had no confidence in himself, and before the decisive battle had virtually broken down and begged the Emperor to make peace at all costs.

The decisive battle was joined on July 3rd. The Austrians had dug themselves in before the little fortress of Königgrätz and held a position immediately facing what had once been an artillery range, a circumstance which enabled them to know all the ranges in advance. And so, when the main Prussian body began its attack, it was virtually pinned down by the Austrian gunners who were shooting with great accuracy. The Prussian artillery, however, whose steel gun tubes were proving something of a disappointment, was silenced immediately it appeared on the field.

Bismarck on his great day kept close to the King. As a major of Landwehr cavalry he wore his steel helmet and a long grey cloak. So they watched the battle, or what was to be seen of it, which was often little more than columns of Prussian infantry emerging from the mists and then disappearing again. King and minister sat on their horses for the most part motionless and in

silence. The battle orders had been given and there was nothing
to do now but to await the outcome. Moltke, who had a cold,
occasionally applied a red silk handkerchief to his nose. Once
Bismarck asked Moltke whether he knew the length of the towel
whose tip he had contrived to grasp, to which Moltke replied:
"No, there are at least three army corps there, or maybe the whole
Austrian army." It was not a reassuring utterance.

About eleven o'clock the Prussian infantry began to give ground.
Detachments of them were streaming backwards, having obviously
suffered heavy casualties. Once the King rode to meet such a
body and his harsh words sent it back into battle.

The tension grew. The King asked Moltke what disposition
he had made for retreat. To this Moltke gave an answer which,
though almost rude, had a certain dignity about it and was
surely an utterance after Bismarck's heart. "There will be no
retreat. The fate of Prussia is at stake."

It was nearly two o'clock when Bismarck observed through his
remarkably powerful telescope that towards the north-east something which he had taken for a row of trees was moving and
coming nearer. He also observed that a part of the Austrian
artillery had shifted the direction of their fire. Actually what
Bismarck saw was the army of the Crown Prince which by forced
march had effected a junction with the main body and was now
systematically rolling up the Austrian flank.

At that moment, with a certain air of finality, Moltke put his
red handkerchief into the pocket of his coat and moved his horse
to a position close by the King, saying: "The campaign has been
decided—and in your favour." The King asked angrily what
Moltke meant since only a battle had been decided, but Moltke
was not to be shaken. "No," he said, "your success is complete.
Vienna lies at Your Majesty's feet."

Shortly after three o'clock the battle had been won, with the
Austrians in full retreat. It had lasted only a few hours but within
those hours there had been decided the fate of a century. Eastern
and Central Europe still show the traces of its effects and may for
many a year continue to do so.

When towards evening Bismarck was riding across the battlefield along with the King and those of his company, the little
cavalcade encountered the Crown Prince and his staff, so that
Bismarck looked straight into the Prince's fine bearded face. Yet
such was his contempt for the man in whom he now suddenly
discerned a rival that he was unable to force a single word to
his lips but looked through him as though he were made of glass.

Shortly after this, an aide-de-camp, von Steinäcker, gave
expression to thoughts that must surely have been already present

in Bismarck's mind. "Now you're a great man, Your Excellency, but if the Crown Prince had arrived too late, you'd be an out-and-out scoundrel."

As dusk fell, Bismarck parted from the King and, together with a small group of officers, rode towards the little town of Horsitz, where quarters were supposed to have been prepared for him. Everywhere on the trampled corn and in the meadows lay the dead and wounded, often hideously disfigured. This was a moment in which Bismarck grew aware that every political event, however important it may be, has its simple unpolitical human side. He remarked to Keudell: "When I reflect that one day Herbert may be lying like that, I grow sick at heart."

His day ended somewhat grotesquely. The quarters which were to have been prepared for him in Horsitz turned out to be non-existent. Searching for a place to sleep, he passed through a dark doorway into an unpaved courtyard, where he fell into a dungpit. At last he found refuge under a colonnade in the market-place where he was sheltered from the drizzling rain, and made his bed out of the cushions from an abandoned landau. Thus the victor was granted some hours of precarious sleep.*

A second day passed without much incident, but on the morning of the 5th Bismarck was awakened at five o'clock, and now once more a change seemed to come over everything. In the night William had received a telegram from Napoleon, which, although in form a message of congratulation, contained the news that Francis Joseph had surrendered Venetia to the Frenchman and had also asked for French mediation in the conflict with Prussia.

It had been assumed in Paris that the war in Germany would be protracted, and that at the end of it, both parties being more or less exhausted, France would be able to appear on the scene as a mediator, and without any sacrifice of her own would secure the desired alterations to her eastern frontier as payment for services rendered. Now the lightning decision of Königgrätz had completely upset these calculations, and anything that Napoleon might now undertake to do would come too late. If he had only acted differently a week ago while Austria was still unbeaten, if he had then made common cause with her, held back Italy and attacked Prussia in the west, he would for decades have made France the dominant power in Europe. As Bismarck himself was later to remark, to turn the scale he had only to throw sixty thousand troops across the Rhine and join up with the "excellent and most useful" South German troops. Bavaria alone had mobilised a hundred thousand men. She held the fortress of

* Moritz Busch, II, p. 80.

Mainz and so commanded the road up the Main into Germany.
Had, therefore, Napoleon pursued this course of action, he would
have had a force at his disposal which under experienced French
leadership would have threatened the very life of Prussia, which
had no more than forty-five thousand men in southern Germany.

In those last weeks of June and in the first one of July, Napoleon
had had his chance. He had held Bismarck's fate in his hands,
but failed to make the necessary decisions. The fact is that he was
so racked with pain from his bladder troubles that he scarcely
knew what he was about. Indeed, the Empress was already
reckoning with his abdication. It may well be said that in those
days he created the political constellation which led to Sedan and
that he lost that battle four years before it was fought.*

Yet there was danger for Prussia in the very fact that Napoleon's
great opportunity had been missed. Confronted as he was by a
beaten Austrian army on the one side, and on the other by a
victorious Bismarck who now no longer required his services,
might Napoleon not in desperation make an attempt to seize
those Rhenish territories which were as important to his dynasty
as were those of north-western Germany for Bismarck? Might
he not strike there and then while the Prussian force was
still pinned down in the cholera-infested east? To obviate the
possibility, which was still a real one, of having to carry on a two-
front war, it was essential to Bismarck that peace should immediately be made with Austria and freedom of movement thus
restored to the Prussian force.

But luck was again to some extent on Bismarck's side, for
Napoleon had missed the right moment for a French mobilisation.
This was only begun in July, so that he was now hardly ready to
fight. Even so, had he attacked, Prussia would have been compelled to withdraw a hundred and fifty thousand men from
Austria immediately. It is true that Moltke was not overmuch
disturbed by that prospect. He reckoned with holding the
Austrians along the line of the Elbe and taking the offensive in
the west, but Bismarck had little confidence in the plan and
could only hope that there would be no occasion for trying it out.

On the day that Napoleon's telegram arrived, Bismarck had
caused the King to send a temporising reply. But Napoleon was
in a hurry, and when Bismarck awoke on the 12th of the month
he saw standing by his bedside Benedetti, the French ambassador,
who had somehow contrived to make his way through the cordon
of military police. For the next few days and even weeks Benedetti never left Bismarck's side. Thus Bismarck was at length

---

* At a later date Bismarck said that Napoleon had only lacked the courage to do
what, from his point of view, he should have done. Coll. Works, VII, p. 392.

compelled to let him know his peace terms for Austria. These were: the annexation of Schleswig and Holstein and the exclusion of Austria from the German Bund which, in future, would be under Prussian leadership and be limited to Northern Germany. There was to be no annexation of Austrian territory, however. The annexation of the conquered Northern German states was communicated to the Emperor in small and carefully apportioned doses over the next few days. On the 21st Napoleon declared himself satisfied on condition that not more than four million people were affected by the annexations, that the South Germans received the right, if they so desired, to form their own confederation, and that before annexation took place there should be a plebiscite in the northern, Danish-speaking part of Schleswig.

Bismarck breathed again. For Russia had meanwhile become restless. The unilateral dissolution by Prussia of the German Bund had disturbed her government, since the Bund was the creation of the Holy Alliance and guaranteed by Russia. Worse still was the fact that Bismarck had posted up proclamations in Prague in which he had imitated Napoleon's nationality policies and had summoned the "glorious nation of the Czechs" to rise against the Hapsburgs, a proceeding that threw the Czar into a violent rage. What would happen, he argued, if the Russian Poles profited by the Czech example? Fortunately, or perhaps unfortunately, the Czechs remained unmoved by the proclamation, for at that time they greatly preferred Hapsburg rule to rule by Russia or Prussia. The fact that among the Austrian Serbs, Italians and Rumanians similar summonses to disloyalty had been equally ineffective did not lessen the irritation they caused in St. Petersburg.

It was thus obvious that if Bismarck was to give neither the Russians nor the French a ground for intervention he must make peace with Austria as quickly as possible. The spectacle of Bismarck, who had moved heaven and earth to bring on this new war, now advocating equally frantic measures to ensure peace, a peace which he wished to restore with Austria and to maintain with France, is not without its ironic charm.

And now a third enemy arose and attacked Bismarck in the rear—the Prussian generals, who were unwilling to end the war until the enemy had been utterly destroyed, a happy consummation which they believed they were on the point of bringing about. Differences between Bismarck and the King now became severe, for the King was wholly on the side of the generals and was loth to break off after a mere two weeks the great triumphal procession into which he had contrived to be drawn unless, by so doing, he could effect some tangible gain. Bismarck had repre-

sented to him so effectively and for so long that Prussia had been
forced into war by Austria that he now believed in his right to
punish her for her misdeeds. Unfortunately, Napoleon was insisting on the territorial integrity of Austria, which in its turn
was insisting on that of Saxony.

Bismarck was ready to agree to both the demands. The King
was not. Booty had been an integral element of the soldier's
trade since the Trojan war, and that old soldier, William, regarded
his Prime Minister, who sought to deny him this prescriptive
right, almost as he would have regarded a deserter from the ranks.
To make matters even more difficult, the King, unlike Bismarck,
had no fear of the cholera which, now that it was high summer,
was wreaking havoc among the troops, and had perfect confidence in Moltke's plan in the eventuality of an attack.

As a result, the general tone of Cabinet meetings was often such
that Bismarck, to quote his own words, "leapt up, ran out, slam-
med the door, lay down on the bed and *heülte wie ein Schloss-
hund*", an untranslatable colloquialism indicating violent and
more or less audible weeping. In Castle Nikolsburg, in Moravia,
the argument on July 23rd became so violent that Bismarck,
again shaken by a fit of weeping, went to his room and would
have hurled himself onto the paved courtyard below had not the
timely entry of the Crown Prince caused him to desist from this
intention. Fortunately Frederick William was ready to act as a
mediator, and after a great deal of effort actually persuaded
William to agree to a cessation of hostilities, though even then
the King still felt impelled to declare in a scribbled marginal note
that "he had been forced to bite into this sour apple before the
very gates of Vienna and left it to posterity to give judgment in
the matter".

Thus on the 26th Bismarck was able to sign the armistice and
also the preliminary peace of Nikolsburg. A few hours before this
Benedetti had very inopportunely paid him a visit. Napoleon, he
said, considered that his rôle as mediator had come to an end
and felt that he was now justified in presenting a bill. How,
therefore, did Bismarck feel about the immediate restoration of
the French frontier of 1814? In view of the fact that this possibility had already been discussed for years and that Bismarck had
agreed in principle if not in detail to French claims for compensation, he must have reckoned with some such demand. Yet
he put on an air of surprise and, by treating Benedetti's remarks
as merely part of an unofficial private conversation, avoided the
necessity of making an official reply.

Time had indeed already begun to run dangerously short, for
on the following day Russia demanded the calling of a European

Bismarck as Imperial Chancellor

1. Karl Alexander von
   Bismarck, 1727-1797.
   Bismarck's grandfather.

2. Charlotte von Bismarck,
   née von Schönfeldt, 1741-
   1772. Bismarck's
   grandmother.

3. Ferdinand von Bismarck-Schönhausen,
1771-1845. Bismarck's father.

4. Bismarck as a boy.

5 & 6.
Princess Bismarck, Bismarck's
wife, née Johanna von
Puttkamer, 1824-1894.
Married 1847.

7. Bismarck in 1863.

8. Attempt on Bismarck's life, 7 May, 1866. A woodcut.

9. Photograph from Putbus (Rügen) taken in 1866. *Front Row:* Princess Putbus, Bismarck, Countess Rantzau, née von Bismarck. *Back Row:* Count Archambaud-Talleyrand, Prince Putbus, Countess Johanna von Bismarck, Count Moritz Lottum, Frau von Romberg.

10. Frederick III, the Kaiser's father, when Crown Prince.

11. Augusta, wife of William I, the Kaiser's grandmother.

12. Napoleon III and Bismarck after the battle of Sedan.

13. Bismarck with Favre and Thiers at Versailles.

14. Proclamation of the German Empire at Versailles, 1871.

15. The Berlin Congress. *Painting by Anton von Werner.*

16. Attempt on Bismarck's life by the cooper's journeyman, Kullman. Berlin, 13 July, 1874—after a drawing by the eye-witness, the Court painter Karl Arnold.

Darstellung nach einer Zeichnung des Augenzeugen, des Kgl. Hofmalers Karl Arnold

17. Emperor William I with Bismarck.

18. Prince Alexander Mihailovitch Gortschakow,
the Russian Chancellor, in 1880.

19. Bismarck with the Emperor William II in October, 1888.

20.
The Kaiser's mother, Victoria.

21.
" Bismarck is coming ",
cartoon from *Der Floh*,
May, 1891.

22. Bismarck and his family in the park at Friedrichsruh, 1893. *Left to right:* Count Harry von Arnim, Countess Malvine von Arnim (Bismarck's sister), Sybille von Arnim, Princess Bismarck, Bismarck, Wilhelm von Bismarck (Bismarck's son).

23. Bismarck at Castle Rantzau, the property of his son-in-law.

24..Friedrich von Holstein.

25. Von Holstein at Niagara Falls.

26.
Maximilian
Harden and
Professor
Schweninger
in 1905.

27.
Bismarck in the last
years of his life.

28. Bismarck greeted by the populace at a railway station.

29. Bismarck's Funeral at Friedrichsruh, 1898. William II follows the coffin.

conference to settle the terms of peace—this would have meant the interference of the whole of Europe in Bismarck's war. It was only by being able to point to the preliminary peace that had already been signed that he could avoid this disaster which would undo everything he had achieved.

Much has been written about the moderation of this preliminary peace of Nikolsburg, which later became the peace of Prague, but quite apart from the fact that it took shape under the very considerable pressure of time, why should it *not* have been moderate? What Bismarck had sought to gain from Austria he had obtained. Prussia, until now the second of the great powers within the territory of German peoples, had fought its way to the first place and was indeed in strict parlance the only great Germanic power left. What more could he ask? Annexed Austrian territories, such as the King had demanded, would merely have been thorns sticking in the flesh of the Prussian body politic, and Bismarck had never desired an eastward expansion. The expansion he had always sought had been towards the west, where it would achieve the union of old Prussia with its western territories.

In bringing about this last, Bismarck had shown very little of that moderation which marked the Austrian settlement. The territories which lay in his way, though they were political bodies with a history of a thousand years behind them, were, without more ado, converted into provinces of Prussia—as we shall see. Certainly these proceedings were more revolutionary than the entire revolution of 1848, which never dared so much as to touch a single one of the German dynasties. Indeed, what Bismarck did on this occasion more than justified those who had felt that this counter-revolutionary really belonged on the other side of the barricades, and when he thus rode roughshod over the Divine metaphysic on which those ancient dynasties based their authority, he assuredly helped to bring about something of that indifference in such matters that was beginning to mark German ways of thought and feeling—so that in the end Germans accepted the fall in 1918 of the House of Hohenzollern without much inward perturbation.

Even now, they were already taking such things in their stride. Scarcely anyone thought the fact worthy of mention that the so-called Elbe duchies—Schleswig and Holstein—were being forcibly Prussianised, and no one seemed greatly exercised over the fact that many of the more unwelcome provisions of the treaty were quietly ignored. The plebiscite which Napoleon had stipulated in Northern Schleswig never took place at all, nor did the sovereign confederation of South German states which had also been envisaged by the peace terms ever come into being.

The results of the campaign in Italy, however, are not unworthy of note. Bismarck's misgivings concerning his Italian ally did not prove wholly groundless. The Italians were soundly beaten on land at Custozza and at sea off Lissa. For all that, Italy received Venetia from the hands of Napoleon to whom Francis Joseph surrendered it on the day after Königgrätz. One can thus say quite truthfully that Venice was won for Italy by Bismarck.

Thus the world had experienced its first blitzkrieg. Because it took place within so short a space of time there has long been a tendency to under-rate its importance. Gradually, however, we are beginning to realise how right Jacob Burckhardt was when he refused to see in the Prussian victory a mere seven days' wonder but rather discerned in it "the great German revolution". For it is a fact that this, the shortest of all European wars, had consequences more far-reaching than any other fought during that century.

Königgrätz cut off from Germany about a third of the territory which till then had always co-existed with the other two-thirds and had been able to count on that two-thirds for support. Austria unwillingly travelled that road that four hundred years previously had led Switzerland, and, three centuries before, the Netherlands, voluntarily to sever themselves from the German Empire. Whether they called it German Empire or German Bund, some ten million Germans now ceased to regard Germany as their homeland.

Compared with this the consequences of Sedan are relatively unimportant. That battle produced certain changes in the Franco-German frontier which have since been reversed, and destroyed the relations between the two countries concerned, thus poisoning the political atmosphere of Central Europe for generations. But that was as far as it went. Königgrätz, however, cut deep into the very substance of Germany, which it reduced by a third, and caused its intellectual and economic influence, which in the days of the old empire had extended to the Black Sea, to stop short at Vienna which now became a mere frontier post as it had been when Marcus Aurelius pitched his tent on the spot.

Seen from the point of view of world history, it is of little moment that Bismarck left Austria territorially intact, but of very great moment that by excluding her from Germany he delivered her over to the struggle of nationalities which the Germans of Austria —now a minority left to its own devices—were quite unable to control. The weaker their resistance, the more aggressive their enemies became, and the more their confidence in themselves declined. Austria now actually acquired the quality which precipitate progressives had prematurely ascribed to her. She became incapable of survival.

In the catastrophe of 1918 the monarchy was replaced by a conglomeration of linguistic entities each demanding for itself a sovereignty, the right to which was allegedly written in the stars. In actual fact, however, each was as impotent as its neighbour, and collectively they constituted a vacuum that replaced the great dam by which for centuries the Hapsburgs had held off Asia from Europe. The vacuum was filled by the East in 1945, represented on this occasion by the forces of Soviet Russia. The flood reached right up to the castles in the Harz mountains, erected by the old rulers of the Holy Roman Empire.

Bismarck, of course, did not foresee the results that would flow from his policies. He assumed that truncated Austria would be held together, as had been the case in previous centuries (during the Turkish invasions, for instance), by the loyalty of the nationalities to the ruling house. Nor is it altogether strange that he should have taken such a view. Even after the peace of Prague the Hapsburg monarchy was still a mighty structure, and Bismarck was no more blind to the truth than was the Hofburg itself. "We shall certainly get out of Germany," wrote Francis Joseph to his wife, "whether they demand this of us or no, and after the experiences we have had with our dear German allies, I myself think that would be an excellent thing for Austria."

Till now that complex thing, public opinion, of which one can never tell whether it is the creature or the creator of events, had, as we have seen, been hostile to Bismarck. Bismarck had comforted himself with the reflection that you did not shoot with public opinion but with powder and lead, a proposition that is only valid in a very restricted sense. However that may be, public opinion now claimed him for its own with the same assurance with which it had previously rejected him. Indeed it almost claimed the credit of having itself discovered this brilliant mind and of having made its possessor into its leading statesman. Public opinion was, in the main, strongly inclined towards liberalism and coloured by nationalism, but the nationalism of 1866 had nowhere yet attained the dimensions of a popular movement. It was a peculiar property of the higher orders of society from which it was only just beginning to permeate the lower ones. It had singularly failed to spread among the great masses of smaller peasants or among the property-less agricultural and industrial workers who had more pressing and personal cares to occupy their minds. It had also not yet affected the population of such old self-conscious districts as Upper Bavaria and Lower Saxony, which could see no reason for any change in their circumstances.

Nationalist or not, however, public opinion had changed in

Bismarck's favour, and Bismarck was not slow to take advantage
of the fact. The first occasion on which he did so was August
5th, when he appeared before the Landtag that now had a very
different appearance from the one which had been sent home
shortly before the war. The new Landtag had actually been
elected on the day of Königgrätz, and the Conservatives with 142
votes formed the strongest party, while the opposition, the Progressive Party and the so-called Left-Centre, had sunk from 253
to 148. To the new Landtag so constituted Bismarck declared his
intention of asking for an indemnity for all the acts committed
throughout the years, and particularly for all the payments made,
in contravention of the will of Parliament. The King had at first
opposed the idea. During the long railway journey between
Prague and Berlin he obstinately clung to his determination not,
as he put it, to eat humble pie. He completely failed to see that
it was not his government but parliament that would be the loser
if the indemnity were sanctioned, since it would mean that parliament had completely reversed the attitude it had maintained
during the constitutional conflict. For what it would in effect be
saying was that the victory of the Prussian armies had nullified
the breach of the constitution of which Bismarck had been guilty
by their creation. When, therefore, on December 5th the indemnity was approved by 230 votes to 75, Bismarck had really
added the conquest of the Prussian Landtag to that of Austria.

The occasion of this vote produced considerable changes in
the party structure. Those members of what hah hitherto been
the Opposition who could not so quickly forget Bismarck's contemptuous behaviour towards them, parted from those who were
ready to give him their support; and it was from these last that
the party emerged which took the name of National Liberals,
even though their concept of liberalism, that is to say their respect
for the individual, was well nigh crushed out of existence by their
nationalism.

The evening of that same August 5th on which the Landtag
made its offer of peace brought Bismarck face to face with more
intractable problems. During the course of the morning Benedetti
had given notice of a visit, and in accordance with normal diplomatic practice had sent him a document in which the general
purpose of the visit was described. He wanted to discuss Napoleon's very considerable demands for compensation which he
now put forward in the form of a proposed Franco-Prussian pact.
What Napoleon was asking for was nothing less than the Bavarian
Palatinate, that part of Hesse that lay on the left bank of the
Rhine, the Prussian Saar territory, and, as a bridgehead on the
right bank of the Rhine, the fortress of Mainz.

Now we have seen how for years Bismarck had dangled the bait of German and even Prussian territories on the left bank of the Rhine before the French, and surely he must from time to time have said things to Napoleon similar in substance to the remark made to the Italian general, Gavone, "I am much more a Prussian than I am a German and would have no particular hesitation in handing over the whole territory between the Rhine and the Moselle to France."

A few months previously, had he been confronted with a war on two fronts, he would have been quite ready to sacrifice the Rhine if that was the price of saving Prussia. "Do you think," he asked the Hessian ambassador on that occasion, "that I would let Benedek come to Berlin? If he beat us I would offer Napoleon the Rhine." Yet he was now skilful enough, as he had been on a previous occasion, to avoid giving Benedetti a final answer. It is true that he declared the surrender of Mainz, the gateway to the whole of Central Germany, to be quite impossible, and said that the King would never agree to it. But he managed all the more successfully to convince Benedetti that he was prepared to discuss the other demands. "Prussia," he assured him, "was ready to make sacrifices in the interest of Franco-Prussian relations, even if, in the King's view, they were contrary to the national honour."

Benedetti returned to Paris. Once more Napoleon's demands had been turned aside, but how often would Bismarck succeed in repeating the performance? Because he did not know the answer to that question and in order to cover his rear from Napoleon, Bismarck now did all he could to speed up negotiations with Austria. So successful was he in this that on August 23rd, a mere two weeks after Benedetti's visit, peace had been signed in Prague.

Immediately afterwards, and with equal speed, Bismarck set about doing inside Germany what the treaty authorised him to do, and annexed those North German states which had not come down on the Prussian side. Hanover, the Electorate of Hesse, the Dukedom of Nassau and the Free City of Frankfurt were all quietly incorporated in Prussia, which thus was turned into a clearly defined piece of territory with considerably more than twenty million inhabitants. "What we need," he had written a few days earlier to his younger son, William, "is North Germany, and that's where we are going to spread." All the South needed to do was to pay up.*

Anyone who till then had looked on Bismarck as a conservative legitimist, must now surely have revised his views, for northern Germany was indeed undergoing a revolutionary transformation,

* *Bismarcks Briefe an seiner Sohn Wilhelm* (1922), p. 15.

a transformation which Bismarck justified by the thesis which he
dictated to Keudell: "Conquest in a just war is both a just and
a moral title of possession." The various dethronements produced
no searchings of his conscience, for the idea of legitimacy only
existed for him when it had reference to the Prussian dynasty.
Whenever he encountered it in a different context it was the
"Gottverdammter Legtimitätsschwindel" which the reader can
surely translate for himself.

The worst sufferer by far was Hanover, for its personal union
with Britain had been dissolved since Victoria's accession to the
throne. Thus, there was no great European power that was
likely to take its part, as there was for Hesse or Saxony. In
Hanover the state of war was maintained for a longer period than
anywhere else, and it was used to render any person harmless—
by dismissal from his post, by disciplinary procedure or imprisonment—who was suspected of being an opponent of Prussia. This
referred particularly to the "hostile" officials; all officials were
"hostile who did not by their open and honest obedience show
their loyalty to the new order and the Prussian régime". King
George's personal fortune was confiscated and used to create the
Guelph fund. This was placed under the management of Bleichröder and was to be employed in combating "Guelph intrigue".
Since no accounts had to be rendered, the fund soon began to be
used for purposes of general bribery. It received a name appropriate to its chequered history—"the Reptile Fund".

By September both Houses of Parliament had approved the
annexation laws, and among those so approving were conservatives,
who thus showed that they had disencumbered themselves of the
legitimist ideal of their predecessors of 1848. Ultimately, there
was formed a conservative splinter group which, like Bismarck,
was ready to jettison the principles passed on through such men
as Gerlach, and now placed itself unconditionally at Bismarck's
disposal. These men called themselves the Free Conservatives and
represented in particular the great accumulations of capital to be
found within the party. In the main, Junker elements who came
from that stratum of society to which Bismarck belonged had little
to do with them.

Of course the more traditional elements in Prussia did not
accept these developments without some kind of protest. A
pamphlet of Gerlach's attacking the annexations ran into six
editions between September and December and led to his final
breach with Bismarck. With the South German states—which,
like Hanover, had offered armed resistance and so from Bismarck's point of view were equally guilty—he dealt very mildly,
partly because they did not lie in the path of Prussian expansion,

which was westwards, but chiefly because Napoleon had insisted that they should form an internationally recognised southern federation which was to act as a counterpoise to the now Prussian north.

Not that even here everything proceeded without friction. Indeed, Bismarck on one occasion frightened the South German plenipotentiaries so badly by his enormous demands that some of them, in particular Hesse and Bavaria, appealed for help to Paris. But Napoleon delayed in answering their requests, and when the answer came it was that of a tired man who had lost all interest—also it came too late.

For meanwhile Bismarck had hinted to the South Germans that he would treat them very mildly if they would enter into secret alliances with him which, in the event of a war, bound them to place their forces at the disposal of the King of Prussia. The experience of the Bavarian Prime Minister, von der Pfordten, is not without interest in this connection; as he was leaving his Berlin hotel a piece of paper was pressed into his hand on which were printed the words: "Recommended that instead of a sacrifice of territory you offer a full contribution of twenty-five millions and an alliance against all foreign enemies. Please destroy this paper. A Friend."

Actually the South Germans received Bismarck's proposals with a sigh of relief and signed the various secret alliances and peace treaties before a signature had been affixed to the Treaty of Prague, whose provisions guaranteeing unlimited sovereignty to the South German states had already been rendered ineffective before it was concluded. For they had destroyed that very sovereignty themselves when they surrendered the command of their armed forces to a foreign prince.

There seems to be no reason why we should not take Bismarck's word for the fact that at this time he had not yet decided on bringing Southern Germany within his own field of power. Nor can we say with any certainty whether he regarded as provisional or permanent a state of affairs in which Germany was cut in two by the line of the Main. His remarks on this point tend to contradict each other. Presumably, since he had not yet fully made up his own mind, he told each person what that person wanted to hear. Thus he informed the Crown Prince on January 24, 1867, that the North German Bund, which had then just come into being, was a purely provisional arrangement and that he was honestly working for the union of all Germany. One week later, he assured the ambassador of Württemberg, von Spitzemberg, that the South German particularists need have no fears for their autonomy. Prussia had no desire to touch them and no reason

for doing so. In February he told von Türckheim, the ambassador
of Baden, that his wish was to see all South German states make
simultaneous application for membership of the North German
Bund. Sometimes he would say that the present generation had
already done enough for the unification of Germany and even
went so far as to show a distinct dislike of Germany as such.
"We have no desire," he told General Suckow in 1868, "to
unite the heterogeneous elements of the south, where nobody
knows whether the particularists or the democrats are the worst
enemies of Germany." He was also one of those who realised
that the western frontier of Southern Germany was much more
unfavourably situated from a military point of view than that of
the north. "We have no desire," he said, "to become guilty of
the blunder of Piedmont, which was weakened rather than
strengthened by the annexation of Naples." Above all it was
France that made him nervous about any aggression against the
south. Napoleon had made it plain that he attached great importance to the independence of Southern Germany, since it was
this that gave him the assurance that his Prussian neighbour
would not become too powerful.

The fact is that Bismarck was an opportunist who cut his coat
according to whatever cloth a given situation happened to provide,
and it was only in the broadest sense that he had a plan for the
future at all. Nothing indeed could be farther from the truth than
the legend of the school text-books which represent Bismarck as
building up day by day and brick by brick the edifice which came
into being in 1871. Bismarck never had at any time more than
a very general idea of what he ultimately sought to achieve—and
this was the maximum extension and security of Prussian power.
The aim was unalterable, but never the means. Nor was his
choice of means ever determined by principles or dogmas. Indeed,
as Erich Marcks says, "nothing like a consistent doctrine was ever
developed by Bismarck". He had a certain peasant's lethargy (he
himself did not hesitate to speak of downright laziness) as he
waited almost indolently upon events, but whenever they shaped
themselves in such a fashion that he could use them, he struck
like lightning, and he struck directly and with power, indifferent
to all secondary considerations.

In September, as a kind of symbolic climax to the great German
transformation, the army marched into Berlin. Amidst deafening
artillery salvoes, bellringing and the music of military bands,
Bismarck rode through the Brandenburg Gate with Roon, who
was short and stout, on one side of him, and Moltke, who was tall
and gaunt, on the other. Someone had managed to throw a
garland of flowers over his brilliant white uniform, a gesture whose

purpose he made no effort to defeat. In Unter den Linden the stands rose to rooftop level. In that same street he had been shot at a few weeks previously. Now it could not hold all those who wished to cheer him.

But there was to be a reckoning. Immediately after the triumph, his seemingly powerful body showed for the first time all the symptoms of his strange vulnerability, a condition complicated by the old trouble with a vein of his leg. His mood varied between utter listlessness and a well-nigh terrifying irritability, both very puzzling at a time when little was known of the psychosomatic effects arising from extreme expenditure of energy. Though he was only fifty-one, he was already complaining of the disabilities of senescence. "The best thing for me would be to go here and now," he said about this time to Keudell. "I could do so with the knowledge that I have been of some use to my country and could leave that impression behind me. I really do not know whether I can tackle the work that still remains to be done."

In October he went to Putbus on the quiet island of Rügen in the Baltic and there he grew seriously ill, though no one could diagnose the exact nature of his complaint. There is some mention of stomach cramps which could only be subdued by heavy doses of opium. Later there was some improvement which could be maintained so long as he could stay in the open and watch the blue rollers move inland and enjoy the still air of the dying Indian summer. He idly turned the pages of some illustrated book. Politics, however, wrote Johanna, were a painful subject, and for some time still were to induce feelings of grave anxiety. He returned to Berlin at the beginning of December but still wore an air of such exhaustion that Keudell advised him to spend the whole winter on the Riviera. But Bismarck replied, "In Pomerania women say when their time comes 'Now I must face my peril'. That at the moment applies to me."

He was not far wrong. The important thing now was to turn the decisions of the summer into law. Indeed, it was high time for that. But it is always easier to make a successful revolution than to give permanence to its achievements. The constitution of the North German Bund, of Prussian-dominated North Germany, that is to say, had already been drafted by his collaborator, Bucher, while Bismarck was in Putbus, and Bucher had chosen as his models the constitution of the Frankfurt National Assembly of 1849 and that of the United States, at that time the only great power organised on a federal basis.

The North German Bund comprehended all Germany north of the Main, which means that it included also the northern part of the Grand Duchy of Hessen, the three free Hansa towns and the Kingdom of Saxony which had to be impressed into it with a certain amount of force. For the rulers of the aforementioned principalities it was a pleasant surprise, after the dethronements in Hanover, Nassau and the electorate of Hesse, that they still retained a certain agreeable semblance of sovereignty. Only two minute principalities resisted, that of Saxe-Meiningen, whose duke was promptly deposed in favour of his son, and Reuss, the older line, whose regent, Caroline, submitted when her country was occupied by two companies of Prussian troops.

The really decisive clauses in the constitution were those which appointed the King of Prussia as President of the Bund and so to the post of Commander-in-Chief. Thus he was given the control not only of the troops but also of foreign policy and so could decide the issues of peace and war. The individual states were left in control of their own internal administration, of churches and schools, and were permitted to govern themselves according to their own laws. Thus their rulers were in much the same position as the tetrarchs in Palestine under the Roman Empire.

The liberals who favoured uniformity would gladly have introduced the department system of the French Revolution, but Bismarck resisted. He remembered all too well that the history of Germany for a thousand years had been a federal history, so that she could not have endured so sudden and radical a breach with tradition. A saying of his that has a bearing on this matter can be loosely rendered thus: "In dealing with the German states, one must not ask what can be nationalised (*was kann gemeinsam sein*) or how far the great mouth of nationalisation may bite into the apple. One must ask oneself what is there that we simply cannot avoid nationalising."

The Bundesrat, the official central organ of the new body, was a sort of carbon copy of the Frankfurt Bundestag, whose constitution was in part taken over word for word, though with a marked limitation of members' rights. A simple majority was now sufficient to get a measure passed and Prussia could always arrange for that, provided it could secure another five votes to add to the seventeen which it had already. Votes held by others than Prussia were apportioned as follows: Saxony, four; Mecklenburg, Schwerin and Brunswick, two each; all the rest one each. This was, of course, a very different arrangement from that of the American Senate where all states had equal voting powers. Franz von Roggenbach, the liberal Foreign Minister of Baden, and an intimate friend of the Crown Prince, spoke of the North German Bund as "a union of a dog with its fleas", a telling if somewhat indelicate description.

Besides the Bundesrat, there now existed—and here the arrangements differed from those of Frankfurt—a Reichstag based on universal suffrage. This does not mean that Bismarck shared the Liberal theory that universal suffrage was a God-given right. What he saw in it actually was a gift from the Crown. He often declared that he would be quite ready to abolish it if it did not serve his purposes. The Reichstag was elected for three years and had 297 members. Of these 236 were Prussians. It had no independent legislative power. Its only function was to approve and confirm. Its budgetary rights only extended to expenditures by the Bund. Since, however, this was mostly concerned with expenditure on the Army, and the amount to be spent was fixed in a so-called "iron estimate" for four years at a time, the role it played in this matter was of little significance.

The essential feature of any parliamentary system, namely its control over the government, was entirely absent, since the Reichstag could not in any matter go against the Bundesrat, which consisted not of responsible ministers but of diplomats of the various federated governments. Had the Reichstag opposed the Bundesrat, it would have been opposing each of the twenty member states individually, an impossible position.

In discussing the constitution in the Reichstag, the National Liberals, who were now the government party, succeeded in ensuring that the suffrage should not only be universal but secret. It was the first time that Bismarck felt himself forced to make concessions to his new allies. He did it very unwillingly, for the secret ballot prevented the great landowners from controlling their peasants and servants, a power which, so Bismarck had once said to Lassalle, constituted the great advantage of universal suffrage. It was also the National Liberals who compelled him to take over the office of Federal Chancellor (*Bundeskanzler*) himself, although at first he had only attached minor importance to it.

The whole thing was a skilful application of old Prussian principles of government to the whole of Northern Germany with certain unimportant concessions to the theories of parliamentary liberalism and to the federalist enthusiasms of those who could not forget the ancient Empire. He himself said that he had chosen the form of a confederacy but for all tactical purposes had endowed it with the policy of a federal state, and that "this quality expressed itself in various elastic, hidden, but nevertheless far-reaching ways".

His action in this, as in many other matters, disproves a widely-spread misapprehension concerning him, namely that he was a quarrelsome man and found a certain personal pleasure in violent actions. Neither his ancestors on his father's side, who were farmers, well used to waiting on the slow processes of nature, nor the bureaucrats from whom his mother was descended, were the kind of people who sought to disturb others by abrupt and violent conduct. Actually he avoided that kind of thing wherever he could, and would only consent to a serious clash when there was no other way of solving a problem—in which case he would be utterly intransigent. In a word, he was not a man to pick a quarrel over inessentials. Very characteristically he wrote about this time to Roon: "The form in which the King of Prussia should exercise his authority in Germany is a matter to which I attach little importance, but I have used all the strength that God has given me to ensure that he should exercise it."

The central pillars of the new edifice, the educated and propertied bourgeoisie, had little ground for complaint. Business was beginning to flourish to a quite unprecedented extent, especially in those western territories which Prussia had so unwillingly taken over in 1814. It was here, in the pleasant valley of the Ruhr, that one of the world's mightiest industrial undertakings was coming into being. Its growth was helped when freedom of movement was given the formal sanction of law throughout the territories of the Bund, and willing industrial workers were able to move westward in large numbers. The whole trend was undoubtedly assisted by the circumstance that the most active and talented members of the bourgeoisie failed to follow the example of their opposite numbers in England. They had no taste for politics, and in view of the Reichstag's impotence, their disinclination is not surprising. So they went into business, and particularly into industry. They had lost the airy and distinctively German idealism of their parents and grandparents, and their realist perception recognised all the more readily the opportunities for material gain that the world was beginning to offer.

The labouring classes were, of course, still on the losing side. The agricultural workers, who had succumbed to the allurements of industry, entered the factories and so broke the threads which had woven them into society; they thus tasted the loneliness of the insecure proletariat and learned what it meant to be the plaything of chance. Their laborious efforts to defend themselves against their fate were long to remain ineffective. Yet there was already sitting in the Reichstag a certain August Bebel, who had been elected president of the Leipzig Workers' Educational Union. Two years later, in Eisenach, the German Social Democratic Party was founded.

There was now a discernible proliferation of parliamentary activities. The North German Reichstag and the two houses of the Prussian parliament were sitting in Berlin. To these in 1868 a fourth parliament was added, namely that of the Customs Union, and in this, in addition to the North German Reichstag members, sat deputies from South Germany, also elected by universal suffrage. On top of it all, each of the constituent states had a parliament of its own.

Bismarck was quite pleased at these developments. He had once held all that pertained to parliaments in contempt. Now— so Keudell tells us—when he showed himself in the Landtag or the Reichstag, a gloomy narrow building in the Leipzigerstrasse that was later for years to provide a home for the Reichstag of the Empire—one would hardly have recognised him.

He displayed an inexhaustible patience in answering the stupidest of questions, and showed on these occasions "an almost childish friendliness". "An excess of parliament-mongering," he once declared, "would show the electors that even this allegedly infallible panacea had its defects. The people should be stuffed with parliaments much as a pastrycook's apprentice is stuffed with sweets."

In these various parliaments the National Liberals were for long to be his chief supporters; together with the Free Conservatives they formed a reliable and, for the most part, a highly pliable majority. Surveying the domestic scene he could surely be well satisfied. Abroad the prospects were rather less pleasing.

It was obvious by this time that Austria would not accept the defeat of 1866 as final. Francis Joseph had written to his mother, "We were much too honest and very stupid." To ensure that the last mistake at any rate should not be repeated, he invited the Saxon minister Beust to accept service with him, and employed him first as Foreign Minister and then as Prime Minister. Outwardly Beust was a phlegmatic, corpulent bon-vivant, but he possessed an unusually quick and adaptable mind, so much so that he would have been more of a match for Bismarck than any of his contemporaries, had he possessed the same instruments of power. Bismarck was well aware of this and so had compelled the Saxons to dismiss him before they entered the North German Bund. Relations between himself and Beust were governed on both sides by cautious courtesy, but neither was in any doubt as to the true feelings and desires of the other.

Meanwhile, as a result of Austria's failure and their own defeat, the South German states had been affected by something very like paralysis, and become convinced that they would at any moment be forced to enter the North German confederation. None of them, therefore, made any attempt to form the Southern confederation for which explicit provision had been made in the Treaty of Prague. It was only when in the course of time it began to appear that Bismarck would respect the line of the Main that South German confidence began to grow. Then they began to realise that they possessed a more complete measure of sovereignty than they had ever enjoyed before, and the more they grew conscious of this, the greater became their dislike for Prussia, for they discerned in Prussia the one neighbour by whom that sovereignty might be menaced.

So they consistently returned to their parliaments majorities that were hostile to Prussia, majorities which violently resisted the revival of the Customs Union and which, when despite everything the Union came into being, inflicted on the National Liberals a crushing defeat in the elections for the Customs Parliament. In all, the southern states sent no less than fifty declared anti-Prussians to Berlin as members of that parliament, while members who were friendly to Prussia numbered only thirty-five and the friendship even of those was often anything but warm. Both Württemberg and Bavaria began to consider plans for converting their armies into a militia, a measure which would virtually have nullified the value of their military pacts with Prussia.

The question whether to extend Prussian rule south of the Main is one that was constantly argued in those regions of Bismarck's mind into which, he declared, he allowed nobody to look. The anxiety that such an addition of alien and unwilling national groups might to a quite intolerable extent change the character of a state that was essentially North German and Protestant never left him. These people were the descendants of the burgesses of free cities of the empire, of proud and self-confident merchants and craftsmen; they were the children of subjects of episcopal states, or of an aristocracy that for the most part had a hundred years ago proved as intractable towards the empire as had the Hohenzollerns. Also the vast majority were Catholics.

Then there might always be danger from France, which had never made a secret of the fact that an independent South Germany was a vital French interest. These were serious considerations, yet it is clear that by the end of the sixties Bismarck was already working to ensure that the line of the Main should not become a permanently irremovable feature of political geography.

Towards the end of 1869 Bismarck began cautiously to circulate a plan for making William emperor. In this he was not unmindful of the fact that the "Iron Estimate" would be running out in 1871, and the new one would have to be sanctioned by a Reichstag which was growing visibly less enthusiastic.

In thus tentatively putting forward his plan, Bismarck was counting on the sentimental appeal which the old, buried empire could still make to both North and South. Since in either case this was equally strong, common ground could be created by a revival of the old imperial title, even if this were to be no more than a matter of an empty name. To create such common ground, even if only on the purely sentimental level, was a great deal better than not doing it at all. There was, of course, little sentiment about Bismarck himself, but he was quite ready to use it when he found it in others.

Lord Clarendon, the British Foreign Secretary, was sounded out and showed himself agreeably sympathetic. The Crown Prince may quite possibly have worked upon him through his mother-in-law. However, Clarendon suddenly changed his attitude and this was, as Bismarck knew full well, because of the opposition that was to be looked for from France.

France's grounds for apprehension were, as Bismarck knew full well, other than merely chimerical, nor could one expect that she should turn a blind eye to a sudden change in the balance of European power, or remain wholly free from anxiety as she contemplated a Prussia which ruled the whole of Northern Germany and had both militarily and territorially been very considerably enlarged. And if France was apprehensive, Prussia was apprehensive of French apprehension, and of the consequences which might result from it.

It was a delicate situation. Even so, after the long intimacy that had subsisted between Bismarck and Napoleon, one might surely say that the Frenchman had a right to see the existing power relations between the two countries preserved. If one of them gained additional strength, it was not unreasonable that he should expect a similar gain for the other—all the more so, now that Napoleon had withdrawn the exhorbitant claims transmitted through Benedetti on August 5th which, he declared, his Foreign Minister Druyn de Lhuys had no authority to put forward. Druyn de Lhuys's successor, Rouher, worked hard to establish good relations with Prussia, and even aimed at an alliance. Had this materialised, it would have been possible for Bismarck and Napoleon to dictate jointly to Europe.

France's new proposals had already been submitted to Bismarck on August 23rd. They had been relatively modest. There was to be an offensive and defensive pact; Prussia was to have a free hand in Southern Germany, while France was to enjoy the same privilege in regard to Belgium and Luxemburg. Thus, there was no longer any talk of surrendering German-owned territory on the left bank of the Rhine. In principle, Bismarck raised no objection to these arrangements, and he had even advised Napoleon to use the same methods in acquiring Belgian territory as his own King had employed in the case of Schleswig. And indeed,

Bismarck was never particularly adverse to such territorial horse-trading, a practice which, in point of fact, had often saved peace and with it countless human lives.

Bismarck's illness and protracted convalescence had caused the negotiations to be interrupted. However, his relations with France continued to be friendly in the extreme. Shortly before the end of the year, he informed his ambassador in Paris, Count Robert von der Goltz, that since the beginning of his ten years of office, he had regarded an alliance with France as "the natural expression of the permanent community of interest between the two countries concerned" and had treated it as such.

It was not till the beginning of 1867 that the picture began to change. Napoleon had abandoned his plan for the acquisition of Belgium, out of regard for Britain's extreme sensitiveness about any matters touching the North Sea coasts. Now all his efforts were concentrated on Luxemburg. Unfortunately, news of this had leaked out and produced a somewhat noisy reaction.

For the Grand Duchy of Luxemburg had once been a part of the ancient German Empire, though it had become independent once the latter had ceased to exist. Thanks to a personal union, the King of Holland, whoever he might be, was automatically Grand Duke of Luxemburg. Luxemburg was a member of the German Bund and its capital was regarded as a confederate fortress and garrisoned by Prussian troops, and now that the Bund, in its turn, had ceased to exist, Luxemburg had lost all connection with the German states. When, however, it became known that Napoleon was intending to purchase the place from the King— Grand Duke William III—for some three hundred million francs, this touched the sensitive nationalist nerve. Luxemburg was regarded by the Germans as a piece of German soil, which the Dutch Serenissimus who, so it was now said, simply needed money for his mistress, wanted to bargain away to Germany's hereditary enemy.

Amid the thunder of protests, nobody thought of doing the obvious thing, which was to ask the people of Luxemburg how they felt about it themselves, and the whole matter was made even more complicated by the fact that Luxemburg still had its Prussian garrison. For the first few months of 1867 Bismarck took no notice of the growing public ill-will. He was concerned to get the whole business settled as quietly as possible, so that he could confront the constituent Reichstag, which was just foregathering, with an accomplished fact, and complete the drafting of a constitution for a North German Bund at the earliest possible date.

Meanwhile, Napoleon, relying on Bismarck's silent consent, had begun open negotiations at The Hague. It was high time for him to turn up with some striking success in foreign policy. The contrast between the development of Prussian power and the disquieting shrinkage of the power of France was becoming all too evident.

The King of Holland, calling to mind the regrettable results that just such a personal union as that with Luxemburg had recently produced for his opposite number in Denmark, was quite eager for a deal, and for that very reason was anxious to be certain of Bismarck's concurrence. Napoleon reassured him on this point, and since Napoleon in those days was still rated as the confidant of the enigmatic Prussian, William allowed himself to be reassured.

While negotiations were in progress, Bismarck suddenly disclosed the existence of the secret military treaties with the South German states. Nobody now knows why this was done at this particular moment. Formally, the disclosure was a reply to a question, but even if the question was not prearranged, there was no need for such a disclosure to be made. There can be little doubt, however, as to the effect, intentional or otherwise, which it produced in France and even less as to that produced in Holland. William indeed was reduced to near panic and abjectly requested the Prussian ambassador to assure Berlin that Holland would take no step without Prussia's knowledge.

This, from Bismarck's point of view, may not have been altogether fortunate, for it threw the whole responsibility for Luxemburg openly onto his shoulders and it may well be that he would have preferred to remain in the background and left the active shaping of events to others. It may even be that he might have wished events to take a different shape from that which they assumed. As it was, however, he seems to have accepted the dictates of the situation and—this time there is no doubt about the matter being pre-arranged—got the deputy Bennigsen, who was something of an adept at this kind of rodomontade, to put a question in the Reichstag couched in flamboyant terms. ("Was the government aware . . . ancient German soil about to be torn from the fatherland, etc.")

Bismarck replied with exquisite ambiguity, but there was nothing ambiguous about the telegram sent to the Prussian ambassador at The Hague, urging him to advise most pressingly against the sale, since in the present state of public opinion, its completion might lead to war. And so, with the thunder of Bennigsen's periods continuing to reverberate round the political heavens, the entire project was dropped.

Whether or not it was intended to do so, the whole affair constituted an appalling humiliation for Napoleon, and it is still something of a mystery what lay behind it. It is just possible that it was simply an experiment, something in the nature of a trial of strength, which was to show Bismarck just how far he could go. A more simple and obvious explanation is that Bismarck blundered, or at any rate, miscalculated. It is possible that he simply did not foresee the effect that his plan would have on national sentiment, and that when this was made plain, he preferred to pacify domestic opinion, even at the risk of giving offence to France, rather than lose its support. Such an explanation conflicts with the image of the infallible Bismarck, but, if anything, that is an argument in its favour.

There is, however, a possible third explanation, which lies midway between these two. This is, that Bismarck was indeed taken by surprise by the popular reaction, but that when it came, it afforded him a welcome pretext for getting out of his bargain. If that is so, it explains a remark he made to Manteuffel that he intended "to use the nationalist swindle as a protection against France".

Actually the matter ended in a compromise. A conference was called in London, Prussia withdrew her garrison and the fortifications were destroyed. Napoleon gave up the project of acquiring Luxemburg, and the personal union between Holland and Luxemburg remained. On the whole, Bismarck had the best of the bargain, but the extreme nationalists continued to be dissatisfied—as did Bebel.

Napoleon made the best of a bad business, and to outward appearances all was harmony and peace. June saw the opening of the Paris Exhibition as planned. The bare Champs de Mars was transformed into an enormous pleasure park in which a fifty-ton Krupp cannon somewhat inappropriately formed one of the Prussian exhibits, while a Prussian military band obliged with musical offerings. Despite all that had happened, "Bismarck Brown" with its differentiation of shades—into "Bismarck enraged" and "Bismarck satisfied"—held its place in the glossary of feminine fashion.

The Hohenzollerns, of course, appeared on the scene, as did all the other European dynasties, and Bismarck was himself treated as an old friend. Once more there was unfolded the somewhat artificial but intoxicating brilliance of the Second Empire, around which echoed the gentle mockery of the melodies of Offenbach, and once more Napoleon experienced the satisfaction of having the oldest of the royal houses treat him as an equal. When he paraded with the troops, the Czar rode on his right, and the King of Prussia on his left.

Yet there were still disquieting factors in the situation. He began to be aware of the fact that his old partner, Bismarck, was being confronted with a very serious choice, a choice between Napoleon on the one hand and on the other that new German nationalism which seemed to be growing stronger every day. Bismarck might quite well give preference to the latter, and very regretfully Napoleon began to classify him as "doubtful" and searched anew for security against his former friend.

In his gambler's imagination he began to visualise an anti-Prussian alliance with Austria and Italy, perhaps even with the South Germans.* Yet despite diligent and somewhat wearisome soundings, nothing came of this but an exchange of letters and visits, whose significance he tended greatly to over-estimate. Napoleon was compelled to realise that all the alliances that he might have entered into before Königgrätz were rendered impossible by the outcome of that battle. Bismarck, whose intuition was much sounder in a matter such as this, made no particular effort to counter Napoleon's activities, but contented himself with ironic comment.

Rather oddly, in the second half of 1866 Bismarck absented himself from Berlin for months at a time. He was following the same instinct that causes a wild animal, when it is sick, to hide itself deep in the bushes. He knew that he needed solitude to restore his physical and mental equilibrium.

Bismarck made use of this therapy with increasing frequency. After the Landtag had voted him a grant of 400,000 talers, he acquired in 1867 the estate of Varzin in Further Pomerania. It was badly neglected, but was much larger than any estate that had previously been in the family, larger, this is to say, than Kniephof or Schönhausen. It was a great place, and through it ran the Wipper, a river rich in crayfish. The house Johanna declared to be a monstrosity that had been too much lived in. It was, she said, a place with ten thousand chimneys, full of crooked floors and ceilings, so that you were always in terror that it would come down on top of your head.

The fields were leased out, but not the great wealth of woodland—beeches and oaks for the most part, and often still a wilderness of primeval beauty. Bismarck's whole heart was in his woods and he had something almost like a personal friendship with individual trees—and in this there was a strange similarity with his contemporary, so different in every other way from himself, Ludwig II of Bavaria. "I have more to tell myself, when I am with the trees," he wrote to Johanna, "than when I am with

* Meanwhile he gave himself up to a strategy of pure illusion according to which one French army was to hold up the Prussian attack while a second was to unite with the Austrians in Bavaria. The French fleet was to take the Prussian North Sea ports.

men," and he felt it most keenly whenever it looked as though because of old age or because it had been struck by lightning a tree would have to be cut down.

Here Bismarck found something of the peace of the old-fashioned farmer, the kind of peace his Junker ancestors had known, and the spiritual shadow of the Mencken inheritance seemed no longer to worry and irritate him, as in other circumstances it was so often apt to do. Here he could at last be the kind of man he wanted to be—the great landlord who was master of his own acres. If the price for all this was a five-hour railway journey, followed by forty miles of execrable roads, he was willing to pay it. Here he lived as the mood dictated, got up late, spent a great part of the day out of doors, walked and rode, ate enormously in the evening and then dealt with the essential papers that came to him from Berlin, working late into the silent, deep, black, country night.

He became one of the many large landowners who, about this time, began to engage in the promotion of certain rural industries. He founded a brandy distillery. His chief investment, however, was a paper factory, and since numerous customers, including foreigners, were eager to buy the product, the factory soon became a flourishing concern. Even so he invariably flew into a rage when demands for the local taxes for schools and roads were made upon him. As to general taxes, he had been relieved of these by a secret order of the King, who knew of his peculiar weakness in this matter.

Every year he visited Varzin and every year he increased the length of his stay, for whenever he returned to Berlin he was invariably assailed by some kind of physical crisis. There can be no question that these had a psychological origin and derived from the fact that his work threw him into states of unbearable tension. To his old friend Keyserling he confessed in 1867 that politics—and that means every form of political activity—inspired him with loathing. In that same year he said to one of the members of the parliamentary opposition, that his nerves were in shreds and that he was always on the point of bursting into tears.

The disability lasted throughout his life. When Richardson, the English artist, asked him whether he was, indeed, the man of iron that he was reputed to be, he replied, "No, my hardness is something that is consciously acquired. I am all nerves and that to such a degree that the one task of my life is self-control."

In the 1860s, however, his staggering success developed new facets of his character. Amongst other things, an absolute self-assurance towards the outer world. But he also began to acquire at that time a kind of playful exhibitionism which, amongst other things, expressed itself in continual changes in his outward appearance. He often changed the cut of his moustache and, by way of sartorial variety, took to wearing military uniform, namely that of the 7th or so-called Yellow Cuirassiers—though even in this he was something of a law unto himself, for he often combined it with a black civilian waistcoat. He declared that he preferred a military attire, because military uniform covered his chest and so protected him from catching cold, but we need not doubt that the real reason was his desire to endear himself to the Prussians, who, he rightly surmised, had a liking for that kind of thing. The practice was perhaps a little unfortunate, for it helped in the course of time to fashion the image of the jack-booted Chancellor, with all its preposterous and monstrously misleading implications.

The beginning of 1870 was marked by an interesting event. On January 2nd, while the Prussian Crown Prince and Crown Princess were visiting Paris and were being received with the kindness to which they had grown accustomed—a fact expressly noted in Frederick William's diary—a new Cabinet had been formed by Emile Ollivier. In 1858 Ollivier had entered the Imperial Chamber of Deputies as one of five lonely Republicans. By elevating him to the Premiership, Napoleon was endeavouring to show that he was entering upon the final stage of the transformation to an "*Empire Libéral*" for which, so, presumably, he thought, the time was now ripe.

Ollivier had married Blandine, the daughter of Liszt, loved German music and had an understanding for the peculiarities of the German character. Before taking over the premiership, he had argued to the Emperor that France must not oppose a union of Northern and Southern Germany—why should she prevent the Württemberg democrats and the Bavarian ultramontanes from making difficulties for Bismarck in his Parliament, since in the event of war the whole of Germany would in any case be united against France?

Actually, Napoleon had himself already determined on this line of policy, because his physical disability was growing more serious and because he knew that his health needed watching. Also, the much needed Army reform, which he had entrusted to Marshall Niel, had proved exceedingly unpopular because of the extension of conscription which it involved. When Niel had died in the preceding year, it had been quietly abandoned. The progress of Napoleon's plans for an Austrian and Italian alliance had been equally unsatisfactory. For all these reasons, Napoleon had for three years now considered it imprudent to raise the

delicate question of compensation. Everything about the Emperor
had an autumnal air, an air of silent resignation.

In May there was a plebiscite. What influenced the voting
was not so much the *"Empire Libéral"* as the prosperity and
internal peace which had been enjoyed over the past decade.
The result was an astonishing vote of confidence both for the
dynasty and for Ollivier's peace policy. Despite a few malcontents in Paris, whose voices attracted undue attention abroad,
there can be little doubt about the temper of the country as
a whole.

To Bismarck, also, the probability of a war with France appeared
at that moment more remote than ever. In August of the previous
year the French military attaché, Lieutenant-Colonel Stoffel, had
declared with great emphasis to his government that neither the
King nor Bismarck had the faintest intention of attacking France
and would always do everything in their power to avoid a war.
Six months later, Bismarck was explaining to Waldersee, the
military attaché in Paris (Ollivier was just beginning his experiment), that politically they were at that moment living in an
idyllic state of peace. The French had much too much to occupy
them internally for them to think of external complications.

And what purpose could Bismarck have had at that time in
waging a war? What did he stand to win and what did he
stand to lose? He stood to lose the North German Bund, a body
only recently created and still far from secure, and with the
Bund he stood to lose all hope of extending Prussian rule over
Germany within foreseeable time. What he stood to win, however, since no French territory tempted him, was nothing more
than a free hand in the joining of South Germany to the North
German Bund, a step which France had always opposed. Yet
he felt sure that the sensible French would not be willing to
bleed forever for the preservation of the line of the Main. According to Lord Acton, whose remarks tend admittedly from time to
time to be a little fantastic, Bismarck believed that if he could
manage to keep the peace with Napoleon so long as the latter
lived he would never have to fight.

Of course, Bismarck never wavered in his aim of extending
Prussian rule over all that was left of Germany after the exclusion
of Austria. But he believed in patience and in allowing himself
plenty of time. He spoke of five, of ten, of twenty years, of
entire generations which might have to pass away before that
aim was achieved. There was none of that boldness and energy
now, which, blow by blow, had brought the North German Bund
into being. "You can put the clocks ahead," he now grew fond
of saying, "but you don't make time pass any faster by doing

so." Moreover, as we have seen, Bismarck, East Elbian and Protestant that he was, could not overcome the feeling that these various South German races were alien and even incomprehensible. If ever North and South Germany were to be united, this could only be brought about by a process of slow growth, like grafting on a tree, a process that could be watched, and to some extent even controlled, but could not be expedited by any action from without.

Bismarck's feeling in this matter is well illustrated by his reaction when a National Liberal named Lasker moved a surprise motion in the Reichstag that Baden should be joined on to the North German Bund. In the Grand Duchy of Baden, which was in perpetual fear of its two neighbour states of Württemberg and Bavaria, the desire to lean on Prussia had always been particularly strong, and shortly before this Bismarck had already remarked to Roon, "This silly unrest in Baden comes blundering into every political calculation, with disastrous effects." (" *Tölpelt in jede politische Berechnung störend hinein.*") Lasker's motion produced in Bismarck a stomach cramp, and he replied to him with a sharpness of tone which would have been wholly incomprehensible had not patient waiting at that time been the very essence of his German policy.

Bismarck's progressive strengthening of the armaments of the Bund is not out of keeping with the complete absence of any aggressive intention. He wished to make it plain to France that it was to her own interest to avoid war. But he was running no risks, and when in that hopefully calm spring of 1870 Daru, the French Foreign Minister, submitted through Lord Clarendon, his opposite number in London, a scheme for general disarmament, a scheme which would particularly affect Russia and France, Bismarck decisively rejected it. He declared, among other things, that the King was before anything else a soldier, and it was quite impossible even so much as to mention such a plan in his presence.*

Yet though Bismarck's intentions were certainly pacific, and though there was no conceivable reason why they should be anything else, there was continual whispering—it had been going on ever since the Luxemburg affair—that war was coming. Even such a man as Bismarck's assistant, Abeken, a quiet type of higher civil servant with a humanist background, could say that there was a general feeling that there never really would be peace till there had been a war with France. The Crown Princess wrote much the same thing to her mother, Queen Victoria. In France

* There are some who think that Daru's action was taken at Beust's inspiration, who naturally had Austria's interests at heart. This would not change the facts.

the last words of the dying Duc de Morny, Napoleon's half-brother and old fellow-conspirator, were "Sire, beware of the Prussians". Both in France and in Germany "inevitable war" became a pot-house cliché.

In due course Daru was replaced by the Duc de Gramont as French Foreign Minister. Gramont was a sort of French Sir Charles Grandison, a man of exquisite manners, a model of dependability and rectitude and almost, one feels, a little too good to be true. There were, of course, the disparaging voices that this type always seems to provoke and Gramont was denounced by some as vain, arbitrary and capricious. Bismarck referred to him as the ideal figure of a Cuirassier but as he failed to explain just what was implied by this somewhat Eleusinian classification, the remark contributes little towards an accurate assessment of the man.

Amongst these divided opinions Napoleon himself remained uncommitted and, with that engaging aptitude for going to the heart of a matter, observed that it was of little moment whether it was Gramont or another, since everybody had made up his mind to do nothing whatever.

Even so Ollivier was cautious. Gramont, he was told, was very pro-Austrian and anti-Prussian, but Gramont promised to leave his prejudices at home and to support Ollivier's policy of peace. Nor did Bismarck have any misgivings when Gramont was appointed. In June he wrote to Bernstorff that he could not share the apprehension some people entertained about the imminence of war, at least he could not do so so far as the immediate future was concerned, and in so far, of course, as political calculations of the future were possible at all. He was quite convinced that Napoleon realised that acquisition of the left bank of the Rhine was perilous in a high degree both to himself and to his family, for Napoleon knew that such an enlargement of French territory would raise all Europe in coalition against him and that such a coalition would be permanent. "That is no mere conjecture, but the necessary consequence of the position in Europe and the conclusion to which experience must inevitably lead."*

Three weeks later Ollivier put forward a motion in the Chamber for the reduction of the French army by ten thousand men. "Wherever we look," he said, "we can see no causes for any quarrel that might give us ground for anxiety. Nor has there ever been a time when the maintenance of peace in Europe was better assured."

That was on June 30, 1870. Three days later, on July 3rd,

* Bismarck, Collected Works VII(a), p. 301.

nothing of this remained real, for the world had suddenly changed. On the afternoon of that day the Agence Havas brought the news that in Spain the Cortez was about to elect Prince Leopold of Hohenzollern as King, and suddenly France saw herself confronted by that uncannily successful Bismarck not only in the east but in the south-west too. The news produced an upheaval far more violent than the occasion justified, for it represented the climax of all the diplomatic defeats France had suffered at the cunning Prussian's hands.

8

FULFILMENT

Since September 1868, after Queen Isabella had been driven from Spain and the whole House of Bourbon along with her, the government of the country had been conducted by a Provisional Committee, or, to be more exact, by the War Minister, General Prim, while the question of a succession preoccupied all the chancelleries of Europe. For Prussia the matter was hardly a major issue, and it was only insofar as it indirectly touched France that Prussia attached any importance to it at all.

Even so, the situation held interesting possibilities. The expelled Bourbons were Francophiles, and the fact of their expulsion was something of a blow for Napoleon. Bismarck would have liked to have seen a Spanish republic, not because he believed republics to be by nature weaker than monarchies, but a republic in Spain might well prove infectious so far as France was concerned and might conceivably produce internal disturbances there. With the help of such distractions it might well be possible to effect a union with the South German states, and to do so quite bloodlessly and without fear of serious French objections.

Certainly Bismarck's interest in the Hohenzollern candidature awakened at an early date and soon led him to take positive action. It may well be that a mere chance in the form of a letter to Princess Charles, the King's sister-in-law, first set things in motion. The letter was written in February 1867, nearly two years before Isabella's fall, and came from von Werthern, the Prussian minister in Madrid. It stated that if a Hohenzollern were to ascend the Spanish throne, this would mean that here, too, the rising dynasty was succeeding the failing Hapsburgs. The matter first became the subject of public discussion in the Bavarian Press after Werthern, a gentleman with a distinct taste for the eccentric, had been made ambassador to Munich. In Spain itself the matter was first raised in February 1869, in a pamphlet by a certain Eusebio de Salazar, a Counsellor of State.

Before that, however, in December 1868, two months after Isabella's expulsion, Bismarck was arranging for an exploratory mission to go to Spain, led by Bernhardi, though actually this did not set out till May. If credence is to be given to Lord Acton, who was half a German and had much background information, Bernhardi spent no less than £50,000 in Spain from the Guelph fund which—it will be remembered—Bismarck was able to administer much as he pleased. The money was almost certainly used for bribing members of the Cortez. Indeed, the fact that in his first report Bernhardi stated that nobody in Spain took the Hohenzollern candidature seriously, lends colour to this view.

The undertaking was quite in accordance with Bismarck's general policy, for, as everyone knew at the time, he was greatly concerned to increase Prussia's military superiority over France. If, in a war, French troops were pinned down in the Pyrenees, and the forces that could be used on the eastern frontier were further weakened, the probability was increased that France would be even more concerned to avoid war, and that this disinclination would persist even if, one day, Bismarck considered that the moment had arrived for a union with South Germany. Moreover, he had already established one Hohenzollern on a non-German throne, and this had worked out very successfully. In March 1866, while the great powers were taking counsel together on the choice of an incumbent for the newly-created throne of Rumania, Bismarck, behind the backs of Russia, Austria and Turkey, though with the approval of Napoleon, had despatched a Prussian officer, Prince Charles von Hohenzollern Sigmarigen, from the South German branch of the dynasty, to Bucharest, where he had promptly ascended the newly-manufactured throne and had remained decorously seated on that piece of furniture ever since.

Bismarck now thought of Prince Leopold, a brother of Charles, as a highly suitable King of Spain. Leopold was a Catholic, he was married to the sister of the King of Portugal and related to the Bonaparte family. His father's mother had been a niece of Murat, while his mother's mother was a daughter of Stephanie Beauharnais, Napoleon I's step-daughter. Because of this, Napoleon III had shown both liking and confidence towards the young Prince, whose family was as closely connected with his own as it was with the Prussian Hohenzollerns.

Bernhardi's mission did not very long remain a secret from the French. In March 1869, before Bernhardi had even left the country, Benedetti was making enquiries at the Prussian Foreign Office. He was turned over to State Secretary von Thile, a man so timid that in diplomatic circles he was known as the "mute of the seraglio". Thile did exactly what Bismarck had instructed him to do. He assured Benedetti there was not a word of truth in all these rumours. It was not till May 8th that Benedetti contrived to speak directly to Bismarck, who treated the whole thing as a joke, and whose only serious remark was, "King William would most certainly not advise the Prince to make such a choice."

But already the Hohenzollern candidature was being pushed in Spain itself. The Cortez had already accepted a monarchical state in principle, and in September the indefatigable Salazar appeared in person at the Hohenzollern Castle of Weinburg on Lake Constance. He was confronted with well-nigh impossible conditions made by Leopold himself and Prince Charles-Anthony, his father. Only if Napoleon could be induced to suggest the candidature himself to King William, and only if King William concurred, would the Hohenzollerns agree to it.

But Salazar was not to be put off so easily. In the following February he renewed his attack, armed on this occasion with a letter of General Prim's addressed direct to Bismarck. Bismarck had spent almost the whole of this time in Varzin. He had undergone a cure with Carlsbad water which had reduced him to a very low state, and only returned to Berlin in December because his son Herbert was down with erysipelas. How, in these circumstances, he managed to keep abreast of the Spanish question is difficult to say.

Prim's letter, however, made a difference, and it was reserved for State Counsellor de Salazar, of whom, incidentally, history knows very little, to shape the destiny of Europe. King William refused to receive this ambassador of the revolution. Bismarck, however, not only received him, but after his visit gave orders that during the evening he himself was not to be disturbed. The result of these solitary hours of reflection was the resolve to give the Hohenzollern candidature his wholehearted support. What had hitherto been unofficially explored now became the official, although secret, policy of the Prussian government, though it was a policy vigorously opposed by those who were to be principally concerned with it, namely, Prince Leopold and his father, and, to an even greater extent, the King. When, towards the end of February, Bismarck first mentioned the candidature to him, the old man felt "as though lightning had struck him from a clear sky". But the king added, "We must confer about it, although so far as my own feelings are concerned, I am against the thing."

The conference, to which the King had alluded, was tacked on to an all-male dinner, which was given on March 15th at the Royal Palace. Besides the King, Bismarck and the two Hohenzollern princes, there were present the Prussian Crown Prince, Moltke, Roon, the Minister of the Royal House, von Schleinitz, and the two State Secretaries, Thile and Delbrück. There were thus present all the Crown's most intimate advisers, who would normally have been called upon to deal with the Spanish question

under the presidency of the King. Since, however, their meeting
was a mere adjunct to a dinner, Bismarck is definitely right when
he later denied that a Crown Council had taken place. However
that may be, Bismarck explained that in view of his Rumanian
success, he desired to use the element of surprise also in Spain.
There was no mention of French approval, on which Charles-
Anthony had hitherto insisted, but the risk of war was also passed
over in silence, in order not to frighten the King. As against this,
Bismarck did not hesitate to play on the latter's dynastic jealousy
by telling him that Salazar had threatened to look around for a
Bavarian prince if the Hohenzollerns failed him.

In the end, all the King's advisers supported Bismarck, and
even the two Hohenzollerns, father and son, began to waver in
their resolve not to exchange the peaceful life of great South
German gentlemen for the crown of a country torn by civil war.
The King alone remained obdurate. He closed the conference
by making a note on Bismarck's memorandum to the effect that
he could not, as a matter of personal conviction, order the princes
to take up the candidature, and that the discussion must therefore
be regarded as closed.

The nature of Bismarck's motives in this matter has been the
subject of endless discussion, but it is fairly safe to assume that
at this time he had nothing more in mind than increasing the
pressure under which Napoleon already found himself. One day
after Salazar's visit he dictated to his journalistic supporter
Busch, "Napoleon has been friendly till now, but he is changeable. We could wage a war with France, and do so successfully.
But four or five wars would result from it, and so it would be
folly, if not a crime, to do this, seeing that the whole thing can
be settled by peaceful means."

The crucial matter now was to win over the King, and after
the King, the two Hohenzollerns. By April 4th he had brought
the King to the point where he was willing to agree to the despatch
of two Prussian experts to Spain, Bucher and Major von Versen,
a major of the General Staff.

Shortly afterwards Bismarck contracted jaundice in Varzin and
grew so ill that it hurt him "either to speak or hear a single
word". Throughout five weeks he had no papers sent to him
and was not visited by any official of the Foreign Office. It was
not till May 21st that he again made a short stay in Berlin.

Here he met Bucher and Versen, who had returned from Spain
and who, since they knew very well what Bismarck expected from
them, were full of favourable accounts. The King, sound sceptic
that he was, called these reports "rather overmuch *couleur de rose*"
and remained unchanged in his opposition to the plan. Not so

the two Hohenzollerns. The intoxicating accounts of the two Spanish travellers, combined with ceaseless pressure from Bismarck, had brought about a change of heart. "The knife is at our throat," was how Leopold expressed himself, while Charles-Anthony, with a more pronounced talent for verbiage, declared that a rejection of the candidature would be tantamount to a misunderstanding of the historical situation. Subject to the King's concurrence, Leopold would accept the candidature.

Now the King, who at that time had been convinced that nothing could change Leopold's determination to refuse, had said that he would in no circumstances interfere with his wishes. He now, therefore, felt honour-bound to sanction what Leopold proposed to do, but he felt that it was Bismarck who had caused the young prince to change his mind, and because of this there was, for several days, considerable ill-feeling between the King and his Chancellor, an ill-feeling which did not diminish when both set off on June 2nd to greet the Czar in Ems. It was planned that, after the meeting, William was to undergo his yearly cure here.

Meanwhile, Bismarck, without the knowledge of the King, sent Bucher back again post-haste to Madrid in order to get agreement on the steps now to be taken. In Bucher's instructions there is one sentence, the sincerity of which we can surely accept, since it was written purely for the recipient and not for posterity. "It is possible that we shall arouse some hostility among the French and, no doubt, we shall have to avoid anything that could produce or increase it." In Madrid, which Bucher reached on June 9th, Salazar was so delighted with the turn things had taken that he accompanied Bucher on the latter's return, and on the 19th he was able to wire from Sigmarigen to Madrid that Leopold had accepted.

On the 22nd Bucher made his report in Ems to the King, and skilfully adapted it to the royal mentality. The Prince, he said, would be particularly welcome to the Spanish army as one who had taken part in the war of 1866. "And what an army," exclaimed the King, "an army that has made all the revolutions in the last forty years." The report took an hour and a quarter, then at last the King gave way "with a very heavy heart", as though he already felt that at this time of the summer solstice he was setting out on the road that was to lead to two world wars and to the destruction of his state and of his dynasty.

The plan of Bismarck and of the Spanish cliques associated with him was to push Leopold's election through the Cortez with maximum speed, so as to create a *fait accompli*, and to do this, if possible, before the end of the month. When, however, on the 26th, Salazar came back to Madrid, he found that the Cortez had gone into recess three days previously so that no election could take place.

People have put the blame for this contretemps, which completely upset Bismarck's plans, on a Prussian cipher clerk who had grown sleepy during the summer heat and had mixed up June and July, but it may well have been Prim's intention to delay the election so that he could have time to visit Paris and assure himself of Napoleon's concurrence.

Prim was at this moment hunting near Toledo, and days went by before he could be brought back to Madrid to reconvene the Cortez. The matter, however, had now been dragged out too long for the great secret to be kept. The President of the Cortez, Zorilla, passed the news on to his friend, Escobar, the editor of *The Epoca*, and so it became public property. Prim appealed to Mercier, the French Ambassador, to help him (it was now July 2nd), and to prevent Napoleon from wrecking the whole affair, which, so Mercier telegraphed next day to Paris, had already reached an advanced stage, though the final details might still be lacking. Hereupon followed that publication in the Agence Havas which set France into an uproar.*

The French Cabinet found itself in a difficult position. The time when the House of Hapsburg had held French territory in its grip from the direction both of Germany and Spain was not a happy memory for any Frenchman. The excitement of the French that started on July 3rd was so extreme that it surprised even the most experienced of politicians. A *fait accompli*, once the initial shock is over, tends to produce a positively pacifying effect, a fact which Bismarck had definitely taken into his calculations, but the *fait accompli* had remained unaccomplished and that, if anything, made matters worse. To take account at one and the same time of an enraged public feeling and of the demands of common sense is not easy, and it was this, and nothing less, that Ollivier was called upon to do.

Gramont found that he could adjust more easily to the situation. Indeed, he welcomed it, for, after so many defeats, it presented him with the opportunity of at last achieving diplomatic victory over Prussia without having to fear, as he had had to do in the case of Luxemburg, an upsurge of German nationalist sentiment. It was, to say the least, unlikely that a purely dynastic matter like that of the Spanish succession would prove capable of inflaming nationalist feeling.

So sure did he feel of this that he committed a serious blunder.

---

* That events took this course, which we have long been inferring they did, has since been confirmed by the publication in England of documents of the Berlin Foreign Office.

Instead of dealing with the problem through diplomatic channels, where it would either be solved or die of slow suffocation, he brought it up publicly in the Chamber of Deputies. On July 6th Gramont read from the tribune a statement which had been approved by the Cabinet. France, he said, relied on the friendship of Spain and the good sense of the Germans for a peaceful removal of the difficulties which had arisen. Should this hope prove vain, however, then "with your support, gentlemen, and that of the nation, we shall know and do our duty without weakness or hesitation", a sentence that in itself constituted no more than a sharp warning, but was so passionately underscored by the Press that to the layman it looked like a threat.

Professional diplomats, of course, put a different interpretation on it. The British ambassador, Lord Lyons, for instance, reported after Gramont's speech that neither the Emperor nor his Cabinet desired war or expected it. Nor was it without significance that four days previously there had been a consultation of Napoleon's doctors, after which Nelaton, the leading surgeon of his day, declared it would be folly to think of war; the Emperor was ill and could not even ride; his condition was serious.*

Bismarck read Gramont's speech in Varzin in the papers at breakfast. He was astonished by it and said that it looked almost like war. Gramont's language was more clumsy and presumptuous than he would have expected. The Prussian Press was to make a thoroughly rude reply. But Bismarck spoke without excitement and his remarks seemed to be the fruit of quiet reflection. In actual fact, he did not attach overmuch importance to the speech. He regarded it as something designed essentially for internal consumption. Certainly he was resolved to remain mute until the election in Madrid had produced the *fait accompli* which he desired, for he knew nothing of the delays that had occurred. Once Leopold had been elected, everything would quieten down.†

Meanwhile he was anxious to ensure that no one should say anything to anybody that would mean anything in particular, and made especially certain that Benedetti should have no opportunity of doing anything of the kind. He himself had withdrawn to Varzin, the King was in Ems, Prince Leopold was somewhere or other clambering about the Alps and wholly beyond reach, while Benedetti himself was in Wildbad. And so Benedetti's representative, Le Sourd, could only find the bashful

---

* Schlagintweit, *Napoleon III* (1949).
† Many years later, when these events had led to a personal triumph for himself, he spoke of them in a much less casual tone, and Gramont's speech became an "official international threat made with the hand on the sword hilt".

von Thile at the Foreign Office, who, scrupulously observing Bismarck's directives, informed him that the Spanish affair was a matter that concerned the family of the Hohenzollerns alone, and that the Prussian state had no interest in it.

It was, therefore, not altogether unnatural that Benedetti should now receive instructions to visit the head of this family, namely the King, in Ems and to ask him for an assurance that he did not approve of Leopold's candidature and would cause him to abandon it. There was nothing unusual in this. Benedetti had been in Berlin since 1864, was well liked in Court society, for he was intelligent, industrious, conscientious and "capable of saying something unpleasant without becoming unpleasant himself". As an ambassador, it was his privilege to ask the King directly for an audience.

So Benedetti went to Ems, the little watering place that is squeezed into the dark wooded valley of the Lahn. The King immediately granted his request and invited him to join him at dinner, of which he was just about to partake. Everything seemed to be going very well. The King stated that he would be perfectly content to see Leopold renounce the candidature. However, he had nothing to do with his action in the first place and could, therefore, not cause him to abandon it. So far the King had spoken the truth. Only two days previously he had written to the Queen "*Entre nous soit dit*" he would be quite happy if Leopold failed to get elected. He diverged a little from the truth, however, when he stated that the Spanish venture had been a purely family affair; actually it had long been something with which his government had been concerned. However, he had to play the part as Bismarck had written it for him, though he was continually haunted by a vague feeling that events might be shaping in such a fashion that they would be too much for him. He would gladly, so Abeken tells us, have had Bismarck by his side. Bismarck, however, was telegraphing that he was ill or that he wished "that people would only send him communications that did not annoy him, or, at any rate, such communications that he could read without having to think about them much, and need not answer", or that he was "annoyed that so much ink from Ems was being poured into my Carlsbad water". Whereupon the King remarked with a sigh, "Yes, that's the way the gentlemen are. The things they pour into *our* Ems water nobody seems to think about." The feeling of being compelled to be a little less than honest was getting on his nerves, and he was beginning to long for nothing more passionately than for an end to the whole wretched business of the candidature.

To fill his cup to overflowing, an ambassador's report from St. Petersburg had reached him on the 9th, informing him that the

Czar begged him most urgently to disavow the candidature. Two days previous to that, a telegram with a similar message had arrived from Queen Victoria, but, above all, Southern Germany was showing its quite marked distaste for being dragged into a war for the sake of a foreign dynasty.

Yet Paris continued to be dissatisfied. The impatient Gramont found William's conduct equivocal, and suspected that the delay which it involved was being used for purposes of Prussian mobilisation. The growing excitement of the Paris boulevards made a deep impression on him. He was an aristocrat and an old diplomat who had spent the greater part of his life outside France, and he did not know how little real weight is to be attached to noisy demonstrations in a great city.

So, on July 11th, Gramont once again sent Benedetti to see the King. He was to ask for a formal declaration that he had advised the Prince to abandon the candidature. William refused to agree to this, but assured the ambassador that a final answer from Leopold himself would be available within twenty-four hours. He could speak with some assurance on this matter, for he had secretly sent a Colonel von Strantz, who was a member of his military suite, to Sigmarigen, where the colonel had failed to encounter Leopold. But he had met Leopold's father, Charles-Anthony, and had described to him the King's misgivings. It was Charles-Anthony who, on the morning of the 12th, in the name of his still inaccessible son, wired to Prim that the candidature was being withdrawn. That afternoon William wrote to Augusta, "I have just had a curt telegram from Colonel Strantz who, in veiled words, tells me that Leopold is withdrawing. What a weight off my mind." (*Mir ist ein Stein vom Herzen.*) "But don't tell anybody." Meanwhile the news had reached Paris, and a radiant Ollivier appeared before the Cabinet. All grounds of quarrel had disappeared.

Bismarck had passed all these days in Varzin, with the express intention of drinking his Carlsbad water in peace, after which he proposed to visit a seaside resort. He had ordered the various offices to disturb him as little as possible, but the news from Ems gradually persuaded him not to leave the King alone any longer. On July 11th he set off, cheerfully confident that all was going as he wished it to go. When, however, he arrived that afternoon in Berlin, from where he was to journey on that night to Ems, he heard the wholly surprising news of the Hohenzollern renunciation of the Spanish throne.

This was a defeat for him to which the whole world was witness: German princes beating an unconditional retreat—at least that was how the thing looked—because of a speech by a

French minister! The dimming of the Hohenzollern nimbus, which he had hoped that the Spanish venture would make yet brighter! The uninterrupted personal triumph that he had enjoyed since 1864 now brought to a halt! And it was not only a matter of the collapse of his Spanish project, but the damage to Prussian prestige that this had brought in its train, a damage so great that it was now an open question whether the North German Bund could continue to exist, let alone whether a united Germany under Prussian leadership could, at some future date, be brought into being.

Bismarck's reaction was one of despair. There was, he felt, only one course open to him: to resign. He telegraphed to Ems that the journey to Berlin had so exhausted him that he could not travel any farther for the moment. There followed a sleepless night and a day spent in dark brooding. That on that same day something was to happen in Paris which would at one stroke change the whole outlook he had no means of knowing.

Gramont, meanwhile, was beside himself with joy. At last, under his leadership, French diplomacy had proved itself superior to that of Prussia. But the heady wine of success, of which for so long France had been unable to partake, went to his head and blurred his sense of reality. Unsatisfied with the gift that Fortune had just placed in his hands, he sought to impose on it yet a further crowning ornament—and did something which, had he been directly under Bismarck's orders, could not have better served the latter's interests.

For what Gramont now did was to instruct Benedetti to make two further demands on the King. He asked that he should explicitly approve Leopold's renunciation of the candidature and should also undertake in future never again to sanction a candidature of the Hohenzollerns for the Spanish throne. Gramont's instructions to Benedetti were sent without Ollivier's knowledge and only after a long debate with Napoleon. Shortly after midnight they were in Benedetti's hands.

The consequences followed quickly enough. On the morning of July 13th, William, in excellent spirits—for the Spanish nightmare seemed at last to be dispelled—was taking his usual walk after drinking the waters, when he saw Benedetti sitting on a bench. He went over towards him and gave him the *Kölnische Zeitung*, which reported the Hohenzollern renunciation of the candidature. Obviously he expected Benedetti to be pleased and to say so, and was bitterly disappointed when the ambassador merely told him of Gramont's new demands. The first of these, namely that he should approve Leopold's renunciation, he immediately accepted. The second, in which he was called upon to commit himself for all time, he rejected as impossible.

It is conceivable that William's disappointment caused an undertone of irritation to creep into the talk, and that this irritation was further increased by the persistence with which Benedetti clung to his demands. However, the King ended by promising to inform him as soon as he had official information about the Hohenzollern renunciation, but added that guarantees for a future which was unknown were something he could not undertake to give. With a kind of injured sense of family pride, he then remarked, "Repeat to the Emperor that I know my cousins are men of honour. If they withdraw from a candidature which they have accepted, they certainly would not do so with a secret intention of taking it up again at a later date."

As the promenading public became aware of what was going on and the King's escort could only with difficulty make them keep their distance, he terminated the conversation with the words, "Mr. Ambassador, I can and will not give an undertaking of that kind. I must reserve the right to weigh all the circumstances in any eventuality that may arise. I have given you my answer and have nothing to add. Perhaps you will now excuse me." A courteous raising of top hats concluded the talk, which had proceeded in unimpeachable form, accompanied by the light-hearted strains of the orchestra from the bandstand.

About one o'clock the King received a letter from Prince Charles-Anthony who officially confirmed the renunciation of the throne. As promised, William thereupon sent Prince Radziwill, one of his adjutants, to Benedetti to tell him the news. The ambassador, however, took the opportunity of again asking for an audience, so that Radziwill had to visit Benedetti a second time and inform him that the King approved of the Prince's renunciation, much as he had approved of his original acceptance, and that the first of the French demands had thus been fulfilled. As to the second one, however, and the audience which Benedetti had requested, the King had nothing further to add.

When Radziwill returned, the King was about to go to lunch, but before doing so ordered Abeken to follow the usual routine and inform Bismarck of the day's events by telegram, after which he dined with an excellent appetite. When the meal was over he sent Radziwill a third time to Benedetti to assure him that as far as guarantees for the future were concerned he could not again resume the discussion. He had agreed without reservations to Leopold's renunciation. Obviously, as Lord Acton remarks, he wanted to be finished with the whole business and for the future leave it in the hands of his ministers.*

Meanwhile Abeken's telegram had reached Berlin, and here

* Acton, *Historical Essays and Studies* (1907), p. 235.

Bismarck's situation seemed completely hopeless. He had now only the choice between an international humiliation and a war which would certainly be accounted a war of aggression, which would therefore almost certainly have to be waged without allies and which, on top of everything else, since it only concerned the private interest of the Hohenzollerns, would be extremely unpopular. He seemed to expect a new and far worse Olmütz, after which there would be nothing left for him except resignation and the end of his political career.* He had invited Moltke and Roon to dinner and all three were in a melancholy mood, and this was certainly not made more cheerful by the arrival of Abeken's dispatch, which reached them just as they were sitting down to the meal. This read as follows:

"His Majesty the King has written to me: 'Count Benedetti intercepted me on the promenade and ended by demanding of me in a very importunate manner that I should authorize him to telegraph at once that I bound myself in perpetuity never again to give my consent if the Hohenzollerns renewed their candidature. I rejected this demand somewhat sternly as it is neither right nor possible to undertake engagements of this kind à tout jamais. Naturally I told him that I had not yet received any news and since he had been better informed via Paris and Madrid than I was, he must surely see that my government was not concerned in the matter.' His Majesty has since received a communication from the Prince" (von Hohenzollern). "Since His Majesty had told Count Benedetti that he was expecting to hear from the Prince, All Highest, on the advice of Count Eulenburg and myself" (Count Eulenburg was the Prussian Minister of the Interior whom Bismarck had sent to Ems in place of himself), "decided in view of the above-mentioned demands not to receive Count Benedetti any more, but to have him informed by an adjutant that His Majesty had now received from the Prince confirmation of the news which Benedetti had already had from Paris and had nothing further to say to the ambassador. His Majesty suggests to Your Excellency that Benedetti's new demand and its rejection might well be communicated both to our ambassadors and to the Press."

As he read out the telegram, couched as it was in Abeken's clumsy German, Moltke and Roon laid down their forks. They had completely lost their appetite. Moltke, so it seemed to Bismarck, suddenly looked "quite old and frail". Yet at that

---

* The Crown Prince states in his diary that Bismarck said on the 15th that he considered peace to be assured, so that he would soon be able to return to Varzin and he obviously meant forever. In 1888 Bismarck denied this. Coll. Works VI(b), p. 363.

moment an inspiration came to Bismarck as welcome as the sight
of a drifting plank to a drowning mariner. Suddenly he saw the
possibility of saving and completing his life's work. Admittedly,
it involved the risk of war, but it was not a war which he himself
would have to declare.

In his *Gedanken und Erinnerungen* Bismarck has described how
he sat down at a small side table and set about editing the telegram. "This is how we'll do it," he said, and then read the new
version to the two generals, the "old bloodshedders", as he
called them, and suddenly he saw Moltke "looking quite fresh
again", for he now had "the war which was his trade". The
telegram now read: "After the news of the renunciation of the
Prince von Hohenzollern had been communicated to the Imperial
French government by the Royal Spanish government, the French
Ambassador in Ems made a further demand on His Majesty the
King that he should authorise him to telegraph to Paris that His
Majesty the King undertook for all time never again to give his
assent should the Hohenzollerns once more take up their candidature. His Majesty the King thereupon refused to receive the
Ambassador again and had the latter informed by the adjutant
of the day that His Majesty had no further communication to make
to the Ambassador."

Already at nine o'clock that evening the citizens of Berlin
could read this version of the Ems telegram in special editions of
the *Norddeutsche Allgemeine Zeitung*, which was being distributed
gratis in the streets and copies of which were being stuck in shop
windows. About eleven o'clock that night it was telegraphed to
the Prussian embassies throughout Germany and at about two
o'clock in the morning to the diplomatic representatives of the
North German Bund in St. Petersburg, Brussels, Rome and other
capitals, with the instruction that it should be communicated as
soon as possible to the governments to which they were accredited.
It was, however, explicitly laid down that this should be done
verbally. Bismarck was therefore quite right when he said later
that no note or written document had at that time been handed
over.

It is worth comparing the two versions of the dispatch. Actually
Abeken's telegram was not altogether truthful. It said that
Benedetti had "intercepted" (*a bgefangen*) the King, whereas
actually it was the King who had first spoken to the ambassador
and not the other way round. Further, Abeken said nothing
about the repeated visits which Radziwill at the King's orders
had made to Benedetti. It creates the impression that the King
had unconditionally rejected the two additional French demands,
whereas in reality he had accepted one of them. Nevertheless,

the impression created by Abeken's dispatch was that the King had no thought of an actual breach in his mind at all. In Bismarck's version there had been an encounter on the promenade in which a blunt demand had met with an equally blunt and final rejection. Thus Bismarck accepted Abeken's omissions, but he also published a great many details which he was not authorised to publish at all, for the King had only suggested that he should publish Benedetti's request for guarantees for the future and his rejection thereof. He had certainly not instructed him to say anything about Benedetti's request for an audience and his refusal to grant it.

From all this the innocent reader would be bound to infer that Benedetti had publicly conducted himself in so unseemly a manner that the King had refused ever to see him again. Indeed, the sharply contemptuous tone of the concluding sentence could hardly admit of any other interpretation. The representative of France was thus made to appear as though he had so importuned the King that the latter was compelled to show him the door as though he were an over-persistent hawker. A dry and somewhat clumsily worded inter-departmental minute dealing with current negotiations had thus been turned into a thunderbolt which the mighty hand of a newly awakened Zeus had hurled into the midst of a terrified Europe.

How was it possible for Bismarck, who had worked so long and so indefatigably for European peace, to release a document to the world whose explosive power was unmistakable? Generations have asked this question without finding an answer. That he knowingly exploited French recklessness and made war inevitable is something which Bismarck never denied. Why did he not bury Abeken's dispatch together with countless other official papers of which the public never learnt anything whatever?

That the German Empire which was to come into being was forged by Bismarck in the white heat of battle is a theme which has often inspired public orators on festive occasions. It is not one on which the critical historian need waste his time. Bismarck knew perfectly well that wartime coalitions have a tendency to end with diminished rather than enhanced feelings of friendship between allies. And if Bismarck did indeed deliberately provoke a war, it was not so that Prussians and Bavarians should learn to love one another.

Actually there were two motives behind the editing of the Ems telegram. In the first place, Bismarck had been compelled to spend two days in a situation to which he was wholly unaccustomed, the situation of diplomatic defeat, and during these days his impotent anger steadily mounted. Abeken's telegram, therefore, constituted a trebly welcome weapon of vengeance not only upon Gramont but upon his own King, the destroyer of his Spanish project about whom he had already spoken to Moltke and Roon in terms of intense irritation.

Apart from these instinctive motives, however, which largely operated in the unconscious part of his mind, there was a clear and rational realisation that his life's task was in danger. That life's task was to bring the whole of non-Hapsburg Germany under Prussian rule, and to save it he was prepared to run any risk whatsoever, including the risk of war. If it came to war, a reason for war had to be discovered which concerned not merely the Hohenzollern family but the whole of Germany, and this was the purpose which the editing of the Ems telegram was intended to serve. The sensitive pride of France was to be so intolerably wounded that no possibility remained save that of war, a war which would thus become a war of aggression on the part of France. The North German Bund would thus be forced into defensive action and this would automatically activate the alliances with the southern states, place their armies under Prussian command and deprive them of the last shreds of their independence.

Actually, even after the publication of the revised Ems telegram, Bismarck was by no means certain that war would come. It was all of a piece with the very high opinion he had of himself that he should have assumed that a war which had not been planned by him could always, even at this late stage, be prevented. Even on July 14th he was still writing in the margin of his *Christliche Losungen* the word "War" followed by a question mark. On the 15th, two days after the Ems telegram, he was instructing the Prussian ambassador in Munich that he hoped to avoid war, "if France would give guarantees for her future good conduct". He was probably well aware that there was no ungovernable desire for war either in Paris or Berlin, and indeed the French Cabinet had heard of the rejection of Gramont's demand for guarantees without losing its calm over the news, news which actually reached it at the very time when Bismarck was redrafting the Ems telegram.

All that had happened was that two nations had just boxed each other's diplomatic ears. It was embarrassing, but it would hardly be a novelty if both sides decided to keep their mouths shut. Napoleon was a very cautious man in foreign affairs. Was it so very preposterous to suppose that having achieved his major object, which was the abandonment of the candidature, he would be quite content to swallow the Ems telegram and say nothing further?

Later, when the war had actually become one of Bismarck's

greatest triumphs, it would never have done to tell the true causes of its outbreak. After the brilliant emergence from that war of the Hohenzollern Empire, it would surely have been quite inadmissible to discern its origin in the fact that a series of chances, miscalculations and precipitate decisions had sent the foreign policy of two great powers right off the rails and so plunged them into a conflict which neither had desired. It was well nigh inevitable that the war should have been treated first by Bismarck's tame Press, then by the official historiography of the day, and finally in his memoirs by Bismarck himself, as an undertaking long and carefully planned by one who had foreseen that it was indispensable if the new German Empire was ever to come into being.

But we are already anticipating an age whose character in those hot summer days of 1870 nobody could foresee. Even on the morning of July 14th the influence in Paris of the pacifically minded was still paramount. On the preceding night Ollivier had at last managed to sleep, something that for a long time he had been unable to do. People would have been quite ready to forget about the guarantees which William had refused to give. Unfortunately, before these feelings could be given formal shape in any decision, the text of the Ems telegram had been wired from the French embassy in Berlin and its effect was that of an exploding bomb.

William's first knowledge of the garbled despatch came from a newspaper from which he learned of it while walking on the Ems promenade. He read the passage over very carefully twice, then handed the paper to Eulenburg. "This," he said with a shudder, "is war."

Despite the provocation, Napoleon and his ministers could not make up their minds. Indeed, they forbade the Minister of War to call up reserves. Only when it became known that the Prussian diplomats were communicating the text of the despatch to foreign governments, thus giving it an official character, was a change in their mood discernible. Even now, however, it was in the final analysis certain personal and imponderable elements that probably turned the scale.

Napoleon was a sick man and the desire at all costs to avoid war was very strong, but the public humiliation was one which his authority might not survive—and then what would become of his dynasty? He was also moved by other considerations. He was some eighteen years older than his beautiful and passionately active wife. What would be the effect on her if he showed himself lacking in virile determination? The thought had never ceased to haunt him. And so, though he was well acquainted with Bismarck's devious political methods, he failed to avoid the trap.

Late on July 14th the French decided to mobilise and parliament voted the necessary credit on the following day. On that same July 15th King William ended his cure at Ems. He received Benedetti once more at the railway station and courteously raised his hopes that the conversations which had been broken off between the two of them would be resumed by their respective governments. His journey to Berlin, the astonished man wrote to his wife, was like "a triumphal procession. I never thought such a thing was possible. I am terrified by this enthusiasm."

Bismarck, who entered the train at Brandenburg, observed with some disquiet that the demonstrations had failed to produce any effect whatever on the King. He made his report to him in a very serious tone and as the Crown Prince remarked, "without any of the jokes which he usually liked to introduce". He employed a technique rather similar to that which he had used before the Princes' diet in Frankfurt, and sought to convince the King that he had been most grievously insulted. But his success was far from complete. For even with Bismarck the old man could at times be very obstinate. He had been irritated and annoyed at having his holiday disturbed by the all-too-persistent Benedetti. But the worst that he could find to say about him was that he had been "almost impertinent". There can be no denying the fact that the King had not felt himself insulted by Benedetti nor Benedetti by the refusal to grant him an audience. It was Bismarck's luck that the voting of the war credits in Paris, of which they learned when the train reached Berlin, and finally the declaration of war on the 19th saved him from the necessity of turning a supposedly insulted sovereign into a *casus belli*.

William signed the mobilisation order while still at the railway station. The streets and the windows were full of the faces of people who wanted to greet him, but the uninspired old sceptic wrote to the Queen, "If cheering could do the trick, we should be quite all right, but it can't."

Once war had broken out, Bismarck threw himself into it with all the passion and fire that was in him and, indeed, if anybody was bound to tolerate no doubt as to the justice of his cause, he was that man. In a circular letter to the Prussian diplomats, he admitted that the Ems telegram had unleashed the war, but this, he declared, had not been an official document but only a Press notice that had been sent to those governments that were accounted friendly in order to keep them informed. An offer of mediation by Gladstone's Cabinet, which reached him on July 18th, was rejected by Bismarck. The same treatment was accorded the Papal intervention of the 22nd. It should, however, be added that these offers suffered a similar fate in Paris.

After he compelled France to assume the role of the aggressor, he threw all his energies into isolating her. He arranged for the editor of *The Times*, Delane, to be shown a Franco-German draft treaty for the partition of Belgium which Benedetti had committed to writing in 1866, but was very careful to say nothing about the date. The result was that the whole of Britain gained the impression that it had only just been written down and recoiled in pious horror at such cynical French duplicity. The document also helped to cool the French sympathies of the smaller European powers.

In Italy Victor Emmanuel seemed not disinclined to make common cause with his old friend Napoleon, but was rendered powerless by the opposition, and particularly by Garibaldi and Mazzini. Bismarck got into touch with the latter, oddly enough through the socialist, Karl Blind, the stepfather of the young man who had shot at him in 1866 and then committed suicide. Nor did Bismarck hesitate to resort to bribery, a practice that was rendered relatively easy by the fact that Italy was a poor country which had been devastated by war.

In Vienna Francis Joseph and his Chancellor, Beust, would gladly have used the opportunity to get their revenge for 1866, but as a result of that catastrophe the Hapsburg Empire had been so transformed that Hungary was now a state that enjoyed rights virtually equal to those of Austria herself. Although the majority of Hungarians sympathised with France—"France's victories are our victories," wrote the *Pester Lloyd*—the powerful agrarian nobility of Hungary had natural affinities to that of Prussia and was able to nip every movement against Prussia in the bud. Hungarian pressure thus forced the dual monarchy to remain neutral.

The story that Austrian neutrality was the result of Russian threats is a myth, though Bismarck often acted as though he believed it. Actually the Czar had let it be known that he would march with three hundred thousand men if Austria intervened in the war. However, he made not the slightest military preparations to carry that threat into effect. Russia was, of course, as Gortschakow was later to admit, militarily very weak.*

France was able to obtain war materials from the United States in the shape of obsolete weapons from the Civil War, but Washington had not forgotten Napoleon's intervention in Mexico and was, as the French ambassador reported, *"plus Prussien que les Prussiens"*. In short, the whole civilised world was either neutral

* Speaking to the French ambassador, the Czar said that this affirmative reply to King William was merely a matter of form. After all he could not quarrel with his uncle. Aubry, p. 702.

or positively hostile to France. Only Sweden and Turkey gave assurances of their old friendship, and so France stood alone with at most 300,000 men facing 450,000 Prussians and South Germans.

Late on the afternoon of July 31st citizens of Berlin who happened to be passing that way saw with some astonishment their Federal Chancellor going off to war. He was dressed in the blue overcoat of the Heavy Landwehr Cavalry, and wore on his head a steel pickelhaube and on his legs boots which covered the upper part of his thighs like those generally worn in the Thirty Years War. Thus attired, he got into the carriage which took him to the railway station. The train took him as far as Mainz. Here he had his quarters in the house of the champagne manufacturer, Kupferberg, who remarked on his enormous capacity for consuming both food and wine.* And it was here in Mainz, in a corner of the sandstone castle of the ancient clerical Elector-princes, that Bismarck had a collision with the King in which we catch a first faint glimpse of problems which were to weigh heavily on Germany at a later date.

The matter turned on a letter from King Ludwig of Bavaria who was asking for an assurance that he would not be "media-tised" after the war. Such apprehensions were not altogether without foundation, for the annexationist appetites of King William were not unknown. Even at this critical moment he refused to give Bavaria an unqualified affirmative answer. Bis-marck had to point out to him that if he persisted in such conduct, Ludwig would probably withdraw his troops and in doing so would be legally in the right. It was, so Bismarck says, "a tough business" (*es ging hart her*).

When the King left Mainz for the front, Bismarck was determined never to let him out of his sight. He followed behind headquarters, "for the most part directly behind the King's wagon train", in a landau drawn by four requisitioned brewery horses who were driven by two mounted postilions.

In the August fighting at Weissenburg and Wörth, Prussian and South German troops fought side by side, with results that satisfied the exacting Prussian command beyond expectation, though behind the front relations between the allies left something to be desired. Thus, when there was a parade of Saxon troops before King William, the hurrah of the mounted guard regiment was stated to be "in drawing-room tones", while the officers

* Kupferberg said of him, "That man'll drink me under the table", while Bamberger, the deputy for Mainz in the customs parliament, wrote on August 5th when the victory of Weissenberg was known, "Bismarck took occasion from the victory to do some whole-hearted boozing. That is Germania." Feder, *Bismarcks grosses Spiel* (1932), pp. 141, 148.

consisting of the Saxon and Hanoverian nobility barely raised their sword hilts to the level of their faces.*

On the evening of August 16th Bismarck was informed that his son Herbert had been killed during an attack by the Guard Dragoons, while his second son, Bill, had been seriously wounded. In silence he mounted his horse and rode through the night in the hideous wake of the fighting, much as he had ridden at Königgrätz, but what he had then only seen in his mind's eye as a possibility seemed now to be hard fact. It was only after day had broken that he found Herbert lying on a pallet of straw with a not too serious wound in his thigh. Bill was unwounded.

On that same day he wrote to Johanna that the command "misused the courage of the men and their indifference towards death. It's all fists and no head— and still we're winning." All his old dislike of generals broke out afresh. He damned the useless sacrifice of the cavalry, among them of the Cuirassier regiment, whose uniform he wore, and the decimation by Canrobert's artillery of the Prussian Guard, which for him seemed to incorporate a piece of old Prussia. He spoke of these things as "nonsensical, impossible and criminal" ("*unsinnig,*" "*unmöglich,*" "*verbrecherisch*").

But despite the failures, real or imaginary, of the generals, their strategy succeeded. Metz was surrounded and the army of Bazaine immobilised inside it. By the end of August only one French army, that of MacMahon, was left in the field, and this moved westward to protect Paris. Suddenly it changed direction towards the north-east, possibly in the hope of relieving Metz. But soon it was trapped between the Belgian frontier and a half circle of German troops with double its numbers. At the centre of the French position lay the relatively unimportant fortress of Sedan.

The battle began in the first shimmering mists of a September morning. Repeated attempts by the French to break out were without result, but the death-defying courage of the French cavalry charges drew cries of admiration ("*Ah, ces braves*") even from the old soldier who was King of Prussia. Surrounded by an enormous suite, among them twenty German princes, William was watching the battle spread out before him from a hill near Frenois. Bismarck from time to time seated himself astraddle on a camp chair and studied papers.

On the other side, through the drifting smoke clouds which covered the French positions, Napoleon was moving among his troops. He set his teeth as he tried to endure the pain that riding caused him, hoping all the while for the mercy of a bullet. Shells

* Holstein, I, p. 45.

exploded so near to him that his face was blackened, but not a splinter touched his skin. He stood his ground till evening then he hoisted the white flag.

Some hours later, in the sitting-room of an unassuming dwelling in the suburbs, French and German officers were meeting together. Bismarck, Moltke and the French commander, General Wimpffen, moved through the crowded room by the dim light of a single petroleum lamp, scarcely recognisable amid the press of uniforms. Negotiations went on for two hours, only to prove abortive, then everybody got up and called for horses, and during the deep silence that followed Wimpffen remarked, "Well, then, tomorrow we'll start the battle again." "At four in the morning," said Moltke, in an even more formal and colder tone than was his wont, "I shall open fire."

Again there was silence. Suddenly Bismarck turned to Wimpffen. "Certainly," he said, "the French tomorrow will again perform miracles of courage. But what purpose will that serve?" Tomorrow, he said, the situation would be exactly the same as it was then—except that Wimpffen would have on his conscience the shedding of useless blood. Bismarck's sensible advice saved the negotiations.

There was a move back towards the house, the conversations were resumed and agreement ultimately reached. Early next morning Napoleon and 84,000 men became prisoners of war.

Bismarck was awakened very early on that day, which was September 2nd, and was told that a French general had appeared and said that Napoleon wished to speak to him. Bismarck rode off immediately, unshaven and without breakfast. His assistant, Busch, found his room in complete disorder. On the toilet table lay one of the two books of devotion which, according to his servant Engel, he took with him everywhere.

Bismarck rode down the street at a headlong gallop and, shortsighted as he was, only recognised Napoleon's halted landau at the last moment. Bismarck pulled up his horse just in time, dismounted and first gave a military salute, after which he followed the French practice and took off his cap. He then approached the carriage and asked ("exactly as I had done in St. Cloud") for "Your Majesty's commands".*

He was not usually so gentle with fallen princes, and on this occasion incurred much criticism from the German Press for behaving as he did. But Napoleon, although he may have been a prisoner-of-war, was the only representative of France who could at that moment be recognised in international law. He was, in

* Based on a statement made by Bismarck to the artist Anton von Werner. Werner, *Erlebnisse und Eindrücke*, p. 406.

a word, the only one with whom they could deal when in the very near future—so Bismarck believed—they would conclude peace terms.

In a workman's cottage by the roadside the two men sat next to one another on rush-bottom chairs. Their conversation was often halting, for as soon as it became clear that the Emperor was more anxious to speak with the King than with Bismarck, it was difficult to find subjects of conversation which were not in some way offensive. So the talk was confined to trivialities.

Next day Napoleon went off with his entire court to Kassel, where he remained a prisoner. On the same day the King ordered the troops to march on Paris. In that city on September 4th Napoleon was declared to be deposed and a "government of National Defence" was set up, the life and soul of which was the Italian-born lawyer, Gambetta.

It was precisely because operations had progressed with such unexpected speed that Bismarck felt the ever-increasing necessity of furnishing the war with an aim. Its immediate purpose, which was to halt the French attack, had been achieved, but now the fundamental difference between this war and those of 1864 and 1866 was made clear. For the aims of the two last-named wars had been clearly defined and plain for everyone to see. The aim was the union of old Prussia with its western provinces through the annexation of the states that lay between, and the extrusion of Austria from Germany. In 1870, however, there was nothing of the kind, and it is not difficult to understand how it came about that a very obvious idea should begin to recommend itself to Bismarck's mind.

Centuries ago the French provinces of Alsace and Lorraine had been a part of the old Holy Roman Empire. They were a tangible piece of ground and represented an idea which could be grasped by the humblest of German infantrymen. Actually a demand for the annexation of these territories had of late been growing steadily more vocal. Even as far back as July 13th the *Berliner Börsenzeitung* had declared that after a victorious war it would be quite impossible to allow Strasbourg to remain a French city.

After long hesitation Bismarck at length resolved to follow the popular cry. It was not that he was less intelligent than Gladstone who, on that occasion, immediately remarked to his Foreign Secretary Granville that the annexation of Lorraine and Alsace spelt the beginning of a new and most unhappy phase of European history. Bismarck knew as well as the next man that the two territories which had for centuries been an integral part of France had no wish to be anything else, and had never shown the slightest sign of that fiery irredentism that the world had become familiar

with in Italy. Moreover, Bismarck was one of the very few
Prussians who had doubts about the utility of the Polish partitions,
although he considered the accomplished facts to be unalterable
and did not want them interfered with. This alone made him
disinclined to strengthen the Polish opposition in Prussia by
allowing it to ally itself with a French one.

It was now two years since he had told his friend Keyserling
that even if Prussia were victorious over France it would lead
to little good. If Prussia won Alsace she would have to defend it
and always keep the fortresses garrisoned, and ultimately the
French would find allies and then things might not be too rosy.

On September 5th, during a nocturnal walk through the
medieval streets of Rheims, he opened his heart to Keudell for
the first time. Without Strasbourg and Metz, it would be impossible to make peace; the purpose of holding them was not to
win back Alsace and Lorraine for Germany but to deter the French
from a new war of aggression. The acquisition of Lorraine was
something that, politically speaking, he did not want at all, but
the military held the view that Metz was indispensable and was
the equivalent of 120,000 men.

One thing is quite obvious. German popular nationalism and
its related myths of a submerged Germany made no impression
whatsoever on Bismarck any more than did the learned professors
who endeavoured to extract juridical titles from the history of
past centuries. He roundly rejected such arguments as "professors' ideas". He knew only too well that it is as easy to prove
one thing from dusty archives as it is to prove its opposite. He
was guided by one thing alone, the wishes of the military, though
usually he had no high opinion of them and was very much afraid
that their influence might lead to dangerous territorial extensions.
He was in one of those situations where he was confronted by two
equally disagreeable alternatives, situations to which he tended to
react by violently losing his temper. He knew very well, he said
on this occasion, that the population of Alsace and Lorraine was
against Germany. So much the worse for Alsace and Lorraine.
"Wir werden ihr kein Vergnügen machen und sie uns auch nicht." (We
will afford them no pleasure, neither will they give any pleasure
to ourselves.)

It was these words that on September 20th he addressed to the
grey-haired Jules Favre, a Paris lawyer who had grown famous
because of his stubborn resistance to Napoleon, and now he
appeared in Rothschild's castle at Ferrières as head of the delegation from the new French government. At the time it seemed not
unreasonable to suppose that after the disappearance of the
Napoleonic system, its two enemies, who now met, would make

peace together. Shortly before this meeting Favre, in a circular letter, had admitted France's war guilt and declared that her punishment through defeat was just. But he had also added that he would not yield a foot of French soil nor a single stone of any of France's fortresses, a vow that could scarcely be reconciled with Bismarck's annexation policy.

On that occasion Bismarck first hinted that he could get as satisfactory a peace, if not actually a better one, by dealing with Napoleon rather than with the Paris delegation. The Emperor had never abdicated, whereas the Paris government had no mandate from the French people. One might think that he was merely using this threat in order to put pressure on Favre. Actually he would have greatly preferred making peace with Napoleon to making it with anybody else. Within a short time, however, as we shall see, the whole situation had grown so tangled and complicated that there was very little chance of a peace settlement that conformed to any of the dictates of common sense. Immediately after Sedan, even before the meeting with Favre, Bismarck had established a connection with Napoleon, and, what was even more to the point, with Eugenie, who had fled to England, and with Marshal Bazaine, who was locked up in Metz by the army of Prince Frederick Charles.

Bazaine recognised no authority save that of the Empress, and had been created a Lieutenant of the Empire by her. There were therefore distinct possibilities in the idea of allowing Bazaine to march out of Metz with his army on the understanding that he would promise to overthrow the Republic and make an early peace. Meanwhile the Empress was to settle down in a man-of-war in some harbour town that had remained faithful to the Empire and summon the two Houses of Parliament to meet there. Moltke and Frederick Charles naturally opposed such plans. They could not understand that Bismarck was anxious to prevent the French from developing a people's war, foreseeing as he did that the longer such a war lasted the more the nationalist passions of France would become disastrously inflamed.

The programme, however, came to nothing owing to the wholly unexpected surrender of Bazaine on October 27th. Bismarck thereupon permitted Eugenie to pay a visit to Napoleon at Kassel which lasted several days. Its purpose, obviously, was to enable them to make new plans for their life. Even as late as March 1871, when the preliminary peace with the Republican government had already been signed, Bismarck was still negotiating along this alternative line and would certainly have made peace with Napoleon if it had been possible to reach agreement with him, despite the fact that public opinion in Germany was still feeling the effects of the propaganda directed at the beginning of the war against the Imperial pair. When Johanna asked in horrified tones whether he was content to see Napoleon remaining on the throne, he answered "I might be at that".

In the end, however, it all came to nothing because Napoleon, well aware that he could not return with empty hands, asked for a partial mitigation of the peace terms. To achieve this, however, in the teeth of the opposition which would certainly come from the King, the Army and, indeed, the whole of Germany, was something which Bismarck now felt was wholly beyond his powers. For a long time, however, he continued to see in a return of the Bonapartes the best solution of the difficulties that were bound to ensue between France and Germany.

However, hard facts prevailed, and he was compelled to treat with the representatives of the Republic. At first his efforts in this direction achieved nothing or rather, as he wrote to Herbert, "the French negotiators got such a bellyache over Alsace that we had to break off the talks".

This rather jovial tone employed towards his son was obviously intended to disguise the very real crisis which confronted him. Bismarck, in default of any other war aim, was compelled to insist on the annexation of the two French provinces and the war went on. Conversely, the longer the war continued the more Bismarck had to insist on these territorial claims. For only thus could be he assured of the loyalty of German public opinion, which he so despised but which he could never entirely refuse to obey. Bismarck took these matters very much to heart. He was deeply depressed and seemed utterly weary of it all. He told Busch that he loved the country and took pleasure in the forest and in nature, that he would gladly pack up tomorrow and go off to Varzin for good, but his life was not his own. "And yet," he said, "why, save that it is God's commandment, should I subordinate myself to these Hohenzollerns? They are a Swabian family that's no better than mine and with whom I personally have no concern."

Meanwhile, the war went on under Bismarck's growing disapproval, for he would gladly have ended it as rapidly as he had ended that of 1866. The military saw in their march on Paris only another mopping up operation. Moltke had already notified his Silesian estate that he was coming to shoot hares. Only the old King, with his sound soldier's instinct, had said immediately after Sedan, "Wait a bit. The war is only really beginning."

Bismarck, too, was of the opinion that the correct strategy for an army such as that of Germany, confronted as it was with almost the whole territory of a throughly hostile great power, was to use all its strength in holding on to territorial gains, perhaps occupying a defensive position along the line of the Ardennes. Certainly it should not undertake any crazy trip to Paris (*wie unsinnig nach Paris . . . laufen*), and dissipate its strength by fanning out. It should leave Paris alone and use its concentrated power to destroy any French force that showed signs of putting up a fight.

Nobody took him seriously, but his quarrel with the High Command became an open secret, and certainly he was forthright in his expression of his feelings. Prussian officer material, he was fond of saying, was good enough to supply regimental commanders. Beyond that, it simply wasn't up to the mark. The best Prussian generals, Scharnhorst, Gneisenau, Moltke, had come from foreign armies.

Of course, the general staff was now also beginning to realise that its tasks were much more difficult than it had anticipated. The rapid advances of the summer were over. Half of its effectives were pinned down in front of Metz, Strasbourg and the other fortresses of Eastern France. The other half was beginning to surround Paris in a wide circle. The city showed no signs of wanting to surrender, indeed it seemed grimly determined on its own defence.

Soon it began to go hungry, but it did not waver. More important, the Republican government of unknown lawyers and journalists, which had been elected by nobody and among whom the aged Thiers alone enjoyed an international reputation, was displaying a wholly unexpected energy and creating new armies out of nothing. At the beginning of November one of these armies crossed the Loire, threw back the Bavarian troops that it encountered near Coulmiers and seized Orleans. It was a minor victory for France. Moltke no longer thought of shooting hares. Indeed, it was not long before he was remarking that "nobody could say how long this terrible war will last". For an entire nation in arms was not to be under-estimated. By the new year they might well have to reckon with a million French soldiers.

Meanwhile headquarters had followed the army that was besieging Paris and had established itself in Versailles; the mighty palace was turned into a Prussian hospital. Bismarck made his home in a villa in the rue de Provence which belonged to a certain Jessé, a textile manufacturer. It was a yellow building with white curtains, and Landwehr men, whose long pipes hung down over their beards, kept guard at the gate. Now a form of life began to organise itself around Bismarck: a wartime billet, a bachelor establishment, a diplomatic office and a centre of internal politics were curiously mingled. A single room, always overheated, constituted his living and sleeping quarters. Smoking endless cigars, in a uniform which was lined with doeskin, and often in a dressing-gown, he frequently worked right through the night and then slept till noon.

At dinner, round about six o'clock, he was joined by all his officials. They used tin dishes and candles were stuck in wine bottles. His appetite was excellent, which explains his frequent complaint that one didn't get enough to eat at the royal table. Later in the evening Keudell had occasionally to perform on a very indifferent piano.

Meanwhile, the task which Bismarck had set himself ever since he had entered politics, that of making the King of Prussia into the master of Germany, was ripening rapidly towards completion. Since the catastrophic fall of France, no earthly power could prevent Northern Germany from uniting with the South. All that remained to be settled were certain matters of form, things that had never greatly interested Bismarck, though they now involved him in a vast amount of work. Ancient conflicting ambitions between the various German peoples and states had at least to some extent to be harmonised, while at the same time the mighty upsurging wave of unifying nationalism had to be duly allowed for in his calculations.

Yet though he certainly had to take account of it (it would have been folly to do otherwise), the concept of nationhood still meant very little to him. Indeed, the very fact of its origin in the French Revolution caused him to look at it askance. As to a German nation, he doubted its existence and even its ability to exist, as many other Germans have doubted in every age. In Goethe's opinion it was impossible that the Germans should ever form a nation, and this was no random utterance.

For Bismarck a nation was not a real fact at all. It was not a constant factor that could or should be taken into one's political reckoning. Only the German states were for Bismarck realities. It was with these alone that his practical work was concerned. Whether the supposedly transcendent reality of the nation was a figment or otherwise, the idea that every nation, or rather every group of human beings that designated itself as such, had a divinely guaranteed right to existence and even to unity, was for him pure mythology.

For Bismarck it merely introduced supremely unimportant and superfluous issues. There was, for instance, the question of a flag for the new political entity which was about to be born. His ambassador in Munich had dwelt upon this matter at some length, only to receive the telegraphic reply that people who boggle over that kind of thing are immature. To Busch he remarked, "I am quite indifferent to colour schemes. As far as I am concerned, you can have green and yellow and any nonsense you like, or if you prefer it the colours of Mecklenburg Strelitz." Only the "black, red and yellow" was ruled out as "contrary to the Prussian tradition". The word "Kaiser" (Emperor), in so far as it might apply to William, was one which at first he sought to keep right out of the discussion. Even at the beginning of August he had written to the Prussian Minister of the Interior from Mainz, "Newspapers which . . . speak of 'Kaiser ideas' do harm to our policies and are liable to spoil our understanding with our South German allies."

In October he had to begin to decide on the legal form which the power structure envisaged by him was to assume. On the 20th he was writing to Johanna, "Tomorrow the South German ministers are coming to consult with me concerning the new thousand-year Reich." It was apparently impossible for him to refer without irony to any part of the system of ideas so cherished by the nationalists at home. He was anxious to have negotiations with the South Germans in which the latter, appearing on this occasion as partners of Prussia, would formally declare their membership to the North German Bund, a membership which was in reality already a fact. What they were really to do was formally to confirm the shift of power which to their not inconsiderable disadvantage had already taken place.* Indeed, precisely because Bismarck was in such a position of strength, he could cause pressure to be indirectly exerted on them, say through the King of Saxony, to take the initiative in opening negotiations in which they actually had very little interest. Such apparent spontaneity might always help to provide Bismarck with an alibi.

This also explains why he treated the South Germans with exemplary patience and consideration. He may, among other things, have feared, as did many of his assistants, that these allies who, in name after all, were still sovereign states, in their desperation might—if they were too roughly handled—declare the alliance to have lapsed and withdraw their troops. Once, however, they were members of the Bund, they would have lost their sovereignty and all escape would be cut off.

This whole matter became the subject of a violent altercation between himself and the Crown Prince who, as a strict liberal "unifier", was quite ready to employ armed force against what he called the "disaffected princes". Bismarck opposed the Prince with great vehemence, and became so excited that he shortly

---

* Very soon a sort of sour gallows humour came into evidence among them, as when young Prince Georg Albert von Schwarzburg, whose nickname was Prince of Arcadia, joined the assembled potentates with the greeting, "Good day, fellow vassals." Holstein, I, p. 77.

afterwards had a bilious attack. He referred to the Crown Prince as "the stupidest and vainest of men" who "would one day die of his Kaiser-lunacy".

Each delegation was received separately by Bismarck in the very bourgeois drawing-room of the Villa Jessé, with its plush furniture, its numerous mirrors, its piano and its bronze clock on the mantelpiece. He skilfully isolated each from the rest and frightened each by suggesting to him that the others had already given much more ground. As a final means of pressure—should it be required—he had a number of packing cases in the cellar which had been discovered by the German troops in Rouher's house, and which contained correspondence between Napoleon and the South German governments. As sovereign states they had a perfect right to correspond with anyone they pleased, still you never knew if there might not be passages which, if published, would at that particular moment prove highly embarrassing. Wearing and irritating as these negotiations often proved, he always contrived to preserve an unimpeachable courtesy—which only impaired his self-control when dealing with his own subordinates who often had the impression that he was going to throw the inkpot at them.

Meanwhile Bismarck's attention was being diverted to the diplomatic field, for Russia, which after the Crimean War had surrendered its right to maintain warships in the Black Sea, now declared that it would no longer be bound by this clause in the peace treaty. Bismarck had already assured Russia of his support for such a step in September. Now his promise was placing him in a very difficult position. He dare not do anything to obstruct this most important of neutrals, and at the same time he must do everything in his power to prevent France from taking part in any conference which might have the right to come to a decision on the Russian claim. For France would undoubtedly bring the present war into the discussion, would break out of the isolation into which he had so skilfully contrived to manoeuvre her, and subject the results of continuous Prussian successes to international interference.

Strenuous efforts had to be made (a threatening private letter from Bismarck to Jules Favre being among the means employed) before France could be prevented from attending the so-called "Pontus conference" in London. It was only after the conference had ended, and when there was already a truce between the combatants, that Bismarck agreed to Jules Favre adding his signature to those of the other conference members.

As time went on, relations between Bismarck and the general staff grew steadily worse. Bismarck was continuously complaining in his letters about the "victorious intrusion of the *Soldateska* into civil business. The gentlemen from the army," he wrote home, "make my work terrifyingly difficult. They engross tasks which are rightfully mine, ruin them and then I have the responsibility." Success had given the generals "imperial delusions" (*"Kaiserwahnsin in die Krone gefahren"*), while Moltke had "become old and was letting things slide. It's the rank and file that'll see us through, not the generals."

Meanwhile the generals did all that they could to keep Bismarck away from military decisions and this enraged him all the more, since he thought that in military matters his judgment was as good if not better than theirs—as indeed it sometimes was. However, his confidence sometimes over-reached itself, as when he urged the bombardment of Paris, a proceeding which offended the moral sense of the time without really yielding any military dividends.

When for a time this course was opposed, Bismarck suspected sinister influence to be at work, especially that of the Crown Prince, though he could never produce any proof of this. "There is a web of intrigue over the whole affair," he wrote to Johanna, "spun by females, archbishops and academics" (*"Weibern, Erzbischöfen und Gelehrten"*). Whereupon Johanna spread the report in Berlin that it was the Crown Princess who was preventing the bombardment on orders from her English mother. Most certainly the Crown Princess was against it on humanitarian grounds, but it would have been contrary to every Prussian tradition if Moltke had allowed himself to be governed by the views of a lady, however princely her blood, in any case where he expected a military success to result from the opposite course.

For all that, Bismarck's impression that the high command no longer measured up to its task was undoubtedly correct. At the beginning of the new year the German forces were faced by three new French armies: one in the west under Chancy, one in the north-west under Faidherbe, and one in the east under Bourbaki. They were no longer armies with a kernel of professional soldiers but levies which had been very rapidly armed and trained —a militia known as the *Garde Mobile*, supplemented by *franctireurs* and various other voluntary bodies.

More and more the war became a war of the people, something which the Prussian general staff had entirely failed to foresee. Moltke's defensive strategy was still able to halt the attacks of these new French armies, but he was unable to destroy the armies themselves. Some fifty years later Ludendorff was to write, "I can't help saying that the German conduct of the war of 1870–71 was quite helpless when confronted with an entirely new phenomenon."[*]

[*] Ludendorff, *Der totale Kreig* (1936), p. 4.

It was because Bismarck was thoroughly alive to this fact that
he pressed with increasing urgency for an ending of the war. On
the day after Christmas Waldersee states that he found him in a
very bad state of health. He cursed the secrecy-mongering of the
general staff and "worked himself up into a really violent temper.
His eyes grew larger and larger and the sweat ran down his face.
He made a thoroughly disordered impression."

Actually his relations with the general staff had now reached
their nadir. On the journey to the front he had overheard a
conversation that took place between Generals Roon and Pod-
bielski in a neighbouring compartment, a conversation in which
they expressed their satisfaction that this time Bismarck would
not, as in 1866, be allowed to take part in military discussions.
Indeed he was deliberately kept in ignorance of military matters
wherever possible, and "a military boycott" was imposed on
him.

The fury which the military began to feel towards him is shown
by the diary of Lieutenant-Colonel Bronsart von Schellendorf,
head of the operations department of the general staff. Here we
see him referred to as "that civilian in a curassier's coat who is
always becoming more impertinent". He is called a "talented
but inwardly mean man who would never rest till he had utterly
crushed any other person who had any right to survive alongside
of him".

At length, under pressure from the King, Bismarck was given
the right to attend a war council, though this did not happen until
the beginning of February. Moltke reports that he had simply
allowed Bismarck to talk, with the result that a matter which he,
Moltke, would have settled in two minutes, took an entire hour.

For weeks now Bismarck and Moltke had avoided each other.
The Crown Prince had endeavoured to bring about a rapprochement between them by asking both to dinner. Bismarck on that
occasion spoke of the possibility of signing a peace with the
Empress Eugenie which only provided for very small territorial
annexation. Moltke was silent, but opposed Bismarck violently
when he said that he had no intention, when Paris fell, of putting
a German garrison into the city. The incident throws the difference between the two men into sharp relief. Bismarck, as was his
wont, was dealing with the realities of the situation. He wanted
an early peace, if possible with a Bonapartist dynasty. Moltke,
however, hag-ridden by an idealist conception for which world
history and world judgment were interchangeable terms, felt himself to be the representative of an avenging Nemesis.

By the end of November the treaties which incorporated the
South German states in the North German Bund had been con-

cluded. The final negotiations, particularly those with Bavaria, had cost Bismarck three sleepless nights. When the signatures had all been appended he told his assistants that he could probably have demanded much more than he had. The South Germans would have been compelled to sign. But, he added, *"was sind Verträge wenn man muss?"* (What are treaties when people sign them under compulsion?)

As to the name the new entity which he was shaping should bear, Bismarck was never in any doubt, but here a difficulty had already arisen, for if it was to be called a Reich (or Empire) its head would have to be called Kaiser. But William was by no means prepared for this. Not that he had had any scruples when it was a case of enlarging his territories. Catherine Radziwill, who knew him very well, tells us that he contrived to combine great greed as a ruler with selflessness as a man. Even Bismarck once remarked to the Bavarian diplomat Lerchenfeld that in 1866 William would have "annexed the entire world if it had been possible to do so and had I let him have his head".

Nevertheless the title of Emperor which he was now asked to assume caused him grave conscientious misgivings. He would have been quite happy to call himself Grosskönig or "Grand King" of Prussia, or possibly King of Greater Prussia. But that he should pay for his dominion over Germany by accepting the imperial title, that is to say by putting aside the ancient Prussian one, was to him quite intolerable; much as it had been intolerable to Enrico Dandolo, the Doge of Venice, to assume the title of Emperor of Byzantium, since he knew no more exalted one than that which he already bore.

The King was already beginning to suffer from severe depression as a result of other causes. The reverses near Orleans were leading him to believe that the troops besieging Paris had already been surrounded, and his nights were oppressed by nightmares in which he dreamt of a retreat which was very nearly a rout. In the middle of December Bismarck could still remark that it was he alone who managed to keep the King's nerves under control. One month later, however, he was compelled to confess, "I believe I have not seen Serenissimus for nearly three weeks." Clearly his relations with the King were growing tense and difficult.

The King's adjutant, Count Lehndorff, tells the following rather astonishing story: "One day Bismarck appeared to report, but the King was suffering from a headache and would not have him admitted. Ill-luck would have it that the Court Marshal, Count Perponcher, slipped into the royal apartments just ahead of Bismarck. Bismarck was beside himself with rage, and hurling down his briefcase, cried out, 'What, that man's admitted and

I'm not. If anybody else can put up with that, let him. I'm going
home.' Then he stormed away.

"Lehndorff rushed to the King and told him what had happened and received the order to catch up with Bismarck and tell
him that the King commanded him to return immediately. Lehndorff managed to reach the Chancellor on the stairs, pushed his
briefcase under his arm and opened the door to the King for him
as though nothing had happened. But when the audience was
over Bismarck sank down on a sofa in the anteroom and gave
way to a violent fit of weeping."

Ludwig II of Bavaria was second in rank among the German
princes and there was a strange relationship between him and
Bismarck. He did not hesitate to treat Ludwig as just another
German prince as soon as reasons of state seemed to demand this,
but he displayed on occasion a unique understanding for this
rather odd creature. In Bismarck's memoirs no one cuts so good
a figure. It was as though the Chancellor felt that there was something Shakespearian in Ludwig's personality, much as there was
in his own, and there are no other personalities in recent German
history of whom that could be said.

Ludwig II, at that time twenty-five years of age, was a shy,
proud man, of great physical beauty. He was essentially a
medieval feudal lord born out of his time. None of the contemporary German princes was so jealous of the sovereignty of
his state, yet hardly one of them longed more ardently or more
honestly for the rebirth of the ancient empire. Since Bismarck
frequently led him to believe that this precisely was his aim and
expressed from time to time an intention, which he certainly did
not seriously entertain, of restoring old Wittelsbach territory in
the Palatinate, there were often times when Ludwig was prepared
for a partial surrender of sovereignty.

It was this king, then, that Bismarck chose for the task of overcoming William's dislike of the imperial title; he made use of a
certain Count Holnstein, the Bavarian Master of the Horse, as
an intermediary. Holnstein was in Versailles at the time, and he
and Bismarck understood each other perfectly. It was not long
before Holnstein was on his way back to Bavaria with a draft
letter in Bismarck's handwriting in his luggage, couched in terms
that would lead most likely to the persuasion of William to accept
the imperial crown. When Holnstein arrived back in Munich he
found that the king had withdrawn to Hohenschwangau and was
lying in bed with a bandage round his face suffering from the
effects of recent dental treatment. But the Count was nothing if
not persuasive, assuring his royal master that unless he agreed to

sign, the Bavarian army would revolt and there would be nothing left for him but ignominious flight and exile. At last, possibly still under the influence of the dentist's drugs, the king surrendered. The letter was copied in the royal hand and signed, though Holnstein was strictly enjoined to show it in Munich to all the ministers concerned and only to present it with their concurrence.

Holnstein interpreted this instruction somewhat lightheartedly and contented himself with showing the document to the Secretary of the Cabinet and to the Minister of Justice, who were hardly concerned in the matter at all, but neglected to take into his confidence either the Prime Minister or the Minister for Foreign Affairs. He obviously felt that there was no time to lose, for he requisitioned a locomotive and, hugging his precious prize, put the Bavarian frontier behind him as quickly as he could.

We have still to learn the full truth about Holnstein's mission, but the story that Ludwig simply sold himself for a cash payment out of Guelph funds is, despite the fact that Lord Acton swallowed it, certainly untrue. There is no confirmation of anything of the kind in the records of the fund. Also Ludwig was not that kind of man, and Bismarck knew men too well to suppose otherwise.* All that seems to be adequately established is that shortly after this event considerable payments out of this fund were regularly received by Holnstein. Whether or not he passed these on to the king, we may be quite certain that Bismarck never represented them as being in any way related to the letter which he had got him to sign, though it is just possible that he treated them as contributions to the king's artistic ventures. However, there are some who hold a different view. Count Kuno Moltke, for instance, who for a long time was Prussian military attaché in Munich, believed that Holnstein himself pocketed the money "for services rendered".

William's reaction to Ludwig's letter was distinctly ungracious. The letter reached him during the French Loire offensive and he called it "as untimely as it could possibly be" and, as the Crown Prince noted, was beside himself with ill-will and almost a broken man ("wie geknickt"). For Bismarck's calculation had been correct. If the German monarch who followed him in princely rank asked him to accept the imperial title, he had perforce to accept.

Nor was his irritation diminished when, on December 16th, he had to receive a deputation of the North German Reichstag. This parliament had approved the treaties which Bismarck had made with the South German states and altered the constitution of the North German Bund accordingly. From January 1, 1871,

* Fririch Thimme in his commentary on Bismarck's collected works.

the Bund was to be called the Reich, or German Empire, and its president was to be called Kaiser. The thirty-man deputation was to ask the King to accept the imperial title which in reality was now no more than a matter of form, since he was already president of the Bund. The spokesman of the deputation was Eduard Simson, who, in 1848, had presented a similar petition of the National Assembly in Frankfurt to Frederick William IV, and had been refused. Since the initiative, however, now came from the princes, who at the time of the Frankfurt parliament had been regarded as non-existent, William I found himself helpless. It was this that disturbed him so greatly; when Simson delivered his formally dignified lawyer's address, his eyes were full of tears.

Bismarck's strength, too, was near to exhaustion. He made remarks of a primitive cruelty, such as one might hear among habitués of a pothouse, utterances which were quite unworthy of him. For instance, he said that no more prisoners-of-war should be taken, since "corpses need no shelter or food", that France's African troops, the Turcos and the Zouaves, should be killed out of hand, and all *franctireurs* (the then equivalent of partisans) should be hanged.* To justify this, he said, "I attach no great importance to human life, because I believe in another world. If we were to live three or four hundred years, that would be another matter." He ordered the troops to fire on starving women and children from Paris who approached the besieging troops, and when somebody remarked that the soldiers would refuse to do this, he answered angrily, "Then you'll have to shoot the soldiers for disobedience." His eagerness to bombard Paris, involving as it did the killing of innumerable women, children and old people, is perhaps to be understood in the light of this mood.

Faithful echo that she was, Johanna wrote to him after the truce had been signed with that wild fury to which puritanical Christianity can often lead, "I would gladly have thrown in many thousand fire bombs, shells and mortars until this accursed Sodom had been utterly destroyed for ever."†

Of course such outbursts by Bismarck often represented something other than the irrational effects of a well-nigh incredible nervous tension. There was, for instance, nothing irrational about Bismarck's determination to put an end as quickly as possible, by terrorising the civilian population, to a war that was becoming daily more intolerable. There were, he wrote to the King, to be

---

* Favre informed Bismarck that the Prussian Landsturm Edict of 1813 had served as model for setting up the *franctireurs* organisations. But being the argument of the weaker party it was without effect.

† Eyck, *Bismarck* (1943), II, p. 539.

reprisals of every kind and a "feeling of intolerable pressure" was to be induced; ultimately it was this that would produce peace.

On January 18th, under a clear cold winter sky, the streets of Versailles resounded to the harsh music of the Prussian pipes and drums. About midday an unbroken procession of bright uniforms started to move into the old Bourbon Palace. Here at one end of the vast Hall of Mirrors, resplendent in its white, bronze and gold, a platform had been built whose background was formed by some sixty detachments of picked regiments with their flags and standards standing motionless as pillars of stone, while bearded cuirassiers with their broadswords formed the front of the group. Fires were burning in all the fireplaces, but the air remained chilly and the whole atmosphere seemed to be charged with uneasiness.

On the platform, in front of the variegated colours of the flags, stood King William, surrounded by the German princes and high-ranking officers. His face was chalky white with fatigue, his expression rather sulky, almost grim. An American eye-witness states that Bismarck's anxious gaze was directed towards the legs of his monarch, which sometimes tended to tremble a little. For there he stood, directly in front of the platform, the man who had brought the King from the desperate situation of Babelsberg to the place he now occupied. He wore his great cuirassier's boots, and, as Keudell tells us, his unusual pallor was accentuated by the dark blue of his uniform.*

After a sermon from the Court chaplain and an address of welcome by the King, Bismarck read out the carefully formulated proclamation of the new Empire, but he did so in a comparatively low voice and in a tone which suggested that he would be heartily glad to get the whole business over. Hardly had he finished, when William's son-in-law, the Grand Duke of Baden, called for the first "Hoch" in honour of "Kaiser Wilhelm".

As the new Emperor stepped down from the platform, he deliberately looked past Bismarck, and on that day said not a word to him, for the Grand Duke's "Hoch" had been a compromise. On the previous day William had insisted that he should be proclaimed "Emperor of Germany", which Bismarck refused to sanction, since it would have implied a claim on the territories of the other princes. The only possible title was "German Emperor".

The King had thereupon left the conference table in a rage without reaching a decision. As things were, he believed himself

* Bismarck did not take the white gala uniform of the cuirassier's uniform along with him on the campaign and so he could not have worn it. Anton von Werner's popular picture of the proclamation of the Empire is thus inaccurate.

to be within his rights in instructing his son-in-law to use the title
to which Bismarck had objected. By chance the Grand Duke had
run into Bismarck on the great steps of the Palace just before the
ceremony, and Bismarck had explained to him that "Emperor
of Germany" was impossible and advised him to use the formula
"Emperor William", which implied nothing in particular. To
William this was a bitter disappointment and it was a long time
before Bismarck was forgiven.

It was hardly a happy celebration. The general staff spoke
curtly of it as a piece of mummery. There were too many eyes
to be seen that were red with lack of sleep, too many faces that
showed the signs of embitterment around the mouth, as though
their owners were guarding unpleasant secrets. Those who knew
of the devious roads that had been travelled in order to reach the
present position were too tired to cheer. Cheering was left to the
onlookers and especially to the uninstructed and ignorant at
home. The new Emperor himself wrote that evening to his wife:
"I can hardly describe to you the morose feelings that I have
been experiencing over the past few days, partly because of the
great responsibility that I now have to take on myself, and above
all because of the pain it gives me to see the old Prussian title
pushed aside. I had a conference yesterday with Fritz, Bismarck
and Schleinitz, and at last grew so ill-tempered that I was on the
point of withdrawing altogether and leaving everything to Fritz.
It was only after I had turned to God in fervent prayer that I was
granted the necessary strength and self-control."

That same evening Bismarck discharged some of the fury that
had been mounting up within him by raging against the clergyman whose sermon at the ceremony had actually been in unusually
poor taste. "More than once I thought to myself, '*Warum kann ich
diesem Pfaffen nicht an den Leib*' (Why can I not get at that damned
priest's throat)". Three days later he was writing to Johanna,
"I haven't written to you for an awfully long time. Forgive me,
but this Kaiser-birth has been a difficult one and kings in such
times have their odd desires. They are just like women before
they give to the world that which they can no longer keep for
themselves."

In the new Empire there was only one responsible minister,
the Imperial Chancellor, who was identical with the Prussian
Prime Minister and so was able to dispose over all Prussia's
instruments of power. The various branches of the administration
were under State Secretaries who depended for their employment
even more completely upon the Imperial Chancellor than the
members of the American Cabinet depend on the President. In
these circumstances, Bismarck could afford to have a Reichstag

which consisted of members elected by universal suffrage and secret ballot. He himself was the only minister responsible to this Reichstag, though even that meant little, for his appointment and dismissal depended entirely on the Emperor—a provision which was many years later to prove a trap for Bismarck.

The Reichstag had the right to approve taxes and was to co-operate in legislation. The initiative for legislation, however, remained with the Bundesrat, the diet of princes, in which Prussia only had seventeen votes but nevertheless possessed by far the greater physical power. For all practical purposes therefore power centred in the person of the Emperor-King.

The constitution of the German Empire, unlike that of the United States, was not the product of many months of intensive debate. It was the result of rapid improvisation, for time had been short. Bismarck had incorporated in it such features of the existing order as he thought would serve his purpose. There was the North German Bund on the one hand, the South German states on the other, and these had been joined together in such a manner as would be likely to furnish the minimum of opposition.

Bismarck's most urgent task now was to safeguard his new creation from any of those unpleasant surprises which a continuance of the war was liable to produce, and the spirit in which he entered upon the peace negotiations shows how little this war with France had been an integral element of his programme for the unity of Germany. Even now, after all the brilliance of his victory, he looked upon this conflict, which had resulted from a series of miscalculations on either side, as completely unnecessary. Had he enjoyed the same freedom to speak the truth as that claimed by Thiers, the successor of a fallen régime, he might well have used much the same words as those with which the Frenchman addressed the Chamber of Deputies in July 1871, when he declared that it was not the interests of the country but the blunders of the government that had forced them to go to war.

Bismarck's chief concern was with the effects that the war might have on the future. He had visited France more frequently than any other country and for longer periods. There was no country with which he was better acquainted, and the impressions which he had gathered led him to doubt whether the relations between the two countries could ever again be normalised. France had, of course, suffered other defeats and got over them, but with this latest one, he felt, it was a different matter. And all this disquiet that he experienced found expression in that strange utterance which he made in May: France, he said, was like a fox who has long been shot dead and bitten to pieces by the hounds, the sinews of whose legs had been cut, and who as he is being carried away manages nevertheless to bite the beater's behind.

Occasionally he submitted to the current cliché that the French were "too vain" ever to forget their defeats, so it did not matter whether the terms of peace were harsh or otherwise. They would, whatever one did, be a source of mortal peril for Germany. The logical inference from this was that Germany would only be safe from France when it had not only removed the latter from the map but from the surface of the earth. Bismarck knew very well that that kind of thing just doesn't happen, that none of the old European peoples has ever completely exterminated another. As an East Elbian, he was well acquainted with the case of Poland, whose life continued despite all the partition, even though for long periods it had to do so underground. He therefore never seriously doubted that he would have to come to terms with France's continued existence. Should she prove irreconcilable, he would have to keep the sword permanently pointed at her throat.

To Bismarck's flexible mind such an unfruitful and inelastic attitude was profoundly distasteful. That is why in January he had drawn up a long memorandum to the King advising him to try and make peace with the Bonaparte dynasty, for no other government would find it more difficult to make a fresh war in the future. A Bonapartist régime would be the only one that would have to depend for moral support on Germany. Every other government would necessarily be committed to enmity towards that country and would be added to Germany's opponents in any diplomatic combination. A French Empire would be able "to take up the attitude of a government friendly even though not actually allied to Germany". This would naturally not be popular in Germany itself. But it had not been an aim of the war to prevent the return of the French Empire. The peace conditions therefore which he proposed to the King were mild ones—an indemnity and the surrender of the government district of Strasbourg, which meant only the city and the fortress and the territory that was accounted part of the fortress.

Naturally Bismarck must himself have doubted whether so sensible a solution could ever actually be adopted. The feverish atmosphere in Germany had lasted far too long for that. If the worst came to the worst he would, of course, have to accept the French Republic, make peace with it and let the French defeat take such a form that there was some hope that in the course of time she would be reconciled to it. But even here there were difficulties, for the demand for Alsace and Lorraine, which he himself had made on purely technical grounds, now stood in his way and utterly refused to be conjured out of existence.

The problem of annexation was probably the most intractable among all those with which in that late winter of 1870 he had to wrestle—to wrestle to the point of utter exhaustion, often in loneliness and silence. For he surely recognised its importance for the future quite as much as the rest of the civilised world, which, horrified at the idea of annexation, took a certain malignant pleasure in the predicament in which it involved him.

The suggestion that in place of the two provinces Germany should accept certain French colonial possessions, say in Indo-China, was rejected by him outright. Here again, it was his sound East Elbian instinct which made him realise that his new creation, powerful as it appeared to be, lacked certain of the prerequisites necessary for a power with overseas possessions. "Colonies," he said, "for Germany are like the sables possessed by noble Polish families who have no shirts."

Negotiations for surrender and a preliminary peace began in Versailles at the end of January, and along with Favre came Thiers, who had already attained the rank of an important statesman when Bismarck was duelling in Göttingen. The two men had meanwhile become acquainted and had a high opinion of each other.

Bismarck, for whom the war had no longer any point whatsoever, would have been ready now to make considerable concessions, but, unlike 1866, the generals on this occasion had their way, for the Emperor was on their side. In such questions as the drawing of the frontier, Bismarck had to give way to them completely. He had his moments of rebellion in which he loudly and bitterly cursed the fate which had not permitted him, as it had permitted the first Napoleon, to unite the direction of military and political affairs in his own hands.

In negotiating with the French he showed himself much more pliable than the Press made him out to be to the public at home. The artist Wagner had been busy at Versailles and one of his paintings had become well known throughout Germany. This shows the French negotiators as broken men, while Bismarck, gigantic in his cuirassier's uniform, stands before them, making a gesture with his open hand as though to say "whether you like it or not".

Actually the scene was quite untrue to life. Though at that time Bismarck was suffering from neuralgia in the face and the trouble with his leg had returned, he remained courteous and obliging, particularly towards Thiers. When one day he found the tired old man asleep in his ante-room, he covered him up with his huge cuirassier's overcoat. "He is a sensible and very pleasant man," he wrote home, "witty, brilliant, but without a trace of the diplomat. He is much too sentimental for that trade. Indeed,

he is quite unsuited to be a negotiator, even a horse trader. . . .
Also I'm quite sorry for him, but all that won't help."

Until a few days before the actual signature, Bismarck was still
worrying about the unforeseen results that the annexations might
bring in their train and was trying to find ways of mitigating
them. Even as late as February 22nd he said at table, "If they
give us another billion, we really might leave them Metz after all.
We should then use eight hundred millions and build a fortress a
few miles further back, possibly by Falkenburg or Saarbrücken.
We should then actually make a profit of two hundred millions.
I just don't like having so many Frenchmen in the house who
don't want to be there."

The instrument that was actually signed partook of the nature
of a compromise and pleased nobody. The French succeeded in
reducing the war indemnity, though hardly anybody believed
that they would be capable of paying even the new amount. They
also succeeded in saving the fortress of Belfort, the only one that had
never surrendered. As against this, they agreed to the Germans
marching into certain parts of Paris for a period of two days. The
population maintained silence and remained behind closed shutters.

Very little notice was taken at the time of the iron ore deposits
of Lorraine which now passed into German hands. The iron of
Lorraine was at that time not rated very highly because of its
high phosphorus content. Nobody guessed at that time that
within a few years the Thomas Gilchrist process would be invented
which made it possible to use this iron on a very extensive scale
and it was really this that turned Germany into an industrial
power of the first rank.

The final peace was signed in Frankfurt on May 10th, after
the Reichstag had approved the constitution six days previously.
Bismarck's work was finished. The Kaiser gave him the title of
Duke of Lauenburg and also the large estate of Friedrichsruh,
which was ten times the size of Varzin, in the "Sachsenwald",
near Hamburg.

This was the peak period of Bismarck's life. The whole world
knew his face, the face of a man who had built a new state of a
kind entirely different from any that had existed before. From
the first day onwards, he continued to be fearful for the future of
that which he had created. And this is not surprising in a man
who, like Bismarck, had recognised that all that is young is only
young so that it may grow old, that every new-born child already
possesses the organ from which sooner or later death will come
forth. He asked for permanence and security for his work, and
knowing more clearly than most that these things are not granted
to any creature, he had his misgivings till the day he died.

Part III

AFTERNOON SHADOWS

9

THE NEW RULER

The new state, which had the trappings and nomenclature of the ancient Empire but was so unlike it in fact, was in the main quite readily accepted by the public. Indeed the nation, if this term may now be used, was definitely grateful for the prosperity which, the authorities assured it, lay just ahead. It is true that their optimism did not last very long. In 1871 76,224 Germans had emigrated. In 1872 the number had risen to 128,152, while in 1873 it reached a total of 220,902. It was only then that the figure once again began to drop.

Meanwhile Bismarck was encountering more difficulties in the new Germany than he anticipated, for there were many who had solid grounds for hatred—the dependants of the fallen German dynasties, particularly in Hanover, the hundred thousand Danes who had been incorporated in the Empire without being asked. There were the inhabitants of Alsace and Lorraine, amounting to several hundred thousand, and, as always, there were those two million Poles, though feeling was equally strong in old Bavaria which felt itself to be quite as badly treated as the latter. Among such people as these Bismarck encountered an outright rejection of all he had done, but there was also resistance where social conditions were particularly bad—among the newly-born industrial proletariat, for instance, and among the rural workers in the poorer parts of Silesia.

Among the latter, young Gerhart Hauptmann, the son of a well-to-do middle-class family, discovered a mood of downright nihilism. "The joy of victory, German unity, the intoxication of success . . . have here only created a quiet rage and a dark and determined hatred. Bismarck, Moltke and the Kaiser, it is said, do nothing for the poor. The Reichstag consists of a crowd of swindlers and idlers."* In that same Silesia, moreover, and all over East Elbia as a whole the black and white Prussian flag alone was shown and no one had any regard for the black, white and red banner of the Empire. The East Elbian conservatives mourned the death of Prussia, and did not realise the extent to which Bismarck's empire was nothing more than Prussia enlarged.

* Gerhart Hauptmann, *Das Abenteuer meiner Jugend* (1937), I, p. 474.

The head of this opposition—had not destiny happened to make him Emperor—might well have been William himself, for he was unable to find in the new Empire any of the things to which he had grown attached or any of the old traditions that he knew. He could not even reconcile himself to changes in the Court cere-monial. When the Crown Prince, speaking of his mother, said that the Empress had said this and that to him, his father would ask "When did you see the Queen?" When shown designs for the coronation robes, he pushed them aside saying that he "did not want to look like a priest of Baal". It irked him most grievously, so we are told by Princess Radziwill, "to find out that even only in form he had to share his authority with other monarchs (i.e., the other German princes) whom he secretly despised". But he had learnt to control himself in the school of ancient courtly tradition—and in this at least he was Bismarck's superior.

Meanwhile Bismarck was turning into something like a legen-dary figure, not only at home but also abroad, and the image of him which the world created for itself was formidable indeed—a giant of a man, whose eyes moved hither and thither with the menacing watchfulness of a bulldog, a huge head with a walrus moustache, and inside it a brain ready, like that of a crafty ele-phant, for every kind of devilry. The descendant of barbaric Junkers who until recently had been slave owners, a cold, cal-culating brute devoid of all human feeling, a man best pictured in a stone monument which showed him as a huge corporal of cuirassiers with the spike of his Pickelhaube reaching up towards the heavens. All the world, even that part of it which could neither read nor write, was familiar with this sinister picture, and Bismarck himself, since he was thus far better able to conceal the truth about himself, was quite anxious to give it permanence.

For between Otto Bismarck the man and his popular image there was no connection whatever save the name. He was indeed fairly tall, and broadly built, though he was by no means a giant, and had the odd habit, whenever he was in Berlin, of observing the world through an old-fashioned lorgnette with polygonal lenses. In the country he wore spectacles; he used to say that in the country there was more to see. In relation to his tall figure and his ever-increasing corpulence, his head did not seem unduly large, nor the brow particularly high, though it was well developed and there were wildly luxuriating eyebrows over his eyes. He had a small, snub nose whose distended nostrils suggested something of the eager curiosity of the born empiricist. The mouth, finely moulded, was largely invisible under the moustache. His voice was surprisingly high-pitched. In private conversation, Keudell tells us, it was "soft, in the baritone range, and agreeable". But when he was excited it could easily become shrill, though when he so desired he could impart to it a quality that was strangely soothing.

The general impression was one of robust health, though, as we have already seen, his nerves were a constant source of trouble. Fundamentally his physical constitution was excellent; considering the strain under which he consistently placed it, he would hardly have lived well into the eighties had it been otherwise. Subjectively, however, it was a very different story. He was continually complaining of being "unwell" and morbidly preoccupied with real and imaginary ailments. In 1846, when he was troubled with a cough, he believed that he had "a weak chest", the usual euphemism at that time for consumption. In 1872 he wrote to Lucius, "My oil is used up. I am at the end of my strength." To Roon, "My feelings have told me for months that I shall never again enjoy my old health. . . ." Actually he may well have spent half his days either physically or mentally in very poor condition. Johanna was in the habit of speaking of him, a little incongruously perhaps, as a "poor sick chicken".

Even so, he was healthy enough to develop the most appropriate methods of therapy out of his own inner consciousness. Instinctively he knew that he needed solitude and that it was essential for him from time to time to get right away from official business. There was always some connection between the complaints from which he suffered and the nature of his work. When Moltke in the winter of 1870 refused to bombard Paris, Bismarck was plagued by a pain in his foot which lasted several days. At Versailles, when he grew excited at meals, he afterwards had a vomiting fit. At one time these things were believed to be the results of his immoderate eating habits. Today they would most certainly be ascribed to psychological origins.

Not that Bismarck did not eat to excess, for he most certainly did. Ernst von Leyden relates that he was once summoned to Bismarck's house by Struck, Bismarck's personal physician, because Bismarck had allegedly had a stroke. Actually—both doctors are in agreement on the point—he had simply been overeating, having on the previous evening consumed eight hard-boiled eggs and a great quantity of ices.* For one so concerned about his health, he took very little care of himself. He never sought any protection against the wet, never used an umbrella or overshoes, and till extreme old age always travelled in an open carriage.

As he grew older, he cared less and less for the graces of life, and there are innumerable stories about his habit of constantly going about in a dressing-gown. Even in Frankfurt he received diplomats attired only in a black and yellow dressing-gown and a pair

* Treue, *Mit den Augen ihrer Leibärzte* (1955), p. 383.

of underpants, while in Versailles he spent the greater part of the day and night in this comfortable article of clothing. In Varzin his dressing-gown was light grey and violet, and indoors he never seems to have taken it off at all. The elegance which in Frankfurt he had still regarded as of some moment now completely ceased to interest him. As to Johanna, she never really got away from her puritanical pietistic background or her contempt of what she called "mere externals". Consequently, wherever the Bismarcks lived, their home showed no signs either of care or taste. Bismarck was in the habit of remarking that where there was fine furniture the food was bad.

In the woods of his new estate there was an inn much favoured at weekends by people coming from Hamburg. Bismarck had it converted into a dwelling-house but left the rotten wood-work standing and never dreamed of doing away with the petro-leum lighting or the numbers on the doors. Certainly the reason for this was not lack of funds, though he was in the habit of remarking that, having been a wealthy Junker, he was now a poor prince.

Actually, of course, this was nonsense. He was now an owner of a great deal of land and his industrial activities were steadily growing. His brandy distilleries and paper factories were multi-plying. He had entrusted the paper factories to a friend of Bleichröder, a certain Behrend from Köslin, who soon contrived to get the business of the imperial Post Office and of the railways; he was also an active exporter of pit props and cattle.

Was Bismarck a happy man? Holstein, who was able to observe him at close quarters for thirty years, writes: "I have hardly ever known a man who knew so little joy." In conversation "there was really never any undertone of pleasure. When there was merriment it was always at someone else's expense."

Yet he had so managed matters that what seemed to him the most valuable thing in life, independence, was certainly his, and he combined it with a degree of power enjoyed by none of his contemporaries. He had indeed succeeded in making his life conform to the lordly wish he had expressed as a young man. "I would make music which I think good or none at all."

There was hardly a single thing to which he had to pay regard. Among other things, he became increasingly careless of his duties towards the spirit and etiquette of a royal Court. When he received the Grand Cross of the Hohenzollern order with dia-monds, he told the whole world, "I'd rather have a good horse or a barrel of Rhine wine." When he was speaking to the Crown Prince, Princess Radziwill tells us, "his excessive arrogance was quite deliberate. He hardly answered the Prince when spoken

to" and "got him to say what he had to say two or three times
over. He really acted as though he were the master of his master-
to-be". When speaking to the Crown Princess Victoria, however,
who "treated him without particular friendliness but also without
coldness or stiffness", he looked as though he felt uncomfortable
and embarrassed. He bowed very deeply "playing nervously
with the long gloves of his cuirassier's uniform".

Before the wedding of Frederick Charles's daughter, the whole
world waited maliciously to see how Bismarck would get along
with the Torch dance, a sort of minuet which, according to ancient
tradition, the ministers of Brandenburg Prussia had to dance in
knee breeches, holding burning candles in their hands, at every
Hohenzollern wedding. This was a ceremony that, in the course
of time, had become faintly ridiculous. Bismarck solved the problem by absenting himself from the wedding on grounds of health.

The façade of Bismarck's empire was that of the parliamentary
state which was normal to the people of that time. The Imperial
Reichstag was elected for the first time in March 1871 on the
basis of what was then the freest electoral system in the world,
though, since the Reichstag's own powers were extremely limited,
this last was of very little account. The crucial fact was that, as
we have seen, the Reichstag had no means of controlling the
Chancellor and that there was thus no reason why Bismarck
should have been afraid of it.

The Bundesrat had a faint, though deceptive, resemblance to
a House of Lords, but, as in the case of the North German Bund,
it was directed by the very skilfully built-in superiority of Prussian
power, a state of affairs which constitutional lawyers referred to
as "legal hegemony". Although, therefore, the new Empire was
most certainly not a parliamentary régime in fact, Bismarck
attached great importance to the circumstance that it resembled
one. He had no wish to repeat the experience of anti-parliamentary government of 1862, during the so-called "time of conflict".
Not only did he wish to avoid a dissipation of his strength, he knew
how much remained to be done, if the Empire, as yet no more
than a loose concatenation bound together by diplomatic links,
was ever to become a living organism.

To achieve this he needed peace at home and a strong government party which would always assure him of the full support of
the Reichstag. The mighty National Liberal Party was just such
an instrument. It had 150 votes out of 382 and was the strongest
party in the Reichstag. Together with the closely-associated
German Progressive Party on its left, with its 45 votes, it had an
absolute majority. It rightly referred to itself as the party of the
Empire's foundation, and also as Bismarck's Party.

This last was perhaps a little odd, since it also claimed to be the heir of the Frankfurt National Assembly. But back in 1848 it had had no real power and had consequently been unable to create the new Empire that it desired. Now under pressure of war Bismarck, by the very plenitude of Prussian power, had given a certain support to the National Liberal ideology, thus giving some substance to the illusion that it had drawn him into its ranks and that the party had now triumphantly attained the goal which their fathers had failed to achieve.

Bismarck submitted to all this with courtesy and good grace, for he was certain that the party would confine itself to rhetoric and outward show, move on the surface of events, leave undisturbed all the deeper and more vital functions of the state, and only deal with those tasks that he entrusted to it. Indeed, he rode the party with a loose rein, confident that it had neither the courage nor the temper to take the bit between its teeth. But he had as little sympathy for National Liberal doctrine as he had for that of Garibaldi at the time of the Italian alliance. It remained for him the "nationality swindle", and the members of the National Liberal Party continued to be the privileged object of his jibes.

Of course, the National Liberal Party of 1871 had little in common with its fathers of 1848. The password of the latter had been Unity and Freedom, two things which are, in actual practice, rather difficult to combine. Their sons had solved the dilemma by declaring for Unity, that is to say for national power at the expense of the individual's right, based on Christian teaching, to the possession of his own soul. They still called themselves the party of culture and property. Unfortunately, the first of these attributes was tending to disappear, along with the world of the German classics and romantics, while the feeling for property and the desire for it grew steadily greater.

Meanwhile the spontaneous patriotism of the fathers had been turned into an artificial, forced and, finally, cruel nationalism which was the very negation of freedom, and the words of such a man as Karl von Rotteck, "I would rather have freedom without unity, than unity without freedom", would now have been accounted a blasphemy. So the great concept of freedom had shrivelled, until it meant no more than freedom for business enterprise.

At that moment, however, it certainly seemed as though there were good reasons why there should be free enterprise. The new Empire had created a vast new trading area, and since the opening up of that area was associated with the growth of power, there was an unlimited enthusiasm for both. In this respect at any rate

Bismarck's empire was something which was very much to the National Liberal taste.

Meanwhile, Bismarck's estrangement from the Conservative Party, his political home, was steadily growing. In particular, that brand of East Elbian nobility from which he was himself descended looked upon him as a son who had gone astray and from the very first would have nothing to do with his new political creation. Ruthless egoists though they were, the extreme nationalist spirit was utterly alien to them, and from the very beginning they held Bismarck's grave violations of the legitimist principle against him. They referred to him as Mirabeau, the prototype of the aristocrat who had made a bargain with the revolution and ruined his king.

Bismarck felt the enmity of the Conservatives more keenly than he admitted. He attributed their motives to envy, which was neither true nor particularly helpful. The first real breach, which he describes as a "very noisy" one, came in 1872, when he sought to transfer the inspection of schools from the local clergy, which had till then been responsible for it, to the state. The law was passed, but in the voting the Conservatives joined in opposition with the Hanoverians and Poles. He had already had angry passages with his old friend Gerlach, and now had him prosecuted for "insulting the Imperial Chancellor". Gerlach, who was president of one of the highest courts in Prussia, resigned his office; his resignation was accepted and, under pressure from Bismarck, not a word of thanks was said to him by the Emperor—this after sixty years of service.

Yet despite the enmity that was growing up between himself and a very powerful group, he knew it to be the enmity of men to whom he was no longer bound by any strong spiritual tie. Indeed, it is eloquent of his assessment of the East Elbian Junker's character that, while in Versailles, he quite openly discussed the question whether the Junker type could not be loosened up and made easier to get on with through marriages with Jews. Where such marriages had already taken place, the results, he said, "were not at all bad". Rather than have Jewish men marrying into Junker families, it might be best if one "brought together a Christian stallion of German breed with a Jewish mare. There is no such thing as an evil race, and I really don't know what advice I might one day give my sons".

There is a marked change here, one might remark in passing, from the attitudes of his youth, when he had been susceptible to anti-Jewish prejudice and had, in the Landtag, spoken against the complete civil emancipation of the Jews. "I am quite prepared," he said on that occasion, "to grant all rights to the Jews, save that of holding high office in a Christian state." How completely he had changed in this respect is shown by the number of Jews whom he had put at the head of departments. He preferred to employ Jews as his lawyers and doctors, and we have already seen to what extent he depended on his banker Bleichröder. The Jews in Germany were, for him, just another racial group like the Hessians or the Pomeranians, save only that they added to the mingling of races "a certain *mousseux*".

How deep this enmity between Bismarck and the Conservatives had gone was shown when Bismarck altered the constitution of the Prussian administered districts, according to the wish of the Liberals, in such a fashion that the great landowners lost their local police powers. Here the Prussian Upper House, the strongest citadel of the Junkers, was most determined in its opposition, opposition which Bismarck could only overcome by getting William to pack the Upper House with twenty-five new members. This was a step which the King, himself a dyed-in-the-wool Conservative, took with very ill-grace.

The fury of the victims was boundless, yet not all of them were to prove irreconcilable. For just as a group had broken off leftwards from the Liberals, so it was with the Conservatives. This splinter group, originally an offspring of the Free Conservatives of the North German Reichstag, called itself German Reichs Party, and here a very important part was beginning to be played by those Silesian aristocrats who owned mineral deposits. The fact is that the value of these deposits was only now becoming apparent, and the men in question were tending to become large-scale entrepreneurs. They were thus beginning to realise that they had much more in common with the industrialists of the West than with the poor, unenterprising Junkers, say, of Brandenburg.

Many members of this nobility, which had been here since the Austrian period and so was Catholic, had, of course, joined the newly-formed Centre Party. This was a somewhat novel organisation which had come into being when it became apparent in the winter of 1870 that the Catholics, who counted for 52 per cent of the population in the old German Bund, now only represented 37 per cent of Bismarck's new Empire. There had in recent months been all too many incautious remarks in the Press and elsewhere which represented the war as a victory of a Protestant Empire over Catholicism, and though the new party had no intention of opposing the Empire as such, it sought to afford protection to its Catholic and other minorities. Thus having no clear economic or even denominational basis, it became the gathering-point of all those who considered themselves to have been swept aside by Bismarck's triumphal progress.

The party contained aristocratic, petty bourgeois, and working-class elements, and even a Protestant like Gerlach was able to join it. Within a year it was the second most numerous party in the Reichstag, which was not surprising. Those who had lost their anchorage in the Christian Churches, sought to find a new one in their idolatry of the state; either they worshipped the ideal state of the Socialists, or Bismarck's National State. Those, however—and they were many—to whom neither of these alternatives appealed found a refuge in the Centre Party, which under the unimpeachable motto "*Justitia Fundamentum regnorum*" couched its programme in very general terms.

Bismarck's instinct caused him to look on the new party with disfavour, and from the start he watched it with suspicious eyes. The programme angered him largely for personal reasons, because the first signature was that of Savigny, who as a Prussian diplomat had been his closest associate up to 1866. The second signature was that of Windthorst, who had been the Royal Hanoverian Minister of Justice, a dwarflike figure of astonishing ugliness, but a man who, nevertheless, was a rare combination of fidelity and skill, a tough and courageous fighter. Bismarck had every ground for fearing him. There can be no doubt that he was apprehensive about the new party, precisely because, like himself, it was committed to no clear, mundane principles and consequently was incalculable. It was not yet actually his opponent, but it could become that from one day to the next.

The parties who could be relied on always and in any circumstances to oppose Bismarck, were only feebly represented in the Reichstag and were thus unworthy of any serious consideration. They consisted of the Hanoverian delegates, the Danes from Northern Schleswig, who were still expecting that the plebiscite which had been promised them in the Peace of Prague would become a fact. Then there were the Poles, who immediately refused to take part in the debate on the address in the Reichstag, since it was only "a demonstration of specifically German feelings and was concerned with specifically German interests". In the Second Reichstag of 1874 they were joined by fifteen Alsatian autonomists, whose first utterance was a protest against the annexation of their country.

The strongest minority in the Reichstag owed its origin not to political but to economic considerations. This was the Social Democratic Party. As far back as 1870, in the last elections of the North German Bund, the Socialists had polled 3.3 per cent of all votes, and in the First Reichstag they had only a single representative, Bebel, the turner. Now in the first year of the Empire wages of industrial workers rose, but not to a point that would have turned their recipients into satisfied citizens. On the contrary, the more wealth increased, thanks to the opportunities offered by the new dispensation, the more marked became the division between the workers and the rest of the nation. The workers rejected Bismarck's state as a prison and a workhouse, administered by the bourgeoisie and the nobility. The elections to the Second Reichstag brought them as many as 340,000 votes and nine new members.

Bismarck's work in parliament was therefore not too difficult. He could always be certain of a majority, and the permanent opposition was very small. There were, of course, a number of uncommitted parties, but these usually backed him in the end. What really mattered now was the consolidation of the Empire. Bismarck saw that the problems involved here were essentially organisational and economic. He gladly left these to the National Liberals, who were exceptionally well qualified to deal with them, and it was this that caused him to treat them more or less as a government party. He kept their leaders informed of his plans, in accordance with normal parliamentary procedure, and, wherever possible, sought to make legislation conform to their wishes. In the end, however, he made his own decisions and looked to them to give these their unconditional support which, in point of fact, after a great deal of twisting and turning, they never actually refused. Both believed that they needed each other, but for all that they remained strangers, though their feelings in this respect rarely led to more than the soft and courteous expression of a doubt. It was not often that there was actual anger in their words.

Now and then, when his mood was more than usually light-hearted, he dangled before the National Liberals the enticing picture of a ministerial position, as though for all the world he was working a real parliamentary system. "I am ready to wager, Herr Doktor," he once said to the Deputy, Lasker, "that we'll yet be colleagues," which brought forth the ready reply, "I can't imagine that Durchlaucht intends to become a lawyer." He can, of course, never seriously have contemplated making ministers of parliamentarians who brought nothing with them but the confidence of some local majority, or have preferred men such as these to those sustained by the confidence of the Emperor who belonged to the whole people.

On one occasion, years later, he was talking to Bennigsen, who had stood by him so staunchly in the Luxemburg affair, about the possibility of a ministerial appointment, although he must have known that such an appointment would never be confirmed by William I. Bennigsen misunderstood the situation and believed that Bismarck had at last realised the necessity for having a genuine parliament, and therefore made it a condition that there should be a number of other National Liberal appointments in addition to his own. Bismarck, however, was only interested in Bennigsen as an individual, and the matter was dropped.

Perhaps in any case Bismarck's policy was not far wrong, for if appearances are anything to go by, there was, in the Germany of that day, neither among the National Liberals nor among the members of any other party, an élite capable of conducting the already highly-complicated affairs of this newly-created state. The authoritarian rule which Bismarck exercised was not only made fairly easy for him by circumstances, it was the only form of rule that in those circumstances was really workable at all.

For all that, he showed a large measure of tolerance to his colleagues. Economic affairs did not interest him in the least, and he left them wholly in the hands of Delbrück. When the new coinage was being debated in the Reichstag, he went out riding, because, he said, he understood nothing whatever of the subject. It was the same with educational matters. He did not feel that they touched any interest of state, and thought that in this field too he could give the National Liberals their heads. Thus though the law for school inspection by laymen was personally distasteful to him, he was ready to make this concession to Liberal anti-clericalism.

We shall therefore not be far off the mark if we think of this period of German history as a Liberal era under authoritarian guidance, and speak of a balance of Liberal and authoritarian principles. Thanks to the reasonably smooth working of the government, the Empire was able fairly rapidly to set up adequate machinery and to put flesh on its bones. Bismarck had started off with only two Imperial offices, his own and that of Foreign Affairs. Soon, however, a number of other departments were called into being, particularly in relation to business and transport, each under its own State Secretary. These last, however, were the Chancellor's subordinates and not, like the Ministers of Prussia, his colleagues.

It looked as though things would go on the way they were going for a long time. However, peace was disturbed much sooner than anyone anticipated, and just in one of those spheres in which Bismarck thought he could allow Liberalism a free hand. For there soon began that strange spectacle that seems as though it were somehow suspended midway between the spiritual and material world. The spectacle which historiographers have cursed with the singularly inappropriate name of Kulturkampf.

10

FICKLE FORTUNE

Neither the Syllabus Errorum of 1864 nor the Proclamation in 1870 of the Doctrine of Papal Infallibility did much to disturb the even tenor of Bismarck's mind. He had, of course, at that time other things to think about. Doubtless, also, the fact that he himself had largely been the cause of the Pope's becoming a prisoner in the Vatican (it was, after all, the war with France that had brought about the withdrawal of the French garrison from Rome), inclined him charitably towards the victim of that calamity.

Despite the fact that in Bismarck's recent wars papal sympathies had been markedly on the side of his enemies, he was almost touchingly eager to bring aid and comfort to the fallen. If the Pope found certain inconveniences in his present place of residence, he would, he let it be understood, be delighted to have him settle, say, in Fulda or Cologne. This might mean, he subsequently conceded to some of his anxious compatriots, that a number of Germans would turn Catholic, but what would that matter so long as they remained Christian? And in any case he had no intention of becoming a Catholic himself.

However, the Church of Rome was one thing, the Centre Party quite another, for the Centre Party, as we have seen, always made him vaguely uneasy. Since he could never tell exactly what it was up to, it was natural for him to assume that what it was up to was in some way reprehensible. Could it perhaps really be that it was what its name represented it to be, a centre or rallying point for all those whom Bismarck had offended, and that its functions were to present the bill on behalf of those at whose expense the Greater Prussian Empire had been created?

Everything that the party did aroused his suspicion. It had but to make a request—and some of its requests, such as the one that the Prussian constitution's guarantee of civil rights should be taken over by the Empire, were surely miracles of sweet reasonableness—for that request to be rejected out of hand. So powerful an irritant was the party's mere existence that it warped Bismarck's judgment, causing him on one occasion to remark that the party's policies were viewed with disfavour by the Vatican itself, an observation which, no doubt, he considered unlikely to draw comment from the Holy See, as the plight of the Papacy might at any time cause the Pope to appeal for his aid. But in this he was mistaken, for the Vatican reacted with disturbing speed, declaring that it had no intention of allowing itself to be used as a weapon against the Centre Party.

The late summer of 1871 was disastrous for Bismarck, his policies caused both Centre Party and Vatican to form a single solid front against him. His position was like that of a general whose probing attack reveals his opponents to be in possession of vast, unsuspected reserves which, if he is not to beat an ignominious retreat, he now finds himself compelled to engage. In many ways he felt this new war resembled that which he had waged against France a year before, a war which he felt he had never desired to wage but which, through force of circumstances, he had been compelled to fight; as on that previous occasion, he threw himself into the battle with ruthless determination.

Bismarck's official Press now declared all-out war against the Centre Party, adding that Bismarck would go over to the offensive not only on the home front, but against enemies outside the country. Everyone grasped the meaning of that. On July 8th, the "Catholic section" of the Prussian "Kultusministerium", the section which had been created under Frederick William IV and whose duty it was to safeguard the special interests of Prussian Catholics, was dissolved. In August Bismarck met Beust in Gastein and expounded his further plan of campaign. There was no question of limiting his attack to the Centre Party, he was going to develop it against the Church itself.

There now followed—like the successive crashes of a thunderstorm—laws, orders, regulations of the most varying kind. For the most part Bismarck's anti-Catholic legislation was confined to Prussia and passed by the Prussian legislature, but Prussia was so much the predominant element in the new Germany that the effect was shattering.

The state increasingly usurped the supervision of clerical life. In March 1872 the clergy were barred from the supervision of schools. Regular priests were forbidden to give any kind of instruction. At length came the notorious "May Laws". Among other things, these compelled the clergy to sit for a state examination in science before accepting any clerical appointment. They also severely restricted the Church's disciplinary powers. Then came the so-called "pulpit paragraph" which made it a criminal offence "to misuse the pulpit in such a manner as to endanger public order".

Various other measures were introduced. Civil marriage was made compulsory. The Jesuits were suspended and ultimately expelled from Prussia. The unauthorised exercise of clerical office, i.e. the conducting of divine worship by a priest who had been suspended, became punishable by loss of citizenship and even by expulsion. It was only in the case of this particularly illiberal piece of legislation that the left wing of the Liberals withheld its support.

The Church, attacked along a broad front, defended herself by passive resistance. In the Vatican Council the German bishops had unanimously rejected the Dogma of Infallibility, but after the resolution had been passed, they accepted it, together with all their clergy. Being now wholly of one mind with the Sovereign Pontiff, they refused to co-operate in the execution of the various laws and accepted, with patience, the many penalties with which the power of the state now visited them—the expulsion of religious orders, the suspension of pastors and bishops and the sentencing of the latter to periods of imprisonment.

At length, in 1873, the Pope sought to approach the Emperor, of whom it was generally known that, like the old Prussian Conservatives, he thoroughly disliked this battle with the Church. Pope Pius was, however, not altogether fortunate in the wording of his appeal, saying as he did in one passage, "Everyone who receives baptism belongs in a certain measure to the Pope." Bismarck had no difficulty in appealing to the Protestant pride of his old master and getting him to reply, "The Evangelical faith which, as Your Holiness is aware, like my ancestors and the majority of my subjects, I myself profess, does not permit us to accept any other mediator in our relations with God, than Our Lord Jesus Christ"—an utterance which earned him a veritable storm of applause from all over Germany.

Yet, strange to say, the rapid success which usually had come to Bismarck in his wars deserted him on this occasion. The campaign dragged on from year to year. Churches stood empty because numerous priests were in prison; over wide areas church bells were silent; baptisms were continued and marriages were solemnised, though by priests whom either the state or the Church refused to recognise. The parish registers, the only record of their kind at that time, fell into hopeless confusion. Soon nearly all the bishoprics in Prussia, nine out of the twelve, lacked the presence of a bishop. From 1875 onwards, bishops of whom the state disapproved were deprived of the allowances which it normally made them. But all that happened was that they turned to voluntary gifts; the embittered fidelity of lay-folk strengthened them in their resistance.

Today it is clear that Bismarck's defeat was inevitable, for he did not know his opponent. What it meant to be a Catholic, at least, what it meant to be a Catholic worthy of the name, was something into which Bismarck had never troubled to enquire and of which he was, therefore, ignorant. Nor did he realise that, for the Catholics, certain matters lie wholly out of the sphere of discussion. It was this ignorance that lost him the battle, and one can't help asking what it was that induced him to commit himself to it with such frantic intensity.

Other heads of state, who were no more prudent than he, had contented themselves with a formal protest against the offending dogma, if, indeed, they did not ignore it altogether. Why did the equanimity with which Bismarck had at first regarded it give way to such frantic opposition? The Empress Augusta noted the sharpness of this transition when she wrote, in March 1872, to her husband that Bismarck, who had always treated ecclesiastical matters "with great moderation", was now showing a "morbid sensitivity about them".

We may, perhaps, discover the clue to the mystery if we remember the vacillating feelings with which, between 1866 and 1870, Bismarck regarded his plan for a Greater Prussia, and how hesitantly and with what measure of indecision he regarded the union of South Germany with the North German Bund—right up to the moment when he was suddenly confronted with the necessity of creating a new political organism overnight.

Now, no doubt, he was tortured by the feeling that it was to himself alone that the Centre Party owed its existence. If the line of the Main still divided North from South Germany, the closed ranks of Protestantism in the North German Bund would not have been disturbed by its Catholic minority, and had he not granted the Empire universal suffrage, it would have been impossible for such parties as the Centre to come into being at all. Even before the Empire was created, he had already given expression to such misgivings. Perhaps he now realised that they were far from groundless, and that it was for his own mistakes that he was now being punished. But what was done was done, and he had made it a rule never to admit an error, and if he had been guilty of one, to use all means that would help to prevent it from being discovered. This may, indeed, be one of the reasons why he now carried the war so passionately into the enemy's camp.

Another possible explanation may, perhaps, be found in his anxiety, on this as on other occasions, to bring the war to a conclusion as quickly as possible. He had special reasons for this. For the rift, which was now beginning to divide the new Empire into two, made utter nonsense of the official legend that the people had longed for the unity which, through Bismarck, it had obtained. It was thus not the state which Bismarck felt to be imperilled by the Pope, but the story of its origin.

How deep was the split, how ungovernable were the passions, was made plain to him when, on July 13, 1874, he was driving through the streets of Kissingen in an open carriage. A shot was fired at him and a bullet grazed his cheek and slightly wounded him in the hand. The would-be assassin was a young cooper's apprentice named Kullmann. Like millions of Catholics, he believed that Bismarck was threatening the existence of the Church. Needless to say, he acted on his own and had no accomplices. For all that, in December of that year Bismarck made the accusation in the Reichstag that Kullmann was "hanging on to the skirts of the Centre Party" and that they would never "be able to shake this murderer loose". It was, of course, a monstrous accusation, but he spoke—or seemed to speak—with such fiery indignation, although the incident was now five months old, that nobody dared question his sincerity.

Even so, it was during this period that his strong common sense gradually asserted itself against his passions and made him realise that his battle with the Church was leading him up a *cul-de-sac* from which there was no escape. Yet, the restoration of peace was not easy, for Pope Pius proved somewhat obdurate. It was only after his death, in 1878, and the succession of the wise Leo XIII, that even secret negotiations became possible, and these duly took place in Kissingen between Bismarck and the Papal Nuncio Masella. Though there was no full meeting of minds, the parties agreed to a more civilized and considerate form of belligerence. However, the conflict continued through the years, a creeping sickness in the life of the German body politic.

Bismarck, in order to divert public attention, adopted an air of disinterestedness. When asked if he would be attending a session of the Landtag in which the struggle with the Church was on the agenda, he answered in a bored tone "Why should I? The more the thing is left open, the better. They will never put an end to the quarrel, for since the days of Chalchas there have, in all ages and among all peoples, been men for whom the proposition was axiomatic that they knew the will of God better than anybody else."

Very cautiously and with as little noise as possible, the great guns were dismantled as the years went by. In the end, all that remained after the great commotion had subsided was civil marriage, the state inspection of schools and the state's right to make the holding of ecclesiastical office dependent on confirmation by itself. What then had Bismarck achieved? The answer must surely be "very little". Falk, who was Bismarck's nominee at the "Kultusministerium", had dreamed that he would banish the Catholic faith from the universities, but that faith had never grown surer of itself, and had increased its confidence in its highly distinctive culture and in the social unity of all that professed it. Moreover, after the elections of 1881, the Centre Party had emerged as the strongest party in the Reichstag. As against this, Protestantism had been weakened by a grave split—between the orthodox wing, which opposed Bismarck in his Kulturkampf on grounds of principle, and its left wing, which supported him.

The Kulturkampf was the first of the great actions undertaken by Bismarck that completely failed. He had used in the pursuit of his object the means which so far had always proved successful. He had used those means without compunction, even as he had used them to defeat the majority in the Prussian Landtag, to defeat the German Bund and the Hapsburg and French Empires. This time, however, Fortune, which had so far been so favourable to him, had deserted him.

While the struggle with the Church was gradually coming to an end, Bismarck was caught up in yet another venture, which he conducted after the manner of a foreign war, despite the fact that the issue was a domestic one: for it was the fight with the Social Democrats.

The success of the Social Democratic movement in Germany began immediately after the foundation of the Empire and grew so rapidly that its own leaders were astonished. In 1864, under the powerful influence of Marx, the International Workers Association, the "First International", had been founded in London. In 1869 a German branch had established its independence at a congress in Eisenach. In 1866, at the Congress of Gotha, the last remnants of Lasalle's nationally organised following had capitulated before the "Men of Eisenach", so that from now on there was only one socialist party in Germany. In 1876 it already had twenty-four newspapers. In the Reichstag elections, one year later, it polled 480,000 votes.

Bismarck was by no means an enemy of socialism as such; some of his assistants had had a socialist past and this fact was common knowledge to all. This applied especially to Bucher, who remained till the very end his closest confidant. It is also true of such a man as August Brass, whom he made the Editor-in-Chief of the official *Norddeutsche Allgemeine Zeitung*. In 1865 he had already declared that "the Kings of Prussia have never, by preference, been kings of the rich". It was in that same year that he invited Marx, through Bucher, to become a contributor to the

Preussischer Staatsanzeiger. During the days of the Paris Commune he was quite prepared to communicate with the then War Minister, Cluseret.

For the people who had now begun to work in the factories were, to Bismarck, much the same as the agricultural workers with whom, in the main, he had always got along very well. He was, indeed, much more ready to take their part than that of the bourgeoisie, who seemed to have them at their mercy and to whom he was thoroughly alien in spirit. By and large the sympathies of the old-fashioned type of Junker were much more commonly with the workers than with the employers.

But Marx had declared war on the existing social order and sworn to destroy it, and it was only twenty years before Bismarck's birth that the French Revolution had reached its climax and the aristocrats of Europe had not yet forgotten its wholesale murders. It was, therefore, not unnatural that Bismarck should already have felt himself to be under attack and looked round for a means of defence. He did not tend to prejudge on grounds of principle, nor cultivate enmities on ideological grounds, but he was a remorseless enemy of anything or anyone by whom he felt himself to be personally menaced.

During the course of the years, Bismarck had on more than one occasion endeavoured to halt the progress of the socialists by legislation. But his plans were so unconvincing and so vague in expression, that the liberals did not find it difficult to reject them on ideological grounds. Bismarck withdrew them, but not without remarking in earnest tones that the socialist danger was "one of the worms that never die".

A few weeks after he had said these words, it so happened that a young tinker named Hödel fired some shots at the old Emperor's carriage, while the latter was driving down Unter den Linden. The bullets went over the Emperor's head and he was quite unaware of what had happened till his footman jumped from the box and seized the assailant. Bismarck, who was in Varzin at the time, immediately saw the possibilities that the situation offered. He telegraphed that same evening to State Secretary von Bülow whether a new Bill against the Socialists could not be introduced on the strength of the attempted assassination and, indeed, within a week the draft of such a Bill was ready. It was very simple in its terms, so simple, in fact, that the Reichstag's jurists found ample opportunity to complicate it, confuse the issue and so secure its ultimate rejection. Bismarck accepted the new defeat in silence, but it was the kind of silence that, with Bismarck, could portend more danger than an open outburst of rage—as was soon to be made plain.

A few weeks later, while the Emperor was again driving down Unter den Linden in an open carriage, a shotgun was discharged at him and he was struck by thirty of the pellets, and might well have died of his wounds. The assailant was a certain Dr. Nobiling, an intellectual in reduced circumstances, who had fired his weapon from a window, and then inflicted wounds on himself before he could be arrested. He died, and the full circumstances of the crime remained a mystery. However, mystery or otherwise, the whole affair was obviously much more serious than the futile attempt of Hödel.

Bismarck was in Friedrichsruh when the news was brought to him by Tiedemann, the Head of the Imperial Chancellery, and Tiedemann has left us an account of the scene. He tells how Bismarck came slowly towards him through the dusk that was settling down on the fields, with his gigantic Danes gambolling around him; he was obviously not anticipating the kind of message that Tiedemann brought. When he heard what had happened, he stuck his heavy oak stick with all his force into the ground, and cried out, "Then we'll dissolve the Reichstag." He said this in a joyous and triumphant tone without even asking who it was that had made the attempt on the Emperor's life, or, for that matter, enquiring about his condition.

Bismarck's feelings on this occasion must have been very similar to those experienced on that other summer evening in Berlin, when Abeken's telegram arrived from Ems and had similarly rescued him from a desperate situation. On that occasion, as now, he had been wrestling for days with his problems, unable to find a solution, and now, as previously, fate had come to his aid in a manner that nobody could have foreseen. In an instant, all the implications of the situation stood clear before him. Now he no longer needed the Reichstag, whose majorities, everlastingly stumbling over ideological tripwires, had twice refused to turn his anti-socialist Bills into law. And now they were not to be given an opportunity of rehabilitating themselves by having another such Bill placed before them. Now Bismarck could turn to the electors himself, declare his intention of protecting the nation's heroes from the hands of assassins, and obtain a majority which this time would do his will.

For he was sick and tired of his dependence on the National Liberals who were already beginning to presume on that dependence and were making no secret of the fact that they looked forward to the day when they would share his power—in Bismarck's eyes the unforgivable sin. It is said—and the story need not necessarily be apocryphal—that shortly after these events he remarked to some intimates, "And now we've got the scoundrels,"

and when somebody then remarked, "I suppose Your Serene
Highness means the Social Democrats," he burst out with the
truth, "No, the National Liberals."

To secure the dissolution of the Reichstag, however, was by no
means easy. The Crown Prince, as his wounded father's representative, at first refused to sign the necessary authority. He said
he had no desire to make use of the sympathies which his subjects
had for the Emperor in order to secure the adoption of measures
which, as he knew, went contrary to their feelings. At last,
however, Bismarck held the order for the dissolution in his
hands and could communicate it to the Reichstag; one of his
greatest hours had come.

Bismarck got his majority. The liberals lost forty seats while
the two conservative parties won thirty-seven. The passage
of Bismarck's socialist law, which forbade all socialist organisations and their propaganda, was assured.

Outwardly, Bismarck achieved his object. The party disappeared from the soil of Germany. The choral societies, the
skittle circles and smoker clubs, in which it proposed to ensure its
continuance, proved quite insufficient for the purpose. Nevertheless, the subterranean apparatus of the party continued to
function from abroad, and very effectively at that. Sentences of
imprisonment, for which the new law provided a one-year
maximum, were imposed on fifteen hundred people. Much
larger numbers, however, lost their livelihood as a result of the
law. Many decent people, whose only desire was to better their
miserable economic position, had the ground cut from under their
feet, while the door was open to that most contemptible of
creatures, the informer. But the party lived on, and when in
1890—after Bismarck had left the political scene—the socialist
law lapsed, the number of votes given to the proscribed party had
risen from 437,000 to 1,427,000.

But the natural field for the exercise of Bismarck's genius was
that of foreign affairs, and the Prussian guns in front of Paris had
hardly fallen silent before he formed a new resolve. It was that
they were never again to speak at his command. From now on,
the peace of a quiet afternoon was to reign undisturbed over
Europe. For Bismarck realised, with a clarity that was shared by
none of his contemporaries, that despite his staggering success in
founding the Empire, it would need a long period of meticul-
ously careful handling before it had ripened into an organism
capable of survival. Never once did he fall into the popular error
that the mere joining together, under the leadership of Prussia,
which had as yet only hesitantly been accorded great power

status, of a couple of dozen small and medium-sized states (all
with a very precarious economic basis) was sufficient to call a
world power into being.

The very magnitude of his success—and nobody had expected it
to be as great as it was—made things difficult for him. His aim,
which he had slowly but steadily pursued, had been to make
Prussia the paramount power in Germany. Instead of this,
Germany had become the paramount power in Europe. France
and Austria had been weakened by their recent defeats, while
Russia and Britain had their energies absorbed in colonial enterprises, so that the new Germany had suddenly become the only
Continental power fully capable of decisive action.

At the same time, of all the great powers it was the most
imperilled. Due to its geographical position, it could either be
blockaded or attacked on all sides, whereas France, Russia and
Britain lived, as it were, with only their heads in Europe, while
their colonial bodies reached out into every continent—Russia's
into Asia, that of France into Africa, that of Britain into every
part of the globe. Germany simply did not fit into this circle of
giants, any more than Austria or Italy, a fact which later was to
produce a natural community of interest between these three states.

The fact is, that Bismarck's empire offended against geography.
"Our geographical position," he had written back in 1870 to
Bernstorff, "is different from that of any other Continental power."
How he could protect his creation against such malice of circum-
stance was a problem that exercised his mind up to his dying day.

He saw that Germany was in no danger as long as there was
peace in Europe, but that in any war the new great power,
because of its central position, would be compelled to take sides
and risk the championship title which it had so recently and so
laboriously acquired. Therefore, little as this might appeal to the
fire-eaters at home, he wanted peace above all things—peace at
almost any price. And that was why, again and again, he showed
his readiness for compromise. Some words, which towards the
end of his career occurred in a memorandum drawn up for
Frederick III, are very eloquent in this connection. He said that
the chief aim of his foreign policy was always "to remove all
grounds for dissatisfaction before it was too late, so long as this
was consistent with honour".

Not that he was not on occasions pleased to see tensions growing
up between other powers, or even to help produce them. Thus, in
1878, he could write to the Crown Prince, "It would be a triumph
for our statecraft if we succeeded in keeping the oriental sore open
and so prevented any unity among the other great powers; this
would ensure peace for ourselves."

Briefly stated, his dilemma was this. The Empire needed peace as it needed its daily bread, but had not the power to enforce it by simple decree. If, therefore, war became inevitable, he was determined that it should not lead to a two-front war, the catastrophic nature of which, for Germany, was quite clear to him. He could best avoid the contingency of a two-front or any other war by having allies among his neighbouring powers. "Endeavour," he said, "always to be one of three so long as the world is ruled by the unstable balance of five great powers,"* and this throughout was the key to his strategy.

Bismarck's diplomacy was therefore the diplomacy of alliances, though that word must be somewhat loosely interpreted in this connection. As far back as August 1871 he had made his views plain in a report to the King. "Formal contractual arrangements, whether they are public or kept secret, have the disadvantage that they disquiet other countries and at home provide ample occasion for undesirable party manoeuvring." (*Parteiumtrieben.*) That is why his alliances rarely got to the stage where they became solemnly sealed parchment documents. They were mostly understandings, declarations of intention, ententes, gentlemen's agreements, and so on. For alliances now no longer came into being, as did the Holy Alliance, as the result of some permanent community of conviction, but were occasioned by a transient community of changing interests and the purely practical wish not to be alone in a moment of peril.

Objectively regarded, Bismarck's achievement is considerable, and if for decades Europeans were able to enjoy a sensible way of life, it is to Bismarck that a great deal of the credit is due. For this we can be duly grateful, but at the same time we must see the thing in proper perspective. To turn Bismarck on this account, as some seem inclined to do, into a great architect and guarantor of European peace, is to falsify and distort the man's whole character, for he most certainly did not engage in his quest for the sake of Europe, which for him was never more than a geographical expression. He never went back on his angry marginal comment, "*Qui parle Europe a tort.*" The interests he pursued were those of Prussia, whether in its original or later in its imperial form, and the reason for his pursuit of peace is a very simple one. It was that no war could now any longer be conceived from which his state stood to gain, while every war must of necessity threaten it with annihilation.

Bismarck's system of alliances served his purpose very well. The reason is that their effect was a double one. Not only did they enhance German security by strengthening her means of

* Windelband, *Bismarck und die europäischen Grossmächte* (1942), p. 92.

defence, but by engendering the sense of security of others, they further diminished the likelihood of war itself. In this respect the whole system was like the net beneath a tight-rope walker. This too is intended not so much to save the performer's life as to give him that sense of security which ensures that the accident whose effects the net is intended to mitigate does not occur at all. For the more a tight-rope walker feels insecure the more accident prone he is liable to be, and by the same token the more a state feels insecure, the greater the temptation to achieve security by force.

It goes without saying that in this essentially pacific policy military force had its place and function. Bismarck had little love for the military way of life as such. But it did not for a moment enter his mind to abandon the oldest and most primitive means of exercising power, for without power Germany would have found no allies. Bismarck, actuated by this consideration, had in 1874 caused the Reichstag to fix the peace-time strength of the Army at one per cent of the population, which in those days meant about 400,000 men. After seven years it was to be determined afresh and for this reason the law bore the name "Septennat". It was not his fault, but rather the dark destiny of Germany itself, that the pressure of accumulated military power at the centre of the Continent produced a counter pressure at its periphery; Germany's neighbours answered her preparedness by an increase in their armaments, so that in the end Europe became a single great armed camp, waiting for the orders to march.

The greatest obstacle to the normalisation of the Concert of Europe was presented by France, which was in an exceptionally anomalous position. Immune as he was to every form of jingoist claptrap, Bismarck would gladly have entered into close relations with the defeated party as soon as the war was over, and would have welcomed a relationship such as had subsisted between Napoleon and himself.

But France had suffered something more than the kind of reverse which every country experiences sooner or later. That Germany had taken the place of France as the dominant power of Europe was something to which France could have grown accustomed, but that this change had as it were been symbolised by the annexation of the two eastern provinces was regarded by her as an operation on her living body. Co-operation with any European peace system that guaranteed the permanence of this arrangement was therefore out of the question. And because she knew that, under the prevailing power relationships, any attempt to obtain redress by force of arms would be tantamount to suicide, she sought to limit her relationships with her late enemy and, as far as possible, to forget that Germany existed at all.

This suited Bismarck very well. The only question was whether France's isolation could be made permanent, and it was with this agonising question that he never ceased to wrestle. There were times when he seemed ready for some kind of accommodation. On other occasions, he would lose all patience and furiously speak of the "womanish character" of the French, shrug his shoulders and try to reconcile himself to the fact that he had to keep them permanently under the threat of superior force. In 1872 he said to the French ambassador: "You will pay the first two billions, but by 1874, if you're able to do so, you'll be fighting us again." And three years later to Lucius he remarked, "The French are the Chinamen of Europe. We need really not speculate about their future aims and the means they will use to effect them. They will simply fall upon us the moment they think they are strong enough to do so."

To spare French sensibilities, Bismarck refrained from annexing Alsace and Lorraine to Prussia, but by giving the territory the name of the Reichsland "Alsace-Lorraine", gave it the appearance of enjoying something like an independent status within the framework of the confederation. Even so, one third of the one and a half million inhabitants continued to wish to be part of France and six hundred thousand of them emigrated. At first Bismarck spoke before the Reichstag quite hopefully of the "German hearts of the Alsatians" which would possibly be won more quickly than was generally assumed. But the rest of the world did not share this view and grew increasingly sceptical of the permanence of the arrangement.

Before the last of the German garrisons had left, Thiers, for whom Bismarck had much sympathy, had lost the presidency and been succeeded by Marshal MacMahon, a pious Catholic, a monarchist, and a tough, proud veteran, of the kind that every country seems to produce. Bismarck did not welcome the appointment, for he saw in it the replacement of a "weak, civilian anti-clerical" France by one that was "stronger, military, ultramontane and a potentially useful ally" to the enemies of Germany. Added to this, there was his dislike of officers as such, and when at a time in which he himself was in the midst of the Kulturkampf he had to observe how vast crowds of deputies, officers and officials made pilgrimages to Our Lady of Chartres to thank her for the election of the Marshal, this did not seem a very happy omen.

In actual fact, however, there was no change under MacMahon in Franco-German relations. As before, France icily kept herself to herself, and in Paris all the social gatherings were avoided in which there was a chance of meeting Bismarck's diplomats.

Indeed, the change of government in France is noteworthy chiefly because it produced rather disturbing results for Bismarck of a purely personal kind.

Count Arnim, the German ambassador in Paris, believed that a French return to monarchy was in Germany's interests. In so far as Napoleon III was the only likely candidate, Bismarck and Arnim were in agreement. In January 1873, however, Napoleon died in England under the surgeon's knife, and all Bonapartist schemes had to be deferred till the heir of the dynasty reached man's estate. This changed the picture, for Arnim now favoured a Bourbon restoration, and since he had excellent relations with the German Court, particularly with the Empress, he sought to use that influence in support of the scheme, which Bismarck violently opposed.

There was, however, more behind the quarrel than an academic difference on foreign policy. Arnim, a magnificent figure of a man, was widely regarded as Bismarck's successor, and did all he could to confirm that opinion. When Arnim became more or less openly mutinous against his superior, Bismarck ordered him to Berlin, and in the meeting which took place hurled a sentence at him in which his mind is marvellously revealed in all its bitterness and all its weakness for clinging jealously to power even when that power was becoming manifestly useless and almost a curse. "You're conspiring with the Empress," he said, "because you want to sit at the table where I'm now sitting. Well, you'll see one day—there's nothing in it." (*Und dann werden Sie sehen: es ist auch nichts.*)

This was in September of 1873, but it was not till February 1874 that Bismarck was able to persuade the Emperor to transfer Arnim to Constantinople. Arnim, however, delayed his departure and used the time to unleash an anonymous Press campaign against Bismarck. His secret was soon discovered and he was dismissed. Unfortunately he failed to relinquish possession of a certain document belonging to the Paris embassy. He was arrested, brought to trial, and, in a sensational action, condemned first to three, then to nine months' imprisonment. However, he was able to escape to Switzerland, where in 1876 he published a pamphlet against Bismarck entitled *Pro Nihilo.* A new action was started against him in his absence and ended in his being condemned to five years' imprisonment. Arnim died in 1881 in a Nice hotel without seeing his native land again.

Now it would have been perfectly possible to get the Paris documents back from Arnim by instituting civil proceedings. That Bismarck involved him in a criminal prosecution can only be explained by the fact that Arnim had endangered Bismarck's

personal interest. For this was the invariable treatment meted out
to those people who had been guilty of that offence. And it was a
treatment which he accorded to all such offenders, even when they
had long become harmless in themselves.

Many years later, when he was dictating his memoirs, Bismarck
stated that he had not acted from motives of revenge. It was
merely a case of a bureaucrat whose authority had been challenged
insisting self-righteously on having the last word. But this was
not the impression gained by the world. The stir which was
occasioned everywhere by the Arnim affair had far-reaching
consequences. The right-wing conservatives were gradually
beginning to be reconciled to Bismarck. Now they were infuriated
with him afresh. The Arnim family, and all of its wide ramifica-
tions, kept up an unceasing campaign against him. For many
years East Elbian Rittergut possessors went out of their way to
keep Harry Arnim's memory alive.

A man against whom a special odium came to be directed was
Friedrich von Holstein, who had been Arnim's subordinate in
Paris and who is said to have spied on his chief at Bismarck's
direction. How much truth there is in this accusation it is impossible to say. Spying on Arnim would seem to have been a
somewhat superfluous activity since he provided all the proofs
which led to his conviction. Holstein stated in court that the only
steps he had taken against Arnim were to send private letters to
various officials of the Foreign Service which described the
ambassador as a danger to peace. Even so, he remained for long a
social outcast.

In 1877, however, Bismarck withdrew Holstein from the firing
line and transferred him from Paris to the Foreign Office,
ultimately calling him to Varzin as his personal assistant. Here
the Bismarck family soon got to calling him "faithful Fritz", and
liked him so well that Johanna is said to have seriously considered him
as a potential son-in-law. It was only in the eighties that an estrangement took place between him and the Bismarcks, an estrangement which ultimately degenerated into downright enmity.

Even after Bismarck's departure, Holstein continued to serve
in the Foreign Office, distinguished by that correct incon-
spicuousness and slightly Philistine elegance that marks the higher
Prussian official, but also somewhat oddly interested in problems
of the kitchen. Indeed few people who think of him as the
eminence grise of the German Foreign Service know that it was
he who first discovered the gustatory potentialities of a marriage
between a fried egg and a breaded fillet of veal or that the words
"Holstein Schnitzel" keep green the memory of one whom history
has perhaps unjustly blackened.

Yet these were only the transient and venial diversions of a deeply dedicated spirit. The essential Holstein was of sterner stuff. That Prussian Protestant sense of duty which was native to him developed into a fanatical passion, and he lived so quietly— he did not even possess a dress coat—that hardly anybody knew of his existence outside the members of his office. It is these very facts which have caused his influence on German foreign policy to be fantastically exaggerated, though it is quite true that he exercised an unofficial power through an enormous private correspondence which went far beyond his official sphere of duty.

The Arnim affair did Bismarck little good, for it showed the degree to which he was prepared positively to destroy any person who opposed him. The horrified world realised that the old Teutonic demon was still alive in him, that he had on this occasion dealt with a human life precisely as he had dealt with the German dynasties when they stood in his way. Since this was the estimate that men were now beginning to form of Bismarck's character, it was natural for the suspicion to grow that he was only waiting his opportunity to unleash a new war or engage in new acts of robbery, and this made it increasingly hard to believe that he had any real interest in the peace of Europe. Because it produced this reaction, the Arnim affair may really be regarded as the cause of one of the very few miscalculations in foreign affairs of which Bismarck was ever guilty.

The thing happened like this. France had abandoned Napoleon III's conception of a professional army and had gone over instead to the Prussian principle of a mass levy. The necessary legislation had been passed and the result was now that each regiment had four battalions instead of only having three. In the event of war, the country would now have 144 more battalions than before and her forces would thus approximate more closely to the strength of the German Army. The arms budget rose by half a billion.

In Berlin, thoughts of another war with France now began to occupy the minds of the general staff, a war which was to destroy France "once and for always" before the new army laws could be carried into effect. That Bismarck from the very start utterly set his face against the whole idea of such a war is beyond all question. He knew that "once and for always" was a concept unknown to history, and slogans like "the war to end all wars" and "everlasting peace" simply bounced off from his crystalline intelligence.

This, however, was not appreciated at the time. When,

therefore, on April 8th the *Post*, whose connection with the Foreign
Office was well known, published an article under the title "Is
War in Sight?" and answered that question in the affirmative,
everybody took the matter seriously, all the more so since it
synchronised with a number of diplomatic démarches which could
hardly be interpreted otherwise than as a planned offensive on
the nerves of Europe.

The cast for the performance was well chosen, had obviously
been well rehearsed, and threw themselves into their parts with
zest. First Von Radowitz, a high-ranking diplomat known to
enjoy the confidence of Bismarck, remarked to the French ambassador, with something very like a sob, that Germany would be
compelled to anticipate any new French attack. Then Moltke
turned up at the British embassy and sought to familiarise the
ambassador with the idea of a preventive war. Finally, Hohenlohe, who was now the German ambassador in Paris, informed
the French Foreign Minister, the Duc de Decazes, that his government was by no means convinced of the non-aggressive character
of French rearmament.

The effect was all that could be wished. People called to mind
that Bismarck had just ruined a man who was the darling of the
imperial Court because this man stood in his way. What could he
be intending to do now? What would he not be capable of when
dealing with a state which he believed, or was held to believe,
threatened the welfare of his own?

Fortunately for Europe, the Duc de Decazes, an experienced
career diplomat, refused to lose his head. Rather he showed that
he had learned the lesson which Bismarck himself on a previous
occasion had so obligingly imparted to the *Corps Diplomatique*.
He treated his Berlin ambassador's report on the conversation
with Radowitz in precisely the same manner as Bismarck treated
the Ems telegram, the news of which, it will be remembered, he
caused to be disseminated among foreign governments through
diplomatic channels. And precisely as Bismarck had caused Benedetti's draft treaty to be published in the London *Times* so as to
win the sympathies of England, Decazes now made use of a skilful
international journalist named Opper-Blowitz and got an account
published in that same *Times* of Germany's impending aggression
against France.

Decazes's success was greater than he had anticipated. The
Czar announced that he would shortly be passing through Berlin
on his way to Ems and would stop off there and "make an end
of the matter". In London, Disraeli, who had just been made
Prime Minister, sent a circular letter to all the great powers
recommending joint action.

The events that followed, with their neatly timed exits and entrances and their mildly comic interludes, have something of the character of a skilfully constructed play. The Czar, accompanied by Gortschakow, arrived on May 10th, but on the morning of that same day Odo Russell, the British ambassador, had called on Bismarck and informed him that his government would certainly do all it could to prevent a recurrence of the events of 1870. He was about to take his departure when Gortschakow made his entrance, an old man leaning on a stick but still marvellously agile. Hardly had he arrived than he began to talk with needless persistence and at rather needless length, on his hopes that peace would be preserved. He did so in that unctuous and condescending tone which always set Bismarck's teeth on edge. It was his big scene and no doubt he overplayed it a little. In due course Russell took his leave, but not without something of a parting shot, for he remarked as he left that his government would associate itself with any steps taken by the Russian ambassador to assist in the resolution of Franco-German difficulties.

The two Chancellors were thus left alone, and what passed between them we do not exactly know. But this is certain: it was made very clear to Bismarck that in the event of a war with France he could not again count on the friendly neutrality of the great powers. In public after the meeting both men insisted that there was no danger of war. Bismarck in a tone of injured innocence not only confessed complete ignorance of the existence of any crisis—this despite the fact that he had kept the world on tenterhooks for the best part of a month—but almost implied that he did not know the meaning of the word.

It was a good performance as far as it went, but not quite good enough, and there was no disguising the fact that Bismarck had suffered a first-class diplomatic defeat. There had been talk of preventive war and few doubted by whom that talk was inspired. And Europe had risen like a man maddened by a sudden pain and told him bluntly that it would have none of it, and the world, at least the world of diplomacy, knew that he had been so told.

That Bismarck had no intention of preventive war or indeed any kind of war, we may safely take for granted. But appearances were against him and the impression was irresistible that it was the great powers which had prevented him from engaging in one. Certainly Europe had done something which it had not done for a very long time. It had shown that it was something more than a geographical expression.

There is an account in *Gedanken und Erinnerungen* of something that was, or is supposed to have been, for Bismarck yet a further

ground of exasperation. This is alleged to have been provided by
the circular telegram sent by Gortschakow to all Russian diplomats containing the words "peace is now assured", which, of
course, implied that before the Russian Chancellor had taken
action peace had been in danger. In *Gedanken und Erinnerungen*
Bismarck describes at some length how he had visited Gortschakow and had given him what is usually called a piece of his
mind. Actually, however, the circular telegram in question, which
has since been published among the official state papers, does
not contain the objectionable phrase at all.*

There is something of a mystery about the whole crisis of 1875.
It is rather like a phantom comedy whose ghostly producer is
never actually seen. Whether he was seen or no, however, there
can be no doubt whatever that the author of the crisis was Bismarck. It is inconceivable that the various articles in the Press
should have been published or that Radowitz, Moltke and Hohenlohe should have spoken the way they did without Bismarck's
knowledge and express consent. Yet we can be sure that Bismarck never meant these calculated excursions and alarums to
end in a war. Though, however, he wanted no war, he most
assuredly wanted to keep France in fear of one. "The cause of
peace is not assisted," he wrote about this time to the Emperor,
"if France is assured that she will in no circumstances be attacked
whatever she may do."

Yet one still asks just what purpose the keeping of France in a
state of fear was intended to serve. Bismarck could hardly have
believed he could thus persuade the French to abandon their
rearmament plan. One is ultimately driven to the view (which
is also that of Holstein) that Bismarck was moved to act as he
did simply by a desire to inflict suffering, a temptation which
sought to compensate for his own inner emptiness and dissatisfaction, this in its turn being the consequence of his continually
failing health.

Such an explanation, improbable as it seems to us, would not
have seemed improbable to those who knew him. Shuwalow, the
Russian ambassador in London, who was an old friend of Bismarck, saw him as he was passing through Berlin and anxiously
reported that the state of his nerves was "a danger to Europe".
Actually, Bismarck was then just sixty years of age, but gave the
impression of being much older. Facial neuralgia, *tic douloureux*,
as it was called, tortured him in the most cruel manner. Shortly
afterwards, his health became so wretched that he felt compelled

---

* The wording of Gortschakow's actual telegram is as follows: "L'Empereur quitte
Berlin, parfaitement convaincu des dispositions conciliantes qui y regnant et assurent
le maintien de la paix."

to offer his resignation. The Emperor rejected it, as he always did, but allowed him to take several months' leave.

Surprisingly enough, the crisis of 1875 blew over, and relations with France began steadily to improve, due partly to the admirable understanding between those two old aristocrats, Decazes and Hohenlohe; a scepticism which they held in common established a bond of sympathy and even a certain friendly warmth. Bismarck seemed pleased enough at the turn of events. He was also relieved when France finally accepted the Republican constitution and so put an end to all monarchist hopes and, with them, to that promise of national strength which in Bismarck's view a monarchy tended to foster.

A number of other things happened about this time which put him in a more tolerant frame of mind. Gontaut-Biron, the French ambassador and a royalist, a man against whom Bismarck entertained a prejudice which, though largely groundless, made co-operation impossible, was recalled in 1877. He was replaced by Count Saint-Vallier, who rapidly won Bismarck's regard.* In September of that year Thiers died. Bismarck, who was in Gastein, drank a silent glass with Hohenlohe in memory of their sometime enemy. In France, Thiers's opponent, Gambetta, that strange Genoese lawyer who had become a Frenchman, came more and more into the foreground. He had served his adopted country well, for it was largely through him that French prestige, which had been utterly shattered in the first weeks of the war, was once more restored. People saw in him the man of the future. Bismarck was anxious to make his acquaintance. Henckel and Blowitz were among the many eager spirits who sought to make this possible. A meeting was actually fixed for April of the following year. For reasons unknown, nothing came of it, nor unfortunately was it possible to arrange one on any other occasion.

When in 1878 the Berlin Congress was convened under Bismarck's presidency, France, for the first time since her defeat, was represented along with the other great powers and was treated with all customary honours. Bismarck invited the French Foreign Minister Waddington to sit next to himself. What was even more important, he took the occasion of his presence in Berlin to tell him that Germany would be quite agreeable to a French expansion from Algiers into Tunis which at that time was still nominally Turkish, a development which would have been impossible had Germany been unwilling to sanction it.

No doubt he was actuated by purely selfish motives, for if he could divert French energies away from France's eastern frontier he was serving Germany's supreme interest—peace, as indeed he

* Joseph Maria von Radowitz, *Aufzeichnungen und Erinnerungen* (1925), II, p. 29.

was doing by causing a rift to develop between France and Italy which, up till that time, had regarded Tunis as an Italian sphere of influence. For thus he robbed France of the protection of her southern flank should she contemplate a war of revenge, and deterred her even more effectively than before from engaging in one.

In the years that followed he continually showed his desire to give support to France, to protect her rear "from Guinea to Belgium", as he himself put it, on the one condition that the Franco-German frontier should remain outside the sphere of discussion. Thus he certainly hoped by giving France a multiplicity of new interests to induce her to forget the wounds he had himself inflicted. This hope, as we all know, was to prove vain.

Though there were no conflicts of interest with Britain, relations between the two countries were to some extent disturbed by a factor which in other circumstances should have helped to harmonise them. The wife of the heir to the throne was the daughter of Queen Victoria and a woman of great energy, as we have already seen. She was a powerful ally of the liberal-minded Crown Prince, indeed, she was if anything the dominant character of the pair.

When Frederick ascended the throne—and in view of William's age that event could not now be very distant—there would surely be changes in the whole German system of government. This fact caused the seventies and eighties to pass in a continual state of uneasy preparedness. Everything that was done would surely be subjected to fresh evaluation and might possibly be undone again from top to bottom, a circumstance which surely must have occasioned some of Bismarck's formidable outbursts of rage. Certainly this did not sweeten Bismarck's feeling for England, for the liberalism of the Crown Prince and his wife was very much on the English model. To make matters worse, fate decreed that this should be the time of Gladstone's premiership, and there was hardly a statesman whom Bismarck so utterly repudiated. He had a very low opinion of Gladstone's abilities, considered him to be an impractical bungler and also a hypocrite into the bargain.

And yet he had to admit that the idea of a so-called "Gladstone Cabinet" being formed in Berlin was something other than mere irresponsible fancy. He knew that he was strong enough to offer effective resistance to the wild plans of the Liberals of the Crown Prince's party. These plans were similar to those concocted in the Paulskirche and visualised Germany joining with the Scandinavian countries and other Western powers in an "anti-reactionary crusade" against Russia which they proposed to defeat and carve up. The Emperor, in that case, as Bismarck would occasionally point out, would have the standing of an Indian vassal prince. Even so, though these fantasies need not be taken too seriously, it might well be impossible, under the new Emperor, to avoid the application of English ideas to politics at home, and that was a problem that would certainly have to be faced.

Yet England posed an even more searching question. Could she be built into Bismarck's peace system? Might not a power which conceived its mission to be peace the world over, be glad to have the European continent kept under control by the strength of German military might, and be well satisfied to have its rear thus protected? But English feelings were unresponsive. The spirit of Palmerston was still paramount, and Britain was making her way towards that isolation which in years to come she was to designate as "splendid". All these things, as Bismarck plainly saw, ruled out any prospects of a formal alliance.

To tell the truth, the arrival on the scene of Bismarck's German Empire had left Britain largely unmoved. Since the individual member states of the Empire were about as much of a menace as Holland or Switzerland, there seemed no reason to suppose that their conjunction with one another would give grounds for apprehension—for they had long been united in a customs union without thereby endangering world peace. Disraeli saw clearly enough that the foundation of the German Empire would have a vital bearing on the fate of Britain, but in this matter he stood alone.

Victoria, still holding dear Albert's views, or what she conceived to be those views, was a friend to all German states, united or otherwise. It was unfortunate that her eldest did not see things quite like that, for he had married a Danish princess who had not forgotten 1864. Albert Edward, Prince of Wales, therefore tended to be somewhat cool towards German diplomats, and the Germans retaliated by pointing an outraged finger at his private life, which, alas, was not always what it should have been.

Bismarck's personal attitude towards England was affected by that deep mistrust of all that was alien to him—an essential part of his make-up; yet he was not without a real liking for the country, though one is continually being made aware of the fact that, whereas he was very familiar with France and Russia, he had actually seen only little of England. He was thus capable of some very mistaken judgments in matters relating to the island kingdom and prone to accept current stereotypes for truth, the image conjured up by the word Englishman, for instance, being that of a man who when he says "God" means "cotton" and so on.

This tendency to make his appraisals at second and third hand led to some very bad miscalculations—for instance, in the assessment of Britain's military potential, a fact that is all too evident in his well-known remark that, if a British expeditionary force landed in Germany, he would have them arrested by the police. It is not surprising, therefore, that like so many others, he failed to grasp a very important truth, namely that any peril to Britain which threatened to become mortal would draw the United States of America onto the battlefields of Europe.

THE FACE OF THE BEAR

The impression which Bismarck had formed while he was ambassador in St. Petersburg, namely that it was a castle built by slave-labour in a great marsh, had deepened since his departure. When, years ago, he had said *"Ich sehe dem Eisbären ins Gesicht"*, he had experienced a chilly fear, and it was a fear that was never to leave him. Always Russia seemed to him to possess something of the uncanny qualities of the polar bear, with its snow-white colour, the colour of innocence, its silence, its apparently clumsy and indolent movement, which belied the fact that it was incalculable, crafty, an enemy to man and vastly his superior in power. He also understood the instinctive dislike of the Russian people for Prussia, Germany and Austria. It was natural for that vast horde, driven as it was by an expansionist urge, to hate those that stood in its way. For Marx had surely been right when he wrote at the time of the Crimean War, "Russia regards a western frontier stretching from Danzig or Stettin to Trieste as 'natural'."

Bismarck's relations with France, Austria and Britain accorded with the dealings of rational men, and could be developed along the lines of routine. To Russia, however, his attitude was different. It was pliable, accommodating, but immensely cautious, the attitude of a man prepared for anything to happen. He felt no friendship for Russia, and when he adjured his successor not to let the wire to Russia be broken, it was not friendship that was his motive, but fear.

As an ambassador he had, of course, got along very well with Russian society. But it had been a society that still lived within the framework of international forms. That society, however, was dying if it was not already dead. The younger generation "shirked every kind of social effort, was ill-mannered and showed a sullen anti-European spirit". In a word, it was adapting itself to the pan-Slavic urges of the masses and was proving to be ever more hostile to Germany—and, however reluctant he may have been to do so, Bismarck himself added momentum to the trend.

After the battle of Wörth, Czar Alexander II had emptied his glass and joyfully hurled it to the ground, for the defeat of the Crimea was avenged. Shortly afterwards, confident of a Prussian victory, he found himself in a position to break the treaty of 1856, which forbade him to maintain men-of-war on the Black Sea. Here Bismarck disappointed him. For Bismarck, if he was not to endanger his own war aims, could not take Russia's part as wholeheartedly as was expected of him. Indeed, it was precisely at this point of time, as he later declared, that the enmity between the two states began to bud.

Somewhat later, the Czar, who was himself related to the Danish Royal House, had urged Bismarck to hold the plebiscite in Northern Schleswig, for which the treaty of Prague provided. Despite the fact that all Germany stood to lose was a little bit of land in the far north, Bismarck bluntly refused, and it is hard to see how he came to commit such a blunder, for the Czar deeply resented his refusal. But Bismarck had always had a rather special feeling where the possession of land was concerned and was particularly sensitive on this subject.

Yet he acted as he did, knowing full well that the cards were already stacked against him and that the very foundation of the empire had been frowned on in St. Petersburg, which naturally enough disliked the idea of new concentrations of power on its western border, and had warned him of the dangers inherent in the whole conception. When it was clear that the warning was without effect, even Schuwalow, who was accounted Prussia's best friend, began to have misgivings and went so far as to say that it would have been better for Russia if France had won the war.

Something obviously had to be done, however insubstantial, to prevent any further increase in the tension, and even gestures were better than nothing. But what kind of gestures? There were strong dynastic sentiments uniting William with the Czar, and there were always the bumbling pontifications of the Holy Alliance. Within limits, these solemn unrealities could serve some useful purpose, and a happy chance enabled Bismarck to make at least such use as could be got from them.

It so happened that the Emperor Francis Joseph had announced his intention of paying a visit to Berlin, and the Czar, by nature a nervous character, discreetly intimated to the German ambassador that he would like to be present on this happy occasion. And so the German capital in 1872 saw the meeting of the three emperors.

There was much festivity and general junketing. The Czar looked magnificent, his knightly bearing successfully concealing a regrettable infirmity of purpose. Francis Joseph contributed youthful good looks, while William, if he did nothing else, could always be relied upon to appear venerable.

In private the three sovereigns exchanged promises which really bound nobody to anything in particular, and it was perhaps unfortunate that during "Retreat" at the Royal Castle eleven people were crushed to death. In the following May William made a return visit to St. Petersburg and signed a convention with the Czar that each would support the other with two hundred thousand men if either were attacked. In June the Czar laid the convention before Francis Joseph, but could only obtain the latter's signature after the meaning of the document had been rendered more nebulous than it was already. The wording now read that should peace be threatened by the aggressive conduct of any power, the three rulers would consult together as to the policy to be followed. When in October William visited Vienna he added his name to the agreement.

The thing that had come into being in this complicated fashion bore the name The League of the Three Emperors. It was an empty demonstration which could offer no foundation for a political edifice of any kind. If William had any faith in it, he was surely falling into the same error as the detested left of 1848.

Like some unquiet ghost, the League of the Three Emperors reappeared from time to time in the diplomacy of the following decades, but it was never more than a creature of mist and fog whose insubstantial nature was made very clear in the very year of its creation when Germany spent seven million talers for erecting against Russia the fortress of Posen. Nor could the League of the Three Emperors prevent the intervention of Russia, so deeply wounding to Bismarck, during the "war-in-sight" crisis of the following year.

But this bemused interlude was soon succeeded by a return to political reality. The exasperated Christian subjects of the sublime Porte, thoughtfully supported by Russian panslavists, were in open revolt against their overlord, and the Eastern Question, in all its pristine beauty, was blossoming forth anew. This meant that Russia, the self-appointed protector of Balkan Christians, would soon be at cross-purposes with Austria and Britain, who considered Russian solicitude touching but not untinged by a certain element of acquisitiveness.

In such a situation Bismarck was in his element. By a feat of contortionism as complicated as his own most complicated metaphors, he combined the activities of an equilibrist with those of a fisherman in troubled waters. The heart of the problem was easy to state. The European balance had, if Germany was to survive, at all costs to be preserved, and so it was really natural enough that when Russia enquired whether, in the event of a war with Austria, Germany would reciprocate for Russia's neutrality during the Franco-Prussian war by remaining neutral herself, Bismarck should have replied with a masterpiece of uncommitment: Germany could not allow a coalition of Europe permanently to weaken Russia's position as a great power; she could not permit Austria to be endangered in her position as a European power or her independence, and so cease to be one of the factors on which Germany could reckon in the European balance of power.

Delicate as was the situation, however, nothing deterred Bismarck from seeking to reap a profit from it by an exquisite piece of brinkmanship. Thus there was the old business with France. Certain military precautions, he explained to Odo Russell, were indispensable for German security, and should the French, so prone to unworthy suspicions, misconstrue Germany's eminently pacific intention, could he rely, he enquired, on England's taking a broad-minded view? As for himself, he would be glad to render any little service in return—moral support in the Near East, for instance, or an attitude of philosophical detachment if the British chose to occupy Egypt; here he displayed the same large-mindedness in the disposal of other people's property, as he did towards the French in the matter of Tunis.

The effect of these manœuvres was not too fortunate. British statesmen were disquieted and perplexed, and matters were not made easier by Bismarck's habit of disappearing for long periods to Varzin and holding himself incommunicado, a practice with which the Germans had, of course, been long familiar but which the British found in the prevailing circumstances a little trying. "When I am told," wrote Lord Beaconsfield to Lord Derby, "that the German (Prime Minister) is in solitude and cannot be disturbed and that the Queen's ambassador is here (in London) because it is of no use being at his post, I listen to eccentricities which must not be permitted to regulate events affecting the destiny of generations and empires." "What," he added a few lines later—and the note of anguish is almost audible—"does he want?"

Queen Victoria, who had indeed never been a friend of Bismarck's, added her voice to the general expressions of displeasure. Writing to her beloved Lord Beaconsfield and expressing herself, as was her custom, in the august third person, she delivered the awful verdict: "The Queen," she said, "thinks that Bismarck is making much mischief," and it is significant that she said this apropos of nothing in particular, a mere concluding obiter dictum such as one might make about the badness of the weather or the spread of measles or any other impersonal calamity that is presumed to have been sent by providence and must therefore be endured. Bismarck, whose delicate sensibility made him well aware that the business had misfired, left the question of his intentions unanswered, and retired from the field.

Meanwhile, things were moving towards an explosion point, and at the end of 1877 Russia attacked in the Balkans. Her progress was at first retarded by sickness among her forces and by lack of funds, and it was not till winter that her troops forced the main Turkish army to surrender at Plevna. Though their munition wagons were empty and their hospitals full, the road was open to Constantinople where the British fleet lay ready and at anchor, while Austria mobilised in her south-eastern provinces, thus threatening Russian lines of communication.

So a Russian-Turkish peace was hurriedly signed at San Stefano, which left Constantinople to the Turks but deprived Turkey of most of the rest of the Balkan peninsula; it was clear to the world at large that European peace was in greater danger than ever.

If it was to be preserved—and none needed its preservation more than Germany—Bismarck himself would have to act. He therefore agreed to offer Berlin as the seat of a congress at which he would, of course, automatically preside. He did so, reluctantly knowing that such a congress would force Russia to relinquish some of her booty, which in point of fact it did, and that some of the odium of this would in Russian eyes necessarily attach to himself.

Public opinion in Germany was, of course, delighted that the German Chancellor should thus, as it held, be made arbiter of the world. But Bismarck vehemently objected to any such title. He was, he informed the Reichstag, no more than "an honest broker", and though Bleichröder assured him that the phrase was a contradiction in terms, he continued to adhere to that description.

And so the world came to Berlin, eager to see the metropolis of this new member of the great powers' club. They found it a very different place indeed from London, Paris or Vienna. The kernel of the old city was still untouched. Here was the Royal Castle, the old Cathedral and the new Guardhouse, throne, altar and military power made concrete and visible. Ennobled here and there by the art of Schlüter, Schinkel and their pupils, the new palaces of the banks, the hotels and the imperial government offices showed nothing of the disciplined restfulness of old Prussian architecture but much self-conscious splendour.

There was obviously plenty of money about and the streets seemed too narrow and the houses too low for all the business that was being done. Of that Prussia that had been proud of having to save so that one day it might be mighty, nothing seemed to be left.

Against all this background of bustle appeared Gortschakow with his years weighing palpably heavily upon him. He was formally Russia's chief representative, yet it was Shuwalow who was the really active power at the conferences; Shuwalow, who had been an ambassador in London and was well thought of by the Emperors both of Germany and Austria, was one of those who had not forgotten Russia's ancient friendship with Prussia. Indeed, he placed rather more confidence in it than events were to justify.

Austria was represented by Count Andrassy, who had taken part in the Hungarian rising in 1848 and had actually been condemned to death. But much water had flowed under the bridges since then, and there had been many changes in the Dual Monarchy. Nevertheless, Andrassy could never forget that it had been Russian troops that had crushed the Hungarian Revolution.

But the man whose personality dominated the conference, who cast an almost magic spell over everybody, including Bismarck himself, was Benjamin Disraeli, Earl of Beaconsfield. He, too, was now visibly an old man, though he continued to dye his hair and beard black. But he claimed that his heart was young in his ageing body, and perhaps it was. For he had, so Princess Radziwill tells us, "that charm which only those possess who have complete confidence in themselves".

Not least among the elements that helped create the nimbus around the man was his authorship. "What amuses rather at Berlin," he wrote to Queen Victoria, "is that almost everybody, certainly all the ladies, are reading my novels, from the Empress downwards. The ladies are generally reading *Henrietta Temple*, which being a 'love story' and written forty years ago, is hardly becoming an Envoy Extraordinary. The Bülow family generally are very deep in my works. Prince Bismarck seems very familiar with them." Indeed, if a note to Beaconsfield from Odo Russell is anything to go by, the sudden demand for Disraeli's books seemed to be regarded as a national German emergency, with which even the highest officers of state had to concern themselves. Beaconsfield was told that Russell had been informed of the matter at the Austrian embassy by no less than three German ministers, those of Public Instruction, of the Interior, and—rather ominously—of Police. "The circulating libraries," wrote Russell, "unable to meet the demands of the public, have bought up all the Tauchnitz editions of your works, both here and at Leipzig, while the booksellers have been obliged to telegraph to

England for more copies of all your novels. The newspapers who publish feuilletons are all advertising translations for the coming quarter of your earlier books."

Perhaps what drew Bismarck most to Disraeli was his realism and his refusal to sentimentalise over the emergent Balkan nations whom Bismarck himself contemptuously spoke of as "sheep stealers", openly declaring that the rights and wrongs of the squabbles of the Balkan peoples were not worth the bones of a Pomeranian grenadier. Beaconsfield would hardly have put it so crudely, of course. But for him, too, the protection of the Balkan peoples from the effects of Turkish misrule was a secondary matter. It was more important to keep Russia away from the Dardanelles. An even stronger bond between the two, however, was their common detestation of Gladstone.

Yet there was much more here than a common dislike or even a community of political principle. The two men took to each other from the start, and the gentle scepticism evident in almost every word Disraeli spoke completely captured Bismarck's heart; Bismarck, indeed, was not so much charmed as bewitched, and one sees him moving among the diplomats and, as though he were imparting some startling, new and altogether delightful discovery, uttering—nay, almost panting—that reiterated encomium: *"Der alte Jude, das ist der Mann."*

Undoubtedly one of the effects of Bismarck's confidence in the British plenipotentiary was to loosen his tongue, as the following letter of Lord Beaconsfield's to the Queen very plainly shows: "In the afternoon at six o'clock great dinner at Prince Bismarck's. All these banquets are very well done. There must have been sixty guests. The Princess was present. She is not fair to see, tho' her domestic influence is said to be irresistible. I sat on the right of Prince Bismarck, and, never caring much to eat in public, I could listen to his Rabelaisian monologue; endless revelations of things he ought not to mention. He impressed on me never to trust princes or courtiers, that his illness was not, as people supposed, brought on by the French war, but by the horrible conduct of his sovereign, etc., etc. In the archives of his family remain the documents, the royal letters, which accuse him, after all his services, of being a traitor. He went on in such a vein that I was at last obliged to tell him that, instead of encountering duplicity, which he said was universal among sovereigns, I served one who was the soul of candour and justice and whom all her ministers loved.

"The contrast between his voice, which is sweet and gentle, with his ogre-like form, striking. He is apparently well read, familiar with modern literature."

"I dined with (Bismarck) alone," Lord Beaconsfield wrote on another occasion, "i.e. with his family who disappeared after the repast, and then we talked and smoked. If you do not smoke in such circumstances you look like a spy taking down his conversation in your mind. Smoking in common puts him at his ease. He asked me today whether racing was still much encouraged in England. I replied, never more so. . . . Then, cried the Prince eagerly, 'There will never be socialism in England. You are a happy country. You are safe so long as the people are devoted to racing. Here a gentleman cannot ride down the street without twenty persons saying to themselves or each other, Why has that fellow a horse and I have not one? In England the more horses a nobleman has the more popular he is. So long as the English are devoted to racing, socialism has no chance with you.' This will give you a slight idea of the style of his conversation. His views on all subjects are original but there is no strain, no effort at paradox. He talks as Montaigne writes. When he heard about Cyprus he said, 'You have done a wise thing. This is progress. It will be popular. A nation likes progress.' His idea of progress was evidently seizing something."

Yet though the congress, as it proceeded, produced in Bismarck these moments of good-humoured loquacity, the circumstances under which he had first to greet his guests on that hot June day had not been pleasant. A few days before, only a hundred yards from the Imperial Chancellor's palace where the congress was taking place, the sovereign had been seriously wounded by a disgruntled subject and was even now fighting for his life. The Crown Prince, at Bismarck's request, had only been trusted with the representation of his father and not with the Regency, and therefore had no authority of his own. The Reichstag was in dissolution and an election loomed ahead, thus neither the sovereign nor parliament could worthily welcome the congress. Moreover, the battle with the Catholic Church was in full swing, while the socialist law was already casting a shadow over everything.

We can thus well understand that Bismarck was not in a good humour when the congress opened and that he made no attempt to disguise the fact. Indeed, his unhappy mood never changed in all that month throughout which the negotiations continued to drag on, the month which seemed, externally, to be the culminating point of his career. He was then sixty-three years old, but the impression that he gave was of a man old before his time, pale, bloated and unhealthily huge. The uniform which he wore always seemed on the point of bursting.

It was only in May that he had recovered from an attack of shingles. He seemed hardly younger than Disraeli and Gortschakow, who were seventy-four and eighty years respectively, old men indeed. Gortschakow had often to be carried into the council chamber, while Beaconsfield suffered from asthma, bronchitis, defective vision and the pains brought on by Bright's Disease. On several occasions during the congress he was confined to his bed and had to be replaced by Salisbury.

Bismarck, who, very much against his will, had been presented with the conductor's baton for this new European concert, had designed a grandiosely conceived programme which envisaged the division of the disputed territories into more or less equal spheres of interest, for Russia, Austria and Britain. He clung to this with iron determination, for though he was not directly interested in the carrying out of such a programme, he was very interested indeed in its indirect effect. What he wanted, as Schweinitz pointed out, was to exploit the Balkan crisis politically in order to achieve a grouping of the great powers, or rather to keep them occupied in such a manner that hostile coalitions against Germany would for a long time be rendered impossible. As we can see from the so-called Kissingen "decree" of June 1877, his purpose was to ensure the equilibrium of the world in which the vital necessities of the great powers were balanced against one another so that "they would be satisfied for a long time with the maintenance of the status quo", and yet preserve certain rivalries which would render them "incapable of participating in coalitions against ourselves".

A great deal later, in 1889, he told the Austrian ambassador, Szögyény, that he had been at great pains during the congress to induce Austria to break up the congress itself by declaring war against Russia, since a war at that moment would be fought with more favourable chances for Austria than had ever existed in the past or were likely to exist again. But, as we know, a great many of Bismarck's utterances dating from that period suffer from a certain historical imprecision.* The congress began in circumstances of some embarrassment, since the London *Globe* published certain secret agreements arrived at between Russia and Britain, the texts of which had come into its possession through the carelessness of the Foreign Office which had entrusted a secret document to a temporary and presumably venal copying clerk. Clearly the two powers had already decided in advance a great number of the questions which the congress was to discuss. By unremitting use of the whip, Bismarck forced the congress to get through its agenda in about twenty sessions, during the whole of which he openly declared that he intended to begin his cure in Kissingen in July.

* Kransnick, *Neue Bismarckbriefe*, p. 56.

On June 20th, however, the congress ran aground. Russian and English claims in the matter of Bulgaria were apparently irreconcilable. Bismarck asked Beaconsfield whether he was prepared to give an ultimatum; Beaconsfield replied in the affirmative and ordered his secretary to arrange for a special train to take him home. To save the congress, Bismarck had ultimately to work quite mercilessly on his old friend Shuwalow and eventually Russia was forced to yield, as indeed her continual yielding was one of the characteristic notes of the congress. The fact is that Shuwalow was no match for Beaconsfield, and Bismarck did very little to come to his aid. For he could not forgive Gortschakow for his intervention in the "war-in-sight" crisis. Holstein says that he never seemed to see Russia any more but only Gortschakow. Indeed he is believed to have said openly to Blowitz the journalist, "Now Gortschakow realises what it has cost him to have treated me as cavalierly as he did in 1875."

Bismarck was rarely present at any of the usual diplomatic junketings which took place on this occasion. He was disturbed by dark apprehensions. He could not do otherwise than adhere to his resolve of strict neutrality and was thus compelled to avoid any step which appeared to favour one of his two eastern neighbours. Thus the congress ended with the palpable defeat of Russia. The Greater Bulgaria that had been visualised in the Treaty of San Stefano, the Greater Bulgaria which absorbed the whole of Macedonia and reached as far as the Aegean Sea, was cut in two, the whole of Macedonia going to Turkey, while the residual Bulgarian half was again subdivided into the principality of Bulgaria and the autonomous province of Eastern Roumelia, both nominally free, but in reality Russian satellites while owing in varying degrees a tribute to the Sultan. For the residual growth of Russian power, such as it was, compensation was granted to Austria by granting her the right to occupy Bosnia and Herzegovina, while England was granted the annexation of Cyprus.

Bismarck himself had little grounds for satisfaction over the congress. His nerves were on edge and the physical symptom of this was a nettle rash which appeared almost immediately after the congress was over. Bleichröder's realistic statement that an honest broker was a contradiction in terms had proved all too true. Everybody was criticising him. The fact that Germany, the only great power that had no interest in the east, went away with empty hands convinced nobody of the selflessness of Bismarck's motives. Indeed, in Germany the overwhelming impression was that Bismarck had let off Russia much too lightly, after which the enmity of the liberals grew stronger, though the clericals, for whom the congress had meant a weakening of Austria's position, were also soon among his critics. Last but not least were the East German magnates who had vainly hoped for a reduction of Russian tariffs.

As to Russia herself, it should have been obvious to anybody of normal intelligence that, but for the Berlin congress, she would have fared much worse than she did. She would then not have been allowed to carry home even a part of the booty that she had appropriated at San Stefano but would have had to defend herself afresh against a combination of Turkey, Britain and Austria. Bismarck had spared her that, but Russia could only gaze at those parts of the treaty of San Stefano concerning which she had had to give way in Berlin.

The Russians raged wildly; Bismarck was to blame for everything; he had proved crassly ungrateful for Russian neutrality in 1870. The Russian Press cried with one voice that Russia had been betrayed, that the congress had been a European coalition against Russia under Bismarck's leadership, and that the League of the Three Emperors no longer existed. Even the Czar himself began soon to nurture these feelings. When he heard that the congress had come to an end, his first remark was, "Thank goodness, now we can be content."* But soon he changed his tune. "I love my uncle, Emperor William," he said, "but Bismarck is a frightful scoundrel."† Bismarck, however, cared little about any of this, for, to tell the truth, his opinion of the Czar was never very high.

One of the most surprising results of the congress was the improvement of relations between Germany and the Western powers. We have already noted how warm were the feelings that grew up between Bismarck and Lord Beaconsfield, and the relations between their countries were further improved. Moreover, Franco-German relations began to be normalised. For now that England's opposition to Russia was clear, Bismarck could view a close understanding between England and France with favour; a France that was tied to England could never become an ally of Russia. With this end in view, Bismarck endeavoured in 1879 to iron out the differences which had arisen between Britain and France over Egypt and to forestall anything in the nature of a breach. He also encouraged France to go into Tunis. Indeed, he prevented a German archaeologist from undertaking a journey to that country so as to forestall any possibility of misunderstanding.

He had already promised the French delegate at the Berlin congress to help France "everywhere where German interests

* Windelband, p. 51.   † Holstein, I, p. 123.

were not involved". Now he instructed his Ambassador Hohenlohe, "We look on France as one of the most important bearers of culture of all time and believe that its influence on the unhappy conditions in Tunis represents an advance of civilisation."* In this he acted with full British approval, and the result was a startling change in public opinion, a change so strong that Prussian consols were bought on a massive scale and their price reached unprecedented heights.

All this ultimately moved Bismarck to work through the German ambassador in London, Prince Münster, to bring about a genuine alliance, that is to say a participation on the part of Britain in Bismarck's security system. But here he was to meet with disappointment. The after-effects of old prejudices were in Britain still so strong that Beaconsfield himself could only venture to give an assurance that in the event of a German-Russian war, he would ensure that France remained quiet. "Nothing else?" wrote Bismarck in the margin of the report, and perhaps that comment would have struck a well-informed contemporary as needlessly despondent, for, like all the world, Beaconsfield was no doubt confident that his government was firmly entrenched for a long time to come, so that the day would not be too far distant when he could meet Bismarck's wishes more completely. He did not guess that the next spring was to bring him a heavy electoral defeat and that Gladstone was to become Prime Minister.

During the electoral battle that brought about this change, two articles, strongly supporting Beaconsfield's party, which had been dictated by Bismarck, appeared in the *Norddeutsche Allgemene Zeitung*. Unfortunately, these merely caused Lord Beaconsfield to be known as Bismarck's lackey. Yet we may be sure that if the election had had a different result, the consequence might have been that European history would have taken a different course from that which it actually followed.

---

* Windelband, p. 227.

12

THE LOST WAY HOME

The Congress had saved the peace, but it had achieved nothing else. About that nobody had any illusions, Bismarck least of all. Indeed, he inspired the *Norddeutsche Allgemeine Zeitung* to say that the work of the congress would not endure for a generation.

The Russian outcries began at once: the German representatives of the border commissions were prejudiced. They claimed that Germany had no interests in the matter, but invariably gave their votes to Austria. Within little more than a year the Czar was telling the German ambassador that things would have to change if the old friendship with Prussia was to continue, and indicated pretty plainly that when he spoke like this it was Bismarck whom he had in mind.

But some imp had got into Bismarck, who, so far from seeking to improve relations, seemed determined by a series of pinpricks to worsen them. A cattle epidemic had broken out in Astrakhan. Bismarck used the pretext to bring the import of Russian cattle virtually to a standstill. When Gortschakow protested, Bismarck found his language rude and forbade Schweinitz to answer him, and Schweinitz himself observed that Bismarck was praying for further epidemics so that he might add to the mounting Russian irritation.

A short while before Bismarck had announced that Austria had, on October 11th of the preceding year, agreed that Article 5 of the Treaty of Prague should be considered void. It was this article which committed Prussia to a plebiscite in Northern Schleswig, and since the Danish Royal House was related to the Romanovs, the withdrawal of the article was an affront to the latter.

The Russian Press was not slow to put the worst possible interpretation on the matter. The honest broker had his price, it seemed. He had bartered his support for Austria over the Bosnian occupation and got Schleswig in return. Actually, the deal had been completed before the congress had met, but to make the whole affair less blatant, Bismarck had post-dated the agreement till after the congress had broken up. The date of October 11th was chosen because, at that time, the Crown Prince was still

247

representing his wounded father, so that Bismarck's tame Press could put the responsibility entirely on the shoulders of the former, who, needless to say, was entirely ignorant of the whole affair.

The reason for Bismarck's calculated provocations remains obscure. Possibly they were due to nothing more than his now deep-seated resentment against Gortschakow. Possibly they were in the nature of a probe, an attempt to assess the strain which Russo-German relations would bear.

Whatever the intention, the effect was to produce formidable concentrations of cavalry and field artillery on the Russian border. Bismarck was slow in recognising the full truth of the matter, which was that Russian enmity was now no mere passing mood, but had become an ingrained and almost instinctive habit of the Russian mind. The shock of this realisation may have been more severe than any he experienced during the whole of his official career.

As usual, Bismarck kept his thoughts to himself, only occasionally allowing a word or two, like a distant flash of summer lightning, to reveal what was in his mind. Thus, for instance, some nine months after the end of the congress, he spoke to Schweinitz of "terrifying new horizons", saying that there was no confidence to be placed in Russia and that good relations must at all costs be established with her enemies.*

In August 1879 he took positive action. The occasion for this was a holograph letter of the Czar's to the Emperor in which he complained of the unfriendly attitude of Germany, saying that there was nothing but Bismarck's personal dislike of Gortschakow at the bottom of it. As soon as Bismarck had news of the letter— he was in Kissingen at the time—he broke off his cure and travelled to Gastein, where he had invited Andrassy to meet him.

What he had in mind was an alliance, but it was an alliance of a rather extraordinary kind. It involved nothing less than a change in the constitution of both Germany and Austria, a change that was to be carried out solemnly and openly with the full consent of the parliaments concerned. It would then be written into the constitution of both countries, that they should jointly wage war against any enemy with whom either was engaged.

This meant, in effect, that so far as external affairs were concerned, Austria and Germany constituted, for all practical purposes, a single entity. Bismarck had long been considering such an organic alliance; indeed, he may well have been doing so from the moment when, in 1866, he excluded Austria from the North German Bund.

* Schweinitz, II, pp. 60, 61.

THE LOST WAY HOME

Andrassy, as soon as he realised that Bismarck meant what he said, is said to have "jumped nearly up to the ceiling" in glee. However, in the end he rejected the proposals. First of all, he had no desire whatever to guarantee Alsace-Lorraine* and possibly become involved in a war with France which might lead to a Russian attack on his rear. There were, however, other considerations. As a Hungarian, he had no wish to see a revival of a greater Germany.

Here, then, was a strange quirk of fate. It was the hand of Bismarck that had brought about the events of 1866, and these had resulted in the *Ausgleich*. This, in its turn, made it possible for a Hungarian to conduct the foreign policy of the Hapsburg Empire, who, because he was a Hungarian, made impossible that revision of the events of 1866, which Bismarck now desired. In the end, Bismarck had to content himself with a secret treaty that only committed the parties to actual belligerence in the eventuality of a Russian attack on one of them. In the event of war with any other power, it merely provided for benevolent neutrality by the non-belligerent partner.

Meanwhile, however, Bismarck found himself engaged on yet another front, for the Emperor was beside himself at the mere thought of an anti-Russian alliance. The old man was now eighty-two and from childhood had regarded the Romanovs, with whom he had numerous ties of relationship, as his oldest and firmest friends.

Once more Bismarck attempted the technique which he had sought to apply on the occasion of the Princes' Diet at Frankfurt and of the Ems telegram. Once more he made desperate efforts to persuade the Emperor that he had been shockingly insulted. For was not a mere suggestion by a foreigner that a German ruler should change his ministers an insult of the most grievous kind? This time, however, such tactics utterly failed to work. Indeed, William, to Bismarck's not inconsiderable annoyance, contrived to arrange for a personal meeting with the Czar at the border station of Alexandrowno, and here the old happy days seemed at last to have returned. Uncle and nephew embraced, kissed each other on the cheek, and there was discreet regal lacrimosity as the Czar begged William to regard his letters as never having been written, while William forgave him with a heart almost visibly overflowing with goodwill.

At the time this edifying scene was taking place, however, Bismarck was quietly pursuing his plans for an Austrian alliance, and on the very day on which William in Alexandrowno was

---

* Andrassy summarised the rebuff Bismarck had received in the "War-in-Sight" crisis, by saying that "we have received peace and the Germans a lesson".

listening to his nephew's embittered complaints about Francis Joseph, Bismarck had the latter's acceptance in principle of the alliance already in his hands.

When William, returning from Alexandrowno, found Bismarck's request to empower him formally to conclude the alliance, he was almost stunned by the blow, and there now developed between the two men a duel that lasted for weeks. As during the Ems negotiations, Bismarck kept at a distance from his sovereign, while his agents worked diligently on the old man, continually whispering the dreadful word "resignation" in his ear. At last (it was now September) they contrived to wrest an "approval in principle" from him, Bismarck being given leave to proceed to Vienna, where he was splendidly received by Francis Joseph and hastened to complete his business as quickly as he could. Since Andrassy was on the point of retiring, he had to conduct some of the negotiations with his successor Haymerle. Within three days the text of the treaty was complete and all that was now needed was William's signature.

When the old man discovered that the treaty was even more explicitly directed against Russia than he had been given to understand—directed, that is to say, against the very country whose ruler had just renewed his ancient friendship with his house—his fury knew no bounds and he flatly refused to sign. To take any other course, he declared, would go against "his conscience, his character, his honour". And so the whole miserable wrangle between the two men reached its strident climax.

Ultimately the Emperor fled to Baden-Baden. Bismarck sent one of his aides in hot pursuit, armed with an ultimatum in which, as he himself says, he applied the very embarrassing expedient of the *Kabinettsfrage* (Bismarck's official threat of resignation): the aide, being asked to request an immediate decision and, whatever the reply, to return forthwith.

William knew he was beaten, though he was anything but convinced by Bismarck's arguments, and on October 3rd gave his assent to the treaty. He felt incapable of any further resistance, and he was resigned to accept whatever calamity fate might have in store. He wrote on the papers, "Let those who have forced me to take this step answer for it above, when the time comes."

Two days later some natural element of toughness within him caused him to rebel. Let them try, he said, at least to get the treaty to cover the eventuality of an attack by France. But Bismarck refused even to transmit such a request to Vienna. The Emperor then asked that the memorandum in which he proposed to interpret the new agreement to the Czar and which, as was customary, would be written in French, should be accompanied by a German text so that he would be protected from malignant tricks by translators. But this, too, was refused him. Full of bitterness, he wrote in the margin of the documents, "There isn't a thing I can do under the present administration" (*Nicht das Geringste kann ich erlangen bei der jetzigen Geschäftsführung*),* and one feels that the remark did not wholly lack justification.

At last he resigned himself to his fate and authorised the ratification of the treaty. A letter to Bülow shows the state of his feelings. "My whole moral strength is broken. I don't know what will become of me."† It was an outcry not unlike that anguished utterance to King John, when Bismarck had compelled him to absent himself from the German Princes and he had thrown himself weeping on the sofa. On that occasion, we are told, Bismarck was so exhausted that his legs were trembling. He was exhausted now, for the exertions of the past few weeks had made cruel inroads on his strength. And so he took a long leave and went off to Varzin. This time, however, there was no trembling of the legs, or, if there was, the fact has escaped record by the historians.

As was to be expected, the alliance with Austria improved Germany's relations with both Western powers. In France, Waddington's markedly anti-Russian government was still in power, while that of Freycinet, which followed it, and behind which loomed the shadow of Gambetta, placed greater value on good relations with Bismarck than it was prepared to let its electors know.

Bismarck availed himself of such good political weather and encouraged France to increase her strength in the Mediterranean and North Africa, and it seemed logical to suppose that, after the excellent understanding established between Beaconsfield and Bismarck at Berlin, relations with Britain should be even more cordial than those with France. Where with the French there had been a gentle but perceptible budding of good will, there should be a positive flowering in England—and not only a flowering but a fruit. Yet it was not to be.

Actually, Bismarck had always hoped that, as an old ally of Austria, Britain would more or less automatically be brought within the context of the new alliance. As we have seen, he had had enquiries made in London as to what the attitude would be in the event of a Russo-German conflict, and we noted Beaconsfield's answer that in such a case Britain would compel France to remain neutral—which was certainly not a negative reply. Yet suddenly—and almost inexplicably—Bismarck found this answer

*Windelband, p. 83.
† George W. F. Hallgarten, *Imperialismus vor 1914* (1951), I, p. 189.

insufficient and instructed his ambassador in London not to press
the matter any further.

One asks why Bismarck should so suddenly have called a halt.
Yet his action is not hard to understand, if we take account of
the fact that, at this very moment, probably to Bismarck's own
astonishment, a prophecy which he had made to the Emperor had
actually come true. For what he had told William was that Russia
would accept the existence of a German-Austrian alliance and
would make the best of a bad business, and would actually
approach Germany with a view to coming to a better understanding with her.

Now this was exactly what happened, and really there is no
good reason why it should not have happened. Russia was
politically isolated and still suffering from the economic effects
of the war with Turkey. Russian state bonds had fallen to rock
bottom prices. Whether she liked it or not, Russia was in desperate need of peace and of support from the West. Already in
the summer of 1879, Bismarck had been approached by Prince
Orlow, the husband of the unforgotten and unforgettable woman
who had actually died four years before, and had shown himself
ready for conciliatory conversation. Shortly after this, another
letter from the Czar reached William, full of an astonishing understanding for the circumstances which had compelled him to
enter into an alliance with Austria. Simultaneously, the Ambassador Oubril, whom Bismarck had thoroughly disliked, was replaced by Saburow, with whom, at this stage at any rate, Bismarck
managed to get along very well.

Slight as they were, these were signs of a change. Whether,
indeed, there would now be a second Spring of Russo-Germanic
friendship, nobody could say, but the chances seemed good enough
to Bismarck for him to abandon the possibilities of a solid,
British-German entente, a fact which it is difficult to explain
objectively, but which is, nevertheless, subjectively not unin-
telligible. For to Bismarck, the East German nobleman, to
Bismarck, the great landlord, the neighbouring empire, unreliable
and irresponsible though it might often prove itself, was something
more familiar and understandable than the Atlantic Western
world of money-lenders and traders. There was here a sense of
kinship at work. The great plains of his homeland passed imper-
ceptibly into the vast Russian steppes, and he was distrustful of all
that lay beyond the water. It was instinct that made him break
off the talks with London and fall a victim to the new St. Petersburg bait.

It was surely through the operation of a similar hidden and
almost unconscious process of his mind that Bismarck was led

back to the ancient political conception under the dominance of which he had spent the first fifty years of his life, the conception of the German Bund, which he now referred to as a kind of insurance for peace. He did not aim at a pedantically exact restoration of the ancient structure, but at a modern version thereof, in the form of a perpetual alliance.

It is clear, then, that at this period of his life he was more inclined to be guided by his instincts, the reasoned grounds for his action being developed ex post facto. Some writers see in the policies of the decade that starts in 1880 the signs of failing powers, of uncertainty, inconsistency and hesitation. The present writer does not take that view, but holds that the powers of reason and feeling always held equal rank with him, and that it depended on the situation what instruments he used.

Being, as we are, in the possession of more complete knowledge than was at Bismarck's disposal, we need not scruple to say that on this occasion his judgment was probably at fault, that he aroused a mistrust in Britain which continued during the whole of his life. At the same time he provided Russia with a breathing space, during which the forces concentrated on her frontiers remained as numerous as ever, while even the Press did not bother to moderate its language.

As to the Vienna alliance of 1879, it is again very easy to criticise it in the light of events then still to come, but it had features which must have seemed promising at the time and which were indeed by no means unsound in principle. It represented a form of compact, hardly known in Europe, where till now it had been customary to enter into alliances shortly before the outbreak of war and to sever one's connections with one's belligerent partner when the war was over. Here, however, an alliance had come into being in the midst of peace which did not make the prospects of any war more favourable for the contracting parties, but was simply designed to prevent such a war from occurring. Bismarck, whose reputation till now had rested on brilliant improvisations, had apparently returned to his role of the cautious river superintendent of Schönhausen who, like all those that live close to great waters, was building breakwaters and moles out into the sea of the future.

Bismarck had, of course, failed to secure an alliance that was actually written into the constitution. Indeed, the road to the older Germany was one he never found again. Yet if one looked at the actual territories of the two allies on the map, at least the geography of the German Bund seemed to have been restored; it is a significant fact that there was a perceptible change of sentiment towards that vanished edifice which but fifteen years ago had seemed a thing totally incapable of survival. Now it began again to be looked on as a worthy habitation for the German peoples. Metternich's conception—how recently that name had still unfailingly produced catcalls!—the conception according to which German welfare depended on the equal recognition of Prussian and Austrian interests, was now to be the guiding principle of the new alliance.

Yet, if Bismarck had expected to find in Austria the same great power that he had extruded from Germany in 1866, he was surely mistaken. Austria was a weaker thing, subject to new strains and uncertain of herself. For the victors of 1866 were not the Prussians and Italians alone, the Hungarians had also been the gainers. Königgrätz led more or less directly to the *Ausgleich*, and it was not long before so talented a body of men as the Hungarian aristocracy became the virtual directors of Austrian policy, as the case of Andrassy clearly shows. "When I made the alliance with Austria," Bismarck said in later years, "I thought I was allying myself with a powerful Emperor. Instead of that, I see that I allied myself with the Hungarian parliament."* It was, of course, unfortunate that in the final analysis the Hungarians cared little for anybody but themselves.†

Sensitive natures in Austria itself were well aware of these changes. When Archduke Rudolf, the heir to the Austrian throne, visited the New Imperial Court in Berlin in 1878, Princess Radziwill noted a certain sadness in his smile. His hosts had the impression that he was, at least outwardly, a serious young officer, but also a man who realised the futility of any enterprise undertaken within the insecure structure of what was now Austria.

The die, however, was cast, and whether Bismarck willed it or not, the Austro-German alliance determined the future of Europe, for it is never long before a bloc which unites friendly powers also brings about the union of those who are excluded from it. The ultimate encirclement of Germany was thus not due to any malicious intent. Geography had prepared the way for it, and it was the dual alliance which set it in motion.

---

* Holstein, II, p. 375.

† During the war of 1870 Hungarian sympathies were wholly with France. Wherever there was a Zigeuner band they had to follow the Rackoczky March with either "Partant pour la Syrie" or the "Marseillaise" which was invariably greeted with loud cries of "Eljen" . . . French tricolours were waving outside the cafés (Ludwig Ritter von Przybram, *Erinnerungen eines alten Österreichers* (1910–12), I. p. 209.

13

ANXIETY

About 1880 those who were close to Bismarck began to notice changes in his mode of behaviour. There was no question of the fundamental elements of his character having in any way been transformed, or of new traits having come into existence. It was a matter of relative emphasis. Some features seemed almost to vanish away and others became more noticeable. But that which sustained him, remained what it had always been—Prussia, which had now, as the German Empire, became a great power and was, as it were, embodied in his own person.

Bismarck's planning still combined the qualities of boldness and of cool objective assessment of the facts, but the road that led from resolve to execution had become a longer one. The capacity for both lightning speed and hair's-breadth accuracy of judgment was no longer what it once had been. His touch on the reins had become less sensitive, and obstinate stiffness could alternate with excessive laxity.

The extreme caution that marked his foreign policy from 1871 onwards characterised his every action, however much he might still be the Iron Chancellor to the masses who only saw him from a distance. Indeed it is almost touching to read today the instructions he sent to his diplomats, and to note the meticulousness with which every eventuality was considered, including the most wildly improbable. He put no more trust in a friendly chance than he did in his colleagues. And so his load of work grew, till it assumed fantastic proportions. Nothing was left now of the rapid pace of his early triumphs. Everything had to be fought for, nothing was given him for nothing.

In the Reichstag he no longer had a firm majority. He had to apply his strength with much more effort, to concentrate his attention much more sharply than he had ever done before. Even so, his successes only came slowly and piecemeal. More and more, his nights were sleepless, disturbed as they were by intense mental activity. More and more, intercourse with others seemed to him a waste of time, and the more he avoided men, the more he despised them. He could speak respectfully of the workmen on his estates, but the portraits of crowned heads which came to him from time to time, as tokens of royal favour, he placed in the chancellery with their faces to the wall.

He withdrew increasingly into himself. For a dozen years he heard no opera. When he went to see the Emperor the curtains of his carriage were drawn. The most one could see would be a flash of his white cuirassier's cap.

It is scarcely to be wondered at that his character should have suffered, that he should have tended to grow hard and narrow. He felt that people could more easily take advantage of him than formerly, and his attitude became stiff and suspicious. His intelligence was as good as ever, and his courage as strong, but certain ignoble and rather peasant-like traits began to come into evidence: his rudeness to helpless officials, for instance, while self-mastery and generosity, of which lesser men often show themselves capable, were with him very rare indeed, even where common prudence must have told him that a little kindness would have turned away wrath. For anything like that, the elemental power of Bismarck's rage was much too strong.

To place expediency above right was a course which the young Deputy of 1849 had contemptuously rejected as a "theory of the revolution". But Bismarck the prince had long since forgotten that. Whatever or whoever stood in his way—whether it was a crowned head or some petty journalist—he had, as far as this was possible, made to disappear, not under the rules of the Junker's duel but as a result of defamation. Even enmities which had wholly ceased to be relevant were things he was incapable of putting out of his mind. When Lasker, who was a man of excellent intelligence, high courage and personal integrity* but who had certainly caused Bismarck many an anguished hour, died in New York in 1884, Bismark refused to pass on to the Reichstag a vote of condolence by the American House of Representatives. Once he had made up his mind to be hard, that hardness knew no limits. Moments of actual brutality were, of course, rare, and he was wholly lacking the cold and deliberate cruelty of the gangster; that kind of a régime was something which the Germans were only to experience half a century later.

Certainly there were moments when something that was downright and uncompromisingly evil got the upper hand in him. For such forces have certainly always had their place in the shaping of history. There were times when there was a definite will to annihilate, of the kind that may well have moved his ancestors

---

* Eduard Lasker was a member of the Prussian Landtag from 1865 and of the Reichstag from 1883. He was one of the founders of the National Liberal Party and the leader of its left wing.

when they were crushing the Wends. Also, he was too proud to follow the example of weaker natures and hypocritically disguise his hatreds. "I have been hating all through the night," he would sometimes openly confess. Yet, so Holstein tells us, and this at a time of acute personal enmity with Bismarck, "One cannot say that he is a deliberately evil character," and then, as though by way of explanation, "but he makes enemies of people." (*Er verleidet sich die Menschen.*)

Bismarck seems never to have been able to smile, let alone to laugh at himself. Indeed there was nothing that he treated so seriously as himself. Even his massive Nether-German humour had its limits. It never occurred to him to use it as a means of sharpening enmities. Enmities were much too serious things. Where he felt an enmity, he tended to cultivate it with great earnestness, as though it were a decorative plant in his garden.

On the other hand, he had wholly lost the capacity to make friends. It is significant that his last friends were foreigners, the American Motley, the historian and diplomat, and the Baltic naturalist, Count Keyserling.

The heroes together with whom he had formed German history over recent decades had become something very like public monuments on their own account. Age had disfigured them—as no doubt they felt that it had disfigured Bismarck himself. Emperor William's face was becoming ever more like a yellowish wax mask and he was showing signs of senility. Among other things, it was now often impossible to read any intelligible meaning into the confused sentence structures of the letters which he sent to Bismarck. If he did not understand an argument, tears would come into his eyes. Whether he ever really overcame his mistrust of Bismarck, a mistrust which led him to say that Bismarck's politics were those of a high-school boy, is a question to which there is no answer. Bismarck, even in 1877, had called him "as hard as stone and cold". The Emperor, he insisted, felt no gratitude towards him, but only kept him on because he believed that Bismarck could still be of some service.

Roon, to whom Bismarck owed so much, had already in 1873 complained that Bismarck treated him "like a rebellious and inefficient subordinate, which I never was, am not now, nor ever shall be". He was thoroughly ill at ease in the new state, was "stumbling towards a precipice". When he died, Bismarck let himself be represented at the funeral by his wife, while he himself remained at home, quietly smoking his pipe.

Moltke, well on into his eighties, seemed to be drying up like a mummy. The colour of his wig had not been changed since

Königgrätz and he was still Chief of the General Staff. Death was already taking its toll among Bismarck's various foils on both sides of the border. Thiers, Favre, Gambetta, Garibaldi and Disraeli, all these were gone by 1883, as was Harry Arnim, Frederick von Augustenburg and Gerlach, the friend who had become an enemy. Gerlach was run over by a mail coach in that year, which also saw the end of Karl Marx and Gortschakow. Beust died in 1886. The disappearance of these men made Bismarck's world more empty.

The officials whom he gathered around him could hardly have been called colleagues, let alone confidants. He did not take counsel with them, but only gave them directives and could then only hope that these had been correctly understood. He changed his assistants continually, "like knives and forks after every course" (Holstein), partly because they soon began to bore him, and also because he followed the old principle of Philip II of Spain, "He who knows much can betray much." He referred to the Prussian ministers with ironic condescension as his "play-mates".

Thus the various offices were filled with nonentities and the favourites of nonentities—flatterers and hypocrites predominating. Bismarck knew very well how doubtful was their value and let them feel that he knew. Often he showed more respect to his enemies than to those who were supposed to be his allies. He certainly cannot be reproached with showing particular favour to the nobility. His department heads were nearly all commoners, though the Emperor often ennobled them at a later stage.

One cannot, however, help observing that his real intimates came from other spheres than his own. Nay, more, there was something slightly questionable about nearly all of them, the kind of people about whom there were always discreditable whispers.

For instance, there was Guido Henckel von Donnersmarck, a Count from Upper Silesia, later a Prince, who, thanks to mineral deposits on his estate, had become an immensely rich industrialist. He and his wife had lived in Paris during the heyday of the Second Empire. The Henckels went in for Stock Exchange speculation in a big way, and members of the Prussian aristocracy, such as Harry Arnim, were glad to share in their winnings. The couple lived in fantastic style, they had a palace whose stairway of porphyry and onyx was famous, a palace which had once belonged to Morny, Napoleon's illegitimate half-brother.

Henckel's rather equivocal position made him vaguely unpopular in Berlin society, but the very fact that he had some rather shady contacts sometimes made him very useful to Bismarck, who did not in the least object to the eccentricities of the man or those of his family.* Bismarck used him for various discreet bits of political and financial business—in 1884, for instance, to arrange a loan for his old friend Prince Orlow, who was at that time ambassador in Berlin.

This loan, incidentally, seems to have been made by the accommodating Bleichröder, who later got a patent of nobility and who was another strange figure in Bismarck's entourage. Originally little more than the administrator of Bismarck's personal fortune, he gained the latter's confidence to an astonishing degree. He had in 1866 helped him out of a highly embarrassing situation, when the Prussian Finance Minister had refused to make any further payments towards the cost of mobilisation against Austria, and like Henckel he claimed to be the man who had told Bismarck that the war indemnity was not beyond France's capacity.

On more than one occasion he was responsible for supplying considerable sums of money which were needed for political purposes and which the Treasury refused to disgorge. But Bismarck went further than this, and often entrusted him with diplomatic missions which could not be carried out without embarrassment through the normal channels of diplomacy.

This was rather remarkable, since Bleichröder's weakness for indiscretions was as well known as his habit of posing as the intimate confidant of the Chancellor. Yet all this may have served a more useful purpose than one might think, as did the man's appearance, which conformed completely to the stereotype of the financier as seen through the eyes of German caricature. This often dissuaded foreign statesmen from taking his communications seriously—which in certain circumstances could be quite convenient if Bismarck wished to go back on what he had said.

That Bleichröder should have made no use for his own purposes of the information which he obtained could hardly be expected. Apart from this, however, there is strong reason for believing that his firm paid considerable sums to high state officials (and here the reference is particularly to Keudell), for supplying much of the information in question. Bismarck's family loathed the man and felt that they were compromised by association with him. Herbert called him, quite simply, *"ein Mistvieh"*, "a swine with whom no decent person would associate", and it happened

---

* Henckel's sister was also a somewhat wayward woman. She was married to a Prince Carolath, but it is uncertain, according to Holstein, whether the father of her son was a waiter or a coachman. "One must choose between the two." (Holstein, II, p. 211.)

occasionally, that in order to get him out of the house, they would throw revolver ammunition on to the fire, beside which Bleichröder had seated himself while waiting for Bismarck.

In ordinary matters of routine, the man on whom he principally relied was Lothar Bucher. Bucher, an essentially embittered and disappointed man of lower middle-class origin, and of approximately Bismarck's own age, had become a radical in his youth and remained so ever since. In 1850 he had served a prison sentence for not paying his taxes, which caused the Emperor, whenever possible, completely to ignore him. The Emperor was by no means the only one who avoided him and found his society vaguely disquieting. Nevertheless, as early as 1864, Bismarck had made him a *Vortragender Rat*,* and in 1870 entrusted him with a mission to Spain which became world history.

According to Holstein, Bucher lacked the gift to survey and assess a diplomatic situation in its entirety. Also, he tells us that his crude way of talking sometimes moved Bismarck to positive fits of rage. Yet he stayed longer with Bismarck than anybody else, and in the end we see Bucher and Bismarck, now two very old men, sitting opposite each other at Friedrichsruh for hours at a time—until Bismarck was once more moved to continue with the dictation of his memoirs.

To these strange figures in Bismarck's entourage, figures that set one wondering how they contrived to keep the positions which they held, we must add Kuno, Count Rantzau, the career diplomat who in 1878 became the husband of Bismarck's only daughter. Together with his wife, he had contrived to make himself an integral part of the Bismarck household. Whenever Bismarck was in residence in Varzin or Friedrichsruh, Rantzau was recognised as the regular liaison officer between him and the Berlin offices.

Clumsy in thought, mentally undistinguished and not even particularly industrious,† he caused much confusion and annoyance in the conduct of official business. He could afford to do this, for though he was only a member of the Bismarck family by marriage, Bismarck's sense of kin made it impossible for him to be uprooted. In his right to membership of the Bismarck household he was also strongly supported by Johanna, who always wanted to have her grandchildren around her. "Even

---

* Literally "Reporting Counsellor". A title still in use and peculiar to the German Foreign Office. The rank is roughly equivalent to that of Counsellor in the British Foreign Service.

† Bismarck had few illusions about Rantzau. Thus in July 1885 Rantzau remarked at table that if one was called a "Schafskopf" (a blockhead) one had to fight. "Sometimes," remarked Bismarck, "one has oneself the feeling that the other man is in the right." (Holstein, II, p. 239.)

a grandmother," Bismarck used to say, "must always have something to play with."

Unlike Bismarck's two sons, Johanna was of one mind with the Rantzaus in trying to make the time spent in Berlin as short and that spent in the country as long as possible. She thus helped to increase Bismarck's growing tendency towards self-isolation. In the circumstances it was inevitable that the Rantzaus should do their best to diminish the influence of Herbert and Bill upon their father, an attempt which, needless to say, these two strong characters resisted with all their power. So there was not so very much of the peacefulness of country life in the Bismarck family.

There was, indeed, a rather strange atmosphere in the Bismarck household, a mixture in which the nervous tension generated by the everlasting simmering of intrigues was somehow blended with a peculiar sort of philistinism, full of the smell of pipe smoke and great dogs. The external setting was on a grand scale, the servants almost too numerous. The interior of the house, the furniture, china and so on conformed as Lerchenfeld says "to the tastes of the couple, neither of whom had the Muses standing by their cradle". Actually Johanna was satisfied with those primitive conditions to which her parental home in Further Pomerania had accustomed her, and she remained satisfied, even when she bore the title "Durchlaucht". Grand folk like Hohenlohe and his son used to smile at the roughness of the new princely residence, where unmanageable dogs rolled about on the carpets before the guests. The so-called "Imperial Dog" Tyras, a great black brute whom Lerchenfeld speaks of as "a wicked, treacherous beast", was a particularly unpleasant customer. He bit people and killed dogs that were smaller than himself.

This kind of thing and the frequent human clashes could make life with the Bismarcks a somewhat exacting affair, and we know of at least two doctors who declined to go on treating the family because they could not stand the conditions in which they were asked to work. One was von Frerichs, who later became the Director of the Imperial Ministry of Health, and the other von Struck, who wrote to the Prince that the state of his own health would not permit him to expose himself to the kind of incident which the treatment of the Bismarck family seemed to involve. Bismarck himself, wrapped up in the cares of State, may well have been blissfully unconscious of disturbances which were often painfully embarrassing to others.

The tensions in Bismarck's family grew even greater at the beginning of 1881, when Herbert declared his intention of marrying the Princess Elisabeth Carolath, a great beauty and a member of the Silesian aristocracy. Divorce proceedings terminating her existing unhappy marriage had already been initiated. But Bismarck opposed this marriage with downright passion, though the motives behind his opposition are, even today, somewhat obscure. The slight smell of scandal which, in those days, still attached to divorce can hardly have deterred a man who had long ceased to lead any kind of social life. The most plausible explanation is that Elisabeth Carolath was related to the family of the Minister of the Royal Household, Count Schleinitz,* whose confidential relationship with the Hohenzollerns, Bismarck, for a quarter of a century, had been vainly endeavouring to destroy. Thus Schleinitz was the privileged object of his hate. Moreover, Schleinitz's house was recognised as the gathering point of the Richard Wagner clique, the countess being an intimate friend of Cosima Wagner. It is possible that the thought of his son's entering this circle was utterly intolerable to him.

Whatever the reason, he assembled against the unfortunate Herbert every weapon in his possession—frenzied outbursts of rage, terrible appeals to pity, threats of suicide and also threats of disinheritance and loss of livelihood. Almost daily there were wild scenes, which so exhausted Herbert, who was certainly anything but a weakling, that he gave way. The Princess Carolath was duly divorced because of Herbert but was not married by him, a stain on his character which he had to bear for the rest of his life. Many years later he married the Countess Margarethe Hoyos, an Austrian and the grand-daughter of the inventor of the torpedo, Robert Whitehead.

To some extent Bismarck rewarded his son's obedience. Herbert, young as he was, was made First Secretary at the London Embassy, then at that of St. Petersburg, and then Ambassador to The Hague. In 1885 Bismarck called him into the Foreign Office, first as an Under State Secretary, then, in 1886, as State Secretary. The Chancellor now ceased putting in an appearance at the Foreign Office, and during his visits to Berlin would, instead, bury himself in the Imperial Chancellery next door.

Actually, the responsibility was rather more than Herbert could handle and one which even impeded his development. He was a much simpler sort of person than his father, so that the negative Junker elements, arrogance and a tendency towards violence, were much more strongly marked in him. Thus, even in 1885, he was quite capable at Christmastime of firing a new airgun from the garden of the Chancellery into the windows of depart-

---

* Alexander Count von Schleinitz (1807–1885) was employed from 1849–1850 in the Ministry of Count Brandenburg, was Foreign Minister from 1850–1860 and Minister of the Royal Household from 1861–1885.

ment heads in the Foreign Office. His father loaded him down with tasks of great difficulty, and at the same time acted as a tyrant over him. Indeed, when Herbert was already a State Secretary, Bismarck did not hesitate to use such expressions in front of others as, "Don't talk drivel, Herbert." (*Quatsch nicht, Herbert.*) The result was that his son became uncertain of himself, and either sought release in despairing cynicism or made violent scenes.

We must not forget, of course, that these were the years when Bismarck's health was in a very sorry state. Of the various doctors who were consulted, only Frerichs seemed instinctively to grasp the truth when he said that the Prince was perfectly healthy and that his facial pains, for instance, never appeared when his doctor was present. This did not mean that they weren't real, but "it was a matter of Bismarck's mood".

After the Bavarian doctor Schweninger had taken over the treatment, all who saw him agree that there was an immediate improvement. Schweninger, at that time thirty-three years of age, was a strange mixture of the primitive with high intelligence and a rather violent temperament. He had had a rather stormy past, had been country-bred and had been involved in an embarrassing adventure with a village girl, which cost him his membership of the medical faculty in Munich. Since then he had established himself as an outsider, both professionally and socially. Bearded like a satyr, he became something in the nature of a fashionable doctor, and people used to compare him with Kaspar in the "Freischütz".

Schweninger found that Bismarck's sleeplessness, gastric upsets, neuralgic pains and so on were not due to any organic defect but to the fact that he lived on the basis of an assumed primitive Junker strength, which was largely non-existent, and Schweninger's reputed miracle cure consisted in nothing more than preventing Bismarck, to some extent, from ruining his own health.

He succeeded in doing so by establishing himself almost permanently under his patient's roof, whether at Varzin or at Friedrichsruh, and controlling him by day and night. He weighed him, examined him and often roughly criticised him every morning, and did not hesitate to threaten him with complete collapse. The real miracle lay in the fact that he managed to impose his will on Bismarck, whom nobody had ever before ventured seriously to contradict. Indeed his own wife actually encouraged him in his disastrous habits, and all too readily encouraged his gross over-indulgence in food.*

Basically the causes of Bismarck's ill-health were two: the

* Treue, p. 403.

increasing anxieties of his office and his lack of any moderation at table, combined with insufficient exercise. Schweninger contrived to control this enormous appetite—sometimes by very drastic means which, simply because they were drastic, impressed Bismarck. Thus Lerchenfeld tells us that on one occasion, when some heavy Rhine wine was being served, Schweninger gave the brusque order that it be removed, saying that as long as he was in the house no wine of that kind would be drunk. It can hardly be said that Schweninger saved Bismarck's life, but it is nevertheless true that he made the closing decades of it much easier for the old man.

In foreign policy, which was the essence of his very being, his chief concern always remained the eastern frontier. Russia's recurrent symptoms of weakness did not blind him to the fact that this frontier was a mighty dam which held natural forces in check, against which, if they were once released, Europe had nothing to set. The relative importance of all other problems of foreign policy depended on their relation to the Russian one.

He was certain that a war against Russia would certainly mean a war against France—a two-front war—and his sense of realities made him only too well aware that German reserves of strength were quite inadequate to engage in such a conflict. The year 1914, when the victory over Russia had to be paid for with permanent and ultimately deadly paralysis on the Western Front, confirmed the exactness of his calculations.

In 1880 Gortschakow had finally retired, and was replaced by Nicholas von Giers. He was a man of Finnish-Swedish origin, an accomplished European and, for that very reason, fundamentally unable to come to terms with the essential brutalities of the native Russian character. Nevertheless, since through the disappearance of Gortschakow, who died some years later under rather mysterious circumstances,* a considerable psychological obstacle had been removed, Bismarck, too, began to be interested in a new Three Emperors Alliance, which Saburoff, the Russian ambassador, had recently informed him was being drafted. In Vienna, he met some opposition, since Austria felt herself more secure in a simple alliance with Germany, than in one which also included Russia.

Andrassy's successor Haymerle, an essentially slow and rather over-cautious man, refused to consider any kind of agreement that went beyond the limits of the Berlin congress. Yet, disagreeable

---

* Gortschakow died in 1883 in Baden-Baden from phosphorus poisoning. It was, however, never determined whether this was secretly administered to him by prospective legatees or whether he took an overdose as a means of rejuvenation. Bismarck was of the latter opinion. (Brauer, *Im Dieste Bismarck* (1936), p. 187.)

as the negotiations became, Bismarck refused to give way, and one wonders why, for months on end, he loaded himself with this extremely tough assignment which needed all his hard-bitten determination to carry out. He knew full well that the value of the new Three Emperors Pact was purely decorative, that it could never be more than a show-piece for festive occasions.

The only rational explanation is that his concern over the threat from the east was so great that he refused to neglect any thread, even the veriest gossamer, that might conceivably link him to his eastern neighbour.

At last, in January 1881, Saburoff could report his master's readiness to sign. Whereupon Bismarck managed to persuade his Emperor to go behind Haymerle's back and communicate directly with Francis Joseph, who on the 31st of that month declared himself agreeable in principle.

Some weeks later, however, Czar Alexander II was murdered and everything that had been attained to date was destroyed. For though the new Czar, Alexander III, had much personal respect for Bismarck, he was highly suspicious of his tactics. Only a few months previously he had remarked to the Crown Prince that he was convinced that Bismarck had his eye on Russia's Baltic provinces. Moreover, as the husband of a Danish princess, he could never forgive the Chancellor his Danish war, a feeling which was, as we have seen, to some extent shared by the Prince of Wales, who had married the Czar's wife's sister. Thus, the Danish War, which was regarded at the time as a relatively minor adventure, had consequences which lasted for many decades, consequences which were hardly balanced by the acquisition of a small piece of territory.

Yet Alexander realised that if Russia was not to be wholly isolated, she had to choose between two equally unpleasant alternatives. She had either to associate herself with the Austro-German pact or enter into some kind of a bond with the French Republic, a thing profoundly repugnant to her conservative instincts. At length, when Saburoff returned from the funeral of Alexander II, he was able to state that the new Czar intended to follow the foreign policy of his father.

Bismarck now applied all his energies to concluding the affair as soon as possible. The pact was signed in June. Compared with its predecessor it was an even weaker instrument. There was no longer any mention of possible military aid. It merely committed the three contracting parties to neutrality if one of them should be attacked by a fourth power. In other words, Russia had to be neutral in the event of a Franco-German conflict, and Germany in the event of an Anglo-Russian one.

Yet even in this, the value of the pact was largely illusory, as Bismarck must surely have known. For we cannot but suppose that even at that stage he was aware of the truth that he later uttered in his memoirs. "No great nation will ever be persuaded to sacrifice its very existence on the altar of fidelity to its treaties, if it is forced to choose between the two." In the present instance, the most that Bismarck could have expected from this treaty, should a serious situation arise, was some chance of delaying the ultimate catastrophe. Nevertheless, Bismarck had succeeded in inveigling Russia into a bond that at least bore some superficial resemblance to her bygone friendship, while at the same time he deterred her from active hostilities by giving the dual alliance the maximum possible military strength. Actually, though it was renewed once more in 1884, relations with Russia during the lifetime of the Three Emperors Pact of 1881 became steadily worse.

From the close of the seventies onwards, the pressure of Russia upon the West, which was essentially a natural phenomenon and so independent of any change of government, had occupied the central place in Bismarck's thoughts. To an ever-increasing extent his conduct became essentially a reaction to Russian behaviour. He continued, of course, to seek ways of escape from the peril and clung to the belief that the ultimate issue could be decided and the ultimate crisis suppressed by the surface methods of diplomacy. In the background, however, stood a kind of alter ego who knew the uselessness of all attempts to smooth matters over, and when people said that the business of a Russian war would one day be settled, just as that of a French one had been settled in 1870, it was this alter ego that replied to such folly with the profound remark, "We shall never have the Russian war behind us."*

When Russia was the subject of discussion, Bismarck's tone would be irritable and bitter, but he would be quite remarkably cautious. Much of what he knew, he kept secret from the German public, and wherever possible he prevented disturbing utterances by the Russian Press from being reproduced in Germany. When he spoke in public he tended to represent the situation as being much healthier than it actually was, whereupon he would immediately communicate his true views secretly to the German embassies. Where Russia was concerned he moved with the thoughtful timidity of a wise old elephant, but for all that it became ever more obvious that he was deeply concerned. Some kind of premonition seemed to be telling him that at the end of everything there would be a great calamity. Ultimately he

* Holstein, II, p. 14.

would take refuge in a kind of enforced stoicism, telling himself and others that he would rather accept an apparently unequal battle than play a dishonourable part.

It was, of course, inevitable that the cautious nature of Bismarck's Russian policy should produce disagreements with Austria, for it was in the nature of things for Austria to put a very wide interpretation on German duties to secure her from attack while that of Bismarck tended necessarily to be narrow—particularly when he suspected that Austrian activities with the Balkans might leave him with a Russian war on his hands. So great was his anxiety that it sometimes looked, during this period, as though he was seeking to escape from the Austrian alliance. But the very fact that German interests themselves made this obviously unthinkable caused his tone towards the Vienna Cabinet to become perceptibly sharp. The Austrians, for their part, recognised with a kind of melancholy clarity that destiny itself had made Russia the enemy of their ruling house, and even in Bismarck's view Russo-Austrian hostility derived from "political causes which no human power is capable of setting aside".

Yet despite everything, Berlin showed no signs of breaking away from the tradition of friendship with Russia, and, indeed, used every opportunity to confirm it. This made the Austrians timid and mistrustful, and often somewhat devious in their dealings with Germany. Thus, a Serbo-Austrian alliance, concluded a few days later than the Three Emperors Pact, was kept a secret from Bismarck, who only found out about it through Haymerle's successor, the Hungarian Count Kalnoky, a skilful and a harder man than his predecessor and equally mistrustful of both Germany and Russia.

Bismarck extended the external scope of the dual alliance by the somewhat surprising inclusion of Italy—surprising because Italy's failure in 1866 had sadly depressed her credit. Italy, said Bismarck, had a great appetite but bad teeth. But Bismarck did not seek the Italian alliance because of its military value. He knew that the country had unstable governments, that its people were politically indifferent and lived in great poverty, and that in consequence Italy was unable to incur large expenses for armaments—which was unfortunate, since the Austrians in 1866 had sunk the greater part of her fleet.

What Bismarck was concerned with were two things: to secure Austria's southern frontier against Italy and so increase the Austrian defensive strength against Russia by four army corps, and, secondly, to prevent France becoming allied with Italy and so providing herself with an assembly platform against the dual alliance. The task was not an easy one since Victor Emmanuel was equally unpopular in Berlin and in Vienna. He was accounted a barbarian peasant smelling of garlic and the stables, who painted his cheeks red and dyed his mighty moustache black, and who, if Cavour had not intervened, would have chosen a buxom drum-major's daughter as his queen. What was even more important was that Italy never sought to conceal her desire for the ancient Austrian territories of the Trentino and Trieste, and this opened up a veritable abyss.

Yet strategic considerations were, for Bismarck, not the only decisive ones. Indeed, what he believed was that England had an interest in seeing that there were only weak fleets in the Mediterranean, that is to say, across its road to India, and would therefore be prepared to assist second-class Mediterranean powers such as Austria and Italy against great powers like France and in particular against Russia. It seemed to him that an Austro-Italian maritime alliance could be certain of British support. This meant that whether she desired it or not Bismarck was already treating Britain as a silent partner in an anti-Russian system of alliances.

For all that, his relations with England remained what they had always been, and that country remained to him something that was, at one and the same time, attractive and strange. He always felt, as did Frederick the Great, that the logic of facts necessitated a co-operation of the two greatest Protestant powers of Northern Europe, the continental and the maritime. Yet this was an idea that he feared to realise, for if he were even to give the appearance of being closely tied to the island kingdom, this might well serve to increase the enmity of Russia. When, therefore, the two brothers-in-law, Crown Prince Frederick William and the Prince of Wales, sought to persuade him to enter into a formal entente, he politely evaded the offer.*

Another circumstance that militated against any such project was the return, about this time, of Gladstone to power, for wherever Bismarck might be, Gladstone was invariably in the opposite camp. For all that, his courtesy towards Britain was marked and unfailing. "He hates Gladstone," wrote Holstein, "but he is afraid that by striking at him he will strike at England." He treated the occupation of Egypt by England more as an intelligent administration of a bankrupt estate than as a military undertaking. After Tel-el-Kabir, he sent London his formal congratulations.

His relations with France, however, were never marked by that wholly problematical character that bedevilled those between himself and England. Indeed, in retrospect, one marvels at the

* Haselmayer, *Diplomatische Geschichte des zweiten Reichs* (1956), II, p. 97.

success of his policy with France, which because of sensitive national feelings in both countries had to be carried out in the strictest secrecy and which, simply because in the end it failed, was never really made known to the public. It should be added that the inspired historiography of both countries has left this period deep in the shadows. Conjectures have no place in serious history, yet we might surely be permitted to say that if something resembling a sensible relationship could have been established between the two countries concerned, something worthy of their common origin in the empire of Charlemagne, then what might have happened almost staggers the imagination.

The thing which popular demagogy designated as the hereditary Franco-German enmity had for Bismarck no reality at all. For Bismarck the relations between Prussia and France were not determined by great natural forces, as those on his eastern frontier seemed to be. There was a formidable obstacle in the way of good understanding in the shape of the two annexed provinces. Any attempt at a compromise in this problem, so dangerously charged with resentment, would in the end have produced a wild outcry from both the countries concerned. Again Bismarck found himself trapped in a position which denied him any freedom of movement and slowly, but ever more firmly, the conviction gained ground within him that these two territories were nothing more than a burden which the military had talked him into loading on to his shoulders. He openly admitted to the French Foreign Minister, Waddington, and to the French ambassadors, Saint-Vallier and Courcelles, that the annexation of Metz had been one of his worst political blunders.

By 1882 he had already realised that the hearts of the Alsatians could never be won for Germany. The truth was, he declared in the Reichstag, that France had contrived "so to assimiliate two German-speaking peoples of German origin, that they preferred to wear the livery of France than the coat of the German peasant".

But since within the foreseeable future nothing could be changed here, he granted the Imperial Territories ("Reichslande") as they were called, a constitution, a sort of parliament called the Landesausschuss, and a Council of Ministers. He warmly supported the generous administration of von Manteuffel, the Governor, and it got so far that in Germany people began to take strong objections to what they considered the excessively soft treatment of the territories in question. In particular, the officials and the military who were stationed there grew almost rebellious because of it.

Bismarck, as we have already seen, did his utmost to support

France in her annexation of Tunis. To the *Post*, which criticized this, he pointed out "the absurdity of a German paper's diverting the attention of Frenchmen from Africa to the Rhine". When Sultan Abdul Hamid, till now the nominal master of Tunis, felt that he was performing a master-stroke of Armenian cunning by offering the Tunisian port of Bizerta to Germany, in order to keep the French out, Bismarck did not even consider this offer worthy of a reply.

Meanwhile, in France Gambetta had very cautiously come into the foreground again. In 1881 he became Prime Minister. Many ill-informed people in Germany were suspicious of him, for they continued to see in him nothing but the organiser of the Republican armies of 1870 and so the man who prolonged the war. Now, for that very reason, they insisted that he was an apostle of revenge. Actually, there was not a man in France who worked harder for a satisfactory settlement with Germany than did Gambetta. A common determination to avoid war at all costs drew Gambetta and Bismarck together. Gambetta knew— indeed it was one of his maxims of government—that "to rule France, violence in word and moderation in deed is essential", and this caused Bismarck to reply, rather more sharply in his press than was necessary, to certain utterances of the Frenchman. But it was not long before each member of this strangely ill-assorted pair, the East Elbian aristocrat and the son of a Genoese grocer who had become a Frenchman, recognised in the other a kindred spirit. Both were stout-hearted realists, born politicians, and so the enemies of all sentimentality and romanticizing in politics. A strange personal relationship grew up between the two men; thus, for instance, it was Bismarck's practice to reply to almost every speech of Gambetta's in a dictated article in the official *Norddeutsche Allgemeine Zeitung*. They felt a strong kinship with one another, but to spare the easily excited feelings of their respective peoples they dared not openly confess it. Both were prepared to risk a personal meeting, but although much was done to bring this about, it never took place.

Gambetta's ministry had, unfortunately, only a short life. It fell after three months, but Gambetta was only forty-four at the time. Most tragically he died of appendicitis at the end of the year. Thus, an unhappy fate ended a period of European history that was full of immense promise. Ferry, who came to power shortly after Gambetta's fall, was another man with whom Bismarck found he could work very well, though he lacked Gambetta's constructive imagination and his very Mediterranean recklessness. And though Ferry avoided an actual meeting with Bismarck, which the latter certainly desired, his period of office is generally accounted as one of progressive rapprochement which reached its climax in 1883. In that year Bismarck sent his son Herbert to Paris to assuage the unrest which had been caused by the German-Italian alliance.

Herbert's accounts of the reception accorded him reflect the surprise of one who was used to rather harsher methods. "I must confess," he wrote, "that I was not at all prepared . . . for such a friendly attitude." Certainly there were many encouraging gestures. Léon Say, who was related to the Rothschilds and a big sugar manufacturer, sought to involve him in a plan for a Franco-German customs union, and a journalist named Girardin, who was supposed to receive his inspiration from high finance, openly spoke of a Franco-German alliance against Russia.

Ferry was the real creator of the French colonial empire, and received support from Bismarck with every step he took. It was now no longer merely a question of Tunis, but of France's new ventures in Central Africa and the Far East. When an undeclared war with China broke out and France suffered several reverses, which nearly brought about the collapse of Ferry's Cabinet, it was Bismarck's discreet intervention which managed to get a peace treaty signed in which China recognised France's sovereignty over the disputed territories.

France thus gained its most densely populated colony and also the one that was the richest of all its possessions in natural resources. Even when, after Ferry's fall in 1886, a different spirit prevailed and the Boulanger episode released new waves of nationalism, Bismarck did not really take the matter as seriously as, for reasons of policy, he pretended to do. Excited reports from the Paris embassy he set aside with a cool marginal note that "presumably everything is Blowitz". It will be remembered that Blowitz was the somewhat ill-reputed Paris correspondent of the London *Times*.

The Balkans to Bismarck were an unending source of alternating fury and apprehension; never did any statesman survey that peninsula with a less Byronic eye. In this department, indeed, he was particularly intolerant of nonsense—or what he conceived to be such—and it was certainly as nonsense that he regarded the concept of nationality. Always suspect for Bismarck, even when applied to the great and ancient peoples of Europe, this concept was, when used in reference to the murdering tribes of the Balkan peninsula, merely grotesque.

Yet for all his distaste for this unhappy corner of Europe, he could not completely ignore it, and indeed fitted at least one Balkan state, namely Rumania, into his security system by joining an Austro-Rumanian pact which committed Rumania to intervene if the Dual Monarchy were attacked in any part of its territory that lay near the Rumanian border.

Hungary contained discontented Rumanian minorities, and it was probably Bismarck's intention to secure Hungary against Rumanian aggression in the event of a war between Austria and Russia. If indeed he saw some guarantee for the observance of this treaty in the fact that the throne of Rumania was occupied by the South German Hohenzollerns, he certainly was over-estimating—and that not for the first time—the power of dynastic ties, particularly in the south-eastern countries where the real power did not lie with monarchs, who had been imported from abroad, but with the old and very wealthy native feudal nobility. However Bismarck was taking no chances and made it quite clear that if Rumania behaved herself in "a chauvinist and irredentist fashion, Europe's only interest would be to let her again be submerged". Hohenzollerns or no Hohenzollerns, he would stand no nonsense from Rumania.

Bismarck really only had one proposal for pacifying the Balkans. It was for a line to be drawn running north and south and dividing the Russian and Austrian spheres of interest. But this was rejected by both the interested parties with equal determination, for neither wanted the continuation of the status quo; rather each desired to have a free hand at the expense of the other.

Again and again Bismarck declared that in the currency of Pomeranian grenadiers, Balkan rivalries counted for less than nothing. But he knew in his heart that he was preaching to deaf ears. Indeed, he had a continual dark foreboding that the Balkans would one day be the occasion of a war in which the great powers would shed oceans of their blood. History has proved him right. Meanwhile, most of the Balkan peoples have merely exchanged the Sultan's whip for the scorpions of the Kremlin.

In 1884 the Three Emperors League was renewed for three years. After this demonstration of mutual trust, the three monarchs met in September in Skierniwice, a shabby little town between Warsaw and Lodz in which one of the Czar's castles was situated. It almost looked as though the Holy Alliance had been resurrected, but this time led not by Russia but by Bismarck. And perhaps, indeed, he stood for a few moments at the summit of his power. With the help of the dual alliance, he controlled the territory of the old German Empire. Russia, with its untried ruler and untried Foreign Minister, Russia which would otherwise have been isolated, was now largely dependent upon him. He had fitted Italy into his power system and so indirectly given Britain an interest in that system's continuance. Meanwhile France was engaged in a number of colonial enterprises whose success depended very largely on her continuing to enjoy Bismarck's support.

But just as the renewal of the Three Emperors Pact was little more than a piece of pretentious shadow-boxing with very little that was real behind it, so also the carefully erected security apparatus of alliances which Bismarck seemed to hold in his hand only consisted of possibilities and rather precarious ones at that. If the attempt had been made to realise them, it is most likely that the construction would not have stood the strain.

Nevertheless, faith in the effectiveness of this system, or, to be exact, a suspicion that it might perhaps after all be capable of working here and there, sufficed to enable it to preserve the European peace for nearly thirty years—for nearly fifteen years, that is to say, after Bismarck's death. History can show few comparable achievements.

14

INTERLUDES

For Bismarck there was no policy that was not in the final analysis a foreign policy, and his domestic policies were determined very largely by the consideration that solidarity and contentment on the home front would strengthen the hand of diplomacy while making the home front itself more capable of absorbing shocks from without. Indeed, with this end in view, he often tended deliberately to spread an optimism concerning Germany's internal position which he himself was far from feeling.

It was this anxiety for the preservation of morale—coupled with the desire to prevent the German worker from succumbing to the allurements of socialism—which was perhaps the main motive behind his social insurance schemes, though another strand of motive was the tradition of paternalism which, as an East Elbian Junker, he had inherited with his land. There is ample evidence that his relations with the workers on his estate, though certainly never egalitarian, were nevertheless excellent, and the *nobile officium* of the landowner to care for the people on his land was something that carried great weight with him; it helped determine his attitude towards the working class in general, which was now rapidly being reduced to the level of an impoverished proletariat.

It was this, and also the desire to dispose the worker kindly towards a beneficent state, that made him try to introduce the tripartite system of insurance which is now almost everywhere in operation, the system in which the state bears part of the insurance costs. The National Liberals, however, among whom—this was in 1881—something of the laissez-faire tradition was still alive, rejected this out of hand and, a little paradoxically perhaps, threw the entire cost of the insurance on to the employer.

The whole system of insurance took some time to develop. Health insurance was passed first and without great difficulty, for there was already some machinery in existence. The coverage of the other risks, unemployment, old age, industrial injury, etc., followed over a period of years.

Bismarck became strangely interested in what was really a secondary outgrowth of his insurance system. When it was decided to throw the whole burden of insurance on the employer, it was proposed to set up professional corporations as part of the administrative machinery. Bismarck became increasingly interested in these and began to see in them, when suitably developed, an alternative and superior method of popular representation and one which was far more to his liking than the prevailing system of universal suffrage.* The point is of interest, since it shows that he regarded the whole structure of the empire as an ad hoc affair, something incomplete and provisional which he was at any time ready to change. Ultimately the means became more important than the end and he valued the whole insurance scheme chiefly for the possibility it offered of developing the corporations. When the insurance system failed to achieve the purposes for which Bismarck intended it, when it failed to stem the growth of socialism—the Social Democrats, who under the Socialist Law had not lost their electoral rights, steadily increased their numbers in the Reichstag—above all, when it utterly failed to implant in the German worker any real feeling of affection for the Bismarckian Establishment, he lost interest in it and it is significant that in *Gedanken und Erinnerungen* there is not so much as a mention of it. Yet quite early on Bismarck had realised the importance of the thing. "It is possible," he said to Moritz Busch in 1881, "that all our politics will come to nothing when I am dead, but state socialism will drub itself in." (*Der Staatssozialismus paukt sich durch.*) It was a true prophecy.

Even more than the insurance scheme, Bismarck's colonial policy, or rather policies—for there was here contradiction rather than continuity—were means to an end rather than ends in themselves, and the means served a variety of purposes. Diplomatic blackmail predominated. But there was also Bismarck's rather strange method of making known his affections, which resembled those of a man who declares his tender passion for a lady by heaving a brick at the head of her rival—a kind of diplomatic say-it-with-flowers in reverse. We shall examine these different varieties in turn.

Unlike his work in the domain of social security, there had not been in the case of his colonial policy a long period of preparation. Indeed, for many years he had rejected the very notion of German colonies—starting with that October day in 1870 when the French diplomat Gauthier enquired whether French colonies would be acceptable as a ransom for Alsace and Lorraine and was given the answer, "Oho! Cochin-China, that would be a fat morsel for us, but we can't afford the luxury of colonies, we aren't yet rich enough." Bismarck's attitude was equally clear in 1883, when he

* Bussmann. *Das Zeitalter Bismarcks* (1956), p. 212.

said to Caprivi, who at that time was head of the Admiralty, "I hear you are against colonies," and when Caprivi answered in the affirmative, he rejoined with the words, "So am I."

This negative attitude certainly had nothing to do with any philanthropic anti-colonialism. The founding of colonies, one of the oldest activities of man, could never have been a burden on Bismarck's conscience. Indeed, it carried its own justification along with it, and this applied to the natives quite as much as to anybody else, for these were given the benefits of the rule of law, of improved medical services and the possibility of mental development. Moreover, the solidarity of the white race was something Bismarck took for granted, and, to ensure it, he strove, and strove successfully at the Congo conference of 1885 to secure a ban on the recruitment of Negro troops for European wars.

Yet for a long time he was content to watch, with the detachment of the lone spectator, the rivalries and vicissitudes of others who had been infected with the colonial virus—of England in South Africa and the Sudan, of Italy in the scorching heat of the Red Sea. For the age from which he came was that of the first Napoleon, who traded France's most valuable colonies for a song.

There was, of course, in Germany a certain amount of private agitation to take part in the general colonial scramble. In 1882 Miquel, at that time Lord Mayor of Frankfurt, had founded the *Kolonialverein*, or Colonial Union, but as long as the Imperial government took no notice of it, it remained nothing more than an institution confined to the upper classes of the bourgeoisie. In particular, those sections of German industry which, thanks to the tariff, had undergone a great expansion, poured considerable quantities of money into it.

However, nothing much happened till well into the eighties. In February 1883 Herbert Bismarck mentioned to Pauncefote, the permanent Under-Secretary at the Foreign Office, that a German trading station had been established at Angra Pequena and asked whether Great Britain would protect it. The station had been established by a certain Herr Lüderitz, and Angra Pequena, where it was situated, lay on a part of the West African coast that adjoined Cape Colony but at that time belonged to nobody in particular. There was a reason for Herbert's request, for Cape Colony exercised some jurisdiction over the islands off the coast which had a few traders upon them and had five years previously occupied Walvis Bay. But in 1880 the British government had refused to protect the missionaries who had settled on the uninhabited mainland.

Herbert's entirely proper question was followed by a further communication, equally proper. If the British government would not act, he said, then the German government would do its best to extend to the new settlement "the same measure of protection which they give to their subjects in remote parts of the world, but without having the least desire to establish any footing in South Africa ".

So far, German diplomacy had been propriety itself, and it was unfortunate that propriety should also demand that the British government should refer the matter, via the Colonial Office, to the Cape, this being the territory nearest to the enterprising Herr Lüderitz's scene of operations. The process entailed a delay of several months during which Lüderitz fell foul of an English trader and again asked the German government for protection. And so in September, with the same exquisite politeness, the German government discreetly enquired whether Great Britain had actual suzerainty at Angra Pequena and, if so, on what ground it rested. They further asked, with a perceptible note of disdain for their suppliant, "What view Her Majesty's government would take of the proceedings of Herr Lüderitz and whether they had any objection to them."

Again the wheels began to turn and the matter was referred once more via the Colonial Office to the Cape, and the Cape, after mature reflection, came to the conclusion that, though neither it nor any other branch of the British government had any authority over Herr Lüderitz's trading settlement, nevertheless they objected very much indeed to the presence of a foreign power. They might have added—but did not do so apparently—that they rather especially objected to the presence of Herr Lüderitz of whose character it is unlikely that they had a very high opinion. Count Münster, the German ambassador, was informed of these facts and in December he repeated what Herbert had already hinted at and asked what institutions England had in that part of the world "to give German traders such protection as would relieve the German government of the duty of protecting them itself".

Again the papers pursued their jogtrot way to the Colonial Office and from the Colonial Office to the Cape—and soon it was April. Then on April 24th something rather startling happened. On that day the German consul at the Cape received a wire instructing him to announce that Herr Lüderitz and his property were under German protection. A similar message was handed in to the British government on the following day. Lord Granville, the Foreign Secretary, who, incidentally, now heard the name of Angra Pequena for the first time, was completely non-plussed by this communication and, still believing firmly that Germany neither had nor could possibly have any colonial ambition, concluded that Bismarck was annoyed at the British failure to protect German nationals. He consequently assured the chargé d'affaires, who brought him the communication, that he would try to get the Cape Colony to assume responsibility for the safety of Germans.

There for a time the matter rested and Bismarck, with one of those convenient fits of amnesia by which he occasionally was affected, forgot all about Angra Pequena. Instead of this, he suddenly brought up a new subject, Heligoland, and in May Bismarck authorised his ambassador in London to raise the question of Heligoland as the price of German support for England over the Egyptian question. A fortnight later the ambassador received instructions to forget all about Heligoland, and a fortnight after that Angra Pequena once more leapt into the news.

It will be remembered that Granville had promised to oblige the Germans by trying to make the Cape assume responsibility for the safety of the excellent Herr Lüderitz. He was, unfortunately, entirely successful, for what happened was that the Cape announced that it would now extend its sovereignty over the whole coast as far as the Portuguese border; thus it would be able to give protection to the German nationals at Angra Pequena. Whereupon the German ambassador was instructed to say that the German government could not recognise the Cape's action.

The British government was thrown into hopeless confusion, and once more the anguished cry that had been uttered by Lord Beaconsfield echoed through the ministries: "What does Bismarck want?" Eventually Herbert came to London and thrashed the matter out during three visits to Granville, visits in which he was persistently and quite deliberately as rude as he could be. Agreement, however, was at last reached and the terms thereof sent to the British ambassador in Berlin for presentation to the German government, it being distinctly laid down that Germany "had no intention to establish state colonies but merely to give protection to her subjects". But the matter was not over yet by any means, for no sooner had the Germans received the note than they came back with a request that the phrase about Germany having no intention to establish colonies should be deleted, a request which sounded as if it had been made from considerations of domestic policy, since the note would be made public and might give offence to the colonialists.

Whatever meaning he read into it, however, Granville, now desperately eager to do almost anything that might put Bismarck in a better mood, promptly complied, whereupon the Germans equally promptly announced that their own protection now reached up to the Portuguese border, which meant that Lüderitz's little settlement had been expanded to form what soon became the colony of German South-West Africa. That Germany should thus be presented with the key to the backdoor of Cape Colony can hardly have been welcome either to the colony or to the British government. But that government accepted the fact, and its acceptance was duly communicated to the government of Germany, and one can almost hear Granville's sigh of relief at being done with the business.

But Bismarck had still not been won over and was still determined to pose as an injured man, and so the British government was told that this was indeed a "first step in the direction which he hoped British policy would take. He could have wished, in the interests of the present and the future, that it had been taken earlier"*—after which there was really nothing for poor Granville to do except to resolve to do better next time.

In the meantime, the Germans had been able to mark up yet another kill. They had seized the Cameroons. Till now the British had not thought the place worth bothering about, and, though invited to do so by some of the native chiefs, had refused to annex this territory, though the British consul at Oil Rivers exercised a vague *de facto* jurisdiction over it. But to refuse to occupy a territory yourself is one thing; to let another power do so, is, as we saw in the case of German South-West Africa, quite another, and it was unfortunate that the British consul did not get wind of what was afoot in time. As a result, when a certain gentleman with the pleasing name of Herr Nachtigall hoisted the German flag, it was five days before the consul found out about it.

Having for the moment temporarily exhausted the possibilities of remunerative, or apparently remunerative, annoyance in Africa, the Germans now looked elsewhere.

The island of New Guinea, which lies to the north of Australia, is mountainous and poorly equipped with harbours. The western half had long belonged to the Dutch East Indies. The eastern part was at that time owned by nobody, though the inhospitable character might well have recommended it to some European power as a penal settlement. The Australians were anxious that this should not be allowed to happen and had repeatedly tried to get the British government to annex the place. Now at last the government took some notice and prepared to make the eastern part of New Guinea a British protectorate.

Anxious, however, to cover itself in every way, and in view of the fact that the German ambassador in London professed to have heard of some apparently quite supposititious Germans

---

* Quoted by A. J. P. Taylor from a Foreign Office Minute. *Germany's First Bid for Colonies* (London, 1938).

in the neighbourhood, it suggested that the whole matter should be made the subject of informal talks between Herbert Bismarck, who was then in England, and a British representative. And when the Germans showed themselves almost incomprehensibly dissatisfied with the plan, they declared that for the present the British protectorate would be limited to the south coast.

The Germans did nothing for three months, then it was made known that large tracts of the north and north-east coasts had been placed under German protection. Needless to say, the Australians were furious, while Bismarck answered the expostulations of the British not so much with argument as with that sententious moral deprecation which he could turn on whenever the occasion demanded it. England, he said, had vast possessions and it was unworthy of her to grudge Germany a settlement on the coast of New Guinea, and so on and so forth.

Indeed, during the whole of this business the Germans can hardly be said to have argued at all. They inflicted the maximum of annoyance and then, when asked to explain, or merely to say what they really wanted, threw up a smoke-screen of irrelevance and prevarication. Thus when, during the Angra Pequena business, a nearly demented Granville wrote to Herbert Bismarck and asked him to state quite frankly whether there was any matter between the two governments on which a misunderstanding might exist and which might easily be cleared up, Herbert replied *inter alia* with the following gem, which, in a context remotely like the present one, must surely be unique in the annals of diplomacy: "I remember having heard my father say that on the whole the best plan to maintain and strengthen existing good relations between the two countries was to treat each other in a gentleman-like way, and I am sure that you thoroughly agree with him."* Coming to London shortly after this, Herbert indignantly refused to visit Granville on the ground that he had left this letter unanswered!

In the course of a single year Germany laid the foundations of her colonial empire, for in the same year in which she acquired German South-West Africa, the Cameroons and New Guinea, she also acquired Togoland and started that long wrangle over Zanzibar which led her to her East African possessions. It was an empire that Bismarck most certainly did not want and that he acquired with the maximum of quite needless provocation.

What was it that made Bismarck act like this? What made him ask for colonies he did not desire and what made him set about acquiring them in a manner calculated to inflict the maximum of

*Quoted by A. J. P. Taylor, *op. cit.*

annoyance on the one power that more than any other could help
him to attain his wish—assuming that he really entertained it—
and was in point of fact eager to do so.

That anything had happened which seriously changed Bismarck's views about the value of colonies we have no reason whatever to suppose. For it never escaped his perspicacity that a state
which wishes to be accounted a great power can only maintain an
overseas empire commensurate with that status if it is in a position
to defend it. Thus he was faced with the alternative: either there
must be a German fleet so large that its squadrons could be
present on all the oceans of the world—which for Bismarck was
merely the revival of the sentimental naval enthusiasms of 1848,
enthusiasms that had so miserably come to nothing—or it meant
dependence on an ally who was great in sea power. Neither
alternative was acceptable. For him as a Prussian who was
accustomed to concentrate all his energies on firm ground, the
fleet need be no larger than that of Holland. It was for him no
more than a kind of auxiliary force designed to serve the Army,
which was why he appointed infantry generals to its supreme
posts. He was still capable of saying, somewhat tentatively it is
true, that in a war the fate of the colonies would be decided by
land armies. But it is unlikely that he really believed this himself.

Nevertheless one of the things he would certainly have had to
take account of was the appearance of a strong anti-British
sentiment, a sentiment which became more marked as with set-
backs in the Sudan and the threat of a clash with Russia in Asia,
British power seemed to be becoming more precarious. It was as
though the Germans resented her continuing to cling to it, when,
as was claimed, she had forfeited the right to do so.

Treitschke was the man who most disastrously set the tone here.
This man's family had originally come from Bohemia, and it was
almost as if the wild excesses of the Hussite temperament had
flared up in him anew. The hegemony of Britain, he declared, of
this senile country of hypocrites and hucksters, was at an end.
Justice demanded that the world be divided up anew and that the
German master race should get the lion's share—theories that
somehow flattered the self-esteem of the young state, which still
badly needed such psychological support, but ultimately expanded themselves into sheer insanity.

Bismarck himself was of course completely unaffected by this
nonsense, but he may well have been ready to capitalise on it. He
needed a weapon at the election against the bourgeois left and the
Social Democrats, both of whom were enemies of colonialism,
and he may well have hoped to inflict heavy damage on them
if he pilloried them as allies of Britain and so made them a target

for anti-British feeling, while himself posing as the champion of anti-British grievances. He said to Boetticher* in September 1884: "The whole colonial business is a swindle, but we need it for the election."†

Another powerful motive behind Bismarck's colonial policy may well have been the desire to drive a wedge between Britain and the German Crown Prince, so that when the latter came to the throne, which might be quite soon, it would be impossible for him to adopt a policy which was markedly friendly to Britain. In Skierniewice, in September 1884, Bismarck actually confessed to such an intention.‡

There can be little doubt, however, of the main reason for Bismarck's conduct. It is to be found in the fear, which always haunted him, of a two-front war, and it is this that certainly prompted him during this critical period to seek for an entente with France. Relations between France and Britain were at that time gravely disturbed by the Egyptian question, but Bismarck's purpose would not have been achieved by merely giving France his support over Egypt. He had to convince the French that he had his own independent and deep-seated quarrel with Britain. That would establish a clear community of interest and provide the basis for a solid understanding. Even if France could never wholly forget the peace of Frankfurt, she might at least allow the memory to pale. Surely his experiences with Austria must have encouraged him in such a belief.

At the same time Bismarck knew that he must not commit himself too deeply and that here, too, the principle of reinsurance should be applied. Should France prove unresponsive to his wooing, he had necessarily to show that he could compete with her, and compete successfully, for Britain's favour, and that if a Franco-German entente were rejected, an Anglo-German one might well take its place.

Now that the various documents, the minutes and the memoranda of the governments of the countries concerned have been thrown open to inspection, this is precisely and quite unmistakably the pattern that emerges. If France showed herself responsive, pressure was applied to England; if reluctant and coy, Whitehall was treated to the faintest and most wintry of smiles. The sudden temporary emergence of Heligoland into the discussion fits perfectly into the above scheme. It was made at a time when Bismarck was doubtful about French willingness to cooperate and was faced with the possibility of having to abandon

---

* Karl Heinrich von Boetticher (1833–1907), State Secretary and Prussian Minister 1880–1907.
          † Lerchenfeld, p. 211.   ‡ Holstein, II, p. 174.

the whole manoeuvre. He was at that time in the midst of the Angra Pequena dispute which, should the French not prove amenable, would have to be dropped, not only because it was causing needless annoyance but because he could make a much better bargain with the British. To come home with the *"Ur-deutsch"* island of Heligoland in his pocket would be a triumph indeed. But France, for the time being at any rate, appeared ready to go along, and so Heligoland was dropped and the policy of pinpricks renewed.

Of course, the game was a dangerous one. We possess some illuminating correspondence which shows that at least three of the initiates, namely Holstein and Bismarck's two sons, were very much alive to the magnitude both of the risk and of the stakes. Holstein took the line that Bismarck was not being sufficiently drastic so long as he failed to make the French quite definite offers. It need not be Alsace-Lorraine, but could well be Egypt or Morocco, and, so long as he failed to do this, France would ultimately be driven into Britain's arms and Germany would fall between two stools. The unity of these two western powers, however, would not only attract the United States but also Italy and Russia.

Herbert, who defended his father, denied this. Bill, however, with that sceptical phlegma of the very fat, was more clear-sighted than the erratic and ambitious Herbert and sided with Holstein. "Papa finds the present policies convenient and likes to play off one side against the other," he wrote. "That will work for a time, but the moment will come *où il faut prendre une resolution.* The game is too obvious for either party not to have noticed what is going on, so naturally both are distrustful. . . . England will not always have such stupid statesmen as she has now, and once the conviction gains ground with the leaders of either side that both countries acting in conjunction could determine the nature of any overseas constellation, they will come to an understanding without war." The fatal prophecies of Holstein came true after thirty years, those of Count Bill within twenty.

What Bismarck really wanted, of course, was not colonies but a quarrel about colonies, and it must be admitted that he played his cards brilliantly, all the more so since the British, though they took umbrage at his methods—"there appears to be an element in him which I do not wish to characterise," said Mr. Gladstone— were almost desperately anxious to give whatever he asked, which of course was the very last thing he wished them to do. For in those days German stock stood very high in Britain, while the possession of an empire was still accounted slightly shameful. The apparent exception to this feeling, according to A. J. P. Taylor, "namely the aggressive imperialism of the late nineteenth century, was merely part of the diabolism of the naughty nineties with Chamberlain as the Oscar Wilde of politics".*

As to the Germans, British statesmen were continually and apparently quite sincerely declaring that there was nobody whom they would rather have as neighbours—though they may well have desired their proximity in less inconvenient places. Even in the matter of New Guinea, Mr. Gladstone found grounds which may today perhaps sound a little odd for actually welcoming the German intrusion, whatever the Australians might say. "I see my way clearly in this: that German colonisation will strengthen and not weaken our hold upon our colonies and will make it very difficult for them to maintain the domineering tone to which their public organs are too much inclined." In these circumstances surely, Bismarck's real achievement consisted not so much in getting a protectorate in New Guinea as in avoiding getting a great deal more.

Such escapades, however, must ultimately be paid for. Sooner or later history presents the bill. What Bismarck wanted, states the above-quoted English historian, was not colonies but a grievance. He might well have added: his punishment was that he managed to get both. For not only did he saddle his unhappy compatriots with what surely must have been the most unremunerative colonial empire in human history, but since all the colonial plums had by that time been gathered by others, the Germans were continually reminded of the fact that they were being served with very second-class fare. (Most of their possessions merely constituted a drain on the German taxpayer. Togoland alone in 1913 managed to balance its budget.) In these circumstances, it may well be that the Germans would have been more free from that aggressive resentment which poisoned the air of the early twentieth century if, instead of having to compare their own meagre rations with the abundance enjoyed by others, they had had no colonies at all.

In the autumn of 1885 Bismarck broke off his colonial activities as unexpectedly and as suddenly as he had started them. There were no doubt a number of causes at work here. His somewhat speculative hope, assuming that he ever entertained it, that he would win the Reichstag elections on the colonial platform, had proved mistaken. The Social Democrats had grown in numbers, the centre maintained its strong position. As before, great masses of the electors were completely indifferent to the colonial issue. Next, Gladstone, whom he detested, fell from power in England and was replaced by Salisbury, with whom Bismarck's relations

* A. J. P. Taylor, *op. cit.*

had always been good. In the main, however, it is safe to say that his policy was determined to a far greater extent by two other events; one of these was the renewed tension in the Balkans which will be dealt with in a later chapter. This made the whole political weather much more dangerous for rash experiment. The most potent cause of all, however, was undoubtedly the fall of the Ferry government, largely due to a military disaster in China.

This had very important consequences, for the collapse of the Ferry Cabinet ended the power of the great financial interests who were always prepared for accommodation, while the middling and patriotic bourgeoisie gained a new access of political strength. These men could not be moved by offers of colonial co-operation and they tended to see the situation very simply. If Germany was really actuated by good will, let her return Alsace-Lorraine. It was quite clear that a genuine Franco-German entente could not be created so long as the tension in regard to Alsace-Lorraine subsisted, which meant that in the then situation it could never be created at all. For a time there was no visible sign of a change. Ferry was succeeded by Freycinet, who appeared outwardly to be following his predecessor's policy, but Bismarck became aware of the fact that he was getting nowhere and that all ideas of a Franco-German entente were an illusion.

Of course, in turning his back on colonial enterprise, Bismarck was certainly following his own tastes and conviction which his most recent experiences had done nothing to change. He had always believed that if there was to be colonial enterprise at all, the British cliché—a very misleading one incidentally—that trade follows the flag, should be applied in reverse, and that it was the trader, not the soldier or the bureaucrat, who should be in the front line of advance.

In this connection he had great hopes of the republican sense of independence that the Hanseatic towns would display, but he was disappointed. The men of the Hansa cities, when left to their own devices in the colonies, clamoured most urgently for the bureaucracy and police to which they had been accustomed at home. When they received these benefits, their conduct was as aggressive as could be, and their mood, in Lerchenfeld's words, "joyously pan-German" (*fröhlich alldeutsch*). "The greed of our colonial jingoes," Bismarck said in 1885, "is much greater than our need and our capacity for digestion." And in this particular, at least, Bismarck's Imperial master most certainly agreed with him. "Every adventurer," the latter once said, "asks for German protection and usually gets it. But nobody has bothered to find out whether this will bring Germany into conflict with friendly governments."

As time went by, Bismarck adhered ever more closely to his original views. "Your map of Africa is very nice," he told an enthusiast in 1888, "but my map of Africa lies in Europe. There lies Russia and there lies France, and we are in the middle. That is my map of Africa." And a year later he said in the Prussian Ministry of State, as we have seen, that "the German colonial swindle" was "clumsily (*tölpelhaft*) disturbing" his work.

One of Bismarck's colonial ventures deserves special mention here, for, though England was this time not concerned in the matter, it illustrates superbly how colonial enterprise for Bismarck was always a means to an end and not an end in itself. In August 1885 the Carolines were occupied, an archipelago consisting of roughly seven hundred coral islands. Spain gave notice that she had rights over this place dating back to 1543 and the German action roused great indignation there. Bismarck immediately gave way, saying that he set much greater store on the preservation of the monarchy in Spain, whose prestige would presumably be damaged by calm submission to aggression, than on any group of islands in the Pacific. He even went further and suggested the matter should be taken to arbitration, and invited the Pope to act as arbitrator.

Leo XIII accepted the invitation and decided against Germany, but presented Bismarck with the Order of Christ, a decoration which no Protestant had ever previously received. In his letter of thanks Bismarck very pointedly addressed him as "Sire", a title only used with crowned heads. Thus an entirely new atmosphere was created between Berlin and the Vatican, which made it possible to put an end with a single swift gesture to the wretched Kulturkampf which had been dragging on for some fifteen years and still refused completely to die. Bismarck's attitude on the Carolines question and his rapid change in August was thus ultimately explained in September. It was a master stroke, worthy of the best things he had done in the past. He had got out of a most compromising dead end, and this surely was a bargain, however many coral reefs in distant oceans he had to give in exchange.

15

TWILIGHT

As yet Europe was unaware that one of its days of destiny was dawning. Only very sensitive ears like those of Bismarck could hear in the dim light of early morning the approach of mighty events to come. Soon they would be there, and in preparation for that moment all muscles had to be tensed and all senses alerted. There was now no time for social and colonial experiment. For soon questions of sheer survival would have to receive an answer.

It began with something that was really nothing at all, with a revolt in the Balkans such as had occurred a thousand times before. Eastern Roumelia, a Turkish province chiefly inhabited by Christians, had at the Berlin congress been granted the right of autonomous administration. Not satisfied with this, it threw out in September 1885 its Governor-Pasha and sought to join Bulgaria, the principality which had also been created in Berlin. With this, however, one of the chief props of the structure so laboriously erected on that occasion had been torn away. For Eastern Roumelia had been forced into its equivocal position precisely so that it should neither join Bulgaria, which was what Russia wanted it to do, nor be handed over to Turkey, which was what the Austrians wanted.

Prince Alexander of Bulgaria, who set all these events in motion, was a member of the Battenberg family which had its origin in the morganatic marriage of the Hessian Prince Alexander with one of the Czarina's ladies-in-waiting, Countess Haucke.* His elevation

* The family of Haucke is descended from a court confectioner of the electorate of Mainz. One of its descendants, Moritz Haucke, emigrated to Poland, where he became a count and Minister of War to Congress Poland and as such was murdered in the rising of 1830. Moritz's daughter Julie became lady-in-waiting to the Czarina and later married Prince Alexander of Hesse, the commander-in-chief of the army of the Bund operating in South Germany in 1866. The children of this marriage received the Hessian title of Princes of Battenburg. Louis of Battenburg, the brother of the prince of Bulgaria, entered the British Navy and became Admiral of the Fleet. He relinquished his German title in 1917 when he assumed the surname Mount-batten and was created the first Marquess of Milford Haven. His daughter was the mother of Prince Philip; his younger son, Louis, Earl Mountbatten, in 1943 became commander-in-chief, South-East Asia, and the last British Viceroy of India. Whereas the House of Hohenzollern disappears amid the commonplaces of the bourgeoisie, the great-great grandson of Julie Haucke, Prince Charles, will one day be King of England.

to the throne of Bulgaria was something which he owed
wholly to the Czar Alexander II who had married a sister of the
Hessian prince in question. Czar Alexander III, who now in 1885
ruled over Russia, was therefore a first cousin of the Bulgarian
prince who bore the same name as himself, but he was, for that
very reason and also on more human grounds, his rival.

For the Bulgarian, now barely twenty-eight years old, was
strikingly handsome, a radiant yet nimble personality, and
adored to distraction by the ladies. The Czar, on the other hand,
was forty-five, a man with many inhibitions and one who had
originally not been intended for the throne, and who, unlike the
other, seemed to spread a heavy and sinister mood. On top of
everything else Battenberg had made it abundantly clear that he
over-estimated the importance of his office—an office which,
according to Bismarck and in view of the prevailing power
relations, was no more than that of a hereditary Russian viceroy.

Instead of this, he had no sooner ascended to the throne when
he began a foreign policy which was definitely directed against
Russia. Russia had, no doubt, liberated the Bulgarians from the
Turks, but she shared the lot of all liberators, which was to incur
the powerful hatred of those whom she had set free. Unlike
Bismarck, the Russians had never grasped the simple fact that
liberated nations are never grateful but always demanding.

In consequence, the Russian government was painfully surprised to learn of the merger with Eastern Roumelia, all the more
so since Giers had only recently warned the prince in the Czar's
name against any venture of the kind. Russia's answer was to
recall all Russian officers from the Bulgarian Army, which thus
was robbed of its backbone. This induced King Milan of Serbia
to take a page out of Napoleon III's book and to ask his Bulgarian neighbour for compensations; when these were not forthcoming he marched his army against him. The unhappy Serbs,
however, were somewhat over-confident and, having prematurely
expended their ammunition, lost two battles and were now in
their turn faced with a Bulgarian invasion.

At that moment—it was October 28, 1885—a special train drew
into the station at Nish, where the Bulgarians had their headquarters—and how much misery for Europe the engine of that
train had dragged over the precarious mountain track! From the
train there now stepped forth Count Khevenhüller, the Austrian
ambassador in Belgrade, and what he had to say was brief and
to the point. If the Bulgarians marched into Serbia, they would
there encounter Austrian troops, and that, for all practical purposes, put an end to the Bulgarian offensive. This intervention
had much more far-reaching effects than Austria had expected.

For, despite the Czar's dislike of the prince, Bulgaria was under Russian protection in exactly the same way that Serbia was under the protection of Austria. Now, however, Russia had left her ward without protection and on the whole was cutting rather a poor figure, whilst Austria was assuming the stance of a protective archangel, complete with glittering sword, which was just the kind of thing that made a strong impression on the simple folk of the Balkans. What had been a slightly comic altercation between a couple of back-garden potentates had thus turned into something very different.

Austria and Russia now stood face to face. The spectators held their breath. It was as though in a circus, after the clowns had done their act, two mighty war elephants had appeared, their howdahs full of archers and the bows of the archers drawn. This time, however, the archers did not shoot.

Actually, Bismarck himself had protested in Vienna against the cavalier treatment of Bulgaria. He regarded it as a breach of the Three Emperors Pact, according to which Austria should at least have informed Russia in advance of the steps she was taking; Serbia had no claim to compensation, and it was not for Austria to levy an execution on her behalf. Kalnoky replied that it was inconceivable that all the Serbs in the Austrian Empire should have stood quietly by while their brother was being strangled to death, by which he was, of course, referring to those affected by Austria's newly acquired occupation rights in Bosnia and Herzegovina.

In the final analysis, nothing very much had really happened at all. A Turkish pasha, at the edge of Europe, had been ousted by a petty princeling, and yet that was enough to threaten Bismarck's security system in this part of the world, thus exposing the precarious nature of the whole construction.

We do not know the exact feelings that all this aroused in Bismarck, but it is hardly surprising that he should have experienced downright hatred for Alexander of Battenberg, whose unfortunate urge to distinguish himself as a man of action had started the whole wretched business. That unhappy young man, whose spiritual home, as a sometime officer of the *Garde du Corps*, was that unreal world in which members of fashionable cavalry regiments tend to exist, became for him forthwith a villain of the deepest dye, a man capable of unimaginable iniquities. Yet Alexander had breeding, intelligence and a certain reckless daring, and in these respects was everything that could be desired, even though he may sometimes have overestimated his value, as when, in 1884, he aspired to become the husband of a granddaughter of William I. But there was more at issue here than the venial follies of a dashing young prince. Alexander had reopened the Eastern Question and no one knew where that would end.

Fortunately it was not too difficult on this occasion at least to restore peace in the Balkans. Turkey, who was really the injured party, with the soft voice of habitual resignation, protested at what had been done, and at the Peace of Bucharest accepted the appointment of the Prince of Bulgaria as Governor-General of Eastern Roumelia, which was, in fact, a personal union of both countries.

It is possible that time would, in due course, have calmed tempers, but for the fact that one year after the Eastern Roumelian affair the world was suddenly startled by yet another Bulgarian explosion. In August 1886 Alexander was arrested by officers of a cavalry regiment with marked Russian sympathies and deposited on the other side of the border. He managed, perhaps inadvisedly, to get back into Bulgaria, and it was at this point that the errors of his anti-Russian policy were made apparent. The results of a rather inept attempt to persuade the Czar to set matters right were negative, as might have been expected, and there was nothing left for him but to renounce the throne.

He removed himself from Bulgaria, leaving behind a Regency Council under the peasant leader Stambulow, and forthwith became a nobody. From now on he led a completely empty life, the only positive element in which was Bismarck's hatred, which continued to pursue him, as it had pursued Harry Arnim, to the end.

By 1886 Austro-Russian relations had attained a state of enraged hostility. This had been provoked by other things besides the intervention of Khevenhüller in Nish. There had also been a rather ill-considered speech of Kalnoky before the Hungarian parliament, in which he declared that if Russia became active in Bulgaria, Austria "would in all circumstances be forced to take up a decisive attitude". By these words, which, of course, went flat against the policy of Bismarck, Kalnoky destroyed the last weather-beaten remnants of anything that constituted a bond between the two empires and destroyed them for good.

Indeed, it now became increasingly clear that Bismarck would one day have to choose between Russia and Austria, which was equivalent to having to choose between Scylla and Charybdis. Like a new Odysseus, he exerted all his pressure upon the steering oar in order to guide his ship safely in between the two. He continued, however, to adhere resolutely to his two-point plan: first, to set up a line of demarcation in the Balkans between the two rival powers, and secondly, by means of the Three Emperors Pact, to keep them united to Germany and so, however loosely, with each other. The pact, he declared, must be spun out as long as there was a thread left in it.

As to the line of demarcation, when the Austrian chargé d'affaires complained that, if such a line were to be drawn, Russia would get the eastern part of the Balkans with its considerable economic potential, while Austria would have nothing more than the inhospitable mountains and their intractable inhabitants, Herbert Bismarck said that if he wanted the whole of the Balkans he would have a war with Russia on his hands, for most Russians claimed the whole Balkan peninsula with the same eagerness as Austrians.

At the beginning of 1887 Herbert had a conversation with Peter Schuwalow, who had not too skilfully represented Russia at the Berlin congress and was now, therefore, seeking for some kind of diplomatic success. It was made plain to Herbert that the Czar only asked for one thing in return for his neutrality in any Franco-German war, namely that Germany should not prevent him from getting hold of the Dardanelles. He had had enough of Bulgarians and Southern Slavs, Herbert was informed, and would now gladly withdraw from the Balkan province as gracefully as he could.* In other words, if Bismarck was ready to forget Austrian and Turkish interests in the Dardanelles, he could rid himself of the spectre of a Russian, that is to say a two-front, war.

Four days later, Schuwalow, together with Paul, his brother, who was ambassador in Berlin, dined with the Chancellor, and here, in the pleasantly relaxed atmosphere of an all-male gathering, it was possible to develop the hints already thrown out by Peter Schuwalow and draw up the draft of a treaty between Germany and Russia. Its main provisions were that Russia could rely on the friendly neutrality of Germany if she should be attacked by Austria, while Germany could rely on the same friendly neutrality on the part of Russia if she was subjected to an attack by France.

Schuwalow returned to St. Petersburg, and a few hours later the debate began in the Reichstag about a new army estimate which was to increase the size of the Army from 427,000 to 468,000 men, and the legislation was again to take the form of a septennate—that is to say, it was to cover a period of seven years. As Chief of the General Staff, Moltke addressed the house, dry and sinister. Let no one deceive themselves, he said, about the seriousness of the situation. The whole world was already asking itself whether there would be a war. For his own part, he believed that if the Bill were not passed, then the temptation to an aggressor

* *Die grosse Politik der europäischen Kabinette* 1871–1914 (1927), V, p. 213.

would be too strong, war would come, and everyone knew that it was in the precarious nature of Russo-Austrian relations that Moltke saw the probable occasion of a conflict into which Germany must ultimately be drawn.

Bismarck spoke next, broad-shouldered and with his cheeks reddened by the winter cold, apparently as confident as he could be—the very opposite of the dry, pessimistic Moltke. Bismarck's speech on this occasion was one of the most remarkable he ever made. In regard to Russia, he assured the house, the prospects could not be more favourable. The Czar only entertained the friendliest feelings for Germany and these were reciprocated. As to Bulgaria, Germany had no intention of interfering. It was a matter of complete indifference to her who her ruler was, and certainly there were no grounds here for a quarrel with the Czar and, he added with an unmistakable reference to Austria, Germany would "*sich von niemandem das Leitseil um den Hals werfen lassen um uns mit Russland zu brouillieren*" ("allow no one to throw a rope round our neck in order to embroil us with Russia"). Nothing, he assured his listeners, could be further from his mind than a preventive war against France, nor was it for that purpose that Germany desired an increase in her armaments. This last was based on one consideration, and one consideration only—a possible attack by France.

The discrepancy between the tone and substance of the Chancellor's speech and the implications behind that of the Chief of the General Staff was so astonishing that Bismarck found himself impelled to inform his own embassies in Germany, that is to say in Munich, Stuttgart, Dresden and Karlsruhe, that he had deliberately represented relations with Russia to be better than they actually were, because his speech in the Reichstag would be reported by the Press. He did not wish his allies to give themselves over to a "feeling of security for which there was no permanent guarantee".* Meanwhile, the Reichstag, to whom this piece of information had not been imparted, was full of mistrust and only legislated for three instead of the seven years that had been requested. Nobody was to know that the purpose of Bismarck's speech in the Reichstag was to prepare the ground in St. Petersburg for the treaty, the draft of which Schuwalow was at that very moment bringing home with him. Nor could anybody know that for the third time he had fallen a victim to that particular kind of wishful thinking which could momentarily persuade him that he could at least delay the Russian peril, even if he could not banish it altogether. One day later the Reichstag was dissolved.

* *Grosse Politik*, V, p. 116ff.

The electoral struggle for the new Reichstag was fierce and would have been fiercer had not France, since 1886, had General Boulanger as its Minister of War.

At the time, nearly a year previously, when the Bismarcks had started building up Boulanger into a kind of bogy man, he was no more than an able and popular young soldier—popular for no other reason than that he had introduced certain army reforms that made life easier for the rank and file and contributed greatly to the raising of morale. The fact that for a time he became a kind of national hero and leader-figure was due very largely to the continued attacks in Bismarck's Press which pilloried him, quite unjustly, as a would-be crusader in a war of revenge, and, needless to say, Bismarck had not forgotten him in his Reichstag speech. "We have," he said, "to fear an attack by France, though whether it will come in ten days or ten years is a question which I cannot answer. . . . It may happen at any time that a French government comes into power, which has risked everything on being able to live by the *feu sacré*, which is now kept carefully concealed under the ashes. . . . If Napoleon III went to war with us in 1870 chiefly because he believed that this would strengthen his power within his country, why should not such a man as General Boulanger, if he came to power, do the same?" That set the tone for the whole campaign.

Boulanger accepted this fake hostility at its face value. He suddenly imagined that France was in danger and began, feverishly, to prepare for war.

All this was, of course, grist to Bismarck's mill. He concentrated all the fire power of his propaganda batteries on Boulanger so that the real enemy, who was, in point of fact, rearming on a large scale, remained concealed. Konstantin Rössler, the same journalist who had created the panic of 1875 with his article "Is War in Sight?" now again published a similar effusion in the *Post*, entitled "On the Razor's Edge".

Herbette, the French ambassador in Germany, advised his government not to take too much notice of what was merely an electoral manœuvre, and stated quite correctly that the military preparations were directed against Russia much more than against France.

Count Münster, now German ambassador in Paris, had also managed to keep his sense of realities. At the end of the year he wrote to Bismarck, "A war with France, as things now stand, could only be caused by ourselves, and it would need very great provocation to persuade the French to start one." Since Münster was sending the Emperor reports about conditions in France which were quite as sober and objective as those he was despatch.

ing to Bismarck, Bismarck ultimately refused to forward his letters to the royal addressee, for, as he quite openly wrote to the ambassador, if the Emperor were to be persuaded to share Münster's views about France, the government would no longer be able to go ahead with its military preparations.

Bismarck, however, won an electoral victory that surpassed the wildest expectations. He had managed to inflame large numbers of these quiet and industrious people in Germany with a positive fury against Boulanger as a disturber of the peace, and in the end his converts formed a bloc which ultimately came to be known as "the Cartel", consisting of Conservatives, Free Conservatives and National Liberals, a bloc that polled no less than 77 per cent of the total votes.

It was the greatest electoral triumph that Bismarck ever scored, and even though Eugen Richter* was not far wrong when he described the new majority as "the product of panic", the fact remains that the strength of his party was reduced by half and that much the same fate befell the Social Democrats. Most important of all, Bismarck had not been forced to name the real purpose of his military preparations. Boulanger had obligingly given him a pretext and a highly plausible one at that. On March 9, 1887, the new Reichstag passed the new septennial law. "I didn't create Boulanger," said Bismarck, "but he has been very useful to me." This was not quite true. For without Bismarck there would have been no Boulanger.

Meanwhile, St. Petersburg was taking its time in dealing with the draft treaty that Schuwalow had brought back with him. At first, the Czar roundly rejected it on the grounds that it was contrary to the general feeling of Russians. It was only after five months, in May, that Paul Schuwalow returned to Berlin with a new draft treaty which, unlike that originally agreed upon, provided for the neutrality of Germany, even in the event of a Russian attack on Austria. Hereupon, to the general astonishment, Bismarck took a piece of paper from his brief-case and read it through from beginning to end. It was the text of the secret treaty with Austria, concluded in 1879, and which ran for ten years.

It is undeniable that by communicating the text of this treaty to the representative of the very power against whom it was directed, Bismarck was guilty of a breach of confidence. He had, it is true, asked Vienna whether it agreed to the publication of the treaty, but the answer, which only authorized publication under certain conditions, could not possibly have been in Bis-

* Eugen Richter (1839–1906), a vigorous opponent of Bismarck's policy of state socialism.

marck's hands at the time his interview with Schuwalow took place.

But if Bismarck committed an indiscretion, it was an indiscretion well worth committing. It brought him Russia's acceptance of the principle that both Germany and Russia should be given the benefit of friendly neutrality in the event of either power finding itself at war with a third. This arrangement, however, would not apply if the war was a war of aggression on the part of Russia against Austria, or on the part of Germany against France—which, of course, raised the ancient and fundamental question, how one can definitely distinguish between a war of aggression and a war of defence, and that question remained unanswered, as it has always done.

The most important and explosive provisions, however, were confined to a highly secret supplementary protocol. According to these, Russia was to be given a free hand by Germany in the Dardanelles.

Russia finally accepted the treaty in June 1887. On the 18th of that month, the day of Belle Alliance, the last battle of the great war which the three monarchies of Prussia, Russia and Austria had fought together, the signatures were appended.

The new treaty, which has become known as the Reinsurance Treaty, did not by any means spring forth from the brain of its creator in all its ultimate perfection, like Pallas Athene from the head of Zeus. It was gradually tortured into shape by the mutual distrust of the Cabinets concerned. Viewed superficially, it was a sort of complementary arrangement to the Dual Alliance, yet in reality it was something rather different. For while the former was strictly a pact of mutual defence, the Reinsurance Treaty was something which might come dangerously near to being an actual betrayal of Austria.

According to the letter of the law, it was, of course, nothing of the kind, but if we examine it a little more closely, the treaty has rather a different aspect. For if Russia were to threaten Austria's position in the Balkans, possibly through an offensive against Bulgaria or Constantinople, and Austria thereupon were to declare war, Germany would in such a case be obliged to remain neutral.

Moreover, the secret agreement of Germany to give "moral and diplomatic support" to Russia should she make a grab at the Dardanelles was contrary to the whole spirit of the Dual Alliance, all the more so since it was a guiding principle of Austrian state policy only to allow a weak state to be master of the Dardanelles. An additional complication was provided by the fact that, at this very time, through the active agency of Bismarck, the Mediterranean Agreement was concluded between Austria, Italy and Britain, the express purpose of which was to protect the status quo in the Dardanelles. Bismarck, therefore, had at one and the same time committed himself to ensure the closing of the straits and also to give moral and diplomatic support to one who proposed to break the lock.

Actually, so long as he was in office, Bismarck did not attach great importance to the document in its final form. It was only later, when his successor refused to renew the treaty, that he took a different attitude in the hope of discrediting him. When the treaty was signed, Herbert wrote, and most certainly he must have been expressing his father's views, that he did not expect anything from the treaty, save only "that in an emergency, it might keep the Russians off our necks for six or eight weeks longer than otherwise might have been the case".

Bismarck was always in doubt whether the Russians would keep to the terms of the treaty, for Russia, in 1807, had cold-bloodedly deserted her Prussian ally and, in 1762, her Austrian ones. "*Was sind Verträge wenn man muss?*" he had said in 1870. "What use are treaties when signed under compulsion?"

Yet if we are really concerned to judge the Reinsurance Treaty by ethical principles, we will be unable to overlook the fact that in the final analysis not only this treaty but the whole system of alliances was really designed to nullify itself. If everything went according to the wishes of its author, no single pact could come into operation without bringing other pacts into play which would automatically prevent it from functioning. Thus wars would be, so to speak, throttled at birth or would, at worst, remain localised.

There can be no doubt that Bismarck entered into treaties in which he virtually promised to break his engagements to others. This was a risk which he deliberately took upon himself, because he assumed that he would never be called upon to redeem such promises. All these treaties, including the Reinsurance Treaty, were in form preparations for war; in intention and fact they were designed to prevent it.

"What a pity," Alexander III had often remarked, "that we cannot go along with Germany. Unfortunately Austria stands between us."* Now things were changed, and it was the strictly secret Reinsurance Treaty that had made all the difference.

In other respects, however, the world presented to that monarch a less encouraging aspect. In March 1887 a conspiracy was discovered by which Alexander was to be disposed of in the same way as his father. Among the conspirators who were hanged was

*Grosse Politik, V, p. 108.

a student named Uljanow, whose brother Vladimir later called himself Lenin.

The news from Bulgaria was equally depressing. There the Council of Regency was endeavouring, just as Battenberg had done, to free the country from Russian influence, and another attempt by officers sympathetic to Russia to effect a coup d'état had merely resulted in the Council of Regency rather inconsiderately having them shot. Then Bulgaria, feeling that existing arrangements were somehow less than satisfactory and that it might be as well to regularize them, offered the crown to the twenty-eight-year-old Prince Ferdinand of Saxe-Coburg, from the very rich Hungarian line of the Koharys. It was unfortunate that the agreement of the other powers, which the resolutions of the Berlin congress had prescribed, seemed impossible of attainment. Russia was particularly intransigent. "A Catholic, a Hungarian and a Coburg," said Bismarck. Each on its own was unacceptable to Russia. Ferdinand, however, "had all three Cerberus heads on his body at once".

But the Council of Regency pressed the matter, and so Ferdinand went off to Bulgaria on his own account. He showed himself a more prudent man than Battenberg, but had far fewer of the qualities that make for popularity. The Czar, more in sorrow than in anger, sent him a hesitant note of protest, and then went off for his summer holidays to Denmark—taking no official of the Foreign Office with him. Coburg seemed to be forgotten.

The Reinsurance Treaty soon showed that it could produce no relaxation of tension between Russia and Germany. Hardly four months after its signature Herbert was already saying to the Russian ambassador that Russia had only signed the treaty in order to tie Germany's hands till Russia was ready with her own rearmament. There even seemed doubt whether the very modest prophecy with which Bismarck had recommended the treaty to his Emperor, namely that it would bring three years of peace, was really worthy of belief.

Here then, unmistakably and quite incontestably, lay the key to the matter. However one looked at it all, the problems of Europe really centred on Russia, and this meant that they centred on the person of Alexander III, who was not only in name, but also in fact, an autocrat.

It was unfortunate that just this man, a person of colossal stature and majestic appearance, had not been too liberally endowed either with will-power or perspicacity. He would say: "Am I not master? If I so desire, I have only to bang my fist on the table and all the row will stop." Only, somehow, he never got around to banging his fist on the table.

From youth onwards nothing could shake his belief in certain
things—the superiority of the Slav, of the Greek Orthodox Church
and of the principle of autocracy. Even so, he found difficulty in
ever making a decision and even greater difficulty in abiding by
a decision, once he had made it. He had no real aims, but only
wishes, the most powerful wish of which was never to have to
wage a war.

To have called him an enemy of Germany would have been
extreme, although, like the rest of his people, he had an ineradicable suspicion of Germans and of their nimble-mindedness
and astonishing gifts for civilisation, qualities which had inspired
the popular Russian proverb, "The German invented the
monkey". He was moderately attached to the Hohenzollerns,
but quite free of the sentimental devotion of his father, which
he found rather boring and ridiculous.

One of the best comments on Alexander III's character is contained in a report to Bismarck from his ambassador, Schweinitz.
"For our Gracious Emperor and Master, His Majesty has the
greatest veneration. For His Royal and Imperial Highness, the
Crown Prince, honest respect. For His Royal Highness, Prince
William, he feels friendship, and for Your Serene Highness,
admiration and fear. However, His Majesty's feelings provide us
with no guarantee whatever."

This mixture of fear and admiration made Alexander, so said
his brother Vladimir, "*malheureusement pétri d'un soupçon insur-
montable*", a suspiciousness which international politics had to
accept as one of the facts of life. It was this quality that made him
continue the concentration of troops on the western frontier,
without apparently realising the extent to which this weakened
his policy, which was actuated by a genuine desire for peace.
And although he was convinced that the Press was of no practical
importance, he was never quite certain whether the favourite
journalist of the Russia of that day, namely Katkow, with his
delicate sensitivity for atmosphere, was a person to be loved or
hated. He delighted in the polish of his style, only to be
shocked by his immoderate condemnation of the Three Emperors
Pact, which, Katkow said, Russia had been tempted to sign at the
moment of her greatest humiliation.

Katkow pressed for a policy of the free hand, which could only
mean one of close co-operation with France, and Alexander was
deeply disturbed by such sentiments, for though he was no friend
of Germany he was even less a friend of France. His static mode
of thought abhorred all that smacked of revolution, and the
French Republic was, to him, the very essence of revolution.
Bismarck's fear of a possible Franco-Russian entente would

thus seem to have been without foundation, had not Alexander also sadly lacked any confidence in his own strength.

Bismarck's policy towards this difficult person, who was unable even to come to a decision about his own affairs, and on whom, nevertheless, the fate of Europe could depend, consisted in never forgetting his sensitiveness and in keeping everything from him which could in the least degree irritate him. But it was in vain. It seemed to be a decree of fate that German relations with Russia should never be happy, nor were they. The troop transports to the western frontier continued. What Clausewitz called the Tartaric suspiciousness of the Russians only grew stronger. The Press was full to bursting with jingoist plans of aggression.

The climax came on October 7, 1887, three months after the signing of the Reinsurance Treaty, when the Russian Grand Duke Nicholas remarked in an after-dinner speech on board the French steamer *Uruguay* that France was working to prepare revenge, while Russia was unceasingly striving to eliminate every German influence. It would not be long, and all the obstacles would disappear which now stood in the way of a war carried on against Germany by a Franco-Russian alliance. When Schweinitz protested, Giers merely remarked that the Grand Duke was a completely brainless person and left it at that.

Francis Joseph had already in August told the German ambassador that Germany was wasting much loving kindness on Russia and would get no thanks in return. The Russians would not attempt any concrete adventure, once they were convinced that they would meet determined opposition. But if they were allowed to have their way, their conduct would be increasingly brazen as the years went on.* It is possible that the Emperor had a better insight into things on this occasion than Bismarck himself, preoccupied as he was with the excessive refinements of his alliances.

For some time Bismarck was silent, but a month later he suddenly drew back to deliver a heavy blow against Russia, this time in the economic field. In May of that year the Czar had issued a ukase that no foreigner was to acquire landed property in the western provinces. There was some reason for this, for the freeing of the serfs by Alexander II had virtually turned numbers of those liberated—namely, those whose holdings were too small to support them—into proletarians. To give them a place in society, industries had to be set up, and for this there was an insufficiency of Russian capital. As a result, for some decades now Russia had been importing capital, and the policy had paid off very well. To protect the young industry a tariff wall had

* *Grosse Politik*, V, p. 106.

been erected, which foreigners found no difficulty in crossing by setting up factories on Russian soil. It was this that the ukase of May 1887 sought to prevent.

The German Government answered with a Press campaign. The damage which the ukase had caused was used to discredit Russia as a country unworthy of trust. The result was a sharp fall in Russian securities and in the value of the rouble. The thing went so far that in November the Reichsbank forbade the use of Russian scrip as collateral.

Bismarck had been warned by experts, and among them Schweinitz, that retaliatory pressures would never force Russia to make tariff concessions. Bleichröder made desperate efforts to change Bismarck's mind, despite the fact that in his private capacity he almost certainly made money by selling Russian paper short.

Virtual exclusion of Russia from the Stock Exchanges of Germany was regarded by her as a declaration of no confidence that had the whole weight of the Imperial government behind it. She felt herself to have been deeply insulted, but suffered little material damage. The export of capital to Russia was much too profitable a business for others not to step in, once the Germans had dropped out of the running. Thus Bismarck's attempt to defeat Russia on the floor of the Stock Exchange proved a failure, and this very fact should lead us to look elsewhere for the ultimate causes that produced the Franco-Russian Pact. Historical changes of that kind are determined by a variety of forces, and cannot be ascribed to the resolutions of a governing body of a central bank. Yet, for all that, if Russia, which he had wooed for decades, Russia for whom he had toiled even as Jacob toiled for Rachel, gave her hand to her French suitor, some cause had been given her— perhaps rather needlessly—by Bismarck himself.

On November 18th, a few days before the prohibition of Russian collateral was issued, Alexander III, returning from Copenhagen, spent some hours in Berlin. The visit had long been prepared for, and then cancelled and finally made after all, the reason for the delay being that his children had measles and were not to be exposed to a sea-voyage. Actually, the whole affair could not have been more chilly than it was. As though things were not difficult enough already, Bismarck was compelled to ask Alexander for an audience, for certain letters purporting to come from the Coburgs had been published, according to which the Chancellor had been playing a double game in Bulgaria and working secretly against Russian interests.

It was not even a first-class piece of forgery, and consequently not too difficult to refute. Bismarck began by saying that he had to speak plainly, whereupon the Czar, with a somewhat forced smile, could only remark "*Allez, allez*". Smoking uninterruptedly, the Czar, after a bare hour and with a somewhat sceptical expression on his face, declared that he was satisfied.

Bismarck got his own satisfaction at the state banquet that evening. He had most carefully drafted the Emperor's speech, and the Czar had never been told the truth in so concentrated and paralysing a form. All the complaints that Germany had had to make against Russia over the past few years were duly recited to him, and, in particular, the grievance that Russia was not only herself continually engaged in preparations for war, but was endeavouring to drag France into a conflict along with herself.

He believed, William was made to say, that the Czar did not want a war, but war would come whether the Czar wanted it or not. If it came, the socialists of the countries concerned would, without any doubt, use the opportunity to bring down the dynasties. The war would, therefore, no longer be a war between governments, but "a war between the red flag and the elements of order and conservatism".

Thus in the midst of the glittering splendour of this scene, Bismarck caused voice to be given to his dark visions of the future, visions that in the sixty years that were to follow were to prove all too true.* The Czar listened with obvious ill-grace, said nothing and left Berlin the same evening, after a visit of barely twelve hours.

He was much too heavy-handed and unimaginative to change his policy. He remained on the track on which he was travelling at the time, like a gigantic locomotive which cannot be switched into a siding, firmly believing that the wish to avoid war, which he most certainly entertained, was sufficient to prevent it from coming. He was a man who walked the road of life with a heavy tread, yet a tread that was so uncertain that, where he was concerned, one had to be prepared for anything.

In the course of these rather depressing autumn days Bismarck received a memorandum from Moltke in which the eighty-seven-year-old Chief of the General Staff pointed out that Russian troop movements to the frontier could only mean that they were assembling for war, and that, consequently, there was nothing left

---

* All this was in itself not new to Bismarck. In a letter to Schleinitz written in 1861 he had described the Russian Minister of War, Miljutin, who was the moving spirit behind the aggressive measures on the western frontier, in the following terms: "The sharpest and keenest mind among the progressives is also the most intense hater of the aristocracy, and conceives the future Russia as a country of peasants with equality but without freedom, though possessing intelligence, industry, bureaucracy and a press." *Bismarcks Briefwechsel mit Schleinitz* (1905), p. 158.

for Germany to do, painful as it was to give such advice, save to anticipate a Russian attack by attacking herself. Bismarck, however, immediately and unreservedly rejected the suggestion. The German generals, he had somewhat cavalierly and certainly unjustly said a year before, only wanted wars so as to get new gifts of money. And most certainly the events that followed justified the refusal to listen to Moltke, for the Russian troop movements, consisting largely of vast swarms of Cossacks, who so grievously disturbed Moltke's peace of mind, lasted for a quarter of a century on the frontier without a war breaking out at all.

It is, of course, possible that there really was something to be said for Moltke's view, and that a quick attack, with superior armaments, which Germany at that time possessed—and with a firm determination not to be drawn into the interior of Russia —would have temporarily, at least, eliminated the Russian threat, even though it could not have done so permanently. There were others on all the general staffs who shared Moltke's views. That Bismarck rejected them so abruptly was not due to any general moral reasons which could be adduced against the resort to preventive war, but to his firm conviction that to engage in a preventive war was to make a professional declaration of bankruptcy. Preventive war was for Bismarck the last expedient of fools who will not realise that the future always holds unforeseen possibilities which it can only do harm to anticipate.

Moreover, Bismarck had lost his old confidence in the Army. A year before, at Christmas, he had expressed his concern in a very earnest letter to the Prussian Minister of War that the legend of the Prussian Army was no more than a legend, that, to take the obvious example, the victory over Napoleon I was to be attributed more to such factors as the Russian winter and the alliance with England, Russia and Austria than to the Prussian Army. In a new war such a fortunate constellation could no longer be reckoned on, so that victory was by no means guaranteed.

Bismarck was not the only one to hold such views. Wherever reasonably well-informed people could speak freely they—not altogether surprisingly—declared that Moltke was too old for his job, nor were their estimates of other high-ranking officers much more favourable. Count Waldersee, Moltke's presumptive successor, elegant and pleasant-mannered, the offspring of a misalliance of the princely house of Anhalt, was no fool, but he was weak and easily influenced.* General von Albedyll, the apparently irremovable head of the Military Cabinet since 1871, who had the appointment of all the higher military posts in his hands,

* Holstein, II, p. 133.

was looked upon as a garrulous courtier. General von Verdy du Vernois was held to be the most gifted of all the soldiers, but was also considered a man of weak character and personally indolent.*

Discouraging as all this might be, Bismarck was compelled to recognize that there were only two expedients by which he could check the unceasing pressure of Russian power on his frontier, and both might, for all he knew, prove vain. One was to expand the fighting forces to the uttermost limit, the other was to perfect his system of interlocking alliances.

In regard to the first of these alternatives, a certain amount could be done. And so a bare five months after the signing of the Reinsurance Treaty, namely on November 24th, the Speech from the Throne announced that new measures were to be put forward, according to which the *Landsturm*, to which all those liable to military service belonged up to their forty-fifth birthday, would be made an integral part of the Army. The latter would thus be strengthened by some 700,000 men, and this meant, as Schweinitz pointed out, as much as the addition of a fourth great power to the Triple Alliance.

There still remained the extension of the system of alliances, but where could a beginning be made? France, with whom quite recently there had been the prospects of a rapprochement, had now, even when the fever of the Boulanger era had died out, become distinctly unapproachable. For power no longer lay in the hands of an indulgently cosmopolitan aristocracy of birth and finance, but with the parties of the petty bourgeoisie and the middle-class intellectuals, who clung to a strict and somewhat suspicious patriotism. They were not propagandists of revenge and, for the present, not propagandists for a Russian alliance. Towards Germany, however, they were anxious only to maintain an attitude of icy correctness.

Actually, clever old Münster was to be proved right in his warnings that a Franco-Russian alliance, like some natural pheno-menon, would come into being at the moment of crisis. With grim humour he recalled an incident in a menagerie, in which a tiger had covered a lioness, and the owners of the animal had explained, "They did not mate from love, but from pure spite."†️ When he wrote in 1889 he seemed to perceive a similar spirit. France, he said, was isolated and its relations with Russia had grown cooler. "From our point of view, this makes no difference, since both powers, even though no alliance exists, are counting on one another in the event of war." It was only a short sentence, but what a terrible indictment of the vanity of Bismarck's untiring struggle against the spectre of a two-front war.

* Holstein, II, p. 139.   †*Grosse Politik*, VI, p. 156.

In England it might perhaps have been possible to come to some kind of understanding with Beaconsfield, that active, unprejudiced and daring Oriental, but he had died in 1881, and Lord Salisbury, his successor, was a rather stiff British aristocrat, with all the qualities and faults of a totally different class. He lacked that air of knight-errantry which surrounded Beaconsfield. He lacked Beaconsfield's capacity for quick enthusiasms and the witty, refreshingly cooling cynicism that always seemed to lie ready beneath the surface.

Moreover, when approaching British problems, Bismarck tended to show himself strangely maladroit. His relations to the island kingdom had something of the coldness of the North Sea, by which the two countries were separated. The kind of intimacy which subsisted from time to time with Austria, France or Russia never came into being at all. Nor for that matter did anything like the intimacy of real enmity.

When Bismarck had turned to Paris, Vienna or St. Petersburg, he hardly ever made a false move. But in London it was quite different. The English form of life and of self-government was something which he never really got to understand and he was always dependent on hearsay. Of the average Frenchman he could form a pretty accurate picture, but when dealing with the British he thought in stereotypes—yes, even, at times, in terms of caricature.

When the Mediterranean Convention between England, Italy and Austria was about to be concluded, Salisbury wished to see a demonstration of Bismarck's active co-operation in this pact, which in point of fact was certainly directed against Russia. He was anxious to prevent him saying, at some later stage, that he had never had anything to do with it. He therefore asked Bismarck for an assurance that Germany would give the Mediterranean Convention its moral approval.

Bismarck's answer, which is dated November 22, 1887, was written in French and very cautiously formulated. It has always been regarded as a veiled offer of an entente with Britain, though in view of the Reinsurance Treaty it had to be couched in more or less cryptic terms. He communicated the text of the treaty with Austria and added, in a suggestive form, a statement of the principles of German foreign policy. Britain, Germany and Austria were, he said, saturated states, and these contrasted with the permanent stirrers-up of unrest, namely Russia and France, which constituted the only danger for the other three. Consequently— and this was the decisive sentence—German policy had necessarily to seek such alliances as it could find in the event of having to do battle with her two mighty neighbours at once.

Salisbury replied a few days later, and precisely because he understood very well what was behind these sentences he very deliberately evaded them. He confined himself to thanking Bismarck for having removed the grounds of his anxieties; in regard to the rest of the matter, however, he displayed a remarkable reserve. For the very fact that for decades Bismarck had been involved with Russia, an involvement from which, in his offer to Salisbury, he was seeking to withdraw, made Salisbury keep silent.

Moreover, the experience of 1879, when Bismarck had suddenly broken off his very promising negotiations with Beaconsfield because Russia had so temptingly come between him and Britain, must further have deterred him. Finally, no doubt, there was alive in Salisbury that very marked tradition which leads the British to combat any immediate peril with all the strength of body and soul, but to avoid wasting their energy in creating safeguards against future emergencies whose exact nature is still unknown.

There thus remained only Germany's old ally, Austria-Hungary, and yet in the Dual Monarchy many things had changed. Since 1866 it had been passing through an apparently irresolvable crisis of adjustment. The old country, with all its reputation for fullness and goodness, could no longer find rest. The loss of spiritual strength, occasioned by the endless squabbles of its nationalities, became ever more apparent and could even be seen by foreigners.

The Germans in the Alpine districts and the Sudeten Germans provided an especial disappointment for Bismarck. They had sunk with surprising speed to the level of just another nationality, and, like the Ruthenians and Slovenes, were only concerned with group interests, and viewed the possible end of the monarchy with indifference in the obstinate belief that, once it happened, they would be welcomed into the Hohenzollern Empire.

Bismarck lost no opportunity of destroying that illusion. "If," he said, and the utterance was one among many, "they love us so much in Austria, then if the non-Germans are to be kept within our alliance they will have to take a different road from that which they have followed hitherto. It is very wrong to allow a partition to come into being between Germans and Slavs. . . . There is place for both them and ourselves on this earth." Yet he was preaching to deaf ears, though he used actual threats and spoke of the "holy duty to send home with bloody heads if necessary" those Austrians who wished to unite their country with the German Empire.

He began to feel increasing concern lest the great complex

of Austria-Hungary, instead of being the weight that drove the clock in his system of alliances, should become a mere lifeless burden. Without in any way desiring it, he had come to accept the degradation of Austria-Hungary to the level of a sort of poor relation who could no longer be permitted to manage her own affairs. Again and again he took towards the dual monarchy the rôle of a guardian and uninvited manager. (We have already noticed his unauthorised disclosure to Schuwalow of the Dual Alliance.) And this was not always to the advantage of his ward.

Thus it was really his doing that in the Mediterranean Convention a provision was inserted that Italy should agree to and receive appropriate compensation in the event of Austrian territorial acquisitions in the Balkans. It was this provision that moved Italy, in 1914, to refuse to act as an ally and to open an offensive on Austria's insufficiently protected southern flank.

Also, Bismarck was continually disquieted by the thought that the Hapsburgs, in the last resurgence of the ancient family pride, might make a desperate attack on Russia on their own. For that reason he kept repeating to the diplomats in Vienna that only a Russian attack on Austria would cause the *casus foederis* to arise. He even went so far as to warn Austria that if she provoked a war against Russia, he would have to anticipate the inevitable attack by France, which meant that he would himself have to attack France, and this would leave no further German troops available for Austria's support. He went so far as to forbid conversations between the general staffs of the two countries, though this would have been a severe military handicap if war had broken out.

During the Boulanger crisis he sent the rather alarming accounts of the German military attaché to Vienna, though he himself did not believe them, the object being to deepen the feeling of faint-hearted melancholy which already prevailed there. No wonder that his ambassador in Vienna reported to him, in 1877, that in Austria there is the "depressed feeling everywhere that they would only be able to count on Germany when they had themselves already been thrown to the ground". At about this time, Count Wedel, the military attaché, was reporting that the mood of Francis-Joseph was serious, and even, up to a certain point, depressed, to which Bismarck coolly made the marginal note: "Rather that, than that he should be enterprising."

Everywhere there was evidence of the feeling that a historical era was approaching its end. The compass needles on the command bridges of Europe were vibrating in a fashion the meaning of which was not altogether plain. Diplomats did not cease to prophesy that war would come within a year, and though it did

not come, people went on announcing the date of its outbreak
as though this was a kind of macabre parlour game.

Bismarck's thinking always kept returning to the point from
whence it started. It returned to Alexander III, the black-
bearded giant, and to Russia, the land of limitless plains that
stretched out from Prussia's eastern frontier and remained to him
a strange land, a part of the world that existed on its own. Whatever happened in Russia depended on Alexander. He alone was
master of its destiny. Or was he?—who could say? For somehow
there was never anything definite or determinate about Russia,
and so it was impossible to say in what direction she would move
next.

Bismarck did whatever lay in his power to avoid disquieting
the Czar, but it ultimately proved useless. Alexander III never
trusted him, however much he might assure him to the contrary.
He was always afraid of Bismarck's mental superiority and
believed that he was being made a victim of the latter's cunning.
Never could he be dissuaded from his conviction—and his entourage strengthened him in this—that Bismarck coveted Russia's
Baltic provinces.

Today it is plain enough that Bismarck never thought of anything of the kind, and had no wish to annex these distant, militarily untenable territories with their very small German minorities. Yet year in, year out, the Russian Press screamed their
accusations against him, and the more he was concerned to prove
the nonsensical character of these charges, the more the Russians
thought of his appropriations in Schleswig, Lorraine and in Inner
Germany and refused flatly to believe him.

The unreliable character of Russia, together with the Czar's
singular inability ever to make up his mind, could not but have
their effects on Bismarck, though these effects were strange. For
something of his opponent's vagueness and unpredictability seems
to have entered into Bismarck himself.

Those around him began to find his policy vacillating—*"entre
la brune et la blonde"*—and at times he appeared quite bankrupt
of resource, then showed a tendency to be over-precipitate. He
changed his purposes more frequently and was less persistent in
pursuing them. What Holstein called "his inward isolation"
grew more marked. Above all, the old condescending irony was
no longer always in evidence, and there were moments when his
mind seemed to move less rapidly than of old.

For all that, he found time for much bureaucratic hair-splitting
in the outward form of documents, and frequently relieved himself by long bouts of swearing, which were embarrassing to those
around him. But his sons were less perturbed. "Swearing amuses

him," said Bill. Even Crown Prince Rudolf of Austria, who saw him comparatively rarely, found in March 1887 that he had changed. He looked more gaunt, was more easily excitable and seemed to be suffering from shortness of breath. "I miss the calm and assurance that I once used to admire in him,"* said Rudolf.

Yet in 1884 there had been a marked improvement in his health. There was much talk of a slimming cure on the Banting method, which he was undergoing, and Schweninger's name was often mentioned. In March Holstein found him "capable of great exertion and eager for battle". But, as Bismarck himself declared, he was "wholly without passion. Since I have no longer any passion for hunting, everything else has gone". A year later, in 1885, Holstein wrote, "He is still more capable than anybody else," but it was obvious that the mere fact of his being the man he was presented something of a problem. "The unfortunate thing," wrote Holstein in December of that same year, "is not that he sometimes confuses things or forgets them—anybody might do that—but that nobody dares to point out his mistakes."

By 1886 he had changed still further. In February, Holstein found, when he was alone with him, that he "seemed completely to have shrunk" (im vollem Einschrumpfen). He was "lonely, nervous, mistrustful and without his old width of vision". On New Year's Eve, at the beginning of the year 1886, which was to be a very eventful year for him, he seemed in a melancholy mood. "I find much greater difficulty in grasping things," he said to Bill, "and I can no longer take in the work as a whole."

He ceased to be a hero for those about him. In the family he was called "Papachen", and in his office S.D., for Seine Durchlaucht (His Serene Highness). Here, however, some of those— and there were not very many of them—who had some acquaintance with the complications of his policy of alliances, began to make mild fun of him and then to be genuinely concerned. They spoke of Haugwitz, the Prussian Foreign Minister of 1805 and 1806, and his perpetual vacillations towards and away from Napoleon which ultimately led to the catastrophe of Jena, and a good, conservative mind like that of Holstein became uneasy when he contemplated Germany's "crisscrossing engagements" and compared them with "the complicated pattern of rails in a great railway station".

Holstein was convinced that the Austro-Russian enmity was incurable, and while Bismarck still hoped for a possible reconciliation, Holstein worked for the inclusion of Germany in the Anglo-Austrian-Italian Mediterranean Pact. Thus a mighty

* O. von Mitis, *Das Leben des Kronprinzen Rudolph* (1928), p. 359ff.

alliance consisting of four powers would have come into being, which would have given Austria a new lease of life, though it would have meant that Germany had finally and irrevocably turned her back on Russia. It was an alliance which, as Lord Randolph Churchill said, might come into being at any time if Germany wanted it.

Holstein had no qualms about carrying on a kind of private foreign policy of his own, since he saw that Herbert Bismarck was doing exactly the same thing, though with an opposite purpose in view. For Bismarck's favourite son had always been an enemy of Austria because, so it was said, as a young attaché in Vienna, shortly before 1866, he had not been too well treated by the aristocracy. He had virtually written off the Dual Monarchy, and when he became State Secretary at the Foreign Office in 1886, did whatever he could to hasten that monarchy's downfall. He told Holstein, "We can do business with Russia, but not with Austria. We'll join with Russia in smashing Austria."

Complaints now began to grow ever more serious; Herbert was dominating his father, was urging him to take sharp measures against Austria in the Austro-Russian conflict and was withholding important documents from him. Holstein, on the other hand, was a patriotic conservative for whom Herbert's policies spelled downright nihilism and who nevertheless was furious to see the elder Bismarck standing "with his hat in his hand" before the Czar, so making every anti-Russian combination impossible the whole world over.

It was made known in 1887—and the news was in accord with the general mood of these disturbed and sinister times— that Frederick William, the heir to the throne, that splendid prince whose shoulders were destined to carry all that was accounted as Bismarck's work, was suffering from cancer of the larynx. The doctors were at first evasive, nobody dared utter the truth, which was that Frederick William would soon be dead. This sealed the fate not only of an individual but of an entire generation in German history.

The skies were indeed clouding over in ominous fashion above the German dynasties, dynasties which were so old that people took them for the eternal carriers of Germany's destiny. A year previously, Ludwig of Bavaria had removed himself by suicide from a world which was repugnant to him, while during a royal hunt in Prussia Crown Prince Rudolf of Austria had brought down a white stag, a thing which, according to an old huntsman's superstition, foretold the early death of the killer, and so indeed it was, for the prince died by his own hand in 1889.

Bismarck had a good opinion of both these men, whose deaths upset the direct succession both in the House of Hapsburg and of Wittelsbach, and when it became known that the eldest son of the German Crown Prince had, since birth, an arm that was too short and was hardly capable of being used at all, a whisper went round as men remembered the old prophecy: "The one-armed man will ruin the Empire."

The first effect of these developments—by this time Frederick William, for all practical purposes, ceased to be counted among the living—was to produce a complete reversal of all Bismarck's personal attitudes. For years he had grown accustomed to the fact that he would serve under a sovereign with whom he was not only at variance over great issues, but who irritated him in innumerable little ways. For instance, it annoyed him almost beyond measure that Frederick William drank his wine mixed with water, and so, as Bismarck said, destroyed the bouquet.

Once Frederick William had ascended the throne, Bismarck had anticipated whole years of struggle for bare survival. Now, however, with the heir to the throne a dying man, all these problems seemed to be solving themselves, without any sort of clash, in a manner highly favourable to Bismarck himself. For young Prince William, Frederick William's eldest son and now the heir apparent, had never ceased to express his admiration for Bismarck to his face. And it is really not difficult to understand that Bismarck should not have been displeased at the prospect of having to deal with a young man who was obviously devoted to him, instead of with a monarch for whom he had neither sympathy nor understanding. Small wonder that he suddenly seemed to have a new zest for life. It was perhaps in the circumstances inhuman to entertain such feelings as these, but Bismarck was never a pattern of human perfection.

Yet the truth was, had Bismarck but known it, that the future was less bright than it appeared. Prince William had recently come under the influence of the Court preacher Stöcker and his Christian Social movement, and Stöcker's zeal for social justice was unfortunately marked by ill-mannered vehemence and crude antisemitism. "An Emperor," commented Bismarck, "who makes his debut under the auspices of Stöcker will find that the results of his first Reichstag elections are such, that no Emperor and no Chancellor will survive." Yet, either because he had lost his old deftness of touch or because of some malignant quirk within him, Bismarck mishandled the matter and, instead of drawing the prince's attention to his indiscretions in a confidential talk, did so before the whole world in an article in the official *Norddeutsche Allgemeine Zeitung*. The prince was deeply wounded and was heard to observe that the present power of the Chancellor could not be allowed to last. "He must be made aware of the fact," he said, "that there is only one Emperor. . . . He must not be allowed to forget that I shall be master."

It is odd that Bismarck, who despised and detested the mischief wrought by any kind of illusion, should have become the dupe of the most disastrous illusions about Prince William's devotion to him. Yet by a strange chance, he whose eye penetrated to every corner of the world knew nothing of these outbursts. Nor did he know that the uncertain twilight over the European scene was not a new dawn, but the light of fading day, the herald of the night.

16

DUAL CHANGE OF THRONE

It was obvious that the death of William I was close at hand. After the attempts on his life his walk had become uncertain, and he had to use a light stick. Since 1885 his condition was continually giving rise to anxiety. One sometimes found him lying on the floor, unable to get up unaided. Everyone in his immediate entourage was equipped with smelling-salts.

In the first days of March 1888, after an unusually hard winter, the Emperor caught cold and retired to bed. It was soon apparent that his strength was now exhausted, but the old man, now 92, whose delicacy as an infant had kept the whole Prussian Court on tenterhooks, put up a tough resistance. On the evening of March 8th the bells in Berlin churches were actually already tolling when he regained consciousness, and it was not till the following morning that he passed away in his sleep.

At noon on the previous day Bismarck had produced documents for his signature. As he was going, the Emperor said, "I will see you again." These were the last words that he addressed to Bismarck.

Bismarck returned in the afternoon and again in the evening and stood by his bed, but the Emperor could no longer recognise him. When, some hours later, he had to inform the Bundesrat of the Emperor's death, there were tears in his eyes. In the Reichstag, however, he forced himself to adopt a cooler and more measured tone, but even here, when he had finished, he hid his eyes under his hand.

So ended that strange relationship between Otto von Bismarck, vassal of the Elector of Brandenburg on the one hand, and his liege lord on the other, a relationship in which the vassal always had the real power of command, while the liege lord quietly confessed that all his decisions were essentially those of his minister. "At best," he would say with a sigh, "it isn't easy to be an Emperor under such a Chancellor."

The real essence of their feelings for one another will probably never be fully expressed. One wonders whether William ever got over that "secret repugnance" towards Bismarck of which he had spoken in Babelsberg in 1862. Sometimes one would hardly have thought so. Bismarck's crude outspokenness, even if he was to some extent acting a part, must have grated horribly on the nerves of a man brought up as a great gentleman of the old school, who valued poise and courtesy above everything.

There are tales of scenes behind closed doors, in which neither the monarch nor the minister attempted to conceal what he thought of the other, for when driven beyond endurance even William could lose his normal phlegm and was capable both of tears of rage and of roaring like a drill-sergeant. Neither, however, uttered a word to anybody else about such things. Indeed, it was quite exceptional for the Emperor to act as he did in the case of Harry Arnim when by way of comfort he told the Count, who was a relative and for whom he had a great liking, that he, Arnim, was being persecuted by Bismarck, "simply because of Bismarck's rancour", which, he said, was his "predominant characteristic. . . . It is sad to have to say this of a man to whom I owe so much."

Yes, he owed Bismarck everything, yet he derived but limited pleasure from what he had received. It was well known that in 1861, William had received the Prussian crown with much ill-grace and would have abdicated in 1862 had not Bismarck prevented him. It was only in the years 1864 to 1870, in the midst of his triumphs and annexations, that the King gained some satisfaction from the office. From 1871 onwards, however, since they had forced the imperial title upon him, he had lost his taste for the business.

Here, then, were further grounds for secret resentment. Nor was his Empress likely to sweeten his feelings. For the enmity between the Empress Augusta and Bismarck which had arisen in that interview forty years ago in Potsdam Castle, would hardly have grown so intense, if that proud woman, the grand-daughter of one of the Czars of Russia, had not had to stand by and watch how the minister kept the King utterly dependent upon himself.

Actually, though the more disreputable scenes do not appear to have been mentioned in public, Bismarck was louder and more frequent in his complaints than was his master. He called William "hard as a stone and cold", yet he could speak of him with a sort of metaphysical awe. "*Wenn die Majestät über ihn kommt, weissagt er.*" (When majesty comes over him, he prophesies.) Surely a strange utterance—for Bismarck of all men—and on March 9, 1888 he wrote in the little notebook, in which he was in the habit of recording very briefly the events of the day, "*Imperator obiit.*" Does the solemn coldness of the Latin denote a certain distance, which had always remained between himself and the Emperor?

In the Dom, a noble, sober structure by Schinkel, which stood next to the Berlin Castle, the Emperor lay in state, wearing the uniform of the infantry of the guard, as he always did when alive, and covered with the black mantle of a general with its red facings. Torches were burning and their light flickered on the sword hilts of the eight colonels who stood motionless as a guard of honour. An unbroken stream of mourners passed the body by day and night.

As the funeral procession moved towards Charlottenburg, where the Emperor had asked to be interred next to his parents in the small family mausoleum, it was observed that there was an empty space in the procession immediately behind the coffin, indicating that this was the place that the new Emperor would have occupied had he not been too ill to do so. Then Prince William could be seen, the new Crown Prince with his hussar's uniform, the mantle drawn tightly around his youthful figure, so that he seemed to be even more slender than he actually was. He looked soldierly and marched quite alone.

After the service in the Dom, Bismarck had gone straight home. He had an ineradicable dislike for funerals and particularly for the spectacular funerals of princes, and it was only with difficulty that he could bring himself to do the minimum consistent with decency. During the evening, however, he sat with his family, thoughtfully speaking of the dead Emperor. He spoke very softly, almost as though he were speaking to himself, and occasionally wiped away a tear. Then he suddenly seemed to pull himself together and in a rather harsh tone of voice, said "and now forward".*

When, towards evening, the funeral procession reached the Charlottenburg Park and moved along the front of the castle garden, there appeared behind a window on the ground floor, a pale, bearded face, that of the new Emperor, Frederick III. Twenty-four hours after the death of his father he had entered the train in San Remo, which was to take him from the Mediterranean sunshine, over the wintry Alps to Germany. On the evening of the following day, Bismarck met him in Leipzig. Before leaving Berlin, Bismarck had requested the surgeon, Ernst von Bergmann, a Balt who had been Russian Surgeon-General in the Turkish War, to come and see him, and had asked him to his face, "How long can the Emperor live?" The answer came, "He will not see the end of the summer."† Now as he entered the Emperor's carriage, Bismarck bent over his hand, to give him the kiss of homage. But Frederick drew him up towards himself, and kissed him on both cheeks.

Now Bismarck could see the extent of the evil thing that had

---

* A. J. P. Taylor, *Bismarck* (London, 1955), p. 231.
† Gustav von Bergmann, *Ruckschau* (1935), p. 17.

attacked this man, who till now had been so splendid a specimen of manhood. The face was shrunken and of a clay-like pallor. The blue eyes seemed to have grown larger. The beard was thin and grey. The coat of his uniform was open. The ribbons of some orders were around his neck, but among them, surrounded by black gauze, the end of a little silver tube could be seen. This was in order to enable him to short-circuit the swollen larynx and so to breathe. The vocal cords were thus, virtually, put out of action, so that the Emperor had to write down whatever he had to say.

Two proclamations had already been prepared. "To my people" and "To the Imperial Chancellor" and these he handed to Bismarck. They were two children of Frederick's spirit, of his honesty of purpose and his goodwill. Bismarck found nothing in them to which he could object. All he asked was that he should not be spoken of as a colleague of William's but as his servant. Shortly before midnight they reached Berlin. In the Baroque castle at Charlottenburg, which had long been uninhabited, Frederick found an improvised domesticity with very little comfort. It was clear that there was no hope for him. Instead of a liberal age that was expected, there was now only to be a one-act tragedy.

Yet the fact that some additional months of life had been granted to the Emperor was largely Bismarck's doing, though he did not know this at the time; for in May 1887, when Frederick's doctors were certain that he had cancer, they had decided that the larynx, or a great part of it, was to be removed, and that Bergmann was to carry out the operation on the 21st May. They did not, however, say anything to the Crown Prince of the risks involved. A number of high officials who had heard of the plan had considerable misgivings, and the Prussian Minister of Justice, Friedberg, brought the matter to Bismarck's notice.

Immediately the Chancellor went to the Emperor and persuaded him, provisionally at least, to forbid the operation. He also visited the Crown Princess and sought to make her see that it was better to fall into the hands of God than those of men.

In the meantime, however, the doctors had already decided to have their diagnosis verified by some authority from abroad and, on the suggestion of the Crown Prince's personal physician, Wegner, had already on May 16th called in the English laryngologist, Sir Morell Mackenzie.* On the afternoon of the 20th,

---

* It is therefore incorrect to say that the Crown Princess had occasioned the treatment of her husband by Mackenzie. It was not till May 17th, one day after the Berlin doctors had of their own accord decided on calling him in, that she asked her mother to get in touch with him. Victoria arranged this through Reed, her personal physician.

at the very moment when Bismarck was having his audience with the Emperor, the Englishman reached Berlin, and immediately after making his first examination recommended that the operation should be postponed on the grounds that he was in some doubt whether the cancer diagnosis was correct.

The real truth of the matter, however, is that Sir Morell probably had very little doubt of the correctness of the diagnosis, but did not believe that an operation in such a case could achieve anything. In his standard work *Diseases of the Throat and Nose* he had written that in the case of cancer of the larynx, the best that could be done was to postpone the inevitable end and make the patient as comfortable as circumstances permitted. Surgery was to be avoided, since in those days nothing could be done to prevent the sepsis which immediately ensued. It was decided to follow Sir Morell's advice, and if he could only achieve his object of preventing a cruel and useless operation by telling a lie, this was surely a case where a lie was justified.

Bismarck at first gave Sir Morell his full support. Later, he moved away from him,* but perhaps only because the Empress Victoria defended the English physician with almost fanatical zeal—possibly because people were saying that the Crown Prince would have been healed if Bergmann had operated on him in time. Those who talked like this, of course, did not know that in such cases there could be no question of operating "in time". In insisting that the operation planned for May 23rd should not take place Bismarck had therefore, to some extent, unconsciously helped to ensure a human solution of a well-nigh inhuman problem and made it possible for the invalid to live another year in relative comfort, the year, incidentally, which brought him the Imperial Crown.

The business of government under the new Emperor went along, said Bismarck, "as smoothly as a game of roulette". That for decades the Crown Prince had been accounted his opponent no longer seemed to matter. A sort of tacit understanding had been formed between the two that their opposition to each other should not come to the surface. This was not so much for political reasons as from the melancholy conviction that it simply was not worth the trouble.

Actually, Bismarck's assessment of the Crown Prince had varied from time to time, according to whether he felt that the slight influence which the heir to the throne could exert was useful to him or not. In Nikolsburg he probably owed his success to Frederick's intervention. In Versailles, on the other hand, he had been incensed by the Prince's unpractical and even turbulent

* Wolf, p. 100–101.

insistence on the restoration of the medieval empire, and had ultimately, as we have seen, cried out in his fury that the Prince was the vainest and stupidest of men who would one day die of his emperor madness.

As against this, the Crown Prince told the Chancellor to his face that the Empire which he had so painstakingly pieced together, was "a cleverly manufactured chaos" and openly disapproved of the pressure which he had used to serve his purposes. In the Prince's view all this should have been achieved by "a moral victory", although in reality the most petty of the German princes would not have been persuaded by moral arguments to abandon any part of his sovereignty.

Frederick III, however, was a child of that age of liberal nationalism that approved of Bismarck's aim but damned his methods, and would not admit that aims and methods condition one another, so that those who desire the one have also to accept the other. After this, on several occasions, Bismarck treated the powerless Crown Prince very badly. When the two attempts were made on the Emperor's life, the fact that the Crown Prince was not appointed Regent but was only given the right to represent his father led to violent arguments. Bismarck, Frederick said later, had on that occasion, done things to him "which no man could forget". For all that, Frederick was never for Bismarck one of those people whom he pursued without mercy, as he did Arnim or Battenberg.

Now that they were entering upon the last phase of their relationship, the situation became much easier. Moreover, Bismarck had gained the impression—and the impression was probably right—that Frederick's liberal tendencies were cooling off, that he preferred to be a hammer rather than an anvil and that he showed signs of becoming "the most reactionary of all the Hohenzollerns". Certainly, a rapprochement had already taken place between the two, simply because Frederick himself no longer had any illusions about his future. When the historian Delbrück spoke to him of some old plans for Berlin Dom, which could now be carried out, "his eyes seemed to redden," so Delbrück tells us, "in a strange manner and with a look that cut right into my heart, he passed his hands several times over the paper before him. 'That's all over and done with,' he said."

Outwardly, however, the dying man continued to exercise strong control over himself. When Bismarck came to report, he would not sit down while Bismarck was not seated himself. Bismarck, whether he liked it or not, could not help feeling that the illness of his sovereign was an unexpected piece of good fortune for him. It is said that during all this period he was in astonishingly good humour and always hopeful and, by reason of this, his manner towards the Emperor was altogether charming, his friendliness being quite sincere.

Of course, in his dealings with Frederick, Bismarck dared never forget the Empress and had always to be on his guard lest she upset his plans. Actually, the first real difficulties between Bismarck and the Emperor were due to Victoria. Certainly, Victoria was no fool. She had at a quite early stage seen through Bismarck, discerned the depths in his character, in which were hidden endless possibilities both for good and evil, and this knowledge created a certain tension between the two. Bismarck himself tells how, even in 1870, at a Court ball, Victoria had asked him for a glass of water, and when he brought it to her, said to the lady next to whom she was seated and pointing to Bismarck, "As much water as there is in this glass, this man has cost me in tears."

Yet the antagonism always kept within the bounds of courtly behaviour. Victoria was enough of a diplomatist to realise that Bismarck's very lack of principle which she detested might cause him one day to change sides and become her ally. He, for his part, had to tell himself that the methods of police and administrative action that he usually employed against his opponents could hardly be used against the daughter-in-law of his King. He could only work underground, by spreading the suspicion among the Berlin gossips that Victoria was betraying state secrets to her mother, the Queen of England, though this was completely senseless, since she had no knowledge of any.

What she had to tell her mother about Bismarck's mental and moral make-up is, however, often of almost embarrassing accuracy. "Bismarck," she said, "always wants the Germans to feel that they would be attacked, ill-used, insulted, betrayed and sold to their enemies, were he not there to protect them. Many would, indeed, give all their rights, their freedom and hope for the future to ensure that Bismarck should be preserved for them. . . . I love honesty and openness, decency and simplicity. I am sick of a system that uses base means, even if it is serviceable to so great a man. Certainly he is a patriot and a genius, but brutal and cynical."

Here, obviously, were two people, each endowed with tremendous energy, neither of whom had learned ever to yield ground, and these two people had been thrust upon each other and condemned to an everlasting war of position. Bismarck was not so far wrong, from his own point of view, when he said "she is a wild woman", and yet, strangely enough, Victoria's own ideals were those of bourgeois mediocrity. She might have been the wife of any wealthy cotton manufacturer. Bamberger, who visited her in the Crown Prince's palace in 1884, wrote "she looks as bourgeois can be, and yet she is natural human friendliness in person".

The character of this woman, who is, after all, not unimportant in German history, is much too complicated to be described in terms of the clichés so often used about her—such as the charge that she had "always remained an Englishwoman", or that "she had been no mother to her son", who later became William II. The last is particularly untrue. Certainly, mistakes were made in the education of the young prince, mistakes so grave that they amount to downright spiritual abuse, but they were not made from her indifference as a mother, but from her conviction that it was her duty to follow certain fashionable pedagogic theories. We are told that on one occasion the Crown Prince had spoken in very bitter terms about his son. Victoria burst into tears, "He is my dear child that I have carried under my heart. He is not to blame for everything. The people who forced themselves between parents and child have estranged him from us."

Perhaps the best summary of her character has been left us by the alleged victim of her errors, namely by William II himself, when speaking many years later with the calm objectivity of age. "In spirit and noble will she was superior to most of her contemporaries, yet she was the poorest and most unhappy woman who ever wore a crown."

The fact that, as an Englishwoman in Prussia, she was nearly all the time on the defensive, has caused the picture of her character to be badly distorted. Through a certain naïve clumsiness and impatience she did herself much harm, and the energy with which she ruled her family and her household could sometimes have the appearance of a lack of love. She even succumbed to the very unroyal vice of stinginess, the well-known Coburg penny-pinching, so much so that even the patient Silesian workmen on her estate in Oels sometimes came near to revolting against her. She was taken for much more subtle and even cunning than she actually was, if indeed, she had these qualities at all.

Now it so happened that Victoria, like her mother, was not insensitive to male beauty, hence no doubt the early passion of the sixteen-year-old girl for the radiant young Prussian Prince. It is often said that she was fascinated by her Head Steward, Count Seckendorf, who was the possessor of magnificent chestnut side-whiskers.* Such little weaknesses, which in her innocence she never endeavoured to conceal, were shockingly exploited by

---

* Count Georg (Gotz) von Seckendorf had in the French war been adjutant to the Crown Princess. He took part in Italy's colonial war in East Africa and had the reputation of being knowledgeable, cultured and excellent company.

Bismarck's tame Press, which almost without attempting to disguise its meaning, attributed to her the man-devouring passions of a Messalina. Bismarck, who was continually bringing actions against newspapers he felt had insulted him, did not dream of trying to protect her.

And now, like many of her non-princely contemporaries, she had been smitten to the heart by the sad fate of Alexander of Bulgaria, the handsome Battenberg. She had resolved that this Apollo beneath the shining eagle helmet of the *Garde du Corps*, should become her son-in-law, a plan which was merely smiled at so long as she was Crown Princess, but which was viewed rather differently when it was the Empress who entertained it.

The princess, whom she intended to make the prince's bride, was a rather boyish-looking young person and something of a flirt. It is said that the princess, finding herself alone with Alexander in the library at Darmstadt, threw her arms around the latter's neck, whereupon both regarded themselves as secretly engaged.

Alexander's feelings were certainly not overwhelming, but such a marriage for the homeless prince was certainly a fabulous piece of luck. He had long been corresponding about this matter with the Crown Princess, and it is a sign of her persistent juvenility, which somehow managed to co-exist with an otherwise excellent intelligence, that this correspondence was carried on through the mediation of her Court Chamberlain under the alias of Gustav Braun.

Now she was Empress and she demanded for Battenberg nothing less than his promotion to general and appointment to the command of the Gardekorps. She also insisted on his receiving the highest military decoration, namely the *Pour le Mérite*, for services rendered in the Balkan Campaign, which so unfortunately had come to grief as a result of the Austrian veto. Finally, she asked that he should be invited to spend Easter with the family, which would have the appearance of an official celebration of the engagement.

It is not surprising that Bismarck shied away from such projects, for even though Battenberg was no longer a factor in politics, the honours with which Victoria proposed to load him might well be regarded in St. Petersburg, where Bismarck was anxious to avoid giving even the shadow of an offence, as gestures of disrespect. To make him commander of the Gardekorps, he said, would be very much as though the Czar had made General Boulanger commandant of Warsaw.

But there was something more directly personal. As we know, he loathed Battenberg, and it was intolerable that he should be received into the Hohenzollern family whose vassal Bismarck claimed to be. It was intolerable that a princess of the Hohenzollern House could find no better husband for her daughter than an adventurer with whom, as Bismarck had known, a singer at the Darmstädter Hoftheater was far more closely associated than she ought to be.

To prevent these monstrous things from happening he felt no means should be barred. He made the grotesque accusation, though it was one which coming from him could be very dangerous, that Battenberg, who if the truth were known had as little talent for politics as he had liking for them, had already been selected to succeed him as Imperial Chancellor in a German "Gladstone Cabinet". So wild was his hatred that he went so far as to throw up against Battenberg the fact that his mother was a commoner, completely forgetting that he, himself, was the son of a Mencken.

Both Bismarck and the Empress now engaged in a sort of game of competitive hysterics, Bismarck swearing that the invitation to Battenberg to spend Easter with the imperial couple, which the Emperor had unsuspectingly approved, would so ruin his relations with Russia that he could no longer be responsible for the consequences—a veiled threat of resignation again. The Empress, when ultimately, under pressure from Bismarck, the Emperor withdrew the invitation, swore that it was all a plot to murder her child.*

The whole business was a little tawdry but also rather grim. The mute Emperor wrote down the words, "I cannot plunge the country into a war with Russia because of this marriage." The Empress, however, was not to be pacified. Even when the unhappy Court Marshal, a man named Radolin, took a hand in the matter and begged her to spare the Emperor, there was a violent scene during which the Emperor had difficulty in breathing, tore open the coat of his uniform with tears of despair in his eyes, and finally stamped with his foot and pointed towards the door. At length Victoria left the room.

Bismarck kept up a succession of memoranda all tending to convey the same bulkily reiterated message—that the Battenberg marriage was iniquitous, improper and utterly inadmissible, and that he would resign if it took place. He had already some weeks previously dictated a letter to the Crown Prince which William was compelled to address to the unhappy Battenberg. In this the writer was made to say that he would treat Battenberg as the Empire's enemy and his own if he pursued the project of the marriage any further.

* Conte Corti, *Wenn* . . . (Vienna, 1954).

Yet, oddly enough, on the day after that letter was written, Bismarck had an interview with the Empress which produced a most surprising result. Bismarck maintained that officially he was compelled to oppose the marriage, but if the two young people were to marry in such a way that he need take no official cognisance of the matter, then he would raise no objections. Whereupon the Empress was very happy and declared that in such a case he could put all the blame on her and abuse her to his heart's content.

Bismarck went even further. He would see to it, he said, that a suitable dowry would be provided for the princess from the estate of William I, and he was as good as his word. On the following evening he summoned Friedberg, the Minister of Justice, and Count Stollberg, the Minister of the Royal Household, and instructed them to arrange that a sum of nine millions should be at the disposal of the imperial pair.

Simultaneously, however, with these acts of fatherly benevolence, Bismarck was putting extreme pressure through diplomatic channels on Ludwig IV, Grand Duke of Hesse and Head of the Battenberg family, to get Alexander to withdraw from the marriage, otherwise the responsibility for a change of Chancellors, to say nothing of a war with Russia, would, he said, rest squarely on Ludwig's shoulders. The Grand Duke passed on the message, but the late ruler of the Bulgars hesitated. Those nine millions were an engaging—nay a beautiful thought. However, as always, the threat of Bismarck's resignation—that political Gorgon's head—reduced Ludwig to abject terror and he so belaboured the unfortunate Alexander that the latter succumbed.* He did not marry his Vicky but the lady from the Hoftheater, with whom it is believed he lived very happily until his relatively early death.

The dying Emperor used all his powers to make himself forget the misery of his condition. He could no longer hope to carry out the great projects of which once he had dreamed—a thorough modernisation of the Army and a genuine understanding with France. His political activities, if one may still call them that, were almost wholly confined to the bestowing of decorations upon men who had supported him before he ascended the throne.

But even here Bismarck obstructed him, for those whom Frederick so chose to honour were mostly men of liberal views.

* Despite the withdrawal of Battenburg, the Empress still clung to the project of the marriage. A few days before Frederick's death she obtained from the Emperor a written directive to Prince William, the heir apparent, in which he was bidden as an act of filial duty to further the marriage. William, however, two days after ascending the throne told Battenburg that he could not sanction the matter (Feder, p. 539). He informed his sister Vicky that although Battenburg was without any importance politically, the marriage would be a misalliance which, as a Hohenzollern, he did not desire.

He could find no good reason for opposing the sick man's wishes but oppose them he did. And, indeed, this was far from being the only occasion in Bismarck's life when the very weakness of the resistance he encountered seemed to bring out the least lovable traits of his character. In the present instance it is difficult to discern any motive behind his conduct save a positive pleasure in inflicting hurt, one of the rather childish characteristics that remained with him to the end of his days.

Meanwhile, Frederick, now schooled in resignation, had accepted the steady development of his disease, and at last there came a June day when a little river steamer bore him across the lakes of the Havel to Potsdam. Here in the Neues Palais, where he had been born, he wished to die. He landed at Glienicke from where one could see on the other side of the river the treetops of Babelsberg. Here, a quarter of a century ago, it had been within his power and his alone to become King. He had only to say a simple "Yes" instead of saying "No" and Bismarck's road to power would have been closed forever.

And it was here in Potsdam that as a ruler he scored his one wretched exiguous success by forcing the removal of Von Puttkamer, Prussian Minister of Interior, who had been guilty of proven electoral fraud. But with that little triumph—little in its practical effect and yet as an assertion of his person, great—the strength that he had sought to gather within himself gave out. On the very day when Puttkamer had been forced to go, Bismarck again asked Bergmann how long the Emperor had to live and Bergmann replied, as before, that he would not outlast the summer.

Bergmann's prognosis was correct. Barely a week later, on June 13th, an inflammation of the lungs set in, after which the decline was very rapid. On the 13th Bismarck saw the Emperor for the last time. On the morning of the 15th, as sunshine and the twitter of birds came through the open terraced doors of the sick-room, there came with them the inevitable end.

Two days before his death Frederick, with an imploring look, had joined the hands of Victoria and Bismarck, who understood very well what the dumb man meant. "Your Majesty can be assured," he said, "that I shall never forget that Her Majesty is my Queen." Yet it is said by those who saw him that he left this audience "strong, lively and erect with the light of triumph in his eyes".

After Frederick's death he forgot the Empress completely, so completely that she did not even receive his visit of condolence. Bismarck was not to be seen in the funeral procession. Only his son Herbert carried the Electoral Sword of Brandenburg behind the coffin.

A small episode, but one that was rather alarming for the older type of Prussians, took place at the opening of the Reichstag. Here, before all the German princes and delegates, here where all Germany was represented, Bismarck bowed his head over the hand of William II, as some months before he had done at the railway station in Leipzig over that of Frederick III. But whereas Frederick would not tolerate such a gesture even in the privacy of a railway carriage, but had immediately raised the Chancellor up to his own level, the young sovereign who now ruled Germany allowed his hand to be kissed by this very old man as though it were a matter of course. Where are we? they began to whisper in East Elbian Prussia. At some Persian Court? Or in the Rome of the Caesars? A new age was dawning—so they had heard and read everywhere, but would it be a propitious one? That was an open question.

As soon as decency permitted, Bismarck left Berlin for a period of many months. This third Hohenzollern whose Chancellor he was to be was, he felt, the most peculiar of the three. It therefore seemed advisable to observe him from a distance. He did not wish, he said from time to time, to force his counsel on the young man or to make him impatient. "There is too big a difference in our ages." Also it would thus be possible for him to carry on his real political business as he thought best without interference.

In outward appearance William II was rather smaller than his father or his grandfather and supple rather than strong. Yet just because of that unfortunate shortened arm he had trained himself to such control over his body that on parades—to give but one example—he would sit for hours on end immobile in the saddle. The tight, rather dashing Hussar's uniform suited him very well, and his moustache stood out against cheeks that had the freshness of youth in two carefully trained semi-circles. His blue-grey eyes were naturally restless, but he had trained himself to keep them set.

His intellectual endowment was well above the average, and yet in his education, despite all their good intentions, his parents had not been too fortunate. William had all the versatility of the Coburgs, a thing that was alien to the cautious Hohenzollerns, and there was a certain erratic quality in his habits of thought which was also noticeable in his mother. He spoke the jargon of the Prussian Guard and had a tendency to coarseness. He lacked the wit that can sometimes lend a charm to frivolity, and when he got excited he could become downright absurd, as when, in unveiling a memorial, he said that Germany rather than lose "a single stone" of its conquests of 1870 would leave eighteen army corps and forty-two million inhabitants upon the battlefield.

Quite early it was said of his character that it was "not handsome"—*nicht hübsch*. Waldersee alleged that he had no heart and that this was a good thing since the future would be hard. Also people were convinced that he was skilled in dissimulation, which was hardly surprising in a lad who had been brought up in the intrigue- and treason-laden air that infected the Court during the last years of William I. It was this that made the young Emperor overestimate the power of dishonesty and untruth. Deliberate malice, delight in hurting other people, let alone deliberate cruelty, were not part of his nature.

He had been forced at a very early age to be hard with himself and now he began to show to the outer world a hardness which was not part of his make-up at all. Yet now he needed this hardness, even if it were only simulated, because it was something to which he could cling and which would not give way. The gravest peril to his character lay in the fact that, to put the matter as a paradox, he feared fear and so displayed a sense of strength towards the outer world which he really did not possess at all.

This was the origin of some very unkingly qualities in his behaviour which caused even his well-wishers to entertain misgivings—his tendency to domineer in his talk, his excited gestures and uncontrolled laughter and the fact that all too frequently he showed a lamentable inability to realise which subjects were fitting occasions for his humour and which were not.

Bismarck had studied his man while the prince was still heir apparent. For instance, he had noted that William always paid particular respect to him when his relations with his parents were at their lowest ebb, which is why, when he thought that it would serve his purpose, Bismarck went out of his way to worsen those relations still further. But he did not hesitate to correct the prince in a manner which was bound to ruffle the latter's sensitive nature.

As for Bismarck himself, he had more than once a foretaste of the kind of thing he would have to deal with. There was, for instance, the interest which the prince displayed—it was the fashion in many officers' messes at this time—in a preventive war with Russia. What really horrified Bismarck, however, was something else! William had drafted, during his heir-apparency, a proclamation which it was his intention to publish at the moment of his accession. The text of this remarkable document is not on record, but we can guess its character from the circular letter to the German princes which was to accompany it and in which the prince intimated in terms that were downright impertinent that he would stand for no nonsense even from aged uncles. Bismarck was horrified, and his answer which he took five weeks to prepare was annihilatory. He recommended "most respectfully" that the document should be burnt "with least possible delay".

On the whole, Bismarck said very little about his anxieties for the future. Indeed, they only came to the surface occasionally, as they did one morning at breakfast when he was discussing the imminent accession of William, and suddenly cried out in a voice of despair "Oh, my unhappy grandchildren"—*wehe meinen Enkeln*.*

Obviously Bismarck believed that he would carry on the business of government as independently under William II as he had done under the latter's predecessors, and actually the young Emperor was fully occupied with state visits to St. Petersburg, Rome and other capitals where the impression he made often left something to be desired. But at least these things absorbed his energies. To be the centre of great public acts was, for one who till now had always had to take a back seat, an altogether delightful experience. His esteem for himself became gigantic, as did his hunger for praise. "*So loben Sie mich doch*" he would on occasion say to Bismarck.

But Bismarck, seeing that the young man was thoroughly enjoying himself, did nothing to hinder him, hoping thus himself to remain unhindered in return. He took it for granted that people abroad would know that all the real decisions in Germany rested, as they had always done, with himself, and that therefore anything that the young Emperor might say was of negligible importance.

For the most part, Bismarck spent the end of that summer and the autumn in the open air, walking or riding as he overlooked the harvests of his fields—perhaps visited the graves of his great dogs in the park at Varzin and of the mare, Röschen, that carried him through the French war. He rarely came home till late in the afternoon, but then he was usually in excellent mood and more at peace with the world than he had been for a very long time. He ate, under Schweninger's watchful eye, rather less than before, but in quantities which were still enormous. Then he sat through the evening with his family and talked a great deal in that low voice of his which could be so strangely gentle.

He did not deal with his papers till the night had come, and even then did not spend much time on them. He made marginal notes which formed the basis of dictated statements made to Rantzau on the following day. The astonishing thing is that he contrived quite successfully to combine with his rural predelections the task of a powerful and important statesman, that he managed to rule a modern, highly-centralised empire from

* Holstein, II, p. 422.

any one of a number of remote estates. "In the country where I live", he would occasionally say in the Reichstag, and in such a simple manner as though it were a matter of course that the Imperial Chancellor should have his permanent residence in the heart of the country and several hours' journey from the capital.

Naturally, this involved a number of irregularities, delays and upsets. No doubt he felt he could carry on in this way because he believed he could rely upon Herbert, who was in charge at the Foreign Office. Moreover, so long as he could depend on the cartel majority, he had no parliamentary difficulties to fear.

Of course, internal administration now went on at rather a jog trot, but to Bismarck that didn't seem to matter very much. He had always had a certain contempt for the routine business of bureaucracy, which bureaucracy itself thinks so important, and made that business increasingly the target of his irony. He had always had a curious sense of the insignificance of human effort, even his own. "It will be as God wills it," he once said, "and it's all a matter of time. Peoples and individuals, wisdom and folly, war and peace—they come and go like the waves of the sea while the sea remains." He said those words in 1859 and he never surely lost that peculiar perspective.

He was a millionaire several times over. In 1885, in honour of his seventieth birthday, a collection had been made all over Germany for the purpose of buying the hereditary property of Schönhausen, yet there was immediately an outcry, especially in the Southern States, against the "Otto-Pence" as they called this collection in imitation of the Catholic Peter's Pence. It was therefore decided to use half the sum for some public-spirited purpose, but the remaining half, totalling some one million one hundred and fifty thousand marks, was insufficient for the purchase of Schönhausen, the value of which was generally estimated at one and a half million marks. Bismarck refused to pay the difference of three hundred and fifty thousand marks himself, so it had to be provided by the bankers Bleichröder and Mendels-sohn-Bartholdy in the form of a mortgage.

It is not surprising that Bleichröder found the position curious. The Bismarck family owed him the acquisition of Schönhausen. "Herbert will get it one day," he said, "and yet I run the risk of being thrown out when I want to visit him."

Bismarck's nose for profit sometimes made people rather embarrassed, though it never caused any embarrassment to himself. Penny-pinching was, for better or worse, the heritage of Junkers of the marshes who had to survive on a very poor soil. He had managed to knock down the valuation of Friederichsruh for tax purposes to a million talers while the real value was three to four

times that. In 1884 he threatened the Kultus Minister that he
would leave the Church because the Church taxes were too high.
He had never raised any objection to the secret order of William I
which had relieved him of all the general state taxes.

He always had the liveliest interest in the sales of spirits from
his distilleries and of the timber of his forests. In 1883 he had no
less than ten such distilleries and they were all doing well while
the paper factories in Varzin which processed his timber continued
to be suppliers of the railways and the post.

When legislation was likely to bring him some personal gain,
Bismarck most certainly did not disregard this aspect of the matter.
Indeed in that strange naïveté which never wholly left him, it
seemed to him perfectly natural that the state, for which he did
everything and with which he really identified himself, should, in
return, let slip no opportunity of conferring a benefit upon him.
Yet he was certainly never guilty of accepting an office for the
sole purpose of milking it dry, nor did he ever look upon public
money simply as though it were his own. Indeed, during the
frequent conflicts between Bleichröder, who administered his
fortune, and the Prussian Minister of Finance, he almost invariably
took the latter's part.

His health continued to improve. He had at last had all his
teeth out, and after this he suffered less from neuralgia. The
colour of his face was not, as is usual with old men, a yellowish
or bluish red, but rather a shining white, which as Lerchenfeld
remarked even Lenbach could not reproduce on canvas. The
subject of Bismarck's health was about the only one on which
the family would always be united, and it soon became apparent
that even a hero like Bismarck could not escape from their
tyranny when he began to grow old. Thus, if on the terrace
of an evening Bismarck refused to put on a little velvet cap which
Johanna had sewn for him she was quite capable of telling him in
the presence of guests, "With your few hairs you ought always to
wear a cap,"* whereupon he obeyed.

In other respects, as we have seen, the peace of the family left
much to be desired. The two sons kept their visits to the paternal
estates as short as possible. For Bill things were made more difficult
by the fact that he had married Sibylle Von Arnim, a daughter
of Bismarck's sister, Malwine, and that Johanna could never get
along with this daughter-in-law of hers, of whose mother she
remained incurably jealous.

Johanna had somewhat prematurely contracted arterio-
sclerosis—actually it was in 1882—which didn't make her more
sociable and strengthened her aggressive tendencies. She was

* P. Hahn, *Varzin*, p. 82.

quite capable of saying at table in front of strangers that she hoped Bismarck's mother, "that worthless creature", was now in the next world undergoing the sufferings she had deserved. Bismarck sought to withdraw from these family tensions. He concentrated upon himself and obviously found pleasure in his own company. He was quite content, he wrote in 1888 to Bill, "to live to see the sun even though I see it through rain clouds, as during the last two months, and to do my poor best to do the duties my office brings along with it".

These months were among the happiest of his life. The fusion of what would have seemed to be two irreconcilable ideals of life—that of the countryman and of the ruling politician—gave him a feeling of quiet power and kept him in high good humour. Schweinitz, who in 1889 visited him in Friederichsruh, states: "The sovereign and yet jovial high spirits, the brutal lack of consideration and the cautious cunning which the Prince unites in his person have never been so drastically and at the same time so humorously in evidence."

Only once were these quiet days interrupted, and the guilty party had to pay dearly for that interruption. At the end of September 1888, Professor Geffken of Hamburg, once ambassador of the Hansa cities in Berlin, published in the *Deutsche Rundschau* extracts from the diary which Frederick III, while still Crown Prince, had kept during the war of 1870. Geffken, essentially a man of good will, though rather a clumsy one, was one of the Crown Prince's political advisers. He had been shown these diaries and had made extracts from them. These now revealed for the first time that the foundation of Bismarck's empire was not the result of some spontaneous outburst of enthusiasm but had been effected under much pressure and harsh treatment.

Bismarck promptly declared the publication a forgery, a statement which he knew to be untrue, and indeed abundant evidence was forthcoming to prove its genuineness; actually Bismarck had in private conversation admitted as much.* However, he was nothing if not determined and, having set out on what was even for him a quite astonishing piece of systematic mendacity, resolved to make the most of it. He obtained the Emperor's permission to publish his "Personal Report" or *Immediatbericht* in the official gazette, and there expressed his horror and indignation about some of the shocking sentiments so maliciously attributed to his late master, particularly the hideous suggestion that Frederick was prepared to use force to make the princes accept the Empire.

Now not only had Frederick never said anything of the kind,

* Busch, p. 243.

but nobody had said he had said anything of the kind. The diary contained no such statement. This passage in the *Immediatbericht* was in fact pure fabrication from beginning to end.

However, so outrageous were Bismarck's lies on this occasion that he had to make some provisions for the eventuality that he might be found out. He therefore inserted almost at the beginning of the report the following amazing sentence: "I did not have the King's permission to discuss the intimate questions of our policy with His Royal Highness, because His Majesty . . . was afraid of indiscretion at the English Court which had such strong French sympathies." In effect he was saying, "The diaries are forgeries and even if they aren't, they are lies, because I wasn't allowed to discuss that kind of thing with Frederick at all, so you can take your choice." In addition, however, this gambit had the further advantage of enabling him to have a dig at his old enemy, the ex-Empress.

The unfortunate Geffken was arrested and criminal proceedings instituted against him. But even the juridical ingenuity of Bismarck's henchmen was unable to build up a case that would hold water, and he was released after what was really a quite unjustifiable detention of nearly four months.

On the whole, it is not surprising that Bismarck should have been annoyed, for one of the things the diaries revealed, though Frederick had not known the whole truth, was that Ludwig's letter of invitation to William I to accept the Imperial Crown was a word for word copy of a draft by Bismarck.

It was about this time that Bismarck began to work up his system of alliances into a kind of climax, and in doing so he almost effected a reductio ad absurdum of the whole business, for he now conceived the idea of passing on the task of checkmating Russia, a project which was always at the centre of his thoughts, to a coalition of powers of which Germany was not to be a member.

Stated briefly, the idea was that Russia should take possession of Constantinople without any kind of interference from Austria. It was this that was behind Bismarck's almost undisguised encouragement to Russia to seize the straits, while at the same time he warned Austria not to oppose such a move, for he reckoned that if Russia was firmly entrenched in Constantinople this would be regarded by England as an intolerable threat to her position in the East and would almost automatically produce an anti-Russian coalition under British leadership, a coalition which would be much more extensive than that of the Crimean War, since it would include Austria, Italy, France, Turkey, Rumania, Bulgaria, Serbia, perhaps even Spain—Germany being almost the only country left out. If such a coalition were to join issue with Russia, this would relieve the pressure on Germany for a long time to come. As far back as 1885 he had said to Kalnoky, "We're talking in private now, so I can speak quite freely and say what I wouldn't otherwise say. A war between England and Russia would be most desirable from our point of view. . . . The result might and probably would be that Russia would be incapable of combat financially and materially for perhaps ten years."*

Had Bismarck had his wish the world would quite literally have been working for *Le Roi de Prusse*. In actual fact, however, every-thing remained in the realm of theory. The people in Russia had long seen through Bismarck's plans and had come thoroughly to resent them. Indeed their reaction soon came to express itself in the phrase, "The way to Constantinople leads over Berlin." In the final analysis Bismarck, through this kind of manoeuvre, lost such little confidence as he still commanded. He made it all too clear, said Holstein, that he was pushing other people forward while he remained sitting in the background himself. That was why "nobody trusted him or us any longer".

After a time Bismarck himself seemed to lose faith in this rather speculative project, and quite suddenly, at the turn of the year 1888/9, he showed that he had quite other ideas in his head. Count Paul Hatzfeldt, the German ambassador in London, had been his guest in Friedrichsruh over the holidays, and returned to London with instructions to make an important communication to Salisbury at his next confidential talk. Bismarck, he was to say, was convinced that nothing would make peace more secure than an official alliance between Germany and Great Britain. So he suggested that the two powers should undertake to come to each other's assistance in the event of one of them being attacked by France, and should enter into such a pact "boldly and openly" —*dreist und öffentlich*—"before their parliaments", for—and here Bismarck followed his accustomed pattern—the purpose of the alliance was not to win a war but to prevent one by deterring from it.

What was, for Bismarck at any rate, wholly new—one might almost say wholly revolutionary—was the tactics he now employed in negotiation. He who always coupled service and consideration so closely together, "move by move", was on this occasion sufficiently large minded, nay, sufficiently reckless, to give a potential British ally an enormous advance of credit. While he strictly controlled the slightest move made by his old ally Austria, he was prepared to allow England immediately a very wide freedom of movement.

* Krausnick, *Neue Bismarck-Gespräche* (1940), p. 34.

Of course, in so far as British world power in those days stretched from the Falkland Islands to the China coast and so could not in any case be controlled by him, he was really only keeping to one of his old guiding principles, never to persuade somebody to enter into treaty obligations which could not, if necessary, be imposed by force. Nay, more, while till now he had always asserted that the right of parliament to be consulted made Britain for all practical purposes incapable of an alliance, he now expressly asked for parliamentary sanctions for the pact. So little did he who was usually so self-controlled hide his impatience, that to avoid a complete rejection by Salisbury he got Hatzfeldt to tell him that even if his suggestions at the moment did not seem practicable, Bismarck's confidence in him would not be shaken; in that case perhaps he would bring the matter up at a more favourable moment. On January 26th, when Hatzfeldt could barely yet have even reached Salisbury, he did something that he certainly was not in the habit of doing, and treated an unfulfilled intention as an accomplished fact by referring in the Reichstag to England as "our old and traditional ally". Since Bismarck insisted that negotiations as far as possible should only be verbal, for he wanted to prevent any actual documents, we only know the outlines of this diplomatic venture which was the last he undertook.

What was it that could tempt a man now seventy-four years old to leave his evening retreat and undertake a venture which, if he had had to see it through, would force him to put everything upon a single card and that his last. There was some correspondence between this astonishing measure of total commitment on the one hand and his assessment on the other of the peril in which he stood, a peril which justified a high insurance premium, payable not necessarily in any material currency but in prestige. It may well be that the key to the whole puzzle is to be found in Bismarck's estimate of his danger, for though his proposal to Salisbury only spoke of a French attack, everybody knew that France would never dare to make such an attack unless she was already covered by an alliance with Russia. Bismarck's project was thus clearly pointed against Russia—which shows how low a value he placed on the Reinsurance Treaty.

The British Cabinet took a very long time examining the proposal. It was not till three months had passed that they sent an answer and that a negative one. Herbert Bismarck, who had come to London for talks, was informed that, in Salisbury's view, the German-British alliance was a most salutary measure for both countries concerned and for the peace of Europe, but any attempt to realise the idea would destroy Salisbury's parliamentary majority and bring his ministry down. Thus every connection between the two Cabinets would cease to exist. He could, therefore, say neither yes nor no, and for the moment could do nothing more than go hand in hand as demonstratively as possible. Nevertheless he still hoped to see the day when he could return to the German proposals.

What decided Salisbury may have been something much deeper than the rules of the parliamentary game, for the community of interest between Germany and England in regard to Russia was perfectly clear. Yet closer observation must have revealed that the co-ordinated protection of these two powers was very difficult to organise. They were, in their respective structures, so radically different that their military potentialities could not help but be affected.

Britain, with the heart of its Empire virtually immune to attack by land forces, had fleets which spanned the globe. Germany, on the other hand, was by nature and through its own will, narrowly concentrated on its own territory with an army that had to be very strong to protect the long land frontiers. Any co-operation that was other than surely symbolic was impossible. What could Germany do for England if England was attacked in India? What could the British Fleet do for Germany if there were a Russian invasion over its long eastern frontier, since Russia was virtually immune to the effects of a maritime blockade? In a word, the willingness to enter into an alliance with Germany and accept the risks involved, the readiness which Beaconsfield had shown, had long disappeared. It had been one of those seconds "that eternity cannot bring back".

When, in later years, Bismarck spoke of this, his last diplomatic action, he—naturally enough since it failed—treated it as a relatively unimportant probe, a feint to make Salisbury declare his intentions, but it is plain enough that it was a great deal more than that.

Actually, nobody can say with certainty whether at that moment, in the spring of 1889 in London, the way lay open towards a better Europe and to a more durable happiness and that this way was missed. But in so far as a purely hypothetical judgment can be valid, this one has all the semblance of validity.

For weeks in Berlin he carried the failure of the English negotiations around with him, and yet he was not unduly alarmed. He remembered the assurance given to Salisbury and declared that time for co-operation with England would come sooner or later. Yet though he told the Prussian Council of Ministers that the supreme object of German policy was the winning of England for the triple alliance, the object was never attained.

Berlin, that egocentric city that was growing so indecently

fast, displeased him on this occasion more than ever. Before the Brandenburg Gate the cellars were slowly being formed of that Cyclopean structure that was to be the Reichstag—a building that Bismarck was never to enter—and not far away stood the great Column of Victory, bearing upon its excessively obese shaft the statue of a winged goddess whose features had—somewhat depressingly for Bismarck—been made to resemble those of the Empress Victoria. An old cart track, which Bismarck had frequently followed when out on his solitary rides, was being transformed by the speculative builder into a sort of Super Boulevard connecting Berlin with Potsdam. It was called the Kurfürstendamm. Meanwhile, a former lieutenant of artillery called Werner Siemens was projecting plans for an elevated electric railway.

All this tended rather to weary the old man and he longed to get back to the country. And so towards the end of April he left Berlin, where the Samoa Conference was in session; Britain, Germany and the U.S.A. were dividing those coveted South Sea Islands up between them. But Herbert could deal with such matters as these, and when the conference came to an end in June Bismarck had already long been back in Varzin.

Part IV

EVENING AND NIGHT

17

"DROPPING THE PILOT"

It was not till October 1889 that Bismarck returned to Berlin. The Czar was making a short stop there, as he had done two years previously, and since Bismarck was resolved to do everything in his power to preserve the goodwill of Russia he was compelled, as he expressed himself, "to crawl into uniform" (*in uniform krauchen*) and even to force himself to attend a performance of *Rheingold* in Alexander's company.

His audience with the Czar at first seemed to pass off much more agreeably than it had done in 1887, until Alexander suddenly asked him, "Are you certain that you will remain Chancellor?" Bismarck replied with what he then thought was the truth, and said that he was convinced of his Emperor's confidence, and did not think that he could ever be dismissed against his will. However, it was obvious that the Czar's question had seriously disturbed him, so much so that the latter immediately changed the subject, which gave Bismarck the impression that the Russian did not fully share the confidence he professed to feel himself.

Whether that confidence was genuine it is difficult to say. Possibly, the many years during which he had been allowed to exercise his office without serious interference had persuaded him that he was irremovable. If that was so, the Czar had shown a sounder instinct.

Yet Bismarck might have guessed that there were changes ahead as early as May. There had been a miners' strike and the strikers had clashed with the troops. There had been casualties and even some dead, but Bismarck had advised that the strike should be allowed to work itself out. The damage which both employers and workers would sustain would provide a useful lesson for both.

But the Emperor knew that it was much more difficult for a monarch to be forgiven for the shedding of blood than it was for a republic, or as the dethroned Louis Philippe had remarked, "A republic's lucky, for it can shoot at people." The Emperor summoned representatives of both parties and ended by giving a peremptory order to the employers to raise wages. They obeyed, and the strike came to an end. Bismarck gave a sardonic smile. To force the money out of the pockets of wealthy subjects and to put it into those of the poor ones was certainly a convenient method of solving the social problem. "Popular absolutism," he remarked, seemed to be the ideal of his young master.

It was unfortunate that the Emperor now began to regard himself as a kind of magician in the sphere of social policy, a king from a fairy tale who won the love and faithfulness of his poor subjects by direct action. His immediate entourage confirmed him in his ideas, for during Bismarck's long absence from Berlin something like a vacuum had come into being around William, and into it there had gradually flowed a wide variety of discontented people.

For the most part they were humanitarians who knew little of the world, like William's sometime tutor Hinzpeter, a somewhat pompous pedant, who nevertheless still carried weight with his former pupil, Count Douglas, a successful speculator in mining shares, or von der Heiden, who had once been an official in a mining concern, and was now devoting himself to the painting of sentimental genre pictures. The only practical politician among so many amateurs was Miquel, the leader of the National Liberals in the Reichstag. Last but not least there was Stöcker, the court preacher with the ungovernable tongue and the dubious reputation, but a man of courage capable of standing before that great city and letting its newly enriched citizens feel how little their heartlessness in the sphere of social relations corresponded with their loudly proclaimed Christianity.

Most important of all, however, was the fact that the new Emperor adhered to the old Prussian practice of allowing the Army to approach the monarch through the military Cabinet, and permitting it when doing so to be entirely free from all civilian controls. The generals made ample use of this opportunity to get satisfaction during Bismarck's absence for many ancient grievances that they nursed against him. Since they possessed, in the military attachés, their own diplomatic corps, it was possible for the gentlemen of the general staff, in all the glory of their raspberry-tinted collars, to play politics on their own. Since 1888, when Moltke, then nearly ninety, retired, their chief had been Count Waldersee, an appointment of which Bismarck had succinctly expressed his feelings with the words: "Moltke has served the Army ill." Waldersee, an elegant Uhlan, who, because of his prematurely white hair, had received the nickname "the White Mouse" and was related to a few of the minor dynasties (the Empress was the niece of Waldersee's wife), was not a bad soldier, but even more gifted in the arts of intrigue. In particular, Waldersee made every effort to draw von Boetticher, the State

Secretary for Internal Affairs and Bismarck's regular representative, on to his side. Boetticher, a homely professorial type, in outward appearance a very ordinary, diligent official, was nevertheless quick in judgment of his colleagues, and as slippery as an eel. He was a creature of Bismarck's, who had saved him from financial ruin,* and Boetticher, now finding himself in a highly invidious position, manoeuvred as best he could and played for time. Meanwhile, Holstein and Waldersee began to feel each other out. Not that they had any mutual sympathies, they were respecters of the realities of power.

The generals stood behind Waldersee as one man, led on by the Prussian Minister of War, Verdy du Vernois, who had been quarrelling with Bismarck since the days of the French war and as a member of the Prussian Cabinet had a knowledge of internal political matters which usually was withheld from the military. Actually, what these experts had in mind was a surprise attack on Russia, which they preferred greatly to launch here and now rather than postpone. The attack was to be launched with such force that France would immediately lose all appetite for participating in any war, and this, in its turn, would avoid the war on two fronts, which they all so greatly feared. "Whatever may be their views on other matters," wrote Holstein, "they all believe that time is working against us, all of them. Waldersee, Bronsart, Verdy, Loë and Caprivi."

Who is to say that they were not right? Russia's armaments were in a most unsatisfactory state, as were her finances and her railways. The revolutionary forces were growing steadily stronger inside her boundaries. In France Boulanger had just had an ignominious fall,† and it was clear that France lacked any desire for war. Moreover, a new aggressive spirit was manifesting itself in the Austro-Hungarian forces, though this may have been no more than the courage of despair. In all such circumstances, might not such a war have had a favourable issue, especially if, as was suggested by the Austrian Crown Prince Rudolf, its object was not to be any kind of territorial conquest, but simply to check the Russian appetite for conquest and terrorism, which was rapidly attaining formidable proportions? Of course, nobody could have expected completely to eliminate Russia as a power factor, but many might well have hoped so

* According to an account of Bleichröder's, Boetticher's father-in-law, Berg, had embezzled a million. Boetticher had no personal fortune but a large number of children to support. He would nevertheless have had to resign if Bismarck had not used the moneys of the Guelph Fund to help him out of his difficulty.

† In 1888 the French government had dismissed Boulanger. He tried to continue his activities as a deputy and an agitator, but without success. Eventually he fled the country and shot himself in Brussels, deserted by all.

to weaken her, that Germany would be able to breathe again for a considerable period of time.

Moreover, Bismarck's aversion to preventive war did not derive from considerations of morality, and was therefore not in the nature of a universal judgment, rather it was part of his conviction of man's inability to forecast the future. Had it been possible to persuade him by some inexorable process of logic, that any particular war could not be lost in any circumstances whatever, he might have been ready to wage it.

A factor which now began to operate against him was his sense of his own unquestioned superiority. For this caused him to despise the various kinds of influence that were being brought to bear on the Emperor to such an extent that they never became a source of great concern to him. Actually he never doubted that the Emperor was still allowing himself to be guided, as he had always allowed himself to be guided in the past, by Herbert Bismarck, and so, indirectly, by himself. The fact is, however, that Herbert's jovial familiarity, which was well enough while William was merely the heir-apparent, was felt by the latter to be unseemly now that he had assumed the crown. William therefore withdrew from Herbert, so that the influence which Bismarck was still endeavouring to cast over him became steadily weaker.

The fact that the old man was unaware of this, and his astonishing over-estimation of the qualities of his son, are among the unsolved riddles of his life, but, as we have seen, he always seemed to have more affection for Herbert than for Bill, the younger brother, who was a much more outstanding character. Indeed, the strange manner in which he opposed Herbert's proposed marriage had about it something of the passion of a jealous lover. Did he never realize the extent to which Herbert was his inferior? Did he not realize that the son completely lacked the father's indescribably delicate feeling for atmosphere, and his capacity for incredibly rapid adaptation to a changing situation? Did he not realize that he lacked that mental pliability of the Menckens, which, when the occasion arose, could make his father irresistible. Herbert was much more the complete and homogeneous Junker than his father had ever been. All that Herbert seemed to have inherited from the latter was a certain bluntness of tone of which he made use as though it were a universal cure-all, while from his mother he had received a bedevilling inheritance of tactlessness and faulty judgment.

Brutality, which in Bismarck represented something like an occasional lapse into the primitive, was with Herbert a second nature. And yet there were moments when the father realized the truth about the son—as, for instance, when Herbert had ridden a horse to the point of utter exhaustion, he remarked to Holstein that Herbert was undeniably the kind of person that loved to torture both animals and men. For all that, Bismarck continued seriously to believe that he would be able to establish Herbert as his successor in the Reichs Chancellery.

Bleichröder tells us that this purpose governed all his thoughts and actions. His old weakness towards kith and kin here assumed disastrous proportions. He not only left the Samoa Conference to Herbert, but the entire Foreign Office.

Now, in the autumn of 1889, Bismarck was occupied with considerations that weighed much more heavily than all the Berlin intrigues. Shortly the Socialist Law would lapse, and soon after the new year the elections for the Reichstag would be due. Bismarck had already in October come forward with the draft of a new Socialist Law, which would not apply merely for a limited time but would have permanent validity. Amongst other things, this .draft contained a provision enabling the police to remove "unwelcome agitators" (*missliebige Agitatoren*) from the district in which they resided, a provision which produced widespread indignation. Since this clause was rejected by the National Liberals, while the Conservatives declared that without it they would reject the entire Bill, the acceptance of the new law seemed in danger.

Bismarck, however, not only believed the law to be absolutely necessary, but did not consider that it went far enough. He was certainly aware of all the objections that could be raised against it. He knew very well that the Social Democratic electors wanted nothing more than a share in the general prosperity of the middle classes, though this was a prosperity that they tended greatly to exaggerate. He knew that they were honourable men who, if necessary, would be ready to go to prison for their convictions and even suffer the loss of their livelihood.

Bismarck also knew very well that the economic position of the labouring classes was still very far from satisfactory, that the immediate results of the victory of 1870 had made them the victims of frantic speculation, which caused a shortage of dwellings and a continuous increase in food prices. Even in 1872 there had been street fighting in the east of Berlin between workers and police, while troops stood by in reserve. Bismarck was prepared to mitigate the consequences of this early crude industrialism, but how far could one go in this?

The Socialist Law, however, was for Bismarck only a detail within a much wider pattern. For though it could make it difficult to build up a Social Democratic Party, it could not interfere with the electoral rights of the individual Social Democrat and so could not prevent the formation within the Reichstag of a group with strong Social Democratic sympathies.

But it was not the German Social Democratic Party itself that was his enemy; he saw in it merely the first of the oncoming waves of Marxist socialism which would ultimately fall indiscriminately over all state boundaries and whose vast possibilities of growth, though one could already feel them, could not as yet be estimated. Very early in this affair he had said that "it was impossible to counter a great world historical movement with petty police methods".* Other means would, if necessary, have to be employed; Lasalle had spoken of these coming developments as "an iron necessity". Iron necessity or not, Bismarck was resolved to oppose them with all the power of his heart and mind, by every means, however radical. To manœuvre successfully for position in this coming trial of strength, that was what mattered now. The danger seemed so great, that he was prepared to go far beyond the Socialist Law. He was prepared to change the electoral law to the disadvantage of the Social Democrats, though this, of course, meant changing the constitution.

That changes would be necessary in the somewhat hurriedly devised Imperial Constitution, he knew from the first moment of the Empire's existence. He was one of the few founders of states who was never left untroubled by the feeling that their work might be faulty. Even in 1871 he had confessed to Waldersee that he had not bothered overmuch about detail, since his object was to call the Empire into being as quickly as possible. Throughout the eighteen-seventies he spoke again and again of "the Empire's constructive dissolubility". By this he meant that in 1871 it was only the governments of the German Monarchies and the Free Cities which had come together to set up a new state—the German Empire—and consequently they, and they alone, had the right to re-shape or even determine the treaty that united them. "We may well reach the point," he said to Schweinitz in 1886, "where I shall be compelled to destroy what I myself have created. People forget that the same thing that happened to the Frankfurter Bundestag in 1866 can happen to the federation which exists at the moment. The princes can withdraw from it, and form a new one without the Reichstag."†

It is true enough that the Imperial Constitution of 1871 came into being through negotiations between the governments of the various German states, the part played by the popular representatives never going much beyond an approving nod of the head. And it is a matter of simple logic that the constitutional

---

* Th. Schieder in P. Rassow, *Deutsche Geschichte* (1935), p. 543.
† Coll. Works, VI(c), p. 433.

power to decide the continuance or determination of a treaty resides with those that originally entered into it. When his attention was drawn to the fact that Laband, an influential authority on constitutional law, was of a different opinion, Bismarck answered that "as the author of the first draft of the Imperial Constitution and as one of those who was principally concerned in formulating it", he was in a position to know the intentions which had been paramount in the treaties on which it was founded. On the strength of this knowledge he could say that the princes and senates were the "members" of the federation and not the "states" over which they reigned. Some years later he expressed himself in even plainer terms. "I shall certainly not allow myself to be talked over by some professor in regard to something of which I myself am the creator."*

It may surely be asked whether the approval of the Versailles treaties by the Reichstag in April 1871, though this may have been a mere matter of form, had not converted those treaties into constitutionally binding instruments. If so, any alteration in them required the Reichstag's consent. In these circumstances, simply to go over the Reichstag's head would surely come very near to a breach of the constitution itself.

Bismarck, however, was deaf to all such considerations. A constitution, for him, was a contract entered into between men and made possible by compromises, like any other. All constitutional life, he had declared before the Prussian deputies in 1862, was a compromise. Changes in the constitution, made on grounds of expediency, were for him like the repairs which sooner or later become necessary in every house. If they could only be made by unconstitutional means, that was unfortunate, but it could not prevent them from being undertaken, and certainly there was nothing particularly tragic about it. The halo that in a democratic parliamentary system belongs to the constitution was, for Bismarck, quite invisible.

These plans of Bismarck's declining years have been the object of unusually harsh criticism in the more popular kind of historiography: the crazy old man had wanted to destroy his own work; it was the madness of one who had over-lived his usefulness, so that he no longer understood the needs of the hour but wanted to meet them by force of arms, whereas civilization had now reached the stage in which the resolution of internal differences in a country by military means had become an anachronism.

Bismarck could make nothing of this kind of criticism. His experience had never taught him anything save that political battle, whether waged within or outside a country's frontiers,

* Hofmann, Ernst, *Fürst Bismarck* (1913), I, p. 227.

was a power struggle, and its ultimate aim, the destruction of
the power of the opponent. Why, then, should he be forbidden
to use the instruments of power in battling with a revolutionary
movement, when that movement itself used such instruments
whenever it was able to do so. All the revolutions of recent
decades had begun by using force against the existing state, the
year-long battles of the Italian Ressorgimento, the South-West
German uprisings of 1849, the Paris Commune and, above all,
that most murderous rebellion of the century, the American Civil
War.

It was thus natural that Bismarck should have said to Helldorf
in November 1889 that the time for blood and iron was again
approaching. At New Year, he wrote to the Emperor that he
regarded internal conflict as being more immediately likely than
any external war, and added that he no longer had quite the
strength to fight it as he had in 1862. Even in April of 1890,
when he was no longer in office, he remarked that at times, true
goodwill could consist in the shedding of blood.* It was, he said,
quite impossible to fight against social democracy by legal means.
Only warlike means would serve.†

The apprehensions of the ageing Bismarck were laughed at by
his contemporaries. Not a single one of his plans was ever carried
into execution. Whether they would have achieved any success,
it is impossible now to say, and even more whether they would
have proved themselves superior to the methods of toleration
which were actually employed. At the end of 1890 the old Socialist
Law expired forever, and up till the end of the Empire not a hair
was touched on the head of the Imperial Constitution.

On January 23, 1890, Bismarck was summoned by telegram
from Friedrichsruh to Berlin. On the following afternoon there
was to be a Crown Council under the Presidency of the Emperor.
Bismarck arrived in Berlin on the 24th, in great ill-humour. A
number of things had helped to produce that condition. The
journey had suddenly been imposed upon him after he had been
living undisturbed in the country since mid-October; he had been
forced to get up early; he had found the train uncomfortable; it
was bitterly cold and there was frost on the trees.

He was even more displeased by the uncertainty of the ministers
with whom he spoke and who professed to know nothing of the
Crown Council's purpose.

The Emperor, who received him shortly afterwards, was
equally uncommunicative. When at last the meeting convened
around the usual oval table, under the crystal chandelier—it was

* Rothfels, p. 384.   † Philipp, p. 181.

now six o'clock in the evening—it was obvious that the Chancellor had to make a considerable effort to control his feelings.

The Emperor opened proceedings by making an announcement which apparently gave him great pleasure. He had decided, he remarked, to continue the social legislation, which Bismarck had initiated, by forbidding Sunday work, limiting the work of women and children, and summoning an international conference for the protection of the worker to Berlin. All this was to be made public shortly, in the form of an Imperial Proclamation.

Bismarck had always rejected the idea of enforced Sunday rest and of any limitations placed on the work of women and children, because he held that the state had no right to deprive workers of possible sources of income. Moreover, as he was later to declare to Lerchenfeld, he saw in the Emperor's plans, "Utopia whose object was to win popularity with the lowest classes." One day the Emperor would regret that, for these classes were thus endowed with a power which would then be lost to the crown. Now, in the Crown Council, he contented himself by warning his listeners that though the state had a self-evident duty to assist those who were economically weak, we should not imagine that we could ever satisfy them. The Emperor's proposals, he suggested, should be first examined by ministers. Somewhat disappointed and very unwillingly, William agreed.

Thus the first part of the Crown Council passed off fairly well. In the second part, however, things became more difficult. Boetticher, in order to change the subject, chose one which was even more unfortunate, namely, the new Socialist Law, which the Reichstag on the previous day had accepted on second reading, though it had struck out the clause giving the police power to expel a citizen from the district in which he resided. The emperor remarked in passing that this was a clause with which the Government would now have to do without, since, if they insisted on it, the entire Bill might be thrown out.

Now Bismarck's high-pitched voice was heard, and, as though all the annoyances of the day had suddenly become concentrated within him, he expressed himself with quite needless force. He did not dream, he said, of sacrificing the expulsion paragraph. He would not, as he said, "lower the flag", and in any case, he would have to lay before the next Reichstag a Socialist Law which was even more severe than the one now under consideration. If the Bill failed to secure passage, there would be a vacuum, during which one would have to manage as best one could, though it might well be possible "that the waves would rise higher and that clashes might occur".

The Emperor was obviously frightened. Did this mean that

there would be rebellion on a large scale? Would cartridges and bayonets rule in Germany? He protested. People would never forgive him if blood were to flow at the beginning of his reign. But Bismarck replied with great calm that the shedding of blood did not depend on the monarch or his laws, but on the revolutionaries. Thereupon the Emperor asked whether the other ministers shared Bismarck's views. At first the question was met with deathly silence. Then, however, the old habit of conforming to Bismarck's will reasserted itself and the ministers all declared for him, though they did so hesitantly and with obvious heart-searchings. Bismarck himself said the last word and it was a weighty one. If the Emperor attached no weight to his advice, he did not know whether he could remain in office.

Furiously and yet still in control of himself, and so quietly that only Boetticher, who was sitting next to him, heard it, William remarked "I am in a trap" and closed the meeting. But the palpable good-humour in which he had opened the meeting had disappeared. He took his leave, and in doing so had obvious difficulty in simulating a friendly air. Thenceforward he began to say that he had no ministers. The only ministers that there were, were those of Prince Bismarck. But Bismarck's nerves also gave way in the night that followed. He spoke of his whole life's work as lost and he wept.

This day, January 24th, was the birthday of Frederick the Great, and the Emperor had for that reason chosen it for a Crown Council which he believed would be epoch-making. And, indeed, the day became a fateful one. For on that day there sprang to life a spark of enmity between the old man, whose single purpose in life had been and remained the exaltation of Prussia, and the man who was to be Prussia's last king.

Once more, during the next few days, there seemed to be a rift in the clouds. The Birthday Audience granted to all ministers, under the leadership of Bismarck, by the Emperor on January 27th, went off perfectly smoothly, so much so as to inspire in Bismarck a perceptible optimism. The moods of a monarch, he said in the Council of Ministers, were like the weather, from which one could not get away.* "I think we'll play ball." (*Ich glaube, wir machen mit.*) And so he began himself to edit the two proclamations which the Emperor wished to make, although their message remained slightly befogged and could mean a great deal, or practically nothing.

Then, at the last moment, Bismarck did an astonishing thing. He refused to countersign them, an unprecedented step, an open revolt of a kind which would have been unthinkable under William I.

* Bussman, p. 239.

The Emperor did not as yet grasp the significance of what had happened, nor did he realise how completely he had misread the situation as a whole. In the exuberance of his untried youth, and overwhelmed by the success of his own initiative, he seriously believed that the elections to the Reichstag, which were to be held on February 20th, would be influenced by his action. He was shortly to have a rude awakening.

Meanwhile, just before its dissolution, the old Reichstag had settled the fate of the Socialist Law. Since the government insisted on including the expulsion clause, it was rejected at the third reading. The old law was still valid until the end of September, of course, but any hope that a new one would be passed in any new Reichstag was as slim as that for the return of the obedient "cartel" majority. And, indeed, since no Boulanger was threatening from without, while the number of vague run-of-the-mill discontents was hugely multiplying at home, the cartel collapsed in the elections and could only save 135 seats out of 220, while the votes of the Social Democrats were almost doubled.

Bismarck was not altogether displeased by this and hoped the Emperor would see that social policy, let alone history, could not be made, as he thought it could, on the cheap. Nor was Bismarck surprised by the election results. If anything, it merely strengthened his pessimism and his determination to fight. He scented the approach of the kind of conflict that had filled the sixties for him, when he was gambling both with the existence of Prussia and with his own. This reanimated him and gave him something like a cheerful self-assurance.

Even at the beginning of the month, he had told the Council of Ministers that he was proposing to resign all his offices except the Imperial Chancellorship. Now there was no thought of that. Rather did he set himself to gather as much power as he possibly could into his hands. In the Reichstag he believed that he would be able to remould the newly created majority, consisting of the Conservatives and Centre Party, into a basis for his government.

Even before the elections he had begun to seek support from abroad. On February 10th, for instance, he had paid a visit to the French ambassador, Herbette, and taken the unusual step of hinting to him that France would be acting in the interest of good relations between the two powers if she did not take part in the Conference for the Protection of Workers, which the Imperial Proclamation had announced. It is quite plain that he had an interest in wrecking the conference, which was the Emperor's darling project. He seems to have hoped that if this was a failure, the Emperor would all the more willingly and obediently submit to the Imperial Chancellor's leadership.

During the visit to the Frenchman he was in high good humour. At the end of it, it so happened that the two men started discussing mythological themes, and the ambassador happened to mention that Medea had ended, in spite of everything, by being reconciled to her husband. Whereupon Bismarck laughed, and remarked, "*On revient toujours à ses premiers amours*," and added, "Who knows, it may yet happen that way with me." Was he thinking of the intimacy which, in the 'sixties, at the time of conflict with Parliament, had subsisted between himself and Napoleon III, an intimacy which had made his position so secure internationally that he could devote all his strength and all his attention to internal politics?

He was even ready to resume relations with so dangerous and so clever an enemy as the Empress Frederick, and, through her, presumably with Britain. The Empress started by refusing to have any discussion with him. There was, she said, nothing to be discussed between them, and if he wanted to make a courtesy call he should bring his wife along. Bismarck accepted this suggestion, though the meeting had no practical consequences. According to King George V, who was the Empress's nephew, the Empress told Bismarck that he was responsible for the fact that she and her son were no longer in touch with one another. So that she could now get nothing out of the Emperor for anybody.

Bismarck accepted her implicit reproaches humbly enough. He said that he could foresee the time when he himself would be misunderstood and slandered, and when Victoria asked what she could do about it, he answered, "Your Majesty, if you then meet me in some drawing-room, you will surely be gracious enough as to recognise me."*

The disagreeable results of the Reichstag elections did, indeed, seem to bring about a new rapprochement with the Emperor who had hoped that his proclamations would produce a very different result. In the first audience that he had with Bismarck after that event, namely on February 25th, William seemed to be very depressed and disappointed. Nor was his humour improved by the news that had just come in, that on the previous day a Russian loan had been subscribed seven times over in France. The Emperor now seemed prepared to recognise Bismarck's cold prudence and to take over his "battle programme", as he called it. Two new Bills were to be presented to the Reichstag, which it could not possibly accept. One was a new Socialist Law, which was even more brutal than the old one, and which authorised expulsions not merely from a subject's district, but from the whole

* Feder, pp. 441-2.

territory of the Empire, and further some new and very costly military estimates. Immediately the Reichstag refused to pass either of these two Bills it was to be dissolved, and the same was to happen to its successor should it continue in that refusal.

This would result in confusion and unrest, which, in its turn, would provide the pretext for the calling together of the German princes, who were the sole real signatories to the Imperial Constitution. The princes would declare that the constitution had lapsed and would replace it by a new one, in which electoral rights would be strictly curtailed.

For all that he neither anticipated nor desired a resolution of the crisis by force, and it is difficult to make a more inept supposition than that he should have deliberately worked for a massacre of the workers. If driven to extremes he would, of course, have been ready once more to let the cannon speak and would certainly have done so rather than accept the defeat of his purpose, a purpose which, he held, should not be abandoned at any price whatsoever. But most assuredly he desired nothing less than to be forced into such a situation.

Nor was there any real prospect of it ever arising. Had Bismarck been in a position to begin his reconstruction, he would surely have called forth a widespread protest on the part of public opinion, but hardly more than that. For to the great majority of German citizens, the idea of going to the barricades to protect the Imperial Constitution, was merely nonsensical. Or is it really conceivable that those two-thirds of the population of Imperial Germany who were Prussians would suddenly have been transported into a state of smouldering rage if Bismarck had introduced into the Reichstag the Prussian electoral system with its three classes graded according to tax-paying capacity? They had been electing the Landtag now, according to those laws, for a quarter of a century. They had realised what they were doing, but never raised any objection. Bismarck was right when he judged that from this quarter, for all practical purposes, there would be no resistance. And who, in the prosperous Germany of that day, would have risked life and livelihood for an Imperial Constitution, when the father of that constitution himself declared that alterations were necessary. Harsh words like "Breach of the Constitution", "Coup d'état", and "High treason" seemed positively to bounce off his person. He had heard them in the 'sixties, till he was sick of hearing them and had gloriously survived the attack.

As we have seen, the unfortunate election results had led to a partial reconciliation between the Emperor and his Chancellor and even induced in William something of that genial pugnacity —real or simulated—that had affected his grandfather on that historic railway journey to Berlin. Bismarck could be assured, the Emperor said at the end of the meeting, that in an extreme emergency, he would not be another Frederick-William IV. The old man breathed again; perhaps prematurely—for he was no longer quite so cautious as he had been in earlier years. He believed that, as on that previous occasion, now so long ago, he would carry his point by appealing "to the Portépée", to the officer spirit of the Hohenzollerns. "No surrender," he said in English, as he departed, and the Emperor, firmly pressing his hand, repeated the words, "No surrender."

And so he was able to report to the ministerial council on March 2nd that "the Emperor had decided to fight" and he could therefore remain at the Emperor's side. He then expounded in all its breadth his "menu" for the new Reichstag, which was based on his old theory of "constructive dissolubility" of the empire and of the possibility to which this gave rise, of getting rid of the basis of the present constitution.* The ministers showed little enthusiasm. They were the kind of men who went along with anyone that happened to have power, but who now were made apprehensive by the confusion existing at the highest levels of the state. As things stood they had little of that appetite for adventure, which at that moment was driving Bismarck forward. The man seemed to have new energies, and at the close of the meeting could still find time to criticise Raschdorff's plans for Berlin Cathedral, which Bismarck said failed to satisfy the demands of a refined taste. He seemed totally unaware of the fact that, during his long absence, there had been a perceptible lessening of the respect in which he was held.

Yet so it was. The right-wing conservatives from whose midst he had himself come had taken umbrage at the leftward inclination of his cartel, had come more and more under Stöcker's influence and fallen away from Bismarck. But even the faith of the great masses, which once had been as firm as a rock, now seemed to be wavering. New generations were coming into being at all levels of society, and these, as always, believed that it was themselves for which the world was waiting. People got into the habit of taking a certain pleasure in enumerating the symptoms of the Chancellor's age. They noted a trembling of his hand, and insisted that this was due to the use of morphia. This story seems to have been particularly popular at the Grand Ducal Court in Karlsruhe. It was, of course, nonsense. In those days of over-excitement it might well have happened that Bismarck wanted

---

* One of the sentences which Bismarck subsequently struck out of the minutes reads as follows: "In this way it would be possible to free ourselves from the Reichstag if the elections continue to produce unfavourable results." (Feder, p. 542).

to be sure of a few hours' sleep, and for this purpose took some kind of soporific. To write him down as a drug addict on this account is ridiculous.

Even so, this kind of thing was characteristic of the prevailing mood, which Bismarck did not fully appreciate, for he never realized how considerable was the extent of his growing isolation. He showed here something of that strange insensibility which on occasion soldiers display when they hurl themselves back into the fray, unconscious of the fact that they have received a mortal wound.

A bare two days after he had expounded his "battle plan" to the ministers, a programme with which, as he believed, the Emperor identified himself, he found that the latter had left him hopelessly in the lurch. On March 4th, to Bismarck's great surprise, William directed him not to submit his new Socialist Law to the Reichstag. The fact is that pressure had been exerted on the wavering monarch, not only from the enemies which Bismarck had at Court but also by two of the German princes, by the Grand Duke Frederick of Baden, who was activated by vaguely liberal and humanitarian considerations, and by King Albert of Saxony, who had a positive horror of possible unrest in his already over-industrialised state, and who already viewed Bismarck with suspicion. They would never get rid of the man, he was fond of saying, "until he dies or goes completely mad".*

Bismarck seemed to take the Emperor's retreat calmly. It meant he would have to forget about the Socialist Law and rely entirely on the military estimates as a means of getting rid of the Reichstag. These last were based on a plan which had been worked out by the Ministry of War in 1889, a plan which aimed to increase the Army by 125,000 men. The cost would be a hundred millions annually, and, to meet this, recourse was to be had to a defence tax which the Reichstag had as a matter of fact already rejected in 1881.

After the manner of old people, Bismarck liked to hark back to his earliest successes, to his battles with the Prussian Landtag in 1862, and this caused him to experience a certain feeling of pleasure as he thus repeated at the end of his career the very thing that he had done at its commencement. For now once again he fairly threw himself into the fight for the passage of some military estimates, even though in this instance—and this was the climax of the general confusion—he was forced to align himself with the very generals who were his habitual opponents and though the fight was one which he was secretly only too anxious to lose.

But the tide was turning against him. Nothing that he now

* Schüssler, *Bismarcks Sturz* (1922).

touched seemed to succeed. Above all, a curious fatality seemed to be increasing his differences with the Emperor. Thus it happened that about this time Bismarck had drawn attention in the Council of Ministers to an order which had been issued by Frederick-William IV in 1852 forbidding ministers to make their reports to the sovereign without prior consultation with the Prime Minister. Bismarck seems to have suspected that Boetticher was playing a double game between himself and the Court Camarilla.

Of course, when in a highly-centralised state like that of Prussia-Germany, the central sun splits as it were into two separate stars, it becomes rather difficult for a high official such as Boetticher was to discern where the path of perfect loyalty lies. The Emperor knew of Bismarck's suspicions and had repeatedly requested him to adopt a friendlier attitude towards the man, whereupon the Prince had at last produced a long list of Boetticher's sins. This unfortunately failed to make any impression on the young monarch, and no sooner had he ended his audience with Bismarck then he presented Boetticher with the Order of the Black Eagle, the highest which Prussia could give.

Psychologically speaking, this suggests nothing so much as the trick of an impudent schoolboy who wants to annoy an unpopular teacher. Politically, it was an affront of the same magnitude as when Bismarck published the imperial proclamations of intended social reform without his own counter-signature. When news of the matter reached him, he contrived to put on an indifferent smile and confine his comments to an apt quotation from Schiller.

Three days later the Chancellor was visited by the gnome-like Windthorst, the leader of the Centre Party, with whom he had had no dealings since the days of the Kulturkampf. The indefatigable Bleichröder had succeeded in bringing about a private meeting which was to determine whether there was any real possibility of the kind of government coalition Bismarck had in mind, a coalition consisting of the centre and the conservatives. Windthorst would have been quite prepared for that, since the rapid growth of the socialist vote filled him with misgivings, but now that he was with Bismarck he began to realise better than Bismarck himself the extent of the opposition that was arising all round him. He knew the extent to which the conservatives had already loosened their ties with him, to say nothing of the National Liberals, the "party of the Empire's foundation" which, incidentally, as soon as it heard of Windthorst's visit to the Reichschancellor, relapsed into a violent anti-Catholicism and announced its intention, though the threat was rather an empty one, of relentlessly opposing any coalition between the conservatives and the centre.

Windthorst came to the conclusion that it was too late for any talk of a coalition. The impression of doom he gained was so strong that after his visit he remarked, "I come from the political deathbed of a great man." It is significant that just about this time the Austrian Ambassador, Széchényi, reported the manner of the old Prince now, alas, to be such "as one often sees in a man *qui aurait perdu la boussole.* A senile 'I want to and I don't want to' combined with an uncontrollable desire to talk, to talk to anybody, no matter who, and sometimes without the dignity that is required of such a man."*

Two more days passed, then on March 15th Bismarck was awakened early in the morning and was informed that the Emperor had suddenly appeared and was waiting for him in Herbert's official residence, a villa in the garden of the Chancellery. Still half asleep, and dressing hurriedly, an ill-humoured Bismarck set out into the dark late-winter morning. Also the Emperor had an air which did not suggest friendly intentions. What made matters worse was that he had been kept waiting.

Bismarck first made it plain that the notice of the Emperor's visit, which the latter said had been sent on the previous day, had not reached him. Why this had happened was not discussed, since Bismarck immediately began his report on Windthorst's visit. The Emperor interrupted him, "And I suppose you threw him out?" "No," replied Bismarck, his duty was to receive any member of the Reichstag who made this request in proper form. "Even," asked the Emperor, and again a kind of boyish malice was discernible, "even if your sovereign forbids you." Bismarck replied with perfect composure that his sovereign's right to say whom he should or should not receive ended on the threshold of his wife's drawing-room.

William then asked whether the visit had been arranged by Bleichröder, adding "Jews and Jesuits always hang together." Bleichröder, Bismarck declared, was a banker, and he himself regarded the Jews as a useful part of human society and had often used them in the transaction of most important diplomatic business. William merely replied that in future Bismarck should first seek the imperial permission in such cases. Bismarck's answer was silence.

The Emperor changed the subject. He had heard, he said, that Bismarck, on the authority of a "yellowing" Prussian Cabinet order, had forbidden ministers to report to the Emperor without previous consultation with the Chancellor. He now demanded that this order, which separated the monarch from his ministers, should be immediately annulled. Bismarck replied that the order

* Schüssler, p. 272.

had been made in 1852 by a king and must be held to be in force
until such time as another king repealed it. In that case, said
William, he wished to have the draft of such a repeal submitted
to him. Whereupon Bismarck explained that the order of 1852
was indispensable if the homogeneity of the government was to
be preserved. The Emperor insisted on having his way. Once
more Bismarck relapsed into silence.

It was as though this conversation were being prompted by the
demons of ruin. Whatever subject he touched, discord seemed
to flare up from it. For now the Emperor, though in a relatively
casual tone, touched on a third subject which was explosive indeed.
He had now decided, he said, in all circumstances to avoid a
dissolution of the Reichstag. For this reason he wanted the costs
of the new military estimates reduced to a point where they could
command a safe majority.* This represented a complete and
wholly unexpected volte-face on the part of William, but for
Bismarck it meant that the whole of his policy had been stood on
its head.

When, a few days previously, the Emperor had rejected the idea
of a new Socialist Law, thus withdrawing from his "no surrender"
agreement with the Chancellor, the latter had actually become
more certain than ever that his master would now stand by the
military estimates, and thus, if necessary, enable him to do away
both with the Reichstag and the constitution. Instead of this,
however, his young sovereign now took the second part of his
campaign out of his hands.

The Emperor explained that there could be no justification
for anything that would further increase popular excitement. But
that was the purpose of the whole thing—Bismarck almost yelled
with excitement—there was to be such confusion in the country,
such a complete state of chaos that nobody would know what
the Emperor's policy was. At least, that is how, a few days later,
William described the scene to his ally, Francis Joseph.

In that moment Bismarck knew that the end had come. The
imperial hunting horn could now sound the View halloo. If the
pack caught up with him, he would have to accept his fate.

Again the question arises whether he was not actually counting
on such a finish as that. The character of William II being what
it was, could he really ever have expected to remain in office up
to the end of his life? A knowledge of men was not his strongest
quality, its growth having been hindered by pride, a pride which
could not bother much with his inconsiderable and rather unprepossessing contemporaries. And now, of course, he realised his
error. Now he grasped the fact that he was no longer dealing

* Haselmayer, III, p. 277.

with William I, the great old gentleman who stood by his word once it had been given even if it made things difficult for him; the man whom he was dealing with was a changeable, immature and quite incredibly spoiled young fellow, who might conceivably have the grace to allow the old man another couple of months of powerless official existence, while the new arrivals, the meddlesome place hunters, took possession of the emblems and machinery of a régime which he had built up entirely for himself.

Nevertheless, although he could do nothing to change the situation, he could still draw back his arm for a retributive blow, using a weapon which, knowing somehow what was to come, he had in those last calamity-charged days laid in readiness like a poisoned dagger.

The Emperor sat at the table with his sword between his knees, smoking cigars and palpably quite glad to be made largely invisible by clouds of tobacco smoke. Meanwhile, Bismarck, as was his custom, walked about the room as he talked, sometimes, in order to emphasise a point, picking up some object, and then replacing it with a certain amount of force. Suddenly he began talking about Russia and of William's forthcoming visit to the Czar. He said that he could only advise him not to go and, as he spoke, he had a large file in his hand which suddenly fell noisily on to the table just in front of the Emperor. Here, he said, were certain reports about Russia transmitted by Hatzfeldt, which confirmed his views. The Emperor asked to see them, but Bismarck did not want to show them to him, because, he said, certain expressions in them might offend him. Whereupon the Emperor snatched at one of the papers and was thus able to read that he who was so proud of his success with Alexander III had been referred to by the latter as "*un garçon mal élevé et de mauvaise foi*".

William was obviously deeply shaken. He went pale under the shock. The barbaric element in Bismarck's nature had come out into the light and, after the manner of revolting slaves breaking out of their cellars, was seeking senselessly to destroy whatever lay in its path. Nevertheless the Emperor noted that Bismarck's eyes were again full of tears.

He took his leave, and in doing so rather languidly extended two fingers of his right hand, which was actually holding his helmet. He reminded Bismarck again of the Cabinet order of 1852 which was to be revoked. When he reached the front of the house it occurred to him that he owed his subjects a bit of a show, and instead of getting into his carriage he ran up the steps and violently shook the Chancellor's hand.

Next day, around noon, General von Hahnke, the new chief of the military Cabinet, appeared on the scene and inquired by order of the Emperor whether the Cabinet order of 1852 had been withdrawn, and again Bismarck explained at some length just why he was unable to comply with the Emperor's wish. Whereupon the general deliberately let the matter be.

This was rather an arbitrary act on the general's part and his courage is, to say the least, surprising. For on the previous afternoon the Emperor had given him and two other generals a full account of what had happened during his morning visit to the Chancellery, and had ended his story with "Weidmannsheil".* It is clear that the Emperor had made up his mind that Bismarck's adherence to the Cabinet order amounted to open disobedience, which justified his immediate dismissal from office.

And so twenty-four hours later Hahnke had to present himself before Bismarck a second time and inform him that the Emperor was not only insisting on the withdrawal of the Cabinet order, but expected Bismarck to appear at two o'clock at the royal castle to tender his resignation. Bismarck replied that he was physically not in a condition to make a personal visit but that he would send his resignation in writing.

For the moment the Emperor was satisfied. In the evening, however, his impatience mounted like a fever and he sent the head of his civil cabinet, von Lucanus, to Bismarck, to enquire what was happening about the resignation. Bismarck, who had just risen from table, replied that it was open to the Emperor if he so desired to dismiss him out of hand, but if he himself was to tender his resignation he would require time to set it down in a form suitable for publication.

That Bismarck should make this stipulation was natural enough. For the formulation of such a document must have been well-nigh impossible even to a great master of the German tongue. For how could one tell the world, and how above all could one tell Germany, of the petty considerations—a Cabinet order on office routine whose author had been dead for years—that had sufficed to destroy the man who was regarded as the creator and guiding spirit of the new empire?

It so happened, however, that on the same day, shortly before Hahnke's second visit, some reports from a certain Raffauf, who was consul in Kiev, were returned to the Chancellery, which Bismarck had forwarded to the Emperor for his information. These reports described Russian troop movements which Raffauf considered to be menacing. Bismarck was familiar with the desire of all too many consuls to raise themselves to diplomatic level by means of startling revelations, a habit which he was apt to call "furor consularis", and so he attached no importance

---

* The traditional greeting to the succ essful huntsman.

whatever to what Raffauf had to say. The Emperor, however, was, or, at any rate, pretended to be, of a different opinion, and in returning the papers to Bismarck added an open note, hurriedly written in pencil on a piece of notepaper. "The reports show quite clearly that the Russians are in full strategic deployment for war. . . . You should have drawn my attention long ago to this terrible danger. It is high time to warn the Austrians and to take counter measures."

The Emperor's note could hardly have reached Bismarck at a more favourable moment, for now it was possible for him to give as the ground of his resignation not a petty domestic squabble but a fundamental difference of opinion on foreign policy. And so, when he sat down to compose his letter of resignation, he passed over in silence the differences which had arisen on such matters as the Socialist Law, the military estimates, and possible changes in the constitution. As to the Cabinet order of 1852, he merely observed that it was indispensable and that if it was abolished at the Emperor's command, this would be certain to introduce an element of inconsistency in the conduct of the government, a pale and rather unconvincing defence.

The Emperor's open note, however, was accorded very different treatment. He referred to this hurried and almost indecently curt document, the fruit of passing ill humour, as "the Emperor's latest decision" and spoke of "a new policy towards Russia" with which he could not associate himself. "I should otherwise," he said, "be rendering questionable all the successes which have been of importance to the German Empire and which for decades our foreign policy, carried on in accordance with the wishes of your Majesty's blessed predecessors, has achieved in our relations with Russia." The concluding sentence reads like pure mockery. He would, he said, have long ago submitted his resignation had he not gained the impression that the Emperor was desirous of making use of the experience and capabilities of a faithful servant of his predecessors. "Now that I am sure that your Majesty no longer stands in need thereof, I can retire from public life without having to fear that my decision will be regarded by public opinion as untimely."

Thus he succeeded in basing his resignation on differences in the conduct of foreign affairs which in reality did not exist at all, or at best only existed in an embryonic state. The reports by the consul in Kiev were of no real importance and would, had they arrived at any other time, have quietly disappeared into the cemetery of dead documents, never to be heard of again.

Attempts to explain Bismarck's dismissal in terms of strict logic have invariably been somewhat forced, and actually the explanation must be sought in the psychological field. Here were two personalities whom chance had brought together and between whom any kind of co-operation was downright impossible. So far from co-operating indeed, they had ended by finding each other intolerable, and whenever they had to meet they trembled with nervous irritation. "A mutual confidence had been shattered," said that very shrewd observer, Lerchenfeld, "and every step taken by either of them increased the tension." Even six months later the Emperor could say, "My nerves were exhausted. I couldn't stand it any longer." Viewed thus, the parting was obviously inevitable and one really cannot attribute actual guilt to either party.

On the following afternoon Bismarck's resignation was on its way to the old castle of the kings of Prussia. It was March 18, 1890, nearly a half century after that March 18, 1848, which for Bismarck had been the day of Prussia's deepest humiliations. Meanwhile, he was riding in the Tiergarten, no doubt with an unconscious desire for ovations, ovations of the sort that he had so often experienced here. But nobody seemed to recognise him. No doubt he had failed to show himself in Berlin for too long. Court society on this particular evening was wholly preoccupied with a performance of amateur theatricals at the Saxon embassy. When the resignation arrived at the castle, the Emperor was sitting at the piano next to Eulenburg, who was singing ballads, while the Emperor turned his pages. He was called outside by one of his adjutants and whispered to Eulenburg when he returned, "The resignation's there," then they went on with their music.

The Emperor accepted Bismarck's resignation in a few hurried lines written in pencil. Naturally he did not permit its publication. It was quite impossible to reveal to the Germans, who were so unsure of themselves as a nation, the existence of this deep division between their two heroes. All that was made known was the Emperor's answer which had originated with Boetticher and which ran: "The grounds which you have adduced for your decision convince me that further attempts to persuade you to withdraw your resignation have no prospect of success." The faithful in all the world were to believe that Bismarck had voluntarily offered his resignation and that the Emperor's efforts to dissuade him had proved vain. The deceit was completely successful. It was only years later, when Bismarck was already dead, that the text of the resignation was published and the whole truth of the matter thus made apparent.

On the evening of March 19th William II informed the commanding generals, whom he had ordered to Berlin, of Bismarck's resignation. Afterwards, when they dispersed and the stairway of the castle resounded to the jingling of their swords and spurs, while the disciplined silence of the old soldiers remained almost unbroken, the voice of the ninety-year-old Moltke, who for a very long time had never so much as opened his mouth, could be distinctly heard. "Very regrettable; the young gentleman will yet present us with many riddles."

Undoubtedly in his final reckoning with Bismarck, William II showed much of that lack of stability in his spiritual make-up which was later to contribute so much to his ruin. Even then, he already showed those characteristically rapid changes of mood and the equally characteristic inability to stick to an opinion once he had formed it. Even so, we must concede, if we look at the matter objectively, that the young man had performed a very considerable feat of daring, even though he may have had to drive himself into it, as a rider drives a horse over a hurdle. Probably he afterwards shuddered at the result of his own courage and longed for someone who would have helped him, without self-interested flattery, to bear the consequences of his deed. It is quite possible that certain sentences in the letter that he wrote to Bismarck when parting from him were sincerely meant, and when he wrote to the Grand Duke of Baden, who had powerfully supported him in all his acts against Bismarck, that his heart was as full as though he had lost his grandfather a second time, this need not necessarily have been pure hypocrisy. We can quite legitimately think of it as an idealisation of a real feeling of loneliness.

Outwardly Bismarck accepted his fall with complete composure. It is possible that his mind needed time to think itself into the new situation. So far that situation had only existed in the realms of fancy. It had been a theory which had never been taken quite seriously, a threat used to break resistance, particularly in the case of William I. Whether he saw that he was actually paying off a swollen debit balance of his own faults, whether he realised that his own deeds—the reduction to impotence of independent political forces and the mighty concentration of power he had effected and placed into the hands of the King of Prussia—whether he realized that all these things had now combined against him, who shall say?

He took no kind of counter-measures. He did none of the things he had threatened in 1888 if he were to be dismissed. He had said that he would stick to his chair and just refuse to go, even if they tried to throw him out. He had said that he would not go if they sent his notice of dismissal right into his own house, because in such a case his counter signature would be lacking.

Had he attempted any of these things, what would have happened? Perhaps he would have shared the fate of Ludwig II of Bavaria. Certainly those in possession of that greater Prussian power which was his own creation would not have stood by him. No one would have taken his part save that great mass of the people who were wholly powerless in his state.

On March 24th, when stepping out from his room, he saw an infantry officer at the end of the corridor whom he did not know. He was told that this was General von Caprivi, his successor, who was inspecting his official residence. Bismarck understood: it was time for him to disappear.

On that same day, however, it was obvious that he had regained his old lordly manner, if indeed he had ever lost it. None other than the Grand Duke Frederick of Baden, the Emperor's uncle —the man who at Versailles had voiced that first "Hoch" for which Bismarck had so skilfully found a formula, but who of late had persistently urged his young nephew to break with Bismarck —arrived for a farewell visit. Very coolly and looking the Grand Duke firmly in the eye, he charged him with usurping the authority of the Chancellor and of bringing him into disrepute with the Emperor. It was therefore he who bore the responsibility of all that must now follow, perhaps for the very severe internal struggle that might shake both the nation and all its dynasties.

The duke, who had never before had such an experience, listened at first in stupefied silence. Then he rose up indignantly, saying he could no longer allow this kind of thing to be said, but that he wished to part from Bismarck in peace and therefore would take his departure immediately.

Two days later Bismarck had his farewell audience with the Emperor, a function which, out of respect for public opinion, was unfortunately unavoidable. And here, too, Bismarck showed that he thoroughly measured up to the situation. For when the Emperor attempted, possibly in an excess of youthful embarrassment, to treat as a reality the legend, according to which Bismarck was retiring purely on grounds of health, the old man refused to play. He quietly remarked that his health had "rarely been as good in recent years as it had in the winter that was just past". People who happened to see him returning from the audience say that he sat motionless in a corner of his quickly moving coupé, that he looked very pale and held a Mareschal-Niel rose to his lips.

On the evening of this same day Bismarck, who had invited a small circle of friends to a dinner, did not hesitate to tell the truth. He said that he had had no wish whatever to retire but had been sent packing by the Emperor. He felt in better health than ever and had looked forward to meeting the Reichstag. He expressed himself very pessimistically indeed about the future. He had no confidence whatever in the Emperor. He held him to be "the man who will certainly ruin the Empire" (*den sicheren Verderber des Reichs*).*

The rumpus occasioned by Bismarck's dismissal was heard far beyond the frontiers of Germany. Everybody knew something about the man—in the Indian wigwams of North America, as on the junks of the Yellow Sea. For the moment the attention both of friend and foe was concentrated on him. Many compared him, not always too appositely, with the heroes of the Nordic sagas or even of the Wagnerian operas. Not infrequently, however, the thought was expressed that only now, after the old oak in the midst of the German forest had fallen, could light and air come in. Bamberger who, as a politician, had opposed him, but still had the self-mastery of a man of the world, declared, "He went away like a great devil who towered above his nation."

In England, the land of nautical tradition, a *Punch* cartoon was widely noted in which an old pilot leaves an outward-bound vessel with obvious feelings of anxiety, while her captain, who had the features of William II, follows him with his eyes, quite unconscious of any perils lying ahead. "An ugly parting," was the Prince of Wales's comment. The embassy in Paris reported that the Press had struck a very serious note. Pope Leo XIII felt uncomfortable. A part of his world had gone. "Mi manca Bismarck," he said.

Bismarck's departure from the Imperial Chancellery seems to have been made in circumstances of some confusion. There were household effects which had accumulated over decades, to say nothing of some thirteen thousand bottles of wine. There were also three hundred cases of official papers, which Bismarck had no hesitation in having packed up with the rest of his things, thus committing the same crime that was imputed to Harry Arnim and drove him to an early death. Bismarck had selected the papers that he wanted together with Bucher, and Bucher had first to smuggle some of them out secretly by night, as no one was certain whether the Emperor was not going to use the same sealing-off methods that he had employed after the death of Frederick III.

But nothing of the kind happened. In the midst of his removal Bismarck got a jeweller to assess the value of his innumerable orders, as though he were afraid of being cast out to starve The amount of the valuation well exceeded a hundred thousand marks. The tables of the Imperial Chancellery almost disappeared

* Lerchenfeld, p. 346.

under the telegrams that came in, and the walls behind the gifts of flowers. On March 27th Bismarck took three roses from the latter, drove to the Charlottenburg Mausoleum and laid them on the marble sarcophagus of William I. On the afternoon of the 29th he left Berlin, three days before his seventy-fifth birthday. The streets were full of dumbly disquieted and uncertain people who were held back by a considerable body of troops in bright dress uniforms. Along the station platform a squadron of the Cuirassiers of the Guard paraded, with their standard and regimental band.

The Lehrter railway station in the northwest of Berlin is not very large, and the crowds, which consisted both of friends and foes of Bismarck, soon filled it up. Besides officials, innumerable unknown little folk had contrived to squeeze themselves in. But the Emperor was absent. The only German prince among those present was Prince Max of Baden, who was destined a generation later to be the last holder of the office which Bismarck had created.

As the whistle sounded the signal for departure, the strains of an old Prussian military march began rather heavily to fill the air, and as the train started to move, some of the tightly packed crowd began to sing "The Watch on the Rhine", while others called "Hurrah" and "Come back". Bismarck stood at the open carriage window and laid his index finger upon his lips, a gesture as ambiguously eloquent as a Delphic oracle. What he intended to convey by it has never been clearly established.

18

VAIN ENDEAVOURS

The move to Friedrichsruh went off without incident. Till August unopened cases continued to fill many of the rooms. Two days after his arrival came the birthday celebrations. The number of presents and congratulations was quite astonishingly large. The Emperor sent a portrait of himself of enormous dimensions. The orchestras of the neighbouring garrisons serenaded him, and every musician left with two bottles of princely wine.

Then came the return to everyday life. Bismarck had found it so difficult to resist the attractions of country life that it became one of the causes of his fall. Now he could have a surfeit of it—and already the first meagre blossoms of the North German spring were throwing their shadows on the insignificant façade of his house, that former inn which stood immediately next to the railway station on the Berlin-Hamburg line. Strangely enough, the noise of the trains never troubled Bismarck. In any case, he said, he was too old to settle down elsewhere. Here he seemed to be attached to every room.

Now he was entirely his own master. Nobody could now summon him to Berlin at an inconvenient time. Till his last day he could listen to the matutinal hammering of the woodpeckers for as long as he pleased, and in the evening to the penetrating song of the cicadas.

The villagers addressed him as they had always done, as "Herr Fürst" (Mr. Prince).

And yet he did not experience the happiness he had anticipated. The real spice of that earlier life had been that he had made one of his estates into the nodal point of German politics—and thus made it the centre of all that happened in Europe. But now only half the man was active—the half that was the great landlord. The other half, the politician, groped about in emptiness. For the machinery of the Prussian-German states went on remorselessly and, much as the Prussian bureaucracy had survived the catastrophe of Jena, so the imperial bureaucracy survived the fall of Bismarck.

When William II summoned General von Caprivi to become Chancellor, he did not by any means make a foolish choice.

Caprivi was descended from a relatively poor family of lawyers, and for twenty years had lived the hard life of a guards officer compelled to manage on his pay. He had worked his way up by sheer merit, first into the general staff, then into the Ministry of War, and finally into the position of head of the Navy.* He was at this time fifty-nine years old, was tall, had a round bald head and a white moustache, and the Austrian ambassador once remarked that he had "a faux-air of Prince Bismarck, which at a certain distance and at first glance struck all who saw him".

He brought to his new office the qualities which among Prussian officers are taken for granted, a Spartan sense of duty, a sober grasp of given facts, a distaste for intrigue, illusions and claptrap. Neither Bismarck nor the Emperor could diminish the obstinate pride of a man who knew that he owed all he had achieved to his own efforts.

He took over the bureaucratic machine that Bismarck had created virtually unimpaired, despite the fact that the Chancellor regarded any man who remained at his post as a traitor. The only important resignation was that of Herbert. His place as chief of the Foreign Office was taken by Freiherr von Biberstein, at the time ambassador in Berlin for Baden and previously to that Public Prosecutor in Mannheim, a competent lawyer, but one who, having moved only within the narrow confines of Baden diplomacy, was unacquainted with the nature of foreign affairs. Salisbury called him simply one of the Kaiser's clerks.

The natural consequence of all this was that the conduct of foreign affairs fell into the hands of Holstein. It would have been easy for him to have become State Secretary in von Biberstein's place, but he preferred to go on working in isolation and so to remain uncontrolled. Holstein, like the rest, had begun to age, though he still held himself like a grenadier. His beard was grey and dark, shaded glasses gave a milder look to his eyes. Nobody was more familiar with Bismarck's ideas and nobody was, therefore—if that necessity should arise—in a better position to depart from them. Nobody was his equal in knowledge of detail or in self-sacrificing industry.

Since he was indispensable for von Biberstein, the two got along well together, and much that hitherto had been Holstein's private policy became the policy of the state. It was the orthodox Bismarck cult that set the fashion of presenting Holstein, who admittedly became estranged from Bismarck during the latter's

---

* In Herbert's view, Caprivi would have been the ideal successor of Moltke as Chief-of-Staff. Moltke, however, had not had him in view for the post because he was of harder stuff than Waldersee. (Letter from Herbert to Holstein of 19th August, 1884.)

final years in office, as a kind of melodramatic saboteur—"the spider in the Foreign Office"—responsible for the Chancellor's fall and so the demon who was to be blamed for all the subsequent failures of German diplomacy.

This is a most unjust picture. Holstein was quite as patriotic as any of his class or any of his colleagues. He was more crotchety than such men are usually wont to be but also more intelligent. His weakness was a Shaman-like obsession which took hold of him when he wanted to push some project through. The result of this was a lack of pliability which caused him sometimes to run aground, and also an insufficient firmness of nerve which made him panic in times of crisis.

In the military sphere, Waldersee, once the favourite of the Emperor, with his dangerous appetite for vague political intrigue, was after only a year replaced by Schlieffen as Chief of the General Staff. This was a good appointment. Schlieffen hated the optimism that had been fashionable till now, and unceasingly repeated that in the nineteenth century Prussia had always contended against weaker armies. In the wars of the future this would not be so, and it would be "the enemy that would be able to adopt our methods of 1870 and not we ourselves".

Something of a stranger in this regime, governed, as it was, entirely by reasons of state, was the figure of Philipp Count zu Eulenburg, yet he was not wholly without power within it. A diplomat by profession, but almost only despatched to the courts of German princes, twelve years older than the Emperor, he was probably the best friend the latter ever had, though his influence on him has been seriously over-estimated. His family had distinguished itself in civil office rather than on the battlefield, and his was a temperament addicted to letters and the arts.

He wrote poetry and composed in a somewhat sensitive vein ballads which celebrated the warlike life of the ancient Vikings. He was a man who had a nameless horror of politics, which he called "the hatching place for snakes' eggs". And yet by reason of his position at Court, he was continually being drawn into them. On the whole his political influence was not unhealthy. He opposed the forwardness of the military clique and would sometimes tell the Emperor truths which otherwise he would not have heard.

At one time he had been very close to the Bismarcks, and in Herbert's unhappy affair with the Princess Carolath he had been the former's only confidant. But in the crisis of 1890, when he was forced to choose between his friendship with the Emperor and his friendship with Herbert, Eulenburg had opted for the former. Since that day, Bismarck said, as soon as the Emperor looked up he was sure that he would see Eulenburg's eyes resting upon him in a dreamy fashion, eyes which he said would "spoil the best breakfast a man could have". But it would be wrong to write down Eulenburg as nothing more than an empty Court favourite.

The beginnings of Caprivi's Chancellorship went off more smoothly than was at first expected, despite the fact that there was a sharp contrast, a contrast which grew ever-more glaring, between this bachelor with his Prussian-Spartan ways and the ostentatious people who were beginning to set the tone of Berlin society. People spoke of a "new course", and indeed the government was revising, although with the plodding competence of mediocrity, the whole structure of Bismarckian politics. Since these had been essentially conservative in spirit, Caprivi's policy had necessarily to adopt a liberalising air, and this produced a strangely ironical historical interlude. Bismarck had always regarded this particular General as a thoroughly aggressive type, and had contemplated giving him the supreme command in the event of any internal disturbance. But now under Caprivi the Socialist Law quietly expired as did the last remnants of the Kulturkampf. And nobody seemed greatly concerned.

It was clear that Bismarck's foreign policy, with all its enormous complications, could only be continued, if it could be continued at all, by the old man himself. Caprivi had remarked that he could only juggle with two glass balls and not with five at once. The first visible result of this piece of self-knowledge was that the Reinsurance Treaty with Russia, which expired in 1890, was not renewed. The Emperor declared that he had promised Francis Joseph to be his faithful ally and that he meant to keep his word. Russia was planning the military occupation of Bulgaria, and if there were a Reinsurance Treaty would be able to count on Germany's neutrality. But that would mean war with Austria whom William could not desert.*

The great majority of Germans seemed as little concerned about these developments as they were about Bismarck's departure. Indeed the Press was much more excited about them than its readers, though an organ which till then had been devoted to Bismarck, namely the *Kölnische Zeitung*, declared that "we should take comfort from the reflection that Germany will not be left without a leader but possesses a forceful and strong-willed Emperor".

And who, indeed, should have mourned for Bismarck? There was no party with which he ever identified himself or which identified itself with him. "There is a comfortable feeling everywhere," wrote Hohenlohe, "that the great man is not to be

* Schüssler, p. 219.

feared,"* while the Minister of Posts, Stephan, remarked that in the last years "it had been terrible. Tiberius and Sejanus in person and both of them on Capri."† Certainly the newspaper readers, who scanned the political news with their eyes half shut, suspected no evil. They had received the impression which the high powers had intended them to receive, that the change of government had been caused by Bismarck's failing health, and regarded this as something quite as normal as when a grandfather retires from some family business. There was a general tendency to breathe more freely. It was not confined to those who, for one reason or another, were opponents of Bismarck. Even the more intelligent of the old Prussian conservatives favoured a policy which kept its feet on the ground. They had noted with growing alarm the perilous paths along which Bismarck's Germany seemed to be travelling.

Only a minority wholeheartedly took his part. For these, Caprivi, who had dared to seat himself upon their idol's chair, was a presumptuous blasphemer, and all his assistants either deceivers or deceived. They were a motley crew, those malcontents, staunch patriots full of fear for a future without Bismarck, to whom were added those whose feelings of decency were outraged by the brusque technique of his dismissal. Finally, there were those who always fall victims to the hollow phrase with a readiness proportionate to the loudness of its repetition. In short, there was here a gathering of full hearts and empty heads of the kind that has so often done harm in the course of history. Such people were less frequently encountered in the East Elbian Junker class than in other parts of the empire.

Bismarck saw in those who succeeded him in office nothing but dilettantes whose clumsy fingers would soon be caught in the cogwheels of his complicated system, and then there would be nothing left save to call upon him to set them free. He noted with astonishment and then with mounting bitterness that this did not seem to be happening. What must have been less surprising was that among the followers who over the years had sworn to be everlastingly faithful to him, hardly one had kept his oath by making any sacrifice on his behalf. Apart from Herbert, only the Under State Secretary, Count Berchem, a Bavarian whose mother came from a family of Jewish bankers, laid down his office in protest. Hitherto he had been regarded as a climber, and he may well have been reckoning with Bismarck's early return. However that may be, he was from now on held in high esteem at Friedrichsruh.

* Hohenlohe, Denkwürdigkeiten, II.
†Fr. Wilh. Foerster, *Erlebte Weltgeschichte* (1953), p. 41.

So life went on, without any notice being taken of Bismarck. The state which he had called into being went on functioning as though he himself existed no longer. The government offices in Berlin went on working as before. The carriages of the ambassadors drove through the streets. The guard paraded every day with loud military music, while Bismarck, whose slightest gesture once had had effects that were discernible in the most remote corner of the world, could do whatever he pleased, for what he did had no effect at all.

His days were ever more uneventful, almost as though time were standing still, the nights, when the land outside looked almost hostile under the cold moonlight, even more so. Then it could be like a liberation when the rattle of a railway train drew near, and perhaps it was for this reason that Bismarck liked to live near the railway line.

Yet it was not as though, being relieved from office, he had also been relieved from what that office had involved. It was not as though those few short lines which the Emperor had scribbled in pencil at the bottom of his letter of resignation had dispelled the anxieties with which for years he had wrestled. Yet it was only later, and very occasionally, that he would publicly put those anxieties into words—as when he spoke to a deputation of students and warned them "carefully to hold fast to what we have, lest we lose it because we do not value it sufficiently. In the past it has happened that Germany has been a mighty Empire, under the Carolingians or the Hohenstauffens. Once it lost this position, five or six centuries passed before it once more got on its feet. Political developments move as slowly as geological ones."*

He sought to gain solace and strength out of doors. The broad plain of his homeland, with its horizons disappearing into the distance, spoke gently to him. Like Ludwig of Bavaria he felt himself bound up with the trees as though they were animate things. "If I did not have my trees," he said, "I don't know how I could live." And how much fairer a thing it would be, when you were dead, to be laid to rest on top of a tree, as was once the custom, than to sink into a dark grave.†

On his estates he liked to observe the migrating birds and note the working of the mysterious law that governed them, while in the autumn he would be tormented by the question whether he would see their return next year. The trees, on which they were in the habit of gathering, he refused to have felled, however rotten they might be.

As for his dogs, he spoiled them outrageously, his preference

* Coll. Works, XIII, p. 558.   † Hahn, pp. 36, 42.

always being for Great Danes—unfriendly creatures, big as calves, which he overfed with the result that they became even more listless and boring than they would otherwise have been. Of the first of these creatures, Black Tyras, to whom patriotic fervour had given the name Reichshund (or Empire Dog) he was long to speak, not without a certain sadness. "He was a strange lad" (*Das war ein eigener Knabe*), he would say. His steadfast habit of letting this living colossus accompany him, was probably intended to enhance the impression of great and, if necessary, brutal power, which was one of the fundamental principles of his policy.

Like the landscape, only perhaps more so, his family were all around him. He seemed, indeed, to have become its centre, though for years he had accommodated himself to Johanna's ordering of the household, which was run on the simple principles customary in Further Pomerania. It was not long before he was the only male living in it, for after his fall his sons disliked sharing his countryman's life even more than they had before.

Herbert had taken over the management of Schönhausen. Of all the family, he was hardest hit by his father's dismissal. He was only forty, and now had to renounce a career which would certainly have been brilliant. The new government would have been glad to keep him in office, not only with a view to emphasizing the continuity of German foreign policy, but because it wished to give colour to the official legend that Bismarck had resigned on grounds of health, and which would have become quite incredible if the healthy son retired simultaneously with the sick father. When, however, Bismarck was asked to try and persuade Herbert to stay, he quoted from "Piccolomini", "*Mein Sohn ist mündig*" ("My son is of age"). But, in any case, Herbert could never have worked under Caprivi. He had taken over his father's prejudice against high-ranking military officers.

So the twists of fortune had brought it about that Bismarck put an end to the career of his favourite son, whose hopes of a marriage he had destroyed years ago, but with whom more than with any other person he felt a real kinship of the blood.

There can be no doubt whatever that, prior to 1890, Bismarck had counted upon Herbert being the second Imperial Chancellor, as had Herbert himself. "I know of no one," the father had said in 1889, "who could replace Herbert. I have made him the depository of all my experience—him and nobody else." Actually for Herbert the end of the Bismarck era represented a more general beginning of the end. He summed the matter up very simply: "This means the break up of the Empire."* In a word

* Ziekursch, III, p. 5.

Bismarck's most intimate associate foresaw the twilight of the Empire while its inhabitants were just beginning to take its unlimited duration for granted.

Even so, Bismarck's assessment of Herbert argues a sad failing of his judgment, for certainly Herbert was not the man who could ever have taken his place. He easily got drunk and was then very open-hearted, though next morning he would approach his work with a hangover and considerable irritation. In 1888 Schweninger spoke of the effects of alcohol on Herbert's nerves and brain. One might add that Herbert was easily inclined both to melancholy and to rage, and harboured the robust conviction that men had to be kicked into working. It was, in fact, only possible to govern properly by means of kicks, and that, he claimed, was something to which he had attended.

There was an external resemblance between father and son. Like Bismarck himself, Herbert was tall and broad, and he had the same bags under his eyes. But there was little else they had in common. Herbert had nothing of that marvellous abundance of contrasting characteristics which make Bismarck easily the most interesting figure in recent German history.

The hatred Herbert had sown showed itself in the moment of his departure, for no one had pity on him or sought to defend him, so that within the shortest possible space of time he stood utterly alone. The management of Schönhausen did not satisfy him as an occupation. He got himself elected to the Reichstag, and here championed a Russian orientation of German foreign policy as energetically as he opposed an English one. During the South African war he openly espoused the cause of the Boers.

Herbert married in 1892 and had three children. After Bismarck's death he inherited the princely title, but only bore it for five years, for he died in 1904. The title thus passed to his son Otto, who is chiefly remembered for a rather curious incident. At the unveiling of a Bismarck bust in the Valhalla near Regensburg, young Prince Bismarck, then eleven years old, collapsed with a loud cry at the feet of Bülow who was Chancellor at the time. Small wonder that many saw in this an evil omen for the future of the state which Bismarck created.

Bismarck's second son, William, always referred to as Bill, has a somewhat different history. In him one could observe flashes of his father's quality of mind much more frequently than in Herbert. Yet there was a cooler air between himself and Bismarck than between Bismarck and his elder son. The massive figure of his father degenerated early in Bill into an incredible corpulence, so that his mother said she felt like a garden warbler that has hatched a cuckoo. When he was only thirty it looked as if Bill would be confined to a wheel-chair—until Schweninger managed to decrease his weight by sixty pounds.

With his huge bald head, Bill looked almost like a caricature of his father. He was easy-going to the point of indolence. Yet the younger man seemed to obtain without effort what Herbert had had to work for with an enormous output of will-power and industry. He was, perhaps, the wiser of the two, for he realized quite early the vanity of worldly activity. He chose to work in the Prussian State Administration and so kept at a distance from those un-bridled passions which were continually at work in the Foreign Office. Even after his father's fall he retained his post as "Regierungspräsident" in Hanover.

His wife Sibylle, who, since she was a daughter of Bismarck's sister Malwine, was also a Bismarck on her mother's side, was accounted somewhat eccentric by the standards of her age, yet it was she alone who, at the final collapse of Bismarck's kingdom, found an end worthy of her name. In 1945 this highly talented woman, then a widow, shot herself as Russian troops approached the family seat.* Shortly after this the victors, by way of a symbolic gesture, razed Schönhausen to the ground.

Bismarck's only daughter, the wife of Count Kuno Rantzau, was externally the same corpulent type as her brother Bill. There were times when she claimed to weigh well over two hundred pounds. She also resembled him in her phlegm, but not in her qualities of mind, which rarely got much beyond good-natured banality. Bismarck, it might be added, remarked of her that he had brought her up more strictly than her brothers.

Since her husband could not forever content himself with the modest post of a "Vortragender Rat" in the house of his father-in-law, he had returned in 1888 to the Diplomatic Service. He became ambassador in Munich, where he was known as "that bit of Bismarck" and was very unpopular. He was another of those who never thought of relinquishing his post when Bismarck fell. As a reward he was promoted to be ambassador at The Hague. Nevertheless, Marie went on living with her three sons in the parental house. The grandparents spoiled the children beyond all reason, allowing them to play noisily with their wooden horse and cart in Bismarck's study while he was carrying on political conversations with visitors.†

Only Princess Johanna seemed to be entirely satisfied with the new turn of affairs. Berlin never made a great impression on her. Its social life was always, for her, a burden. She had become a

---

* Mann, *Deutsche Geschichte des Neunzehnten Jahrhunderts* (1958), p. 311.
† Eulenburg, *Fürst Philipp, Aus Fünfzig Jahren* (1925), pp. 105, 204. Philipp, pp. 61, 70.

thin little woman, with a dark complexion and a large, expressive, though ugly mouth. She was tortured by asthma and liked to wear loose dresses which she herself said looked like night-jackets.*

Bismarck, too, soon adopted a form of dress which belonged to no particular period of time—a coat with long skirts and long trousers, even when he was riding, and a felt hat with a very broad brim, all black. Around his neck he wore a white scarf. Anglo-Saxon observers thought that he looked like a preacher. The principle reason for choosing this attire may have been that it was comfortable, but he may also have reckoned that this mixture of dignity and mourning would have a strong effect upon the masses, and he wore it much as, while he was still in service, he wore his cuirassier's uniform because of the impression it would make on the public.

There now began for him a rather melancholy kind of hermit's life. No longer did the Berlin expresses slow down at Friedrichsruh to throw off bags of mail for him. Instead curious people, and especially people who were making an excursion from neighbouring Hamburg, showed themselves in the neighbourhood of Friedrichsruh in rather larger numbers than previously. Classes of school-children with their teachers would appear there and children's voices would intone uninvited serenades. But those who, a short time ago, would have moved heaven and earth to be received by him, and would have regarded an invitation to Friedrichsruh as something beyond all price, were scared away by the shock of the catastrophe. Those that visited him were mostly foreigners such as Lord Randolph Churchill, who shared with Bismarck a common dislike of Gladstone and who came accompanied by his American wife. No one would have guessed that this couple's first-born son, then seventeen years of age, was destined to play a tremendous part in the destruction of Bismarck's empire.

In the minute sphere of power that still remained to him, he reigned like a true monarch. He received his overseers and foresters for reports precisely as a Prince of the Blood would have received his Ministers, though outside the confines of his estate he had not the power to appoint a nightwatchman. Indeed, every village constable wielded more power than he. Yet, although his business enterprises flourished, Bismarck's territory was very far from being a perfect paradise. There was poverty, though Bismarck did his best to alleviate it. It is said, for instance, that on one occasion Bismarck met an old woman in Varzin eating some bread. It was so hard that she had to knock off bits of it with

* Philipp, p. 93.

a stone. All her nourishment, she told him when questioned, besides this bit of bread, consisted of potatoes. The incident moved him to have a Christmas gift of three hundred marks sent to this woman and to other poor widows.*

There was nothing in the way the Bismarcks lived of that opulence that was becoming characteristic of the town houses of the upper middle class and was now beginning to penetrate to the "Rittergüter". Johanna was a housewife thoroughly used to the bareness characteristic of Further Pomerania, and in Friedrichsruh she had hardly changed anything in the tourist hotel with its sixty-odd rooms that was her home. The walls, covered with a light-coloured paper, were hung with faded portraits of ancestors. In between them were numerous aesthetically unprepossessing framed diplomas. The furniture was heavily upholstered and covered with brightly printed cotton. There were carpets every-where—of varying value—and faded floral tributes from various admirers, the existence of which had apparently been forgotten.

Eulenburg tells us that even the servants were "elderly, slow and very bureaucratic in appearance". The furniture in Bismarck's bedroom could hardly have been simpler had it been that of a young agricultural apprentice. Certainly, such contempt for externals was characteristic of Old Prussians, but in Bismarck's house it lacked the grand style of Old Prussia. Everything had an unloved air, everything was devoid of charm. Once Eulenburg tried to excuse it, by saying, "We Old Prussians have never had any taste," and then again: "The air of petty, not too wealthy country nobility never left Bismarck's drawing-room."†

Holstein sometimes spoke of the Roheit (literally, rawness or crudeness, brutality) of the Bismarck family, which he had got to know all too well,‡ and the ambassador from Baden, von Brauer, who had been faithful to Bismarck to the end, wrote, that the whole tone of the place suggested people that were letting them-selves go. Bismarck himself seemed hardly aware of the fact that his style of living was anything but princely. He no longer had the eye for that kind of thing that he had once possessed—in Frankfurt, for instance.

Was it because he wanted to avoid arguments that he deliberately refused to see the essential ordinariness of Friedrichs-ruh, an ordinariness that suggested, more than anything else, the home of a reasonably well-to-do farmer. When fat Marie Rantzau with the laughing black eyes—Schweninger's arts had here been of no avail—gave a recital on the hurdy-gurdy before her guests, while her children shrieked popular songs at the tops of their voices, Bismarck seems never to have wanted to object.

---

* Hahn, p. 114. † Eulenburg, p. 106. ‡ Holstein, II, p. 236.

We do not do justice to Bismarck if we only see in him the state official or even the statesman. What we must never forget is that what he with gentle irony liked to call his "business" was really an art. "Politics," he said in the Reichstag in 1884, "is not a science, as many professors seem to imagine. Whether you like to call it that or not, it is an art. It cannot be taught, one has to be born for it." And he, too, sometimes fell into the "lovely madness" of the artist, who strives to endow his works with everlasting life. He felt that he was always being called to protect them.

Yet how impotent he was. Indeed, it was this continual urge to activity which could find no outlet that caused him anguish. He could find no solace in the trivialities of his women-folk, nor join in their pleasure of some new vaguery of costume. Bismarck scarcely noticed these things; they formed no part of his picture of the world. What Lenbach, the painter, once said was now more true than ever: "That man lives in a quite different world, and all of us together could only creep and crawl through his visions." (*Wir alle zusammen kribbeln nur so durch seine Visionen hin.*)

For what went on in his mind he showed as little as possible to the outside world. As Bucher tells us, "He was always cheerful at table, ate and drank, told funny stories and flirted with handsome young women like the youngest of those present." In the summer, in Kissingen, he led the old glutton's life, "feasting and drinking every day".*

The summer, which with its resin-sated scent of pines had always made him feel so well, could in 1890 do nothing for him. He fled at the end of July to Schönhausen, in August to Kissingen and then to Varzin, but was never able to get away from himself or from the future that lay before him. Was it always to be thus? Were there always to be these empty days?

One comfort seemed for a time to linger on. However emphatically he declared that he rejected the role of Cincinnatus, who was called from the plough to be dictator of Rome, he was still certain that sooner or later such a call would come. Yet nothing of the kind happened. On the contrary, it grew ever more quiet around him, and as the usual stream of guests sank to a trickle, the servants, whose tips were rapidly shrinking to vanishing point, began to give notice. Even the flood of begging letters and flattering communications began to diminish.

The connection between the power of the state on the one hand and the man on the other, who a short while ago was identified with it, was visible only in one thing; five or six policemen, called *Konstabler*, were always around him keeping just out of sight, and accompanying him on his walks and rides. One

* Busch, III, p. 325.

wonders whether their purpose was to protect him from his many enemies or to keep the authorities posted about his activities. Things reached the point that he began to have the idea that the Emperor would have his house burgled in order to get hold of his papers, and this moved him to ask his lawyer whether, in case of necessity, he might protect his home pistol in hand.

Schweninger had foreseen that the shock of sudden idleness would have an unfortunate effect upon his patient, and had therefore insisted that he should set himself concrete and clearly defined tasks. Naturally what he had in mind was that Bismarck should write his memoirs as other contemporaries of his who had had an eventful life were in the habit of doing as soon as they ceased their normal activities. Bismarck was agreeable, and on July 6, 1890, concluded a contract with Cotta, the publisher of German classics, for a set of memoirs of not less than six volumes. The fee for each volume is said to have been five thousand pounds.

In September the work began. Bismarck invited to Friedrichsruh his old assistant, Lothar Bucher, that sometime refuser of taxes and devotee of Marx, whom Bismarck had nevertheless taken up into the ministry in 1864 and who, twenty-two years later, had left it as the Senior Counsellor in the political division of the Foreign Office. Bismarck counted on Bucher's devotion, on his enormous knowledge of documents and dates, and also took into consideration that Bucher had mastered what was then still the rare art of stenography.

And so the delicate old gentleman with the narrow Puritan's head (Bismarck had long ago told him that he had noticed him among the democratic roundskulls) transferred to Friedrichsruh, leaving behind him his herbaria and his canaries, and had during the winter months to content himself with a room temperature scarcely above freezing point, thanks to which, he claimed, he ruined his health.* The work did not satisfy him. He saw in it "a perfectly hopeless expenditure of effort", something that would leave nothing for history. He worked, as he says, in every respect without success and without pleasure.

That is not difficult to understand, for Bismarck only desired to describe what he called "episodes" out of his life which happened at the moment to interest him, and to relate them "as the spirit inspired him". And so the selection of material was quite arbitrary, and the whole work lacked balance. Bismarck's dictation dragged on. Details kept on being repeated, the descriptions varying with each repetition. Events that had occurred in early youth were dressed up so that they fitted into the present.

* Busch, III, p. 325.

A great deal that is contained in the work seems highly
problematical and must have been simply invented. Bucher had
the task of imparting at least a precarious unity to the whole. Even
so, Bismarck's lapidary formulations are often left standing side
by side with Bucher's officialese. In rummaging through his
memory the Prince was not exactly overmeticulous. Dates in
particular he treated very much as he pleased,* but even if his
memory for objective facts had often vanished away, the feelings
which he had entertained in the past were still as lively as ever;
likes and, above all, dislikes came to the surface, sometimes positive hatred—even for the dead.

Also Bismarck found the work more difficult than might have
been supposed. He wrestled to find the mot juste, and the work
was often wearisome in the extreme. Nevertheless, up to the end
of March 1891 he was dictating for two hours a day. Gradually,
however, the work bored him. He began more and more often
to lapse into silence. Then the two old men would sit opposite
each other, idle and mute.

Bismarck's *Gedanken und Erinnerungen* (Thoughts and Memories)
which thus came into being did not present the world with unimpeachable source material, which indeed from a man of this
temperament could never have been expected. What astonishes
one again and again, however, is the light-hearted way in which
he allows historiography to correct life and thus *a posteriori*
ascribes motives to his actions by which they were certainly
never inspired at the time—as when he translates the crude
Prussian policy of conquest in Schleswig-Holstein into a striving
for national unity. While most of his actions were instinctive and
felicitously improvised, he had now, for reasons of prestige, to
pretend that all that happened within his sphere of activity had
been foreseen and planned. The blame for his failures, if he ever
so much as mentioned them, was with an almost reckless daring
placed on the shoulders of others. "He won't ever admit that
he had a part in anything that went awry," sighed Bucher, after
such a period of dictation, and this was an unpleasant aspect of
Bismarck's character which had already been in evidence before.
Despite all his greatness, he never felt great enough to take
responsibility for all his acts.

Once when he was dictating an account of the candidature for
the Spanish throne in 1870 he stated that this was purely a family

---

* Thus we are told in *Gedanken und Erinnerungen* that when he left Varzin on July
20th, 1870, and was passing the house of the pastor of Wussow in an open carriage,
while the latter was standing in the doorway, he made a violent motion with his
arm as though striking a blow to indicate that war was imminent. Actually this
gesture was made before the pastor's house on May 21st, i.e. two months previously
(Hahn, p. 123), when there could have been no thought of war.

concern of the Hohenzollerns and that the Prussian government had had no part in the affair. Here Bucher contradicted him and reminded him that he himself had twice been sent by Bismarck to see Prim, the head of the Spanish government. But it was in vain. The legend must be preserved intact. Similarly Bismarck contrived to give the impression that his relations with Napoleon III, which over years had been those of the greatest intimacy, were a matter of completely nugatory importance, though in fact they had been so close that after Sedan the return of the Emperor to the throne and a peace treaty concluded with him would have been the most welcome solution of the whole problem. Most certainly the dethroning of Napoleon was not a part of his programme.

It was, of course, well-nigh inevitable that Bismarck's memoirs, since they were intended for the reading public of the nineties, should be the kind of things they were. They were bound to reflect the age in which they were set down rather than the views underlying Bismarck's actions twenty years previously. Was it conceivable that he, whom the whole world had marvelled at, should now tell people the real truth about things, that he should let them know that from Königgrätz to Ems, from 1860 to 1870, the possibility of a war with France had indeed been recognised but had never been regarded as greater than that of preserving peace? That till the moment when war was declared—even after the affair of the Ems telegram—he had hoped to avoid it, and that when the die was irrevocably cast he was quite content to regard the survival of the young North German Bund as an adequate war aim and had not at that time dreamed of founding an empire?

Now, however, two decades later, he was compelled to dictate what had become, over the intervening twenty years, the irrefragable doctrine of official history, namely that from 1866 onwards "it had never been in doubt that a Franco-German war would have to be waged before the final arrangement of Germany could become a reality". Only indirectly had this war been Bismarck's work. Now, however, that its outcome had been glorious beyond all expectations, what could he do but ascribe the sole-authorship to himself?

The circumstances under which he wrote, a man dismissed against his will and forced to defend himself, made objective writing impossible. *Gedanken und Erinnerungen* had no more objective value than the pleadings of one of the parties in a civil action. The psychological background of events hardly interested Bismarck at all, which is one of the reasons why the genuine biographical material gets a disproportionately small share of the whole. The book became an apologia instead of an autobiography, which it might well have become, and a most brilliant one at that. Certainly there were in it autobiographical elements, but they are only the first charcoal strokes on the huge canvas of a self-portrait that was never completed.

But did *Gedanken und Erinnerungen* become anything like a haute école for statecraft? Did it, as Bismarck wished it to do, become something "for the instruction of the future"? That can only be said with considerable reservations. He himself, in 1881, had uttered a warning in the Reichstag that "there are times when one must govern in liberal fashion and there are times when one must govern as a dictator", and his method was that of a continual change of method. All that was unchanged was his confidence in his own intuition which allowed him at a single glance to take in the whole extent of a given situation, and to recognise almost simultaneously all the measures that such a situation demanded. However, this art of the great political engineer is not something that can be taught or indeed described in words at all, and the student, though he will find comments on individual cases, will search in vain for principles with universal application.

It is a miracle that two volumes actually came into existence. They were set in circumstances of profound secrecy, and the galley proofs were treated by Bismarck as though they were a new manuscript. Soon after this he put the work entirely to one side. One of the main reasons for this was certainly that Bucher was now dead. But the fact is that Bismarck's impatient spirit had long since been searching around for a more positive field of action.

Shortly after his dismissal he considered getting himself appointed to represent Schaumburg-Lippe, one of the smallest of German states, in the Bundesrat, or possibly being made Prime Minister of Mecklenburg-Schwerin. In 1891 he put himself up as a National Liberal candidate for the Reichstag in the petty bourgeois constituency of Geestemünde in Hanover, in the land of the Hanoverian opposition, that is to say.

He failed to get an absolute majority and things did not go as he hoped. In the end there was a second ballot in which he was opposed by a Social Democrat, a worker in a cigar factory. This time he was successful, but not overwhelmingly so. When it came to taking up the mandate, he suddenly grew hesitant. The majority of the members of the Reichstag would avoid him, he told himself. Also living in a Berlin hotel would be quite remarkably unpleasant. Above all, since he was an officer, he would have to appear in the Reichstag in uniform and as such oppose the Emperor's ministry. This was something that, save in an extreme emergency, he did not wish to do. Actually he never entered the Reichstag again.

Then had come an invitation from Emil Hartmayer, the owner of the *Hamburger Nachrichten*—and it was one which it was almost inconceivable that he should have refused. For what Hartmayer did was virtually to offer him his paper, an organ of moderate size and reputation, as a tabula rasa—to use as he pleased and in whatever way the spirit happened to move him. The temptation was greater than any man in Bismarck's position could have withstood, filled as he was with vindictive rage, and yet, until Hartmayer came, condemned to silence. Naturally he agreed. Now one of the editors of the *Hamburger Nachrichten*, a man named Hofmann, began to make increasingly frequent visits to Friedrichsruh. Whatever Bismarck said on such occasions—and usually his remarks were violently ill-tempered— would then be quite uncritically published. Bucher himself had observed earlier how Bismarck, instead of dictating to him, busied himself with these relatively unimportant newspaper articles, which of course remained unsigned. But the whole world knew their origin which, incidentally, represented a fine piece of business for the newspaper, although the latter always repudiated Bismarck's authorship of what its pages contained.

The idea of acting as a publicist was not new to Bismarck. There is no question that his talents as a journalist were very great. All through his official life he had really, though acting alone and in silence, very successfully done that for which modern states require a huge apparatus. He had managed to influence the Press without the public being aware of the fact. It is only gradually that we have come to learn just how he contrived to win it over, how sure was the instinct that told him where, when and with what force to use his influence.

For a time he gave himself up entirely to journalism. He read twenty papers, and besides this was overwhelmed with a flood of uninvited printed matter. The picture he presented barricaded behind mounds of paper was not unlike that of a busy newspaper editor. In 1892 the *Hamburger Nachrichten* alone published more than a hundred pieces of work from his pen. And in its wake there sailed an entire fleet of other newspapers which had sworn faith to him—the *Münchener Allgemeine Zeitung*, for instance, whose proprietor was identical with that of the Cotta publishing house, the *Leipziger Neueste Nachrichten* and the comic paper, *Kladderadatsch*. At Friedrichsruh they were glad to see the old man so busy, for when in ill humour himself he tended to make things unpleasant for the rest of the household. Now he had less occasion to indulge this habit.

What he published was invariably harsh criticisms of his successors. He began with Boetticher and von Biberstein but soon went on to Caprivi, and almost continually, though he did so only indirectly, he sneered at William II.

During this period he would also say from time to time that his royalism was getting wobbly and that if he were born again he would be a republican, though no doubt these are fanciful remarks to which too much importance should not be attached. In any case he had long ago remarked that the monarchical system did not necessarily depend on a hereditary monarchy. A president could carry on a monarchical government if he had the power, and certainly Prussia remained more important to him than the dynasty. He never regarded monarchs as anything more than his peers. They were simply men who happened to have got on a little more than the other noble families. They were not their natural superiors, and it is significant for his feelings for the man who at that time wore the imperial crown, that when making a payment of money he placed the coin with the image of the Emperor downwards. He said that he did not wish to see that false face any more.

So it was that Bismarck returned to his natural element, that of political battle, though all too often he wasted himself in long-winded criticism of some trivial speech in the Reichstag or some newspaper article which would otherwise have been forgotten within twenty-four hours. But to be involved in controversy, any kind of controversy, gave him new vitality.

That he thus became immersed in irrelevancies and sank far below his true level seemed to leave him indifferent. Among the motives impelling him—and here we can surely believe him—the principal one was his anxiety lest the political system which he had left behind him should come into unsuitable hands. This anxiety soon gave way to the certainty that nothing that was done under the new regime could possibly be right. Equally powerful, however, was the sense of personal hurt which in so egocentric a personality might well have driven him to the verge of madness. Last but not least were Caprivi's fiscal reforms which damaged Bismarck personally as a landlord and wounded his old if somewhat naïve sense of the sanctity of property. In short, this latter-day journalism of Bismarck was not altogether a happy venture. Moreover, except in a few instances, the general tone seemed uninspired and even sulky.

The victims of his attacks at first showed a considerable measure of indifference, in particular the Emperor, who knew very well that when Bismarck was attacking the officials of the new regime, he was attacking men who did not depend on the confidence of their constituents as they do in a parliamentary state, but wholly on the monarch himself. Aspersions on their competence and honesty therefore were really aspersions on the Emperor.

At first William was not deeply stirred. The apparatus of power which had been his by right since 1888 now belonged to him in reality, and that was all that mattered. Bismarck, he believed, would soon weary and grow dumb. Two years at most should see the end of the business.

At Christmas, at New Year, and on his birthday the usual congratulations and presents from the Emperor would arrive as before. Then suddenly, in 1891, the practice was discontinued. It was a silent warning, but Bismarck was so full of the fighting spirit that he only saw in it a challenge, and stepped up his offensive so that interest in the conflict rapidly spread beyond the confines of Germany and became a spectacle for the sensation-mongers of the world at large.

In these years also another person who was to play a part in this story was laying the foundations of a remarkable career. He was a certain Isidor Witkowski, the son of a silk merchant and an aspiring but depressingly unsuccessful actor and playwright. However, the day came when Isidor abandoned the world of greasepaint and make-believe for the hard realities of politics. Calling himself Maximilian Harden, he became the editor of a weekly called *Zukunft* (The Future), which was very largely written by himself and often contained articles of forty pages in which he showed great courage in exposing very real abuses.

Harden had a highly individual style which smelt somewhat of the tragedian and was loaded with cryptic allusions and particles of recondite knowledge. The upper classes, spellbound as they were at that time by the sacred cow of education, found it very much to their taste. It was a sign of intellectual superiority if you were seen with one of the slender grey-brown volumes in your hand. The first connection between Bismarck and Harden was made by Schweninger, who hoped thus to provide his patient with a certain stimulus, while Harden's lively understanding quickly grasped the fact that on the foundation of the old man's fame he could very conveniently build his own.

By 1891 a true alliance between the two men was already in being. It was the last one that Bismarck was to make and, like so many of the previous alliances, it was made with a man who contrasted quite remarkably with Bismarck himself. But when it was a case of getting a useful ally, Bismarck had never greatly cared where he came from. One has but to think of his association

decades before with Lasalle, another ambitious product of
the Jewish middle class, and, like Harden, nimble-minded,
pliable, cunning, and wholly unable to control his feelings;
also like Harden, full of contempt for that liberal bourgeoisie
from which he sprang, which he was always eager to make
ridiculous and which, for that very reason, proceeded to idolise
him.

The *Zukunft's* political line, however, was very far from being
that of Bismarck. Harden criticised the foreign policy of the
new regime, which Bismarck considered risky, for its unwillingness to take risks. Harden was, in fact, one of the first of those
German imperialists who were prepared for anything. But
opposition to William II, which was common to both men, was
sufficient foundation for a partnership which actually lasted six
years and was only terminated when Bismarck, infuriated by
Harden's indiscretions—at least that was Bismarck's version—*
forbade him the house. By then, of course, Harden had learned
so much from Bismarck that the *Zukunft* for years continued to be
regarded as the latter's platform.

Eight years after Bismarck's death Harden succeeded in involving Eulenburg, the Emperor's best friend, in a discreditable
legal action, and no informed person doubted for a moment that
it was Bismarck who had drawn the pamphleteer's attention to
Eulenburg's unfortunate attraction towards virile men of the
lower classes. The proceedings ruined Eulenburg without serving
any positive let alone any patriotic purpose. For Eulenburg's
influence, in so far as he had real influence with William, was
of a moderating and soothing character. The real purpose of
the action was the personal humiliation of the Emperor through
that of his friend. It was a posthumous act of revenge.

At last, in the spring of 1892, Caprivi, whose patience was
becoming exhausted, saw the opportunity for a counter-stroke.
Herbert's marriage was to be solemnised in Vienna, and it was
known that his princely father intended to use his stay in that
city after his own fashion. What he wanted was to be publicly
welcomed in what was still the brilliant metropolis of the Germany
he had destroyed, and to be received in solemn audience by
Francis Joseph. This would provide a shaming comparison with
the treatment he had received from his own government and his
own sovereign.

Caprivi sought to prevent this by instructing the German
embassy in Vienna to ignore the wedding, and at the same time
persuaded the Emperor to request Francis Joseph not to receive
his "disobedient subject". Though William's letter to Francis

* Poschinger, *Also sprach Bismarck* (1911), III, p. 346.

Joseph remained a secret for decades, Caprivi, in order to protect the Emperor, published his instructions to the embassy—a most disastrous blunder. For now Bismarck's self-pity was suddenly justified in the eyes of the entire world, a situation which he did not hesitate to exploit.

In an interview which was immediately arranged in Vienna with the *Neue Fraie Presse*, he spoke contemptuously of the existing German government, declaring that he had no further personal obligations towards them whatever and that all bridges had been burned. Soon after this he spoke of Caprivi's instructions to the embassy as a "Uriah-letter", recalling thus the general in the Old Testament whom his crafty monarch had delivered to death by means of a letter of which the victim himself was the bearer, and although the comparison is somewhat inapt, this phrase has now nevertheless became an integral part of orthodox history.

Bismarck's success was enormous. Among many who till now had been indifferent, the seemingly misused man gained new adherents. In Vienna in those glorious days of early summer the whole population seemed in high good humour, and everywhere its conqueror of 1866 received ovations. On the return journey the stations were crowded with people who spontaneously expressed their sympathy. He replied with a few brief words, but suddenly, to his own surprise, the expedient of impromptu speech with which he had rarely had much success in parliament proved vastly effective among these great masses of people who had quite unexpectedly gathered together to catch a glimpse of him.

We should try and imagine him as he was seen by eye-witnesses on that day amid the noise and smoke of the stations of Munich, Augsburg and Dresden, as, in his black frock coat and white cravat, he spoke from the window of his railway carriage, palpably a great man, his delicate features slightly reddened, "but also refined and spiritualized".

It was a real discovery for Bismarck that the spoken word can have a stronger and more rapid effect than a printed newspaper article or a printed account of words spoken in parliament. It was also an irresistible temptation, and so, by Caprivi's blunder, he was almost forced into the wholly new role of a popular orator.

At the end of July, at the invitation of the professors of Jena university—and always accompanied, as though by a body-guard, by Haeckel, the herald of popular Darwinism—he spoke several times in the open air to an audience consisting chiefly of students and professors. But when the telegraph wires carried his words from the little Thuringian town into the world outside, there was astonishment and incredulity. For what he said on that ill-paved market-place, while the summer wind played on what remained of his white hair, was the very opposite of everything that Bismarck had championed all his life. How was it possible, for instance, that he, who had always despised the whole parliamentary system, should suddenly know no more urgent desire than to have as strong a parliament as possible.

He spoke in a spirit of mellow patriotism but also with a certain note of self-accusation and quite free from the old gestures of Olympian superiority. Very differently from the Bismarck of *Gedanken und Erinnerungen*, who never in his life made a mistake, and had achieved all his successes according to a preconceived plan, he now stated: "It would be presumption on my part if I were to assert that I had foreseen and prepared the whole course of history." Perhaps, he now said, he had himself unconsciously made the power of the crown in Germany too great and so brought it about that parliament had been suppressed to a point where it was impossible any longer to speak of a parliamentary constitution. So parliament must once again be able to show a constructive majority without which it lacked the authority it required. "The Reichstag should become the focal point of public life. It must be free to criticise, warn and in certain circumstances conduct the government. . . . When popular representation becomes weak and becomes the organ of a higher will, then if this goes on, we would have returned to enlightened absolutism." But it would be "a dangerous experiment if people were today to seek to establish absolutist ideas in the heart of Europe. . . . People might then think they were obeying God while in reality they were obeying some higher civil servant."

All the criticisms which he now felt impelled to utter were directed against the government and not against the Emperor, since, according to the imperial constitution, it was the ministers, and not the Emperor, who were responsible.

Yet once again the Jena speech caused what was in the final analysis the incomprehensible and uncanny element in Bismarck to flare up brightly like the glow of a blast furnace that is suddenly opened. What kind of a man was this, who could suddenly transform himself at a moment's notice into his own opponent? Few people, of course, were rendered suspicious by the suddenness of the transformation. Rather did countless Germans—Germans have always been bad psychologists—rejoice in the happy illusion that Bismarck had recognised his mistakes and had undergone a belated conversion—impossible as such a thing might appear in a man of his character who was nearly eighty years of age.

The truth is that he, too, merely wanted what he had always wanted throughout his life, influence, activity, the rule over men, and if the great ones of the world were turning away their faces from him, he would seek what he wanted with the mass of the anonymous and insignificant. By admitting that his successes were due to lucky chance rather than to any merits of his own, which was precisely the way things tended to happen among themselves, he made them for a moment his equals and gave them the happy feeling that he was stepping down amongst them from the heights and at the same time drawing them upwards towards himself. It was a grandiose and desperate piece of play-acting, but one which might be justified—or at least excused—by his sense of real danger ahead, and by the pain experienced by a proud man who saw himself turned loose like an old toothless dog. The duty to speak, he remarked in 1891—and surely he meant what he said—"seems pointed at me like a pistol".

There were speeches in other towns besides Jena made to a rather different sort of audience, and Bismarck at last began to delight in a new experience. Till now he had associated only with officials and politicians, Junkers and courtiers, and had hardly ever had any relations with the great mass of the population that lived slightly below the level of the propertied bourgeoisie. Now, however, as he spoke to the oddly featureless audiences of thousands, he experienced for the first time the powerful reaction of which such a gathering is capable; the tension as he began his speech, the low-pitched murmurs as their feelings began to be disturbed, and the roaring applause at the end.

Wherever he went he was followed and called on to speak; he was even sought out in his own home. For the sect of Bismarck admirers became a popular movement, Friedrichsruh the goal of streams of visitors who, particularly on Sunday, plodded the Sachsenwald and besieged Bismarck's house. Veterans' organisations, choral societies, marksmen, gymnasts, and skittle groups arrived in special trains.

Innumerable presents were brought, sometimes touching, usually completely useless, presents for which Bismarck had nevertheless to express his thanks in his own writing. There was, for instance, a flag factory which presented him with a package of hideously printed handkerchiefs, as "an expression of their good will". On such occasions it was fortunate indeed that both Bismarck's sons had learned to produce a perfect imitation of their father's hand.

But honours did not stop there. A certain brand of herrings received the name Bismarck Herring; a long light-brown product of the confectioner's art was dubbed Bismarck Oak. Everywhere Bismarck monuments stuck their helmet points up into the sky, and even the smallest town refused to be content unless it had its Bismarckstrasse.

When Bismarck spoke to visitors—he did so in tones of mild, grandfatherly friendliness for the most part—he stuck to the pattern of his Jena speeches. But since he had to remain within the limits of his hearers' comprehension, he could not speak of the past as he had actually experienced it, but only in such a fashion that it could be fitted in to the accepted denatured picture of history which the newspapers had in the course of time contrived to popularise. He was therefore compelled to give his life a much more banal character than it really possessed. The dismissed Chancellor could then strike a more demagogic note than he had ever struck while he was in active politics, though it was only rarely that he hit on phrases which he could hurl into the world like a new Polyphemus hurling rocks. Even now impromptu speeches were often difficult. He himself called this work "torture", and those who watched him attentively noted the effort with which he brought forth his words.

Even so he still contrived so to choose these words that they won him a public over which he had no other power than that of speech, and in choosing those words he certainly threw all scruples to the winds. Thus he did not hesitate to insist that he was no true Junker at all, and had never been accepted as a full-ranking member of their order by the Junkers themselves because his mother was of bourgeois origin. In a word he presented himself as the pitiable victim of haughty nobles' arrogance. Or, since his public enjoyed horror stories, he would tell them how he had seen William I "lying in his blood" after the second attempt on his life, whereas in reality at the time when that attempt was made he was in Varzin and only saw the Emperor some days later.

The situation in Friedrichsruh began to grow slightly grotesque. The peasants of the neighbourhood talked to him in much the same tone that they used to one of their own kind or at best as they would have spoken to a senior forester or to a village constable. The townsfolk, however, seized their hats from their heads with gestures of military stiffness, while their ladies, paling as they attempted to curtsey, breathed out their reverence.

Again and again he was compelled to march along lines of comfortably-rounded citizens shaking hands that had grown cold with awe, giving encouraging nods to maids of honour in their starched white dresses and searching, after the accustomed manner of royalty, for topics of conversation such as the weather, the prospects of the harvest, the number of children and so forth, or asking questions such as "What medal is that?" and "Where did you serve?" Flattery to the point of absurdity had to be endured in silence; not a muscle of his face did he dare to move when referred to, say, as *der sieggewohnte alte Recke*, which might be very loosely translated as the "unbeatable old warrior" but has an air of patronising familiarity, a sort of jolly-old-fellow implication, which must have caused Bismarck inwardly to writhe. Sometimes, indeed, in spite of himself, he would wrinkle his brow, as when a speaker closed his oration with the words, "Hail to Otto the Great." To rob a rather venerable medieval Emperor of his title for Bismarck's sake seemed to him to go too far.

As in other places of pilgrimage, a kind of fair came into being near Friedrichsruh. Hawkers went around with Bismarck soap, Bismarck shirts, Bismarck snuff, above all with portraits of Bismarck as the smith of the empire with his anvil, or, alternatively, as Germany's guardian angel, complete with wings and waving white robe. In the evening the princely family could often see the smoke and flames of approaching torchlight processions. Sometimes the night would be made hideous with the roaring of the intoxicated. Business firms organised trips to Friedrichsruh as they had once organised trips to Lorelei on the Rhine.

To what extent Bismarck was embarrassed by this kind of thing we do not know. Most certainly, however, it was entirely out of keeping with his true nature. In earlier days he had said that ovations of this kind, apart from providing an excuse for drinking beer, merely served to satisfy curiosity. It must have needed an incredible degree of self-control thus to offer himself to the people, to court their favour, and it must have been unspeakably difficult for a man who tended to avoid people, who certainly avoided wherever he could any contact with dull mediocrity, a man who even in Berlin remained almost invisible to the men at the very head of the state and society.

Yet the man, who for all practical purposes had been utterly excluded from power and nevertheless still thirsted for it, succumbed to the passion which caused him to sacrifice a dignity that was timeless for a series of petty temporary external successes. What he now won in popularity from the masses he lost in respect from the much smaller number of men of understanding. Even the present generation will surely agree with the words written by Fontane about Bismarck in 1893: "It is a terrible thing always to subordinate everything to expediency. . . . His genius which shines forth in every sentence delights me again and again and puts an end to my misgivings, but when I am quieter the misgivings are always there and one never can fully place one's faith in him."

The imperial government could no longer remain blind to the fact that it had managed to get into a sort of civil war with Bismarck, a war which was leading both sides into ever more untenable positions. Then chance provided a way out of the difficulty. In the summer of 1893, during his cure in Kissingen, Bismarck contracted an inflammation of the lungs, the effects of which endured till well into the winter. William II, always ready for an improvisation, and for motives in which genuine affection and political prudence were mingled, had von Moltke the Younger, one of his adjutants, take him a bottle of his best Rhine wine. Moltke arrived unannounced in Friedrichsruh and met Bismarck when the latter was for the moment in a mellow mood, and—this is perhaps not unimportant—when his sons were not with him. This made it comparatively easy for Bismarck to say that he would personally express his thanks in Berlin.

Rarely indeed has so commonplace an object as this bottle of Rhine wine created such a panic as that which now arose in Berlin, for the prospect that Bismarck's visit might perhaps lead him back into the Imperial Chancellery caused his successors and the creatures with whom they had filled the various offices to fear a positive massacre of the bureaucrats. On January 25th, almost four years to the day after that disastrous council of 1890, Bismarck, in the imperial state coach, swept through the winter mists of Berlin accompanied respectfully by Prince Henry, the Emperor's only brother. Once again, as on the day when he left Berlin, walls of humanity stood along his way, and there were, no doubt, many who observed how waxen his face was already and with what difficulty—though in the heavy black mantle and steel helmet of the cuirassiers he seemed taller than his wont— he leaned upon the arm of the slender prince in blue naval uniform.

When the Emperor received him, Bismarck showed himself, as the Emperor himself was later to tell, very "forthcoming and friendly". They talked about Bismarck's health, about military matters, though there was not a word of politics.* "Ottochen told stories of the ballroom," Johanna was later to say. He was, in short, treated as the man who officially he was, as a prince that is to say, while the statesman in him was forgotten.

Although there was no warmth in the meeting, the public heart was touched. One could almost hear Germany breathing again. But those who saw deeper, and above all Bismarck himself, must have known that nothing was changed in the realities of the situation.

There was indeed an awkward moment when Bismarck let it be known that he had shared the bottle of Rhine wine which the Emperor had sent him with Maximilian Harden, William's arch enemy. But the incident passed and was veiled in discreet oblivion.

* Eulenburg, p. 268.

Actually, then, what might have had the appearance of a reconciliation was really no more than a precarious truce. Each of the two parties continued to fear the other's power to inflict damage on himself.

And yet the encounter was not entirely without results. Since the Emperor had brought about the meeting behind Caprivi's back, it served further to undermine the Chancellor's position, which had already become distinctly insecure—for he had long succeeded in arousing the dislike of both right and centre. Now, to add to all this, his sober serious mind was becoming less and less attuned to the liveliness of the Emperor, who was always seeking new sensations and found his Chancellor unimaginative. In particular, Caprivi's social policy, although it was identical with that of the Emperor and was the one concerning which the latter had come into conflict with Bismarck, proved to be a failure, since, at worst, it produced a hostile reaction, or at best no reaction at all.

Meanwhile political strikes were becoming more numerous in Europe and there were several anarchist outrages, culminating in the murder of Carnot, the French President, and at last the Emperor began to think of a new Socialist Law. He who in 1889 had condescendingly remarked to Bismarck that the Social Democrats could be left to him and that he would find a way of handling them, was in September 1894 prepared for new emergency legislation. Moreover, he had found in Count Botho Eulenburg, a cousin of his friend Philip, a Minister of the Interior who would not have shrunk from a forcible revision of the constitution. In the end William was occupying the position which Bismarck had occupied just before his dismissal in regard to social legislation. Where, however, the Emperor had stood in 1890, Caprivi stood now. For Caprivi was convinced that the Reichstag would not agree to any emergency legislation and in that case only the coup d'état remained. But this was a measure that Caprivi uncompromisingly rejected.

At length the Emperor demanded his resignation as he had demanded that of Bismarck in 1890. The general obeyed immediately.

His successor, Prince Chlodwig Hohenlohe, a man of seventy-five, and till now the governor of Alsace-Lorraine, had never been regarded very highly by the smart Court at Berlin. He was a member of the very highest aristocracy and therefore felt his own rank to be higher than Bismarck's recent princely dignity. He failed to show Bismarck the immoderate and empty reverence which it had become customary to accord the old man, though he treated him with a certain gentle irony, and was careful to observe all external forms of courtesy. Moreover, whereas the gulf between Bismarck and Caprivi had been unbridgeable, Hohenlohe, thanks perhaps to that indifference that is begotten of age but is accounted wisdom—which well it may be—seemed anxious to come to a gradual understanding.

Immediately on his appointment he was careful to pay a visit to Friedrichsruh, and at the opening of the Kiel Canal Bismarck received an invitation, of which however he did not avail himself. But a gradual change was taking place. Caprivi, that very honest man, simply treated Bismarck as a pensioned, but high-ranking, state official. By Hohenlohe he began to be treated as a power in the state, and the less he approximated to that condition the more emphatically Hohenlohe's conduct implied its reality.

Yet Hohenlohe's delicacy could not change the facts. The world went its own way whether Bismarck liked it or not, and gradually it was borne in upon him that nothing that had happened since 1890 would have happened otherwise than it did. And so it became rarer for him to say or write what was in his mind. He suffered grievously under his impotence. Once, at a time when fortune was favouring him, he was reputed to have said that if a man suffers he ceases to be a politician.* One wonders whether he might not have said that now. For there now came to an end the period of his life that is almost embarrassing yet somehow touching to read about, the period in which the aged man humbly courted the favour of the great helpless masses whom, in the past, he would have considered unworthy of so much as a glance.

The same year of 1894 saw the death of Johanna. She died early one November morning at Varzin, or, to be more exact, she ended on that day a process of dying that had lasted for years. Bismarck, who had been awakened too late to be present at the end, sat weeping by her bed—at least so Harden tells the story—with a thin dressing-gown over his nightshirt.

Johanna's interests had centred exclusively on her husband, while Bismarck's concern, particularly during periods of great political activity, had at best only been partly for his wife. But such vacillations of feeling not only failed to influence Johanna: she was unaware of them. She was always there for him, whether he noticed it or not. And he was not unaware or ungrateful for that constant solicitude.

Bismarck's love for Johanna had none of that violent quality that marked his passion for Marie von Thadden. It had developed gradually, day by day, until it had become a habit, something so deep-rooted that nothing could remove it. That was why her

* Benoist, *Le Prince de Bismarck* (Paris, 1900), p. 194.

death struck cruelly at the old man's heart. "The man who is not married," Bismarck now declared, "offers one target the less for the shafts of fortune." After her death Bismarck wrote to his sister, "Since the catastrophe I am even more tired than before. Tic douloureux has grown worse, it stops me from sleeping, and from going out for any length of time into the open air. Nerves used up. . . ." A few weeks later the widower left Varzin for ever.

Bismarck's eightieth birthday came in 1895. As it drew near, it looked as though, at least externally, peace had been restored between the House of Hohenzollern and his own. This made it possible for the whole of official Germany to put in an appearance at his home and congratulate him. Princes and free cities, four hundred parliamentarians, representatives of all branches of bureaucracy, professors and students of the universities in all their historical mummery—all came about this time to pay their respects. The Emperor arranged for some squadrons of cavalry to parade at Friedrichsruh, while he himself, seated on horseback, resplendent in his cuirassier's uniform, delivered a birthday address to the old man, who had been moved to observe a few days previously that he could no longer bring his old bones across a saddle. So he now stood before the Emperor with his fingers on his helmet at the salute, and had thus, so he tells us, continually to observe a drop of rain that was slowly running down his sovereign's cuirasse. The whole celebration was a somewhat naïve affair, its object being so sedulously to honour Bismarck as an honorary Colonel-General of Cavalry that the statesman was reduced to vanishing point.

The first to come and offer their congratulations were not, as might perhaps have been supposed, emissaries from his native East Elbia, but the Lord Mayor of Hamburg, the great metropolis of trade near which he lived, for whose Press he wrote and whose citizenship he contemplated acquiring. Indeed, it looked at that moment as though he, millionaire, capitalist, manufacturer and exporter that he was, had joined himself to the ranks of Hamburg's merchant aristocracy, having steadily loosened the ties that bound him to his country of origin and to the Prussian Junker provinces.

The congratulatory visits, which went on for several weeks, did not however by any means reflect complete unanimity in Germany. Indeed, the Reichstag by a majority vote—in which the Centre Party, the Social Democrats, the Freethinkers, the South German People's Party, the Hanoverians, the Alsatians and the Poles were all united—had decided to take no notice of Bismarck's birthday, and the same thing happened with the municipal authorities of Berlin. Naturally, this raised a storm of indignation,

and even the Emperor gave telegraphic expression to his alleged
"deep sense of outrage" and assured Bismarck that the Reichstag
resolution was "contrary to the feelings of all German princes
and peoples". Yet one may well ask whether for Bismarck, with
his keen sense of realities, congratulations from parties with whom
throughout his life he had been at enmity would not have sounded
a false note. Perhaps, indeed, the silence of such people had its
uses, for it gave a true picture of the situation, and in a sense the
fact that so many citizens of the German Empire saw no grounds
for making the birthday of its creator an occasion of festivities,
showed how faulty and unfinished the creation still remained.
Bismarck in 1890 had had to leave his work unfinished, but
whether, had time been allowed him, he would have had the
capacity to perfect it, is a question which of necessity must remain
an open one.

All around him a new age was coming into being. After a short
period of maladjustment the new political organism that he had
built into the centre of Europe had adapted itself to its surroundings with astonishing speed and had taken its place in the general
imperialist expansion in which at that time the great powers
were engrossed. Meanwhile, industry was registering an unprecedented expansion and business was booming everywhere. But
it was a growth not without its perils, for the country which
could no longer feed its population but was dependent on imports,
which in their turn had to be paid for by exports both visible and
invisible, peace all over the world was an inexorable condition
of survival, and this was certainly one of the reasons why the
maintenance of peace had always been foremost among Bismarck's
aims.

For the tremendous economic developments that were in progress Bismarck had only moderate interest and no very high
degree of liking. He was an aristocrat and had the aristocrat's
feeling in such matters. He knew well enough that the desire for
quick enrichment made for general prosperity, but he also knew
that it destroyed individuality, caused men to be cut increasingly
after a pattern and made them less sensitive to finer values. It
also brought other consequences in its train which touched him
even more deeply. Some remarks inspired by him in the *Hamburger Nachrichten* in 1891 are eloquent in this respect. German
statecraft, the paper declared, was no longer concerned to avoid
wars, the consequences of which could not possibly be foreseen.
Germany was seeking to play the part of a man who had suddenly
come into money and who, relying on the talers in his pocket, is
aggressive towards everyone he meets.*

* Hofmann, p. 1,381ff.

One circumstance in particular made the German public more inclined than it otherwise might have been to support such short-sighted conduct. This was the false perspective in which as the years went by Bismarck's wars were coming to be viewed. Indeed, so intoxicating did the effects of 1870 continue to be that the public never realised how completely circumstances had changed. It began to be overlooked that Bismarck's wars had been fought against opponents who were weaker numerically and who had already been isolated, that they were wars in which Bismarck would never have engaged had he not first manoeuvred himself into a favourable position—and, it might be added, wars in which the element of luck played a not inconsiderable part.

But the ease with which these wars were won created the illusion not only that German arms were invincible but that fortune had in some way committed herself to accord a kind of most-favoured-nation treatment to this new arrival among the nations, and to make accessible to her here and now all the good things which over the centuries she had granted to the old-established powers. If social or geographical circumstance happened at any time to obstruct the realisation of such wishful thinking, then the malice of rivals was held to be responsible, and this supposed malice tended to be countered by that threat of force which people had so mistakenly come to regard as Bismarck's only weapon.

This whole unhappy trend was further reinforced by the fact that the fighting forces were the Emperor's quite peculiar delight and that he expended on them a disproportionate amount of his energy and time. His continual preoccupation was with military detail, with parades, uniforms, reviews and the like, and whoever wished to win his favour had to cultivate a burning interest in such matters. This caused a distorted view to be taken of the fighting forces' whole place and function in the state. They were no longer a mere tool, as Clausewitz and Bismarck had regarded them, an instrument to be used by the statesmen on special occasions when other instruments proved unserviceable, but the essential and, if not the only instrument available, certainly the instrument that ranked high above all others. Thus the high art of diplomacy was overshadowed and relegated to the background, and since the enlarged army was now recruiting much of its officer material from the rising middle class, such militaristic outlook spread over ever-widening circles.

And so the age of Bismarck tended more and more to be an age of illusion, an illusion which it is inconceivable that Bismarck's penetrating gaze should not have pierced, for there were men— men such as Burckhardt for instance—who seem to have been alive to what was to come. Indeed, there is much evidence that he saw—vaguely perhaps but yet sufficiently clearly—the imminence of the catastrophe that the bright décor of William II's Germany hid from the view of nearly all the others. But he was a beaten man and there was now nothing he could do to avert it, and he was to bear that bitter knowledge to the grave.

19

THE BITTER END

Bismarck had withdrawn into silence, as befits a conquered man who has laid down his arms, and only once stepped forward again on to the stage of actual events. In October 1896, while the shadows of the autumn clouds were racing across the stubble on his fields, one could read in the *Hamburger Nachrichten*—it was little more than hinted at, but the meaning was quite plain—that in Bismarck's day there had been an understanding between Germany and Russia which provided that, if one of the two countries were attacked, the other would practise benevolent neutrality—in a word, there had been the Reinsurance Treaty. Caprivi, however, it was said, had refused to renew the agreement after it had expired, and had thus forced a rapprochement between Russia and France.*

The fact is that on the day before Bismarck signed his resignation, Schuwalow arrived in Berlin to renew the treaty. He found the Emperor quite willing, but since at that moment the change of Chancellors was made known, he waited to see whether there might not be new instructions from St. Petersburg. The delay was a short one, but it sufficed for Holstein to induce in Caprivi his own dislike of the treaty, which he called "political bigamy". Schweinitz, who happened to be in Berlin, held similar views. It was, he said, dangerous to continue with so involved a policy. Even Herbert said, "Only my father can manage a thing of this kind." Caprivi bowed before these experts and, indeed, he was himself convinced that he would never be able to "juggle with five balls". Finally the Emperor came round to the same view. He was sorry, he said, but he wanted above all to pursue an honest policy.

When, in the autumn of 1896, Bismarck let out the secret, though without giving away the embarrassing details, which might force Germany into disloyalty against Austria, William was deeply outraged, though outwardly he remained calm. Nevertheless, the old feud between the friends and enemies of Bismarck flared up again and assumed fantastic proportions. It was even suggested

* Hofmann, p. 1,101.

that proceedings should be taken against him for the betrayal of state secrets. The excitement was tremendous, though it is difficult today to understand why it should have been so great; the Reinsurance Treaty had only been concluded for want of a more effective pact. That Caprivi should have allowed it to lapse certainly was not a matter of world-shaking importance.

That Russia, almost against her will, was forced into a French alliance was a theory which Bismarck naturally was very fond of developing, though he could certainly never prove it, for the Reinsurance Treaty would not have prevented a Franco-Russian alliance, even if it had continued in force, any more than it prevented the continued existence of the Austro-German alliance. It follows that even if Caprivi had renewed the Reinsurance Treaty it would have been perfectly possible for the Franco-Russian alliance to come into being.

Moreover, France's first loan to Russia had been made in 1888, that is to say two years before Caprivi became Chancellor, and the dual and triple alliances co-existed peacefully for some twenty years. Neither fact supports the popular view that the lapsing of the Reinsurance Treaty had, via the Franco-Russian alliance, made the First World War inevitable. Actually, shortly after 1890 Russo-German relations became excellent. Caprivi did all he could to court Russia, ended the tariff war and followed Bismarck's example in refusing to countenance Austria's Balkan aspirations.

Finally, a close personal relationship developed between William II and the twenty-six-year-old Czar Nicholas II, who ascended the throne in 1894. The German Emperor was obviously glad not to be the youngest of all the European monarchs any longer. He assumed towards the Czar the role of a mentor which, at times, had real value, although the pupil did not always show himself obedient.

What was sensational about Bismarck's revelation was not so much its actual content but the mere fact that he felt impelled to make it. Certainly, the Reinsurance Treaty had never really been the apple of his eye, yet it was a secret state treaty and its unauthorised publication, though it was no longer in force, was from the technical and juridical point of view very near to treason. Bismarck himself said that he had acted as he did in order to prevent the falsification of history by the clerical liberal Press which most dishonestly made the government of Emperor William I and of his Chancellor responsible for all the evil in the world. This was hardly a very convincing explanation, however, since it had never occurred to him in all these years to use weapons of this kind. Was the intention simply to discredit Caprivi, who had returned to private life two years previously? Perhaps behind the publication was a kind of malignant whim of idle old age, together with the intention to draw attention to his own continued existence. One can only say that this last action of Bismarck's in the field of foreign affairs is one of many in his life whose motives remain obscure.

And now silence was all around him, and perhaps his very silence induced men to heap fresh honours upon him. He was invited to pompous festivities which in March 1897 were organised to celebrate the hundredth birthday of William I, or to see the cruiser *Bismarck* run off the slips. He regularly refused, giving his health as an excuse, but it might also well be that he wanted to avoid even the appearance of having anything in common with the foreign policy now being pursued in Berlin, a policy which was becoming increasingly incomprehensible to the public, was criticised by the opposition as planless and incalculable, but was in the main accepted by the masses, simply because they found nothing in it that particularly inconvenienced them. Even foreign policy was conditioned by the almost terrifying growth of productive power in Germany. For the directors of business this was, of course, natural and logical; for Bismarck, however, to whom foreign policy was a game reserved for dynasts, aristocrats and a few picked officials and was really the quintessence of politics as such, this commercialised diplomacy was really no diplomacy at all.

He had on one occasion been invited by his neighbours in Hamburg to see their new gigantic harbour, and had stood for some time watching all that deafening activity, but it meant very little to him. With that controlled courtesy of his, he remarked that he was deeply moved, that this was a new age in a new world.* Yet there was nothing of joyous approval in his voice, such as his hosts must surely have hoped for. Rather it seemed that he had had some kind of a sudden fright at the distance he had moved away from the world and the distance the world had moved away from *him*.

The year 1897 was one of destiny for Bismarck's empire. In January Bernhard Von Bülow became State Secretary of the Foreign Office and Admiral Alfred Tirpitz Chief of the Admiralty. Bülow came from an old Mecklenburg family of Junkers and was the son of a diplomat. He had something of a reputation as a wit and a man of culture, but it was a reputation unfortunately that caused him to be somewhat blind to the limits of his talent, for his gifts were inconsiderable and he had no feeling for the continuum of history.

* Fürst von Bülow, *Denkwürdigkeiten* (1930), p. 1,134.

Tirpitz, however, was no Junker, but the offspring of the new propertied bourgeoisie which had pushed its way upward in the social hierarchy. He was indeed typical of that union between the higher bourgeoisie and the feudal elements of society which was a mark of that time. In him were combined the two qualities which even in those days were already bringing success to the German entrepreneur, namely an industry and energy that often reached obsessional proportions and—when this was called for —the slipperiness of an eel.

The Emperor had chosen both these men because they seemed to him to be the right ones for creating a great fleet from the bottom up, which meant the abandonment of the Bismarckian naval plan, to which Bismarck and Caprivi had always held fast. Both Bismarck and Caprivi believed that Germany only needed a "Decency Fleet" (*Anstandsflotte*) no larger than that of Holland, which had colonial possessions far more valuable than those of Germany. Never did Bismarck see in the fleet anything more than an adjunct to the Army, like the bridge trains of the Engineers. That is why as far back as 1887 he had vehemently opposed the Emperor when the latter allowed his brother Henry to become a professional naval officer. A Prussian Prince, Bismarck held, should only be trained as a soldier and an administrator of the state.

From the very start, Tirpitz's effort to exchange a naval plan which was commensurate with political reality for a fantastically inflated project was viewed by Bismarck with the gravest misgiving (the admiral was asking for no less than twenty first-class ships of the line). It was the last time that Bismarck was really carried away by a live issue. Tirpitz's explanation, namely, that German overseas policy had hitherto been executed "on the broad back of British world power", that is to say on sufferance —which in Tirpitz's view amounted to an intolerable insult to Germany—failed to rouse the old man. When he heard that Tirpitz's fleet was only to be strong enough to prevent the British from attacking them, he reflected that Britain had always opposed just such a fleet which might tie off the sea arteries of the island kingdom and had opposed it with all her power. Also he knew enough about human insatiability and ambition to doubt Tirpitz's assurance that twenty ships of the line would be enough. Actually, only two years later, when Bismarck was dead, Tirpitz was asking for thirty-four.

Whenever Bismarck was told that he had to support the building of a fleet, since he himself had acquired colonies which the fleet would have to protect, he replied with the argument that German colonies would be defended by German army corps on the mainland. As to colonies in themselves, we have already seen what Bismarck's attitude was. He had of course opposed Caprivi in 1890 when the latter had bartered a few East African sultanates for Heligoland; but that was an ordinary politician's move which Caprivi countered by quoting an old minute of Bismarck's, which stated that England was more important to Germany than Zanzibar or the whole of East Africa.

Nor did Bismarck ever change his view that the only people to get anything out of colonies were ship-owners and officials whose incomes of course came out of the pockets of the German tax-payer. "For a policy of colonial conquest," he said after Tirpitz's appointment, "I never had any enthusiasm even as a minister, and it seems to me that at the moment the time is particularly unpropitious for such things." Unfortunately few listened to him on such occasions.

He had an uphill fight. Tirpitz was a master of the art of propaganda. He exploited to the full the Emperor's weakness for grand stage effects. "Never," wrote Holstein to Eulenburg, "has any temptation so excited the Kaiser's nerves as this plan for a great fleet." And the broad masses in land-bound Germany, those decent homely folk, what did they know of the sea, which most of them hadn't even seen, or of its importance and its dangers? Therefore it was all the more easy for Tirpitz to win them over.

Nevertheless, Bismarck continued to resist. As he had always been against "the decorative in politics", so now he let it be understood he was against the new fashion of boasting and conquest—*Eroberungs und Renommierpolitik*—which was alien to the German character, and of which the Navy, with its implicit threat to Britain, was a part. The very fact that the threat was bound to be ineffective made matters worse. He detested shams, and for that very reason execrated "the great parade ships, which are only there to advertise our prestige"—and which one might well call lie ships—"*Lügenschiffe*"—"since they achieve nothing".*

It became increasingly impossible simply to ignore Bismarck's opposition, and ultimately it was decided in Berlin to send Tirpitz himself to Friedrichsruh in the hope that his vehement eloquence would bring the stubborn old man to heel. On a rainy autumn day in 1897 the admiral arrived in Friedrichsruh. Bismarck received him very much the Grand Seigneur, although tortured by nerve pains so that he could only speak with difficulty.

The admiral laid all his calculations and tables before him for hours on end, filled by that energy of the expert which can often

* Liman, *Bismarck nach seiner Entlassung* (1904), p. 209.

come close to mania. Bismarck remained polite and cool. Could he guess that he was looking a man in the eye who would ultimately ruin his empire? For today we can surely recognise that the gravest of all the mistakes of Bismarck's successors was their departure from a naval policy that was in tune with realities.

The documents which Tirpitz spread out before Bismarck told him nothing. So long as there had been no alteration in geography, he saw no reason for going beyond the general naval pattern of his own day. He admitted that some increase in the Navy might be needed, but insisted that it should consist of small ships only which would defend the coast "like a swarm of hornets".

In the afternoon, during a two-hour drive, Bismarck suddenly remarked—and because of the coachman he spoke in English—that the admiral might inform the Emperor that he wished to be left alone and to die in peace. His task, he said, was done. There was for him "no future and no more hope".*

Shortly afterwards, in November 1897, Germany was given the opportunity of expanding into East Asia. In China two Catholic missionaries who happened to be German subjects had been murdered by a mob, whereupon, according to the political logic of the day, the German government claimed a right to compensation, which could in such cases usually be satisfied by the cession of a piece of Chinese soil. Accordingly, Germany demanded the Bay of Kiautschou, on which the Admiralty in Berlin had long cast a covetous eye.

To take possession of the prize, men-of-war and marines were dispatched to the Orient and the Emperor, with his inevitable appetite for drama, appointed his brother Henry to the supreme command of this expedition, which was thus dressed up to look like a serious war. The solemn charade was carried out to the end. By virtue of his new office, the prince had for the sake of public opinion to pay a farewell visit to Bismarck. On this occasion, although temperamentally averse to that kind of thing, he had to ask whether he might touch his forehead which his grandfather had so often kissed. Some days later, in Kiel, the Emperor sent him and his expeditionary corps off with a speech whose key sentence was "Fare forth with the mailed fist."

As though there had not already been a surfeit of embarrassments, the Emperor determined to break his journey from Kiel to Berlin at Friederichsruh and make one of his customary quick visits. These usually lasted three hours, of which an hour-and-a-half was devoted to lunch. Bismarck was convinced that these attentions had only one purpose: to show His Majesty how much nearer in the meantime he had come to the grave. Actually, these

* Tirpitz, *Erinnerungen* (1919), p. 92.

visits were due to a warning by Prince Albrecht, an uncle of the Emperor. If Bismarck were to die, he said, without being reconciled to the Emperor, William would never be forgiven.

Unfortunately, on these visits William avoided all political themes and confined himself to Court gossip, verbal puns, militaria and so on. With this approach, of course, he showed something like contempt for his host—as he did when he produced a couple of Grenadiers with a new type of knapsack and asked Bismarck for his opinion as an expert on such matters. These visits got very much on the old man's nerves. The haste with which this unpleasant duty was performed, the almost oriental submissiveness of the Emperor's entourage, and the deliberately exaggerated liveliness of his guest even during the most banal talk, and even the very voice of the Emperor, which was a sort of snarl and had echoes in it of a certain Berlin vulgarity, offended Bismarck.

One December noon in 1897 everything had started as usual. Conversation at table flowed listlessly on. The Emperor led the talk and almost brutally brushed aside all attempts by Bismarck to say something—a strange phantom scene in that darkened dining-room under a winter sky. Suddenly, however, Bismarck, lowering his usually penetrating voice and making it almost sound casual, said: "Your Majesty, as long as you have this officer corps, you can of course permit yourself whatever you please. But when this is no longer the case, it will be very different." It was a voice that seemed to be rising from the grave; it brought the whole conversation to a standstill and made the courtiers who sat around stiffen in their seats. General Moltke the Younger—the man who was destined to lose the battle of the Marne—turned to Tirpitz. "This is terrible," he whispered. Only the Emperor remained apparently unaffected and went on talking.

Twenty-one years later, William II was to learn how accurate had been the old man's vision. In Spa his officers deserted him because they were not the same men whom Bismarck had known and with whom he had won his wars. And, consequently, just as he had prophesied, "everything was very different".

After this Bismarck did not exchange a single word with the Emperor, but when the guests were gone and the house was once more quiet he said that twenty years after the death of Frederick the Great the battle of Jena had been fought and lost, and now, twenty years after his own death, the great crash would come if things went on as they were going. This prophesy came true in November, 1918—almost on the exact date that had been foretold, since Bismarck died in July 1898.

It is not usual for statesmen to die at the height of their power. More often their death is preceded by a period in which their power declines, that bitter time in which the realm of the possible grows ever smaller and that of the "never again" ever greater. The decay of power and of the body seems to proceed simultaneously, and in some dark and barbaric fashion appear to drive each other forward.

Bismarck was no exception. He was convinced that he would never be free of those facial pains which, proceeding from the trigeminus nerve, are so terrible that men can go morally to pieces under them. It was, however, his legs that chiefly gave him trouble, as they had always done since that botched affair with the inflamed vein in St. Petersburg. Even in 1894 he was saying, "Back and legs just don't want to any more." In May 1896 he could no longer walk two hundred paces without growing tired. A. O. Meyer*, who saw him in the summer of 1897, relates that he was "unbowed by age. He took off his hat and bowed—not too little and not too much." But he continues "then he walked slowly with short steps, leaning on his stick, into the house".†

Shortly after this he began to have alarmingly severe pains in the left foot, in the toes, in the heel, and in the instep. For some time Schweninger observed him without saying anything. At length he informed the family that gangrene had set in. It was incurable, but there might be a possibility of slowing down the progress of the disease, and, indeed, Schweninger succeeded in limiting its spread to below the ankle, where it took the form of dry gangrene and was prevented from developing into the more dreaded form of wet gangrene.

Bismarck learned nothing of this. He thought he was suffering from gout. The pain, however, continually grew more intense. "People don't know," he said, "what it means to feel oneself gradually dying off like this and, on top of it all, to have all these different nuances of pain." He felt, he added, like somebody freezing to death in the snow, who actually felt a certain pleasure as the snow flakes covered him.

He now always wore spectacles and, when ladies were present, would remark in his old gallant tone that he did so in order to see them better. ‡ The skin over the bald head and hollow cheeks was smooth and had a sheen like ivory. The nose became strangely sharp. The flesh on the hands, and with it their peculiar softness, seemed to disappear. The eyes remained large but lost their colour; they became cold and took on a certain quality of un-

---

* Arnold Oscar Meyer (1877–1904), historian, held a number of professorships.
† A. O. Meyer, *Bismarck der Mensch und Staatsmann* (1949), p. 74.
‡ Hahn, p. 191.

concern. They gained that distant Triton look that some visitors had long professed to see in them. Thus was formed Bismarck's last face—a face which bore no resemblance to the image of the mighty hero which was how the world still conceived of him.

Often when he could not sleep—and this happened on two nights out of three—he would wander through the house in his dressing-gown. Everything that he had achieved in his life was, during those hours, clothed in the evening mist of doubt, his failures surrounded him like a crowd of eager beggars. Impotent rage tortured him, and hatred of those who had hindered him in the completion of his edifice and whom he now saw engaged through sheer ignorance in destroying it.

On top of it all he was compelled to confess that it was he himself who had given them in this questionable second empire the power to do this disastrous thing. The old German imperial crown with all its accretions of myth lay unattainable beyond the reach of "Kleindeutschland" in Vienna. He had been compelled for practical reasons to replace that ancient crown by a new one which was, however, never more than a product of heraldic imagination, a thing that could be reproduced on stamps and on the shields outside government offices, but had no real existence.

And yet, one day, men might have to fight for this fiction. With sword in hand, he had once written to the prince who now was Emperor, the monarch might have to fight for his rights and die rather than yield, and when he reflected on this, the suspicion naturally arose in his heart that Emperors of that kind no longer existed and that none were likely to come.

Now, as his sufferings increased, and he was less and less able to move, he could no longer escape from the anguish of these night thoughts—or at least have the illusion of escaping—by wandering around. He was confined to his bed, and had to face them as best he could. The circle of his life was closing. He had been born in an old house on the Elbe, not unlike the one in which now he lived. As an infant he had lain helpless there, much as he lay now a very old man, and, as now, the wind from the same river had rustled the trees.

The loneliness which, as a thinking human being, had always been his portion, was now more apparent than ever. When mention was made of him among influential people, they would express a gentle regret that he did not understand the realities of the new age—the same reproach which he himself made against his critics. The new generation was storming forward and cared nothing for what he had to say. And, indeed, was he anything more than an idea—and a vague one at that? An idea before which a certain ritual had to be gone through? It was enough to erect monuments to him in his sky-piercing helmet, it was enough to give his name to streets, squares, hotels and inns.

The public thought it natural enough that old people should have this disability or that, and that they should complain about it, and that, the public felt, was all that was amiss with Bismarck. And so it learned nothing—perhaps because it did not want to learn—of the fact that, from the middle of November 1897, Bismarck was condemned to a wheelchair, a firmly built low vehicle with rubber tyres. Leaning on one of his servants, he could just manage to walk the two dozen steps from his bedroom to his bath, but no more. When the Emperor visited him on what was to be the last occasion, Bismarck had to receive him seated.

The end was nearing. Like an old fallen tree which, as it gradually decays, becomes one with the floor of the forest, and suffers itself to be overgrown by shrubbery and moss until it is entirely hidden, so Bismarck was disappearing from the world.

Engels, on whom the mantle of Marx had fallen, was often asked by his disciples when the great upheaval would come and he had always named 1898 as the year of destiny. Engels himself was now dead, but faith in him remained unshaken, and, indeed, the year 1898 began with some very startling events.

In March the German Colony Kiautschou became a fact on Chinese soil, but it was not a trading post so much as a naval base, the creation of which merely resulted in the destruction of the German garrison in a pointless prestige battle in 1914. Looking one day at the map of Kiautschou in the company of a Bavarian journalist, Bismarck remarked that it was a very small bit of earth but big enough for a lot of silly things to be done there. The Bavarian government should have protested most strongly at such misuse of their people's money.

One month later, in April, war broke out between Spain and the United States and was brought to a rapid conclusion when the American fleet shot the superannuated Spanish fleet to pieces in Philippine and Cuban waters. But the ease with which the position at Kiautschou had been secured misled Berlin into the belief that other equally cheap successes could be scored. The same German squadron which had carried out the occupation of Kiautschou accordingly now appeared before Manila, the capital of the Philippines, and obstructed the operations of the American Navy. "Tirpitz's conviction," telegraphed the Emperor to Bülow, "is firm as a rock that we must have Manila." This was an error which was very quickly put right when Spain handed over the Philippines to America.*

* Eyck, *Das personliche Regiment Wilhelm II* (1948), pp. 208–9.

Meanwhile Anglo-French rivalry flared up afresh in the heart of Africa. While the Dreyfus affair in France was providing new sensational news through the suicide of Colonel Henry, the prosecution's chief witness, and so directing the attention of the world to that country, Major Marchand secretly led a small body of French troops across the African continent and appeared suddenly in the middle of June on the upper waters of the Nile—which Britain had declared to be her own sphere of interest—and planted the Tricolour at Fashoda. Britain exerted increasing pressure and ultimately the force was withdrawn, but Bismarck did not live to hear of this.

Bismarck followed events with undiminished attention, and when he commented on them it was evident that illness had not impaired the power of his mind. The sharpness of his thought was what it had always been, as was his exact assessment of any given set of facts, whether real or imponderable, his unfailing wit and, ultimately, his feeling of personal dignity.

Naturally, he spoke less and less frequently. "When we know the one thing that matters," we read in *Wilhelm Meister*, "we cease to be talkative." Even those who stood closest to him rarely heard him complain in actual words. At most he would make an angry gesture or give a helpless shrug of his shoulders. Only Schweninger relates how about this time he once put both hands on his head and burst out with the words: "If only I could get to grips myself with the mess that they've made (*Könnte ich doch in die Schweinerei hineinfahren*), and tell them what they're heading for. But as you know, my trumpet no longer gives a sound. It's full of holes."*

Yet, just at the beginning of 1898, something happened for which Bismarck had long been working with undiminished persistence. Since 1889 his proposal for an alliance with Britain had been reposing on Salisbury's desk. And now, at last, Britain answered. On March 29th, the British Colonial Secretary, Joseph Chamberlain, remarked to Hatzfeldt, the German ambassador, quite informally at a party, that England was now prepared to enter into a defensive alliance with Germany, for she felt herself unable to continue in her policy of splendid isolation. If Germany refused, she would turn to France and Russia. If, however, an Anglo-German alliance came into being, then the United States would join it—in fact, though perhaps not in name—and this would create a power bloc that would be irresistible.

At last then the situation had arrived which Bismarck had had in mind ten years previously, the situation which had formed

* Liman, p. 214.

the basis of his instructions to Hatzfeldt. "It is not a question," he wrote on that occasion, "of being the stronger in the event of war, but of being able to prevent a war. Neither France nor Russia will break the peace if they are officially informed that they will immediately and automatically have Britain as their enemy."

Had events over the ten preceding years followed a different course, in particular had Bismarck in that March of 1898 been in office—and Chancellor Hohenlohe was only four years his junior—then there might have been a beginning here that could have led us—who knows where? Chamberlain was not a career diplomat but a rationalistic manufacturer of machines from Birmingham, a business man without prejudice, without the lawyer's terror of precedents. Most certainly he meant business, while Bismarck's whole life had shown that he rejected no alliance that served his purposes. Never were his likes and dislikes deducible from the actual alliances he made. Most certainly he would have paid a big price for the partnership of Britain, for when the very existence of Germany was at stake colonial and naval rivalries could be forgotten.

Whatever the cost—that was how Bismarck had long viewed the matter—Britain must be kept from joining a Franco-Russian alliance. She must be won as an ally, at least against Russia, whose strange and frequently terrifying lack of any normal inhibition inspired the same horror in London as it did in Berlin. One thing at least we can say with reasonable certainty: had Bismarck remained in office, Germany would not have had to fight the First World War.

But Hohenlohe was now sitting in Bismarck's seat—a man already tired—while Bülow was at the Foreign Office, convinced that he was a reincarnated Talleyrand. Bülow believed that the essence of diplomatic wisdom lay in putting as high a price on oneself as possible and so he rejected the English proposal. He defended his action by the argument that Bismarck had himself used in the past, though even then it was quite invalid, the argument that treaties with England only bound the particular parliamentary party that happened to be in power at the time.

Chamberlain replied that the pact which he offered would, if Germany agreed, be laid before parliament, which meant that both parties would be bound by it; but Bülow remained evasive, and in this he was supported by the Emperor, who saw his naval plans imperilled by a British alliance, and also by Holstein, who insisted that he was following Bismarck's tradition by refusing all binding engagements and seeking to act as arbiter mundi as Bismarck had done at the time of the Berlin congress.

That tradition was no doubt sound while Bismarck was at
the height of his successes. It was no longer sound when his sun
had already almost set. People in Berlin did not see how greatly
Germany's position had deteriorated—that she could no longer
afford the luxury of a "free hand", least of all now that an
alliance had at last been concluded between Russia and France.
Bülow and Holstein, however, were still hag-ridden by the old
delusion that an Anglo-Russian alliance, an alliance between the
bear and the whale, was for all time inconceivable. Also, both
were afraid of the unpopularity which they were likely to incur
through an alliance with Britain at a time of strong anti-British
prejudice in Germany.

The background of this whole affair is still rather imperfectly
known, but two things are certain—one is that in 1898 the British
most certainly proposed an alliance, and the other that authori-
tative circles in Germany simply did not want it. As far as such
things can be assessed by the human intelligence, this surely was
the most fateful of all the consequences that Bismarck's dismissal
entailed.

It is possible that Bismarck himself knew nothing of all this.
His mind was elsewhere. As the days grew warmer, he sat out
of doors whenever possible, completely motionless, since every
movement might cause pain, and there he remained looking at
his trees as the leaves began to shoot. His hearing was as good
as ever and he could listen to the voices of the migrating birds
as they returned from the sunny south and to the humming of
bees.

It is as though now for the first time one could begin to see a
picture of the essential Bismarck, all those that had at any time
been superimposed on it having fallen away. It was that of the
old large-scale Nether Saxon farmer, rooted in his land and ruling
over it as its supreme lord. It was such a man who had now
returned to his home, to the region of the lower Elbe, that stream
that separates old Germany from what were really her colonial
territories, a frontier which—so Bismarck believed—the Prussian
state had caused to disappear forever.

The whole scope of his existence was beginning to shrink. By
now it had become no more than a constant battle with pain.
Every drive had to be paid for by a sharpening of his facial neuralgia. Sitting in his wheelchair, between blankets, with a fur cap
drawn down to cover his eyebrows—that little bit of life that was
still vouchsafed him seemed more difficult to master than anything
he had known in the past when he had regulated the affairs of
Europe. Brauer, once his colleague in the Imperial Chancellery,
and now a minister in Baden, saw him in June 1898 and recounts

with positive horror that he had seen a decrepit old man, stretched out on the sofa, swathed in blankets, complaining of pain in his legs and face. "With a weak thin voice he made me welcome, and in the middle of a sentence his speech passed over into a soft whimpering. His features became distorted with pain."*

Again and again, as we contemplate this final phase, we ask: How much did Bismarck realize of that which was to come? It is very difficult to find the answer, for Bismarck carefully guarded his tongue. It was only rarely that he gave an indication of what was in his mind on this or any other matter; it was only rarely that he showed his heart—as he did, for instance, at the end of 1897 when he said that it was nearly all over with him and asked what point there was for him to go on living. What he saw of those who were to follow him gave him little pleasure and seemed designed, the longer he lived, to give him even less.†

At times he relapsed into a cynicism that did not ring quite true—as when he said that every time he woke up he hesitated whether to be saddened by the collapse of his life work, which he could clearly see coming, or feel satisfaction over it and regard it as the just punishment for his curt dismissal.‡ At other times a sense of frustration and inadequacy would overcome him, and he would say, as he did to Dilke,§ that he had not been a great statesman at all, and that Cavour and Crispi, yes even the President of the Boer Republic, Paul Krüger, were greater men than he. He had had the state and the Army behind him while those others had had nothing.¶ Yet it was only rarely that the full truth burst out clear and unmistakable from the depths of his heart, as when he made that last despairing utterance to Tirpitz, saying that there was no future left for him, and no hope.

This life, which consisted of nothing but a battle with infirmity, looked as though it would go on for a considerable time. At the end of July, however, Bismarck's condition suddenly took a turn for the worse. There was painful dyspnoea accompanied by lapses of consciousness. Then suddenly on top of all this came an inflammation of the lungs which used up his last reserves of strength.

The sons with their wives were already in Friedrichsruh and were prepared for the end. But July 28th brought a sudden

---

* Brauer, p. 401-4.   † Hofmann, p. 1,244.   ‡ Brauer, p. 400.
§ Sir Charles Dilke (1843–1911) seemed marked out for a glittering political career. After the Liberal victory of 1880 he served in the Gladstone ministry, first as Under Secretary for Foreign Affairs, then as President of the local government board from 1882 until Gladstone's defeat in 1885. In that year he was cited as co-respondent in a divorce suit, and the scandal ensuing from the proceedings obliged him to leave public life for ever.
¶ Taylor, *Bismarck*, p. 258.

change for the better. Bismarck, in his wheelchair, in a fairly placid mood joined the family at supper, and afterwards happily smoked his long pipe. Schweninger allowed him champagne, which he had not done for some considerable time. Bismarck did not go to bed till towards midnight. Schweninger considered —or professed to consider—his condition so satisfactory that he went away that night for two days.

The old man only fell asleep towards morning, and on the following day, the 29th, remained in bed, ate, drank and read as usual, and the same happened on the morning of the 30th. Toward noon, however, a very great weakness overcame him; an acute oedema of the lungs then developed, and around two o'clock Schweninger's young assistant, Chrysander, found that his pulse was failing and gave him camphor injections. Bismarck suffered severely during the afternoon from painful dyspnoea and was tortured by a thirst he could not quench. It was only gradually that some relief was granted him by means of morphia injections and hot sponges on his neck and chest. At length he fell into a kind of half-sleep.

Toward evening the long unequal struggle drew to a close; the fever rose ever higher and the heart was obviously failing. Only a rattling noise of the lungs fighting for air filled the room which still looked like that of a young farmer's apprentice. Over the wooden bed were the pictures of Bismarck's dogs and horses and also a portrait of Schweninger. On the table lay a volume of Schiller's poems. The family gathered round him, waiting and in silence. It was a long time before night came—for this was summer—and it was only then that Schweninger returned. But there was little that he could do. Shortly after eleven o'clock, when for three minutes there had been no sign of either pulse or breath, he declared Bismarck dead.

Of the seconds of his passing we know very little. As his consciousness went into dissolution, it seemed to rise into a kind of freedom. It is said that he carried on half-heard dream-like conversations with himself and that he sang a little—very softly. It would seem that he was granted that parting gift which nature sometimes bestows on her favourites and which medicine calls euphoria. Of the various short, charged sayings which legend has preserved as his reputed last words, nothing is known for certain. They may well all have been invented. It is the author's intention to ignore them.

Meanwhile, there lay over Germany during that week-end the short night of midsummer. The good citizens amused themselves with dancing and music at the holiday resorts. The "little man" who did the heavy toil was looking forward to a fine Sunday and perhaps was preparing for an excursion. He would have set the alarm clock, while the girls got ready their starched white dresses. Nobody cared very much what happened in Friedrichsruh. People knew that Bismarck had long been ill, but it had never occurred to them that his life might be in danger, and since it was Sunday and no papers appeared, the news of his death travelled slowly.

On the big, white, fat-bellied steam yacht, on which the Emperor was cruising along the Norwegian coast the atmosphere was rather different. He had made Schweninger promise to let him know immediately things became critical at Friedrichsruh, but there had been a purpose behind Schweninger's sudden—and in the circumstances very odd—departure from Bismarck's sick-bed on July 28th. The fact is that the family believed that the Emperor was planning some dramatic intervention—possibly a reconciliation scene at Bismarck's death-bed. Anyway the result of Schweninger's action was that if William had any such intention—which on the whole he probably had—the news of Bismarck's death arrived too late for him to carry it out.

The Norwegian summer was as dull and cool as a German autumn, and there was hardly anybody on the promenade deck of the yacht. All were looking forward to returning home. When, on the evening of July 30th, the ship lay at Bergen to take in coal, telegrams arrived from the official German Telegraph Bureau, which reported that Bismarck's condition was growing steadily worse. On Sunday, July 31st, about seven o'clock, the news came from Schweninger that Bismarck was dead.

Most disagreeably surprised, the Emperor ordered the ship to return at top speed. An imperial message of condolence was sent ahead from the ship to Herbert, the closing sentence reading: "I will prepare a last resting place for his remains in the Cathedral in Berlin beside those of my ancestors." But Bismarck had known his William much too well not to guess that he would make a kind of super show of his burial and thus Herbert was able to reply to the Emperor that his wish could not be fulfilled since the prince had made final dispositions for his burial before death. In them he had said he wished to be laid to rest in the small mausoleum in Friedrichsruh and the coffin of Johanna was also to be brought from Varzin. His own coffin was to be closed as quickly as circumstances would permit and, so far as this was possible, nobody was to see him in death. There was to be no photography and no death-mask was to be made.

For the next few hours there took place a grotesque race between the imperial yacht and the funeral preparations in Friedrichsruh. The first mourners, among them Chancellor Hohenlohe, had to wait outside the closed doors of the death room behind which they heard the noise of hammering. When they were admitted, they found the black coffin closed and standing on trestles next to the bed, which had not yet been tidied.

One day later, on August 1st, the Emperor landed in Kiel. On the 2nd he travelled on to Berlin, a stop of twenty-five minutes at Friedrichsruh being provided for. And this was really natural enough, because he knew that his presence in that house was unwelcome and so did not wish to extend his visit over the minimum required.

He must also by now have heard that Moritz Busch had honoured the dead in a disagreeably disturbing way. One day after Bismarck's death he had published the text which, till then, had remained secret, of Bismarck's letter of resignation in 1890. What was the intention of this? Was it a desire simply to make known the objective facts? It is unlikely that Busch alone was responsible, but whether he was actually acting on the instruction of Bismarck or his family is not known for certain. However that may be, he had made all the demonstrations of friendship which the Emperor had made to Bismarck since 1890 appear completely worthless.

When the Imperial train stopped in Friedrichsruh, Herbert and Bill received the imperial pair in the icy attitudes of unbending *frondeurs*. The ladies of the family, almost unrecognisable in their mourning veils, awaited the Emperor and Empress in the house. The coffin, whose forbidding black had now completely disappeared beneath flowers, still stood in the bedroom.

The Emperor laid an enormous wreath upon it and, in doing so, made a rather pitiful and helpless impression as he struggled unsuccessfully, thanks to his short arm, to put the thing in place. The coffin was then blessed, and there followed a sermon by a somewhat embarrassed country parson and afterwards a silent prayer. And then, at a slight jerking of the head by the Emperor, the guests hurried back to the railway station. The visit had lasted less than half an hour.

The closed coffin remained standing* in the bedroom while the mausoleum was being built. It was to be ready in October, but there was delay in completing the building, and so the coffin remained in the house throughout the autumn and winter. For months the family lived under one roof with the remains of the patriarch from which the soul had departed. To keep his coffin in the house as though it were a piece of furniture—a thing that in the course of time becomes a familiar object— certainly this was a robust way of carrying out the last will of

* Westphal, *Bismarck als Gutsherr* (1922), p. 137.

Bismarck, but the word delicacy—*zartfühlend*—Eulenburg was later to write, "had fled from the Bismarck family lexicon as a bird flies away when it hails".

The mausoleum was not ready till the spring of 1899, and it was only then that Johanna's coffin was brought from Varzin to Friedrichsruh, so that on April 1st, which would have been Bismarck's eighty-fourth birthday, the interment could take place. But the enmity between the houses of Bismarck and Hohenzollern was not buried. The soldiers of the King of Prussia were not permitted to touch the coffins. According to Hamburg custom, these were carried to the grave by members of a civic funeral fraternity in black-brocaded costumes of the great Hanseatic past. Prussian Cuirassiers, in the white uniform which was also that of Bismarck, were merely allowed to march alongside of them, the even tramp of their high boots being the chief sound to be heard.

The mausoleum, which was only a short way from the house, and which was a modest structure of tiles in more-or-less Romanesque style, stood on a slight rise in the ground, surrounded by pines and birches. And it was here that, after his unquiet life, all that was left on earth of Otto von Bismarck was laid to rest.

BIBLIOGRAPHY

Note: The student wishing to delve further into the study of Bismarck should not fail to acquaint himself with Professor Gooch's excellent essay on "The Study of Bismarck" in his *Studies of German History*.

The principal biographies
Erich Eyck, *Bismarcks Leben und Werk*, 3 vols (1941–44), available in an English translation under the title *Bismarck and the German Empire*, Allen & Unwin (1950)
C. Grant Robertson, *Bismarck*, Constable (1915)
Max Lenz, *Geschichte Bismarcks* (1913)
Emil Ludwig, *Bismarck* (1927)
Erich Marcks, *Otto von Bismarck, Ein Lebensbild* (1940)
A. O. Meyer, *Bismarck der Mensch und der Staatsmann* (1944)
A. J. P. Taylor, *Bismarck*, Hamish Hamilton (1955).

The amount of published source material is very great. This includes among other things Bismarck's collected works in fifteen volumes.

The following is a selection of other works that deal with various aspects of Bismarck's life and work.
Andrassy, G., *Bismarck, Andrassy and their successors*, T. Fisher Unwin (1927)
Aydelotte, W. O., *Bismarck and British Colonial Policy*, University of Pennsylvania Press (1937)
Becker, O., *Bismarcks Bundespolitik* (1923)
Becker, O., *Bismarck und die Einkreisung Deutschlands* (1925)
Bergmann, G. von, *Rückschau* (1953)
Bussmann, H., *Das Zeitalter Bismarcks*
Clark, C. W., *Franz Joseph and Bismarck* in Harvard Historical Studies, vol. 36 (1934)
Eckardt, Julius von, *Bismarcks Kampf gegen Caprivi* (1920)
Fuller, J. V., *Bismarck's Diplomacy at the Zenith* in Harvard Historical Studies, vol. 26 (1922)
Gradenwitz, O., *Bismarcks Letzter Kampf*
Hahn, P., *Varzin*
Jöhlinger, Otto, *Bismarck und die Juden* (1921)
Krausnick, *Neue Bismarck Gespräche* (1940)
Liman, Paul, *Fürst Bismarck nach seiner Entlassung* (1901)
Mayer, G., *Bismarck und Lassalle* (1927)
Meyer, A. O., *Bismarcks Kampf mit Österreich am Bundestag zu Frankfurt* (1927)

Meyer, A. O., *Bismarcks Glaube* (1930)

Michael, H., *Bismarck, England und Europa 1866–70* (1930)

Mitchell, P. B., *Bismarck's Policy of Conciliation with France 1875–1885*, University of Pennsylvania Press (1938)

Nowak, K. F., *Kaiser and Chancellor*, Putnam (1930)

Rothfels, H., *Bismarck und der Osten* (1934)

Rothfels, H., *Bismarcks Englische Bundespolitik* (1924)

Schüssler, W., *Bismarcks Kampf um Süd Deutschland 1867* (1929)

Schüssler, W., *Bismarcks Sturz* (1921)

Taylor, A. J. P., *Germany's First Bid for Colonies*, Macmillan (1938)

Vogel, Walter, *Bismarcks Arbeiterversicherung*

Windelband, W., *Bismarck und die Europäischen Grossmächte 1879–1885* (1940)

Zechlin, E., *Bismarck und die Grundlegung der deutschen Grossmacht* (1927)

Zechlin, E., *Staatsstreichpläne Bismarcks im Jahre 1866* (1929)

There are many publications recalling memories of Bismarck, some wholly devoted to this subject, others touching on it more incidentally. These are a few of the more important of such works.

Brauer, Marcks, and von Müller (editors), *Erinnerungen an Bismarck*. The collection contains an important contribution by Dr. Schweninger, Bismarck's physician.

Ballhausen, Lucius von, *Bismarck Erinnerungen* (1920)

Bülow, Fürst von, *Denkwürdigkeiten*

Busch, M., Tagebuch Blatter, 3 vols (1894–96). There is an English version under the title *Bismarck, some secret pages of his History*, Macmillan (1898)

Eulenburg, Fürst Philipp, *Aus Fünfzig Jahren* (1925)

Hofmann, H., *Fürst Bismarck 1890–1898*, 3 vols (1913)

Keudell, R., von, *Fürst und Fürstin Bismarck* (1901)

Manteuffel, Otto von, *Denkwürdigkeiten* (1892)

Radowitz, Josef Maria von, *Aufzeichnungen und Erinnerungen* (1925)

Richter, Eugen, *Im alten Reichstag* (1892)

Roon, Graf von, *Denkwürdigkeiten* (1892)

Schweninger, E., *Dem Andenken Bismarcks* (1899)

Tiedemann, Christoph von, *Persönliche Erinnerungen an den Fursten Bismarck* (1898)

Among source material Friederich von Holstein's private papers hold a very high rank, as, of course, does Thimme and Mendelssohn Bartholdy's *Die Grosse Politik der Europäischen Kabinette*.

There are a number of collections of letters to one specific individual. Among the latter are *Briefe an seine Frau und Gattin* (1906), published in England under the title of *Love Letters of Prince Bismarck*, Heinemann (1901); his letters to his sister Malwine and her husband; to his son William; to Freiherr von Schleinitz and to General von Gerlach.

INDEX